PINK-SLIPPED

WOMEN AND FILM HISTORY INTERNATIONAL

Series Editors

Kay Armatage, Jane M. Gaines, and Christine Gledhill

A new generation of motion picture historians is rediscovering the vital and diverse contributions of women to world film history whether as producers, actors or spectators. Taking advantage of new print material and moving picture archival discoveries as well as the benefits of digital access and storage, this series investigates the significance of gender in the cinema.

A list of books in the series appears at the end of this book.

PINK-SLIPPED

WHAT HAPPENED

to WOMEN in the

SILENT FILM INDUSTRIES?

JANE M. GAINES

UNIVERSITY OF ILLINOIS PRESS
Urbana, Chicago, and Springfield

A version of chapter 6, "Are they 'Just Like Us'?" appeared earlier as:
"'Esse sono noi' Ill nostro lavoro sulle donne al lavoro nell'industria
cinematografica muta." In *Non Solo Dive: Pioniere Del Cinema
Italiano/Proceedings of the Non Solo Dive Conference.*
In Italian. Ed. and trans. Monica Dall'Asta. 19–30. Bologna: Cineteca
di Bologna, 2009.
and a version of chapter 1 as:
"Pink-Slipped: What Happened to Women in the Silent Motion
Picture Industry?" In *Blackwell's History of American Film.*
Eds. Roy Grundmann, Cynthia Lucia, and Art Simon. 155–177.
London: Blackwell, 2011.

1 2 3 4 5 C P 5 4 3 2 1
♾ This book is printed on acid-free paper.

Library of Congress Cataloging-in-Publication Data
Names: Gaines, Jane, 1946- author.
Title: Pink-slipped: what happened to women in the silent film
industries? / Jane M. Gaines.
Description: Urbana: University of Illinois Press, 2018. |
Series: Women and film history international | Includes
bibliographical references and index.
Identifiers: LCCN 2017042174| ISBN 9780252041815 (cloth : alk.
paper) | ISBN 9780252083433 (pbk. : alk. paper)
Subjects: LCSH: Women in the motion picture industry—United
States—History—20th century. | Silent films—United States—
History. | Motion pictures and women—United States.
Classification: LCC PN1995.9.W6 G33 2018 | DDC 791.43/6522—dc23
LC record available at https://lccn.loc.gov/2017042174

For Ally Acker, Anthony Slide, and Sharon Smith
who rediscovered them first

CONTENTS

ACKNOWLEDGMENTS

The idea of continuing the research on women in early motion pictures occurred to me in 1994 at the end of a year as Luce Distinguished Professor at Vassar College, for which I have Sarah Kozloff to thank. It never would have occurred to me to take up this particular project if it hadn't been for the legacy of the woman's college in which I was steeped that year. Returning to the Duke University Program in Literature, I was surprised that both graduate and undergraduate students wanted to work on researching the expanding list of women's names, and every student who contributed, along with the staff of the Film/Video/Digital Program, is listed on the website of what in 2013 became the Women Film Pioneers Project online database: wfpp.cdrs.columbia.edu (accessed January 1, 2017). But it was Radha Vatsal who was most dedicated and the project was really hers first.

Between 1994 and 2007, the project was envisioned as a multivolume research tool, and particular thanks go to both University of Illinois Press editor, Joan Catapano, who realized that the output had become too big for a book, and to Danny Nasset, the editor who followed through. It was after I arrived at Columbia University that Rebecca Kennison, director of the Center for Digital Research and Scholarship, saw the possibilities and arranged for Columbia University Libraries to publish the database. This made it a free resource available in every part of the world in which we were discovering women working (not just as actresses) in the first decades of national cinemas—from Europe to East Asia to the Middle East. Librarian for Media Studies and the Performing Arts Nancy Friedland, Metadata Coordinator Melanie Wacker, and Project Manager—now current CDRS Director—Mark Newton helped to implement the Women Film Pioneers Project as an online database. Most indispensable, however, have been the project managers—Sophia Bull at Stockholm University; Maria Fosheim Lund, Diana Wade, Katy Gray, and Kate Saccone at Columbia University; and Julie Buck, who found more irregularities in the credits than anyone.

This book, however, now titled *Pink-Slipped: What Happened to Women in the Silent Film Industries?* has an oblique relationship to the Women Film Pioneers Project, which was for some years as much a hobby as a scholarly pursuit. A year at the Radcliffe Institute for Advanced Study in 2003–2004, followed in 2005–2006 by a year as Kersten Hesselgren Honorary Chair at the University of Stockholm, and a Visiting Lecturer stint at the Technical Institute of Norway in Trondheim, Norway, gave me critical distance on the project of historical research and writing. Thanks here go to Bjorn Sorensen and Gunnar Iverson, as well as Tytti Soyla, for facilitating the turning point and arranging a 35mm film exhibition at the Swedish Film Institute.

Of course, a 35mm film exhibition and archival research is integral to silent motion picture historiography, but public screening of extant motion picture film prints is an especially crucial part of making the argument that not only were women credited on more titles than we knew but also that many of these films survive and, even better, that they have the potential to fascinate contemporary audiences. One of the first 35mm screenings of new discoveries was in 2005 at the restored Kimball Theatre in Williamsburg, Virginia, home of William and Mary College, at the invitation of Arthur Knight. Two programs as part of "To Save and Project" at the Museum of Modern Art in New York launched the Women Film Pioneers Project online in 2013 and, in September 2016, at the Anthology Film Archives in New York, rare prints were screened as part of "Woman with a Movie Camera." Other conferences and 35mm exhibitions from which I learned so much, not only from the screenings but from the papers delivered include: The Women and the Silent Screen conferences from Utrecht University (1997) to University of California, Santa-Cruz (2002); Concordia University, Montreal (2004); University of Stockholm (2008); University of Guadalajara, Mexico (2006); Cinema Ritrovato and University of Bologna, Italy (2010); University of Melbourne, Australia (2013); University of Pittsburgh (2015); and Shanghai (2017). The "Non Solo Dive"/"Not Just Divas" Conference at University of Bologna (2007) was instrumental in discovering Elvira Giallanella's *Umanità/ Humankind* (1919), and the New York Whitney Museum Alice Guy Blaché retrospective (2009), curated by Joan Simon and Alison McMahan, introduced the field to so many Gaumont and Solax films. As vital have been the "Doing Women's Film History" conferences organized by Julia Knight and Christine Gledhill (University of Sunderland), Yvonne Tasker (University of East Anglia), and Laraine Porter and Vicky Ball (De Montfort University). Yet none of these conferences or 35mm exhibitions have come anywhere close to representing the amount or range of work that continues to be discovered in FIAF (Fédération Internationale des Archives du Film) archives worldwide.

The Academy of Motion Picture Arts & Sciences Scholars Program funded both the database and this book. Indispensable were archivists at the U.S. Library of Congress Motion Picture, and Broadcast, and Sound Recording Division, especially Madeline Matz and Kim Tomodjoglou, as well as at the Academy of Motion Picture Arts and Sciences Margaret Herrick Library, Barbara Hall, and Val Almendarez. Collectors Mark Wannamaker, Joe Yranski, Richard Kozarski, and Jessica Rosner have been sharing rare materials for years now. Eminent historian and archivist Paul Spehr pointed me toward Antonia Dickson, the kinetoscope inventor's sister. Talks about early women in cinema evolved from "Mysteries of the Archives" at Indiana University (2005) to the National Film Theatre in London about "Women Writing Scenarios" (2009) as part of the thriving UK/Ireland Women in Film and Television History Network. In the first years of my graduate study of feminist film theory, scholars did not exactly bond over theory, but a community has grown around another generation of archival researchers—all of whom know what I mean—and for whom transformations of the "going story" has become something of a cause: Richard Abel, Mark Lynn Anderson, Connie Balides, Mark Cooper, Marina Dahlquist, Victoria Duckett, Kathy Fuller-Seeley, Annette Fürster, Hillary Hallett, Jennifer Horne, Sabine Lenk, Karen Ward Mahar, Rosanna Maule, Debashree Mukherjhee, Shelley Stamp, Drake Stutesman, and Ned Thanhouser. For their early groundwork, let me also mention Kay Armatage, Antonia Lant, Anne Morey, Martin Norden, Ben Singer, and Tom Slater. For foundation-building I think of E. Ann Kaplan, B. Ruby Rich, Yvonne Tasker, Heide Schlüpmann, Vivian Sobchack, Linda Williams, and Virginia Wexman. The origins of my critical distance on feminist film theory actually go back to the *Jump Cut* "collective" and radical role models Chuck Kleinhans and Julia Lesage. But it was probably Charlie Musser from whom I caught the early cinema bug and André Gaudreault must be thanked for insisting on theory with history as well as Greg Waller who as *Film History* editor was open to my hereticism. Philip Rosen has no idea how indebted I am to his *Change Mummified*, but he will know now. Tami Williams and Mark Williams deserve credit for the Media Ecology Project that has helped to put silent cinema researchers in the digital vanguard. For helping all of us to open our thought to the world, I thank Latin Americanists Joanne Hershfeld (University of North Carolina–Chapel Hill) and Patricia Torres San Martin (University of Guadalajara, Mexico), Mónica Villarroel (Cineteca Nacional de Chile, Santiago), Paulina Suárez-Hesketh (NYU), and Sheila Schvarzman (Universidade Anhembi Morumbi, São Paulo). Patty White (Swarthmore College) early anticipated these world developments in issues of *Camera Obscura* and Esha Niyogi De (UCLA) has now called our attention to Pakistan and the Bengali region of India. More recently, especially for opening up East Asia to the West, I am indebted to Weihong Bao, Hikari Hori, Lingzhen Wang, Yiman Wang, Louisa Wei, and Liu Yang.

Very special thanks to my collaborator Monica Dall'Asta, as I remember the joint talks conceived from the University of Sunderland in the U.K. to Florence, Italy, to Nanjing, China. And to Christine Gledhill, from whom I have learned the absolute most about melodrama as historical mode and even learned enough to know that we will never know enough.

New York, New York,
July 2017

PINK-SLIPPED

INTRODUCTION

What Gertrude Stein Wonders about Historians

In her 1934 University of Chicago lectures on narration, Gertrude Stein asks how historians can write so knowingly about what they cannot have known. Breathlessly running her question into her statement in her perplexing experimental prose she wonders: "how can an historian who knows everything really know everything that has really been happening how can he come to have the feeling that the only existence the man he is describing has is the one he has been giving to him. After all the historian who really knows everything and an historian really does he really does how can he have the creation of someone who has no existing except that the historian who is writing has at the moment of writing and therefore has as recognition at the moment of writing being writing." Then she concludes: "Well I am sure I do not know" (1993, 60). Gertrude Stein says that she does not know how the historian knows all that "he" knows. Neither does she know how the historian can "write" the no-longer-existing historical figure into existence, the moment of writing, and therefore the moment of the writer. She could have said that the only existence the past subject can have is the one given by the writer of history although *that* existence belongs not to the past but to the writer's present.

Gertrude Stein says she does not know how the historian "who really knows" can write about past events. If Stein doesn't know then who am I to insist? She doesn't know and neither do I. It is not clear to me how anyone would know enough from studying the historical evidence of events to write "this happened then." Yet that is what is done. However, to ask *how* it is that the historian "really knows everything" is not to suggest that there is "no knowing." Neither is this to say that the historian cannot *claim* to know or should not attempt to write or to make moving-image works about past events. Is there any other way to "say" without claiming to know? Perhaps not, suggests Gilles

Deleuze who once wondered: "How else can one write but of those things which one doesn't know, or knows incompletely? . . . We write only at the frontiers of our knowledge, at the border which separates our knowledge from our ignorance and transforms the one into the other" (1994, xxi). One historian, even while knowing "incompletely" might nevertheless write with confidence "It is now known that fifty percent of all silent-era films were written by women." But no, another historian now says, that figure exaggerates, implying that those who cite this fifty percent figure *do not know* how many women there were.[1] So what percentage should we now claim?

This book began as a study of events that took place in what we think of as the historical past, roughly the years 1895–1925. Over the course of that study the book became less about events and more about my disillusionment with the historiographic project of researching and writing, of tracking and describing receding events about which I knew too little. Admittedly, methodological disillusionment doesn't make a good advertisement for a work of historical scholarship if only because one assumes that others read to learn more, not to be told how impossible it is to learn enough. Yet one wonders why readers of histories are seldom allowed to share the historian's secret.

Of course, one researches to prove that there is more to know, to add to stores of knowledge.[2] What the historian cannot say, however, is that beyond his or her newly narrated evidence there is absolutely nothing, and that there is nothing because the past "is no more." No matter, the well-trained historical writer can realize past worlds in such fully detailed ways as to make it seem to readers that the historian "who really knows" had been there. Still, that historian keeps the secret that he or she cannot "really know" *all* that happened. What part do archives and museums play in keeping the historian's secret?

Holding the secrets, they keep the secret by enshrining artifactual remnants. Museums and archives, fostering the mystique of loss and working on the economics of artifact scarcity, rely on hard sciences dedicated to restoring cultures secreted in surviving objects. Here, especially in the case of silent-era motion picture film history, our hopes are attached to the "lost" film whose recovery could restore entire "never" worlds to our time.[3] Since the motion picture film print is relatively recent as an archival phenomenon, newly valued as a source and newly recruited as evidence, we have only now begun to think critically about the research implications of our reliance on this object. Thus "Object Lessons," chapter 4, takes up the oddities of the artifactual film object but then considers the equally odd "virtual artifact" (Fossati 2009, 12). Unavoidable here are the implications of using digital means to "bring back" lost detail that is disappearing on deteriorating motion picture archival prints. Viewing these retrieved images we marvel at how much is still there to see on a screen; we're awestruck by the illusion of reality still intact. Or is the historical image not an "illusion" at all? Is it "no illusion" but rather a profound "presence of the past" effectively "transferred" to us in the present?[4]

As a consequence of this famously successful illusion, there is then an extra-special lure of *historiographic knowability* attached to motion picture film and photographic research. And while an entire field has already critiqued a cinematic illusionism that produces the tug of "realism" on the spectator, we have stopped short of applying this critique to our own scholarly research methods. One could, however, argue that moving image historians want to have it both ways, that is, to critique cinematic "realism" as well as "objectivity" but still undertake archival research undeterred.[5] Yet there is evidence of the field's awareness of trouble ahead in writing about modern technologies, as seen in the current turn to Foucault-inspired *media archaeology*.[6] So in the following, I pick up the methodological openness of the "archaeological turn" as well as its break with tradition, its approach to historical events and objects that refuses to claim to know what transpired in the past. Thus, while advocating for archival research and exploration, I am as interested in the historical conditions of "unknowability." But here what intrigues me is a specific sort of "unknowability" as in *which* knowledges are allowable at *what* historical junctures and which are decidedly *unwelcome*. Finally, then, I see a pattern of *precarious relations* between the historical past and the present moment and thus prefer to ask how each present *needs* the very past that it proceeds to make.

Originally, the idea was to explain academic feminism's divergent accounts of women working in the silent-era national film industries in the 1895–1925 period.[7] The wide discrepancy between these accounts seems especially striking, with estimates ranging between nearly "no women" and "many women." Women in the silent era were found to have been "there" in the early 1970s and then "not there" in the mid-1970s. Now, thirty years later, they are understood by historians as more "there" in numbers and influence than in the contemporary film and television industries. Yet we may also conclude that their "being there" is an effect of a contemporary wish to find more historical women, an effect that comes after several decades of "not having found" very many. Or, the question as to whether women were or weren't "there" could be understood as a consequence of commitments to current academic trends. Finally, and most dramatically, there is the evidence of women's contribution to building national film cultures that can no longer be denied because researchers have now witnessed those contributions in the hundreds of whole motion picture films as well as fragments that have come to light in recent years. Extant silent-era film prints housed in the member archives of the Fédération Internationale des Archives du Film/Federation of Film Archives testify to their existence. Recent international exhibitions have evidenced these women appearing on screen as well as named in the credits.[8] There can be no more denying. And yet there is. Today, even with significant ongoing international research, more evidence, although altering the historical record, has not changed the foundational story—the story that men alone founded the national film industries.[9]

HISTORY AND THEORY AS NO LONGER ESTRANGED

The case of the widely divergent accounts of womens' silent-era work is an epistemologically unusual one. Perhaps the easiest way to explain this exceptionality is to fit academic feminism and film (a subfield within the larger discipline of cinema and media studies), into Euro-American intellectual trends where the post-structuralist challenge to the humanities and social sciences has been taken up unevenly.[10] While in the mid 1970s feminist film theory was founded on post-structuralist thought, women's history was established on top of the historicist tradition that post-structuralism sought to critique.[11] When post-structuralism was finally introduced into U.S. women's history circles, it arrived relatively late, and, when it did arrive, it stirred heated debate and discussion (Morgan 2006, 12–13).[12] But if post-structuralism came "late" to history, it had, in contrast, come "early" to feminism and film studies, which meant that historiography came "late" to this subfield, arriving in the 1980s with what has been called the "historical turn" in film and media studies (Butler 2008, 397–399) or the "new film history." From this it might be deduced that the "historical turn" was a reaction against certain post-structuralist positions that underwrote the conceptually powerful feminist film theory.[13] While this case can be made, such an analysis reproduces an old antagonism between "theory" and "history" that we would now avoid.[14] Indeed, for some, the "new film history," especially in its silent-era focus, has been synonymous with "the alliance of theory and history" (Gaudreault 2011, 11–13). Yet Heide Schlüpmann, considering Gaudreault's "theory" and "history," now allied within the "new film history," has wondered. "Theory?" she asks, "which theory?" For in her estimation feminist theory has thus far been left out of that formulation.[15] Schlüpmann's intervention thus explicitly encourages histories of these theories, to which I also add histories of how we have done and continue to do "history," as we will shortly see.[16] Here, then, are several angles from which we interrogate the "new film history."[17] Above all, however, we need to insist that "theory" and "history" are no longer estranged.

Although post-structuralism upended fields like anthropology, challenging scientificity by insisting that scholars, far from being objective, ultimately find exactly what they are looking for, few fields have dared to bring the discursive "construction of everything" too close to empirical research methods on the assumption that one undoes the other.[18] Across the humanities, however, this is difficult to map, historicism's legacy of "objectivity" having been *both* rejected and claimed. Some readers may even wonder what the fuss is all about since today the historian's methodology allows a coexistence of theoretical and empirical approaches within the same study.[19] For one, this book examines the apparent incompatabilities these approaches yield: the theoretical position that there were "no women" as opposed to the evidence of empirical "women" or women theoretically "absent" and then empirically "present" in abundance. To juxtapose these positions is to foreground methodologies at apparent odds. Admittedly, to say something like "Women were *both* 'there' and 'not there'" seems on the face of it a preposterous statement, but the idea is to put uncritical empiricism in check while remaining open to empirical findings that might challenge reigning theoretical paradigms.[20] Recall Judith Mayne's observation about the incommensurability of the empirical "real viewer" and the theoretical ideal female spectator. Since the tendency in the field at the time was, as she said, to "dismiss one or the other," she argued for a theorization of the very difficulty of thinking these two approaches together (1993, 56).

Today, several decades after the "historical turn" introduced empirical evidence as a corrective to film theory, we are in a different moment, perhaps a swing in the other direction (Gaines 2013a, 71). So in the following chapters I deign to say that feminist film historians, after an immense amount of new empirical research, have definitively proven how women in the silent era were "there" in numbers and influence. For the goal here is not to replace the "no women" narratives of the first film histories with ones into which women have been slotted.[21] Why? Because the larger project is to use theories of history to trouble assumptions about *history*, the concept, which entails scrutinizing historiographic method and admitting its shortcomings. Of course, we might ask why one would undertake to write about the difficulty, the futility, of ever really knowing the historical subject of his or her research. To admit the futility, however, is not to say that there is no value in the pursuit of historical knowledge, especially as that knowledge can perplex and surprise. Yet any new findings can only have "knowledge effects" on one crucial condition, a condition that should give us pause. New knowledge can have its effects only on condition that the culture in question defers to something called "history" as authoritative. This particular study, while aware of that authority, is less deferential and treats historical knowledge as especially unstable knowledge. Skepticism gives rise to such questions as: How can we possibly know *now* what we could not have known even then? And given that we can't really know the past "now" either, why would we turn to the past to explain the most mystifying present? And what is the unknowability of the present compared to the complete inscrutability of the historical past? With these questions in mind, I ask whether it is possible for academics to write less knowingly when they are trained to write more knowingly. Now that we think of it, however, there is no easy way to say that one is not certain, especially in the established genre of historical writing where one is expected to assert rather than to equivocate. Consider as well the pressure to choose one interpretation of events over another and the possibility that when one foregrounds such interpretation or writes too tentatively, stopping to qualify too much, one risks breaking the historiographic illusion.

In Phillip Rosen's view, such issues are indicative of the "uncertainties" of the historiographic project, and given that there are so many of these, he urges comprehensive interrogation, asking nothing less than that historiography begin to "historicize itself." Rosen urges us to this project, although warning that the historicization of history is its potential undoing: "If historiography is itself historical, how can it claim validity in the selection and interrogation of sources, much less the construction of an internally unified, developmental sequence or any form of synthesis?" (2001, 127). And so in seeking to "historicize history," in turning the historiographic method back onto "history" to show *that it is situated*, critics may fall back on the very enterprise they would challenge. Such is the case of this book. Undoubtedly, I, too, have relied on the very idea of "history" that I call into question, although I am not alone in my habituated recourse to either the term "history" or to common sense ideas about "history." Then again, neither am I alone in my skepticism.

Theoretical support for this line of skeptical inquiry comes from the contemporary philosophy of history, introduced in chapter 2. This "new" philosophy goes by a number of names; thus while for some it has been *postmodern history* and for others *metahistory*, it might also be termed *metaphilosophy of history* or even *history-writing as critique*.[22] Some theorists affiliate as *deconstructive historians*, and my partiality to this approach stems in part from what I see to be the productivity of combining terms at apparent odds.[23] And "new" here? To call the critical approach to history "new" or "contemporary" separates it from the earlier "philosophy of history" of Marx or Hegel.[24] Although these developments may be "new" as in having appeared in the last half of the twentieth century, they may not all claim to be "philosophy" proper, a nuance I accommodate by referring alternately to "theories of history."[25] Finally, to characterize the irreverence of the radical wing or the deconstructionist, sometimes postmodern approach, consider Keith Jenkins and Alan Munslow who assert that it is to them "wonderful news that historians can never get things right" (2004, 4). But, of course, this is only good news for some theories of history but not others; so at the outset let me register several reservations.

First, as I have argued elsewhere, the history skeptics make something of a "straw man" of the traditional historian and, although conventional textbooks continue to fill libraries, there may be a danger in overstating the case (Gaines 2015a). Second, while engaged in the critique of "history" we would not want to risk warning off "history-as-critique," Joan W. Scott's Foucaultian formulation (2007, 28). Third, and related to the second reservation, new theories of history, given their ambivalence, may have underdeveloped the case for the *study* of past events, and here I persist in asking "why undertake research?" Fourth, now slipping into the proceedings is an acknowledgment of the "presence effects" of historical traces, those traces we may experience as profoundly moving.[26] And my final reservation, related in ways to the fourth, is the very insatiability of empirical desires seen in collecting and hoarding and the appetite for suppressed stories as well as arcane detail. With these reservations, in the following I still take my cue from the new philosophy of history, staging encounters between theories of history and traditions of history writing as well as historical research practices, and reframing the critique of approaches to historical research, which includes the digital upset of the traditional archive. And why? Technological upheaval forces a reconfiguration of sources—material and structural. Why else? "History-as-critique" entails strategic use of past events as the antithesis of what is "thought to be," the opposite of the entrenched and habitual, and this is the spirit in which I revisit the primal research scene.

THE MARGARET HERRICK LIBRARY, 1972

In 1972, Sharon Smith and Anthony Slide, both working at the Margaret Herrick Library of the Academy of Motion Picture Arts and Sciences and looking at the same records, drew a similar conclusion: women had made a significant contribution to the U.S. film industry in the first years. Smith concludes that "women made their greatest impact during the pioneering years," that is, when they were involved in so many aspects of the new business (1985, Forward).[27] Slide's retrospective analysis of the same discovery, however, includes an indictment of feminists. Not only did the discovered records exist irrespective of feminism, he charges, but feminist scholars had a different agenda in the 1970s. Slide thinks that the new feminist academics in that decade were looking everywhere for women except where they could be found—in the archives: "It was far easier to protest about discrimination against women than to accept that there were more women directors at work in the American film industry prior to 1920 than during any period of its history" (1977, 9). Interestingly, the second half of Slide's sentence, to the effect that there were "more women directors" in the silent era than at any period since, has been often quoted, but the first half, the indictment of feminist scholarship, has been left out. Feminism, he wants to say, could not explain a phenomenon inconsistent with the political project of locating discrimination, and that phenomenon, he concludes from looking at the evidence, was that there was an absence of discrimination in the early film industry.[28]

Slide's sources were not, as one might have thought, obscure, for he found his startling evidence in the very trade papers that have been the foundation for U.S. studio film industry. He recalls: "Back in 1972, I was hired to set up and undertake the initial research for the *American Film Institute Catalog: Feature Films, 1911–1920*. As I turned the pages of such early American trade papers as *The Moving Picture World* and *Motion Picture News*, I slowly became aware of the number of films directed by women" (1996a, v). He concludes that there was little to no commentary because a woman directing a film in the early decades was unremarkable: "Not only were women making films, but contemporary observers were making little of the fact. It was taken for granted that women might direct as often and as well as their male counterparts, and there was no reason to belabor this truth" (1996a, v). Much as we might want to applaud this conclusion that women were so integral as to be unremarkable—for its impact alone—further research in the period points to the opposite—the production of their "remarkability." To put it another way, there was publicity value in finding "remarkable" women working among men in the U.S. silent film industry. For another thing, Slide's conclusion that contemporaries "made little" of these women doesn't account for the fan magazine articles championing women as writers, directors, and producers, many of them written by female journalists. These writers treated this apparently "unremarkable" phenomenon as remarkable in its exception to the rule of "men only," making human interest stories out of industry women.[29] Then there were commentators, not quite certain whether women were usual or unusual, who made women in the industry *both* remarkable and unremarkable, depending on the jobs they held, some of whom countered gender expectations more than others. For instance, Robert Grau matter-of-factly observed that women were everywhere and obvious but quite unexpectedly working at the marketing and exhibiting ends of the business where they were least expected to be found at the time:[30]

In no other line of endeavor has woman had so emphatic an impress than in the amazing film industry, which has created in its infant stage a new art wherein the gentler sex is so active a factor that one may not name a single vocation in either the artistic or business side of its progress in which women are not conspicuously engaged. In the theatres, in the studios, and even in the exchanges where film productions are marketed and released to exhibitors, the fair sex is represented as in no other calling to which women have harkened in the early years of the twentieth century. (1914, 41)

Other historical commentators identified powerful women and mentioned them because they were remarkable in their exceptional success or perhaps unremarkable enough to be mentioned along with the men with whom they were seen to be comparable at the time. Thus, some influential women *were* unremarkable, or *had become so* as they were referenced by the first historians of the U.S. film industry. Mary Pickford's financial triumphs are featured in Terry Ramsaye (1986, 741–754), the Clara Kimball Young Pictures Company is mentioned in Benjamin Hampton (1970, 135), and the Helen Gardner Picture Corporation figures in Lewis Jacobs (1975, 91).

Today, over forty years later, however, what might be called Slide's "unremarkability thesis" looks quite different. Whether a woman directing was "unremarkable" or "remarkable" for her time may not then be a function of numbers themselves but a function of the exigencies of the times. Thus we would take into account the historical mindset and climate of receptivity and recognize what I have called the historian's "retrospective advantage," that is, a looking back (2011, 108). A phenomenon "unremarkable" in its time may become "remarkable" in a later time, as, for example, in the early 1970s when feminists saw a woman directing films in the European and U.S. silent film industries as a "remarkable" ideal in comparison with industry employment patterns in their contemporary moment.[31] Karyn Kay's introduction to Alice Guy Blaché's "Women's Place in Photoplay Production," for instance, would claim that as a director who owned her own studio, Guy Blaché was "alone among women in 1914" (1977, 337). More recent research, however, shows that although Guy Blaché does indeed represent an exception as president and co-owner of the Ft. Lee, New Jersey, Solax Company, she was not completely alone since other U.S. women were also directing, writing, and producing motion pictures even before 1914, as chapter 1 demonstrates.[32] In other words, Alice Guy Blaché may have been a singular exception, but she was also part of a phenomenon. What now to call this phenomenon depends upon how the conversation about female executives as well as female film and television directors is framed today.[33] But also it depends upon how feminism and film configures female directors as a contemporary global phenomenon.[34] For instance, as the field takes up the creative work of what Kathleen McHugh calls today's "transnational generation" of female directors (2009, 119), this frame calls up transnationalism's parallels.[35] Significantly here, Lingzhen Wang has charged us with the task of interrogating colonial and neocolonial knowledge transmission but also with rethinking the global interventions of Western feminist film theory (2011, 15). Thus, the multiple angularity of the newly inflected term *transnational*: it locates makers and critics across "uneven" capital circuits and anticipates location of an earlier transnationality beginning with Alice Guy Blaché, who was a French immigrant to the United States, reminding us that for the earliest companies, "market" meant world export.[36]

In the following, I focus on women in the U.S. silent film industry where "What happened?" has been most repeatedly asked, although in the conclusion I gesture abroad and not only because from the first decade cinema was caught up in a world-wide capitalist competition.[37] I look beyond toward women we have *yet to imagine* as having been there in far-flung parts of the world. This is not to say that it is only cultural distance that renders their lives unimaginable. For just as inconceivable have been some women *inside* the dream factory—clerical workers figured in chapter 7, for instance.

OVERESTIMATION AND UNDERESTIMATION

The amount of evidence of women's creative work in the early U.S. industry has increased since the 1970s and continues to grow. For example, in the early 1970s, the number of credits Sharon Smith counts leads her to conclude that "There were more women directors in Hollywood during the teens and twenties than in any other period since that time" and thus to estimate twenty-six between 1913 and 1927 (1973, 77–90).[38] Still, more recent research indicates a higher number of directors, and, following the publication of Karen Mahar's groundbreaking work, an even higher number of aspiring women producers.[39] It is now estimated that, between 1911 and 1927, over sixty U.S. women thought of themselves at one time or another as film producers or producer-directors.[40] Female producers appear even before Hollywood was Hollywood and, later, outside as well as inside the West Coast center of this new industry (Gaines and Vatsal 2013).[41] Yet I would argue that the numerical differential evidenced in increased numbers even worldwide, undeniable as the numbers may be, is not as significant as the conclusions that have rushed in, sometimes in advance of the numbers, at every juncture of interest in the topic of women filmmakers in an industry considered hostile to women. Immediate companion to the lament "no women" has been and continues to be the circular logic of the solution in which without "more women" working in film and television there can never be "more women" (of the remarkable kind) on screen.[42] However, women-in-the-industry is ultimately a matter of what it is that feminists have hoped to see and consequently how they have chosen to deploy employment numbers. What am I saying here? While it may seem contradictory, it appears that when we consider the last forty years of research on women and film, the pattern has been to underestimate as well as to overestimate the contribution of women in the first decades. While we now admit that we underestimated in the 1970s, how could we have also overestimated?

As philosopher Denise Riley has analyzed it, overestimation is an ironic consequence of the achievements of academic feminism (2003, 4). In recent decades we have witnessed a dramatic reversal—feminism coming from behind in the institutional race for viability and finally arriving at the point where feminist discourse is academically automatic. Biddy Martin describes how women's studies settled in as "endless repetitions of the already known," eventually in danger of falling on "deaf ears." (2008, 169–170). Today the familiar position that women are powerful in their own way easily absorbs Alice Guy Blaché's 1914 argument for the female director as "an authority on the emotions" (Slide 1977, 338) and meets no resistance.[43] Still, how strange it is, looking back to the 1970s, to think that feminism, which feels to Riley as though it has exceeded its success, could have overreached its goal. We wonder how feminism could have arrived, become established and institutionalized, and then been so suddenly "over," especially since, as we know, feminism has not met its goal of women's emancipation worldwide. Assessing the academic disciplines, Riley now thinks that, as she says, "There are always too many invocations of 'women,' too much visibility, too many appellations which were better dissolved again—or are in need of some accurate and delimiting handling" (2003, 4). While we might agree that much of feminist discourse in past decades has been written in a compensatory mode, a mode of overvaluation in which women, elevated either by their assigned inferiority or their as-yet-unacknowledged superiority, could "do no wrong," let us also consider the companion phenomenon. This is the way in which women's historical contributions were undercounted, were unimagined, really, by an earlier feminism. There is no more dramatic case of this than that of women helping to start nascent national film industries worldwide, beginning with the first explosion in the United States, the example with which we are concerned here. Consider in this instance the way in which feminism required *both* an analysis of underestimation to support the oppression thesis and a compensatory overestimation in which "women" are now seen to be everywhere. This is not the only issue on which feminism appears contradictory, as I will continue to note.

Overestimation as companion to underestimation is perhaps best exemplified by "writing women into history," the project taken up by scholars so effectively by the late 1980s (Scott 2006, 388). As historian Joan W. Scott has described the work of the first feminist historians, the success of that work has been in the archival excavation of "exemplary" artistic and literary figures, their "invisibility" reversed as they were made "visible" in new narratives of "struggle" (1996a, 1). In this tradition, African American historian Dawn Clark Hine has defended the necessity of the encyclopedic excavation stage as a fundamental groundbreaking, especially in fields defined by knowledge denial where few expected to find women at all, least of all Black women.[44] Anglo-American feminist film studies, however, developed outside the "writing women into history" movement and has been an exception to it in a number of important ways, four of which are the following: First, as I have said, the current archival excavation stage has come relatively late, some decades after "women's history" became institutionally established in history, art history, and literature.[45] Second, as already noted above, historiographic traditions and archival institutional supports were developed later, effectively after

1978, in what is referred to as the "historical turn." Third, a strong feminist theoretical tradition from the 1970s embraced an "anti-historicism" that critiqued the kind of study that might easily, although perhaps too easily, have underwritten archival excavation projects.[46]

Fourth, most interesting of all when we consider women in the early film industries, the favored feminist metaphor of "invisibility to visibility" is oddly invalid. These women, many of whom began as actresses, would have to have been "invisible on screen," so to speak. Not so easily "hidden" from historical view and neither unsung nor inconspicuous, many had been widely known and "everywhere seen." After all, these women's wildest ideas in moving picture form were technologically disseminated worldwide, an advantage no other group of working women in the first decades of the last century could claim.[47] Ironically, the high visibility of a single image could eclipse an entire world phenomenon. One high-circulation female image stands for—but also stands in the way of—many others who, in a sense, underwrote the first one. To give the classic example, "Pearl White" has remained a recognizable name, not only because of her daredevil films exhibited internationally but because more than one actress stepped into the global phenomenon. To see *Pearl White*, however, is effectively *not to see* that she was predated by the American Gene Gauntier's girl spy (Gaines 2010, 293–298) and the French Protéa played by Josette Andriot (Dall'Asta 2013, 75–78) postdated by serial queen imitators like the Chinese Rose White Woo (Bao 2013, 187–221), Indian "Fearless Nadia" (Thomas 2013, 160–186), and French Berthe Dagmar (Spiers 2014).[48] Over time, the screen heroics of French, Indian, Chinese, and U.S. action imitators (Helen Holmes, Helen Gibson, Cleo Madison, Kathlyn Williams, Grace Cunard, Ruth Roland) were effectively conflated into one highly promoted *Pearl White* (Dahlquist 2013a, b, c).[49] In their time, silent-era action heroines were everywhere and invincible and yet, in the 1970s, feminist film scholars *did not know this*. So again, why did feminists not know "what had happened" in the silent era? The question of "what happened" to women in the early film industries is inseparable from the question of "what happened" to the research on these women that began in the Herrick Library in 1972.

What might have been but wasn't? One would have thought that the Leftist historiography associated with E. P. Thompson (1966) and Sheila Rowbotham (1973) that produced British working-class history associated with "history from below" would have had its immediate impact on feminist film studies, given the shared proximity to British Marxist cultural studies.[50] But a warning emerged at the time in the form of the *Screen* magazine position against "historicism." There, Keith Tribe cautions about the "endless quest for the dead heroines of the past," a watchward coupled with a prediction. Because "historicism and humanism" went hand in hand, he argued, cinema histories might reproduce this double problem in which historical work "regresses rapidly into a humanism and its support in which the person is the bearer of the history, the visible agent of historicity, in whose actions are inscribed the truth of the past" (Tribe 1977,

10, 22). By the late 1970s, we see in *Screen* the strong post-structuralist effects of both Louis Althusser and Michel Foucault, and although Foucault's ideas about "history" came to the fore in the intervening decades while those of Althusser receded, the latter comes back and becomes seminal to this study.[51]

WHY WE TOOK THE "HISTORICAL TURN"

Today, safely into the "new film history," it is time to assess the "historical turn" in film and media studies (Gaines 2013a).[52] In one of the first efforts to take stock of changes in the field, Annette Kuhn and Jackey Stacey explain the 1980s "historical turn" as part of a reaction to the extremes of 1970s film theory. That theory included a prohibition against empirical historiography, a taboo condensed into the term *anti-historicism* or the "critical stance towards 'historicism'" (1998, 2). Yet as the idea of theoretical excesses recedes in memory, the "turn" has been characterized less as a corrective to 1970s theory, and more as a turn *toward* historiography. But since historiography may have been a turn back to what 1970s post-structuralism prohibited, it may be time to cast these developments in another way, that is, to ask if the historical turn has been more of a turn *away* from the post-structuralist critique of empirical approaches.[53] Elsewhere, I have suggested that in film and media studies, given its legacy, post-structuralist theory has functioned historically as a kind of antidote to historicism (Gaines 2014c). Yet, while the leading historical works in new film history have been what is often termed *theoretically informed*, there have been too few attempts to foreground, let alone critique, the methods and assumptions that film and cinema historiography picked up along with the professional historian's method.[54]

From all of this, it would seem that today any study of women in film history has not one but three rugs pulled out from under it—film, history, and "feminism". As I have said, in the Western humanities today feminist positions no longer pose the danger that they once did but are rather intellectual givens. This is especially the case in film theory and criticism where feminism was early absorbed (Williams 2003, 1265). So if feminism is passé, what then would be the purpose of continuing to study either the exceptions *to* or the conditions *of* gender inequality in any historical period? After all, as only a feminism after feminism would understand, it is not at all certain that we need another illustration of the foregone conclusions of Second Wave feminist scholarship. In *post-postfeminist feminism* we nail the frustrating ambiguity of postfeminism as it implies feminism exhausted and replace it with feminism revitalized, and most importantly, *itself critiqued*.[55]

At the "*post-post*" moment, acknowledging feminism's incomplete project but facing it with an emphasis on futurity, I have needed a term. In the following, I use *feminist utopianist* to signal a legacy shared with the Frankfurt School and especially Ernst Bloch on anticipation, which I find relevant to the silent era's hopes pinned to the technologically new (Schlüpmann 2010, 220; Hansen 2010, xii). But although a feminist utopianism might describe some recent formulations, including those belonging to queer theory, it is more of a flicker that comes and goes.[56] The strategy of utopianism as an explanatory theory in our time might or might not retain the revolutionary "hope" from Marxist feminist theory.[57] Its first utility, however, is to test the short moment of heightened expectations for women in the "new times" of the silent era.

Here then, where we have apparently hit a wall, and with so many rugs pulled from under us, we may yet find theoretical opportunity. If there is utility to be found in the concept of gender, as Joan Scott maintains, it is because "gender" still presents us with an "unanswered," and even an unanswerable question (1996a, 4).[58] Over two decades after this formulation, Scott continues to maintain that gender is valuable, but "only as a question" (2008a, 1422), yet a question that inspires the subtitle of this book.[59] Thus in chapter 1, "What Happened to Women in the Silent U.S. Film Industry?" I refuse to answer the question posed, using the "what happened?" query to anticipate a theory of history in which past and present are put in constant relation. The first chapter thus postulates interrelated disappearances: 1) Silent-era women as writers, actresses, producers, and directors disappeared from the limelight. 2) They were left out of historical accounts in their era.[60] 3) They slipped away along with silent cinema and remained buried in the 1970s when they might have been uncovered again. But in the present, I intervene, deferring an answer to my question and asking the reader to take a detour through the book's chapters to find out how the "answer" to the "what happened" question eludes us.

Throughout, silent-era female film workers dramatize the unbridgeable distance between what we call "history" and the events of "the past." Chapter 2 introduces Antonia Dickson, sister to kinetoscope inventor William Kennedy Laurie Dickson, an ideal subject for women's history, an approach that the chapter then interrogates with attention to the "ambiguity" of the term "history." The argument here is that because past events are still in motion relative to present events, a historiographic practice, especially a feminist one, needs a theory of historical time. Why? The short answer is because we in the present are what was formerly the future of the women who helped to start the worldwide film industries. The long answer unfolds in the following chapters.

Quite quickly, however, the reader will begin to wonder how foregrounding the difference between historical events and their later narration impacts the research questions historians ask. Thus, in chapter 3, I take up a question in which feminist film historians are already invested: "Did Alice Guy Blaché make *La Fée aux choux* (*The Cabbage Fairy*) in 1896?" Or, what do we do when the evidence of the extant films cannot be made to fit the historical narrative that contemporary scholars want to tell? Historians of motion pictures, I maintain, have an additional burden because, as I am arguing, their object of study itself promises a special kind of *historiograhic knowing* thought to guarantee former existence and confirm a "having happened" in time.

Thus, the survival of motion picture footage from early in the cinema century encourages the empirical certainty we challenge. But does scrutiny of the scientific aspirations of "history," the discipline, apply to the specialized archival sciences so integral to field research today? As I discuss in chapter 4, "Object Lessons," the convictions of empirical knowing return in the film archivist's discourse on analog and digital restoration practices. Without a doubt, the motion picture film print is the artifactual object par excellence, encouraging what I call *indexical certainty*, an intentional redundancy. The issue begins with what is meant by "history" in the archivist's "internal history of the copy" (Cherchi Usai 2000, 147), and ends with film restoration entailing digital conversion to something ontologically unlike motion picture film. Here, I offer a case study of the Dutch EYE Institute's restoration of *Shoes* (Lois Weber, Universal, 1916).

After arguing in chapter 2 for more theories of history, I propose such a theory in chapter 5, "The Melodrama Theory of Historical Time," turning for the germ of a theory not outside but back inside the field to feminist film melodrama theory. There is no denying that historical time has its lived dimension in which the past, present, and future, always at odds, produce the *everyday uncertainties* that plague human beings. But such uncertainties confound historians as well, a condition I address as their *location-in-time quandary* carried over into the companion chapter 6 "Are They Us?" based on Joan W. Scott's question about the historian's relation to historical subjects. The question "What happened to *them*?" leads to chapter 7, "Working in the Dream Factory," and thus to the lower-paid workers left out of the first feminist focus on female directors.

How an earlier feminism "did not know" is picked up again in chapter 8, which opens with film executive June Mathis's 1925 statement that it was women in the U.S. film industry who produced the "voice of the home" that was exported around the world. At stake is a new paradigm—the "voice of the home" as melodrama, the mode. Unlike the empirical point of departure in which the historian is ostensibly open to "finding," I know in advance that I am looking for how women participated in the "new times" when starting a film company that entailed grabbing possibilities open to whomever happened to be there. To study the technological moment of silent pictures from the vantage of women's aspirations is to study a past intent on a future, that is, to study expectations that, for a time, were attached to "newness." It is also to make women integral to the study of moving image innovation in the first decades.

Why *Pink-Slipped*? Given the norm of freelance work and irregular employment in the silent era, no female worker would ever have received a notorious notice of dismissal—a pink slip. Hence, the intentional misnomer of my title. To ask "what happened to them" is to then ask what? I argue that although we cannot know their past we need to develop approaches to it as decidedly feminist theories of film history, theories that even take "history" to task. Thinking more than one historical moment at once allows me to conclude in chapter 9 that in the U.S. industry, women were replaced by the very motion picture narrative technology that they had helped to develop. Women were made redundant by that technology.

Finally, a word about the audience for a book in which historiographic methods are at issue. Hayden White maintains that we must separate the "historical past" from the "useable past," that past claimed by the community, which, after Michael Oakeshoot he calls the "practical past" (2014). My critique of "history" here targets that "historical past" that Oakeshoot thinks is the "invention of historians" (1999, 3). But what do we say about the overlap between the two? What neither White nor Oakeshoot address is the connection between the "practical" and the "professional" uses of the past, especially as communities confirm or contest highly circulated stories. If it were possible I would exempt the "practical " uses of stories about silent-era filmmakers from my critique. For there is a world community of feminist filmmakers and film festival goers who are invested in the "practical" exercise of counting visible women in the international film scene. Although this study does not address that broad community it is, however, *for* them. Its message is that while historical research may stir up epistemological trouble, the stories we choose to tell with our research are always under pressure to line up with the "practical" imperatives of the times.

1
WHAT HAPPENED TO WOMEN IN THE SILENT U.S. FILM INDUSTRY?

"**W**hy did she ever leave the pictures!" laments Epes Winthrop Sargent upon seeing a photograph of actress Gene Gauntier. Quoted in the introduction to Gauntier's 1928 memoir "Blazing the Trail," Sargent cries out on behalf of a generation of audiences (1928, 4). Four years earlier, in the same vein, a *Photoplay* article titled "Unwept, Unhonored, and Unfilmed" bemoans the disappearance of Gauntier as well as of Marion Leonard, Florence Lawrence, Florence Turner, Cleo Madison, Flora Finch, and Helen Holmes (Smith 1924). Such a complaint is nothing new to motion picture historiography. "Unwept," in the best fan magazine tradition, is nostalgia for the forgotten glory of the fading actress and today it could be easily dismissed as nothing more. But buried within the 1924 article are motion picture industry history details seldom found in fan magazine puff pieces. And, as intriguing for film scholars, outbursts of feeling from the women *Photoplay* interviewed suggest another story, one for a new feminist film moment.

Deep within the article we find evidence that these women put their names behind independent companies in the first decade of the new industry. We learn, for instance, that in 1913 Florence Turner left the Vitagraph Company to form Turner Films, Inc., in London (Smith 1924, 65). Further, we read that in December 1912, Gene Gauntier, along with director Sidney Olcott and her husband Jack Clark, left the Kalem Company and started the independent Gene Gauntier Feature Players Company (ibid., 102).[1] In the same article we are told that Florence Lawrence headed the Victor Company and that Helen Holmes was associated with the Signal Film Company (Smith 1924, 103–104).

Florence Turner, actress/director/producer, Turner Films, Inc., 1913–1917. Courtesy Margaret Herrick Library, Academy of Motion Picture Arts & Sciences. Beverly Hills, California.

Over ninety years later, new feminist scholarship tells us what *Photoplay* did not tell fans in 1924. What *Photoplay* doesn't say is that Lawrence started the Victor Company with her husband Harry Solterer in 1912 or that Holmes began Signal in 1915 with her director husband J. P. McGowan, followed by the S. L. K. Serial Corporation and Helen Holmes Production Corporation in 1919 (Mahar 2006, 63–65, 118–120). But that is not all. *Photoplay* doesn't mention comedienne Flora Finch's efforts to start not one but two companies in order to write and to produce her popular action serials—the Flora Finch Company (1916–1917) and Film Frolics Picture Corporation (1920) (Miller 2013a). Marion Leonard is mentioned, but not as the first star actress to start a company, which new research asserts (Mahar 2006, 62). Finally, *Photoplay* features Cleo Madison as an actress although she also directed and wrote at least ten shorts and two features between 1915 and 1917, the creative high point for women at Universal Films (Cooper 2010, 24; 2013a).[2] These are only some of many women who were not just actresses in the first two decades when more women held positions of relative power than at any other time in U.S. motion picture industry history.[3]

Today we have strong evidence to support the assertion that these and other "unwept and unhonored" actresses "did it all"—acting, writing, even editing, sometimes directing, and often producing motion pictures as they attempted to start companies. But here my concern is as much the demise of these enterprising players as it is their ascendance. Their marginalization, shrouded as it is in star nostalgia and cloaked in

Flora Finch, actress/producer,
Flora Finch Company, 1916–1917;
Film Frolics Picture Corp., 1920.
Private collection.

industry euphemism, is awkward to narrate if we want to answer the question in all of its respects. Because our question—"What happened to them?"—is unlike *Photoplay*'s "Where are they now?" Ours is a several-part question for the intellectual history of a field, distilled when we ask not just "What happened?" but "Why didn't we know?"[4] We count not one but three disappearances, first from the limelight and second from historical records, the second a function of the first. Then there is the third, effectively a disappearance in a moment when they might have been discovered and therefore the most difficult for another generation to fathom. While we are not surprised that, fifty years before the advent of academic feminism, *Photoplay* didn't mention key aspects of women's silent-era careers, later generations may wonder why a feminist film historiography did not discover these women in the 1970s.[5] A comprehensive intellectual history needs to explain why, after the reference to women as silent film directors in one of the earliest issues of *Women and Film* (Smith 1973, 77–90), the field still largely assumed that there were very few women and that those few were minor figures. One wonders why, when one researcher uncovered the evidence of many more silent-era women directors in the early 1970s, there was neither fanfare nor follow-up.[6]

Cleo Madison, actress/writer/director, Universal Films, 1915–1917. Private collection.

GENE GAUNTIER:
THE RETURN OF THE GIRL SPY

Seven of the actresses *Photoplay* recalls have a career trajectory in common. They began work early, some as early as 1906–1907, and by the mid-to-late teens all experienced career setbacks. Although some started up again in the late teens and early 1920s, none of these women returned to the top. Summarizing this pattern, a comment in the 1924 *Photoplay* article can be construed as alluding to the conditions of their opportunity as well as to reversals of fortune. Gene Gauntier is quoted on how much more she once commanded than her image on the screen. Perhaps referring to the changes she felt during her contract work at Universal Film Manufacturing Company in 1915, she writes to the *Photoplay* author: "After being master of all I surveyed, I could not work under the new conditions" (Smith 1924, 102). What does she mean by "master of all I surveyed"? And what were these "new conditions"? Yet more difficult to answer is how opportunity, first grasped, was snatched from these early entrepreneurs. And why did most relinquish power silently while at least one, Florence Lawrence, bemoaned in print, "I WANT so to work!" (ibid., 64).

The easiest answer to the question "What happened to them?" is of course that they went the way of all actresses. They faded and aged. But this fading actually veiled the circumstances of their unemployment, leaving intact the widely held belief that women in the U.S. silent-film industry had been *only actresses*. Certainly silent-era actresses were numerous and at least two powerful actress-producers were referenced in the earliest historiographical work on the period—Mary Pickford (Ramsaye 1986, 741–751) and Clara Kimball Young (Hampton 1970, 135). But the idea that there were women in the first two decades of the emerging industry more powerful than some men, even, in Gene Gauntier's term, the "master" of others, is a relatively recent one (Smith 1924, 102).[7] When we look at available sources, what do we find? Gene Gauntier is one of the most well documented of examples, her "Blazing the Trail" telling us how she began as an actress in 1906 at the Biograph Company and by the next year at the Kalem Company was performing her own stunts as well as writing scenarios. Yet even in the published version of her memoir, Gauntier does not give herself credit as codirector or director, or even producer, credit that historians, and she herself, elsewhere asserted. In her memoir, she does not say, as we now do, that with actor-director Sidney Olcott she headed the Olcott-Gauntier unit within the Kalem Company, 1910–1912, or that in 1912, working as a producer with others from the Kalem unit, she started Gene Gauntier Feature Players, which continued for another two years, with the last film to be released *The Little Rebel* (1915).[8] Unfortunately, "Blazing the Trail" narrates neither the circumstances under which she left the Kalem Company nor the breakup of Gene Gauntier Feature Players.

In the 1920s, the public record is mostly silent as to "what happened to them?" and for this reason *Photoplay*'s "Unwept" stands out, breaking the silence if only to instill more mystery.[9] Gene Gauntier seems surprisingly outspoken in the excerpted 1924 letter in which she describes her reaction to changes in the industry as one of "revulsion." However, *Photoplay*'s placement of the phrase "the beginning of my revulsion" produces some ambiguity (Smith 1924, 102). It is thus difficult to know whether the "disillusionment," as *Photoplay* termed it, began in 1912, Gauntier's last year at Kalem, in the Gene Gauntier Feature Players years, 1912–1915, or in 1915, in the last year of her company when she worked temporarily at Universal.[10] And still, Gauntier does not tell us what events took place. Since her remark is not narrated in the excerpt from her 1924 letter, the burden falls on us to interpret her choice of the word *revulsion*.

In the tradition of narrative history, however, the "what happened?" question calls for interpretation by means of narration. Let us not forget, as well, what Roland Barthes calls the "prestige of *this happened*" (1986b, 139). It is thus tempting to try to relate events in Gene Gauntier's life as *this happened* to her, as her "life story." But storytelling entails smoothing over holes in the evidence, effectively covering them up with plausible explanation. What we narrate is, of course, not the same as the life she once lived, even though we may say that that is what it is. Our telling is rather another ordering of events, one not even remotely corresponding to lived events (for that is impossible), but events arranged after the fact—lined up to confirm an argument we would make about historical trends. And here, still in the "new film history" moment as we are, our strongest argument would rely on an economic explanation, as we will see.[11]

Using Gauntier's "the beginning of my revulsion" to support the economic argument, we could use this phrase as evidence of how, as early as 1912–1915, a female producer responded to the beginning of industrial changes that extended over the next decade, changes that would buffet about the women who attempted to negotiate more control over the creative process based on their box office successes, especially those who, in a countermove, dared to start their own independent ventures outside companies that were forerunners of the major studios. Looking for evidence to support this argument, effectively a version of "what happened," we turn back to three documents—a *Photoplay* interview conducted in 1914 and published in January 1915, a trade press announcement in March 1915, and a private letter written in late June 1915. The 1914 interview with Mabel Condon features Gauntier at home in her New York apartment. Although Jack Clark calls from the studio to ask her advice on a scene, she makes no other mention of current work in the old church they are using for a studio but instead refers "cheerily" to future plans for two companies (Condon 1915, 72). In March, *Moving Picture World* reports that Gauntier and Clark have rented their New York studio and traveled to Los Angeles to work for Universal (1915, 1942). In late June, Gauntier writes to "Colonel" William Selig: "I wish to make application, in [*sic*] behalf of my husband, Jack J. Clark, and myself, for an engagement with one of your companies." Of her importance to the Kalem Company in the 1907–1912 years she writes: "For four years I headed their foreign companies, writing every picture they produced abroad, Mr. Clark playing the leads,—in Ireland, England, Scotland, Germany, Italy, Madiera [*sic*], Gibralter [*sic*], Algiers, Egypt, and terminating with the taking of *From the Manger to the Cross* in Palestine. This masterpiece was also conceived, written, and codirected by me as was *The Colleen Bawn*, *Arrah-na-Pogue*, *The Shaughraun*, *The Kerry Gow*, *The Wives of Jamestown*, and five hundreds [*sic*] others." Written on Gene Gauntier Feature Players, Inc., letterhead, this letter might be read as evidence that the company is in limbo. The New York address on the letterhead is crossed out and replaced with a typed Hollywood street address.[12]

While the interview could be interpreted as the kind of cover story that a player plants in a fan magazine, the letter reads like a job application.[13] But how much more can we say? To interpret the interview as covering her disappointment or the letter as trying for a comeback is not to solve a mystery but, rather, to fill in the "what happened" blank with our own contemporary hopes and dreams. What we can say is that the evidence points to the split-up of the original Gene Gauntier Picture Players Company. Sidney Olcott is not mentioned as part of it in January 1915, and, most important, we assume that Gauntier would not leave New York and rent out the studio if the company had not failed to secure the capital to bankroll new production. Why did they leave when they had "plans" for their company, and what happened in the ensuing four months in Los Angeles when they made five shorts for Universal?[14] The hole in Gauntier's motion picture career between the last of her Universal shorts, *Gene of Northland* (1915), and her next, *The Mystery of the Yellow Room* (1919), suggests that her career was over.[15]

Does this mean that her "revulsion" that began in 1912 is complete by mid-1915? The evidence that no films were made could be interpreted to mean that she could not find the capital to continue her company, or that the couple could find no other work, or that the work under the "new conditions" was intolerable for someone accustomed to control over so many production aspects (Smith 1924, 102).

Note that we are relying on motion picture film credits as evidence where little else exists. Gene Gauntier exemplifies challenges particular to motion picture historiography—the difficulty of establishing credits for the years before there were credits, of job titles before there were defined jobs, and, of course, of evaluating so many films when only a handful of prints are extant.[16] But since, in Gauntier's case, beyond her few published credits there is relatively more evidence of her career in the fledgling motion picture industry than that of others, we are doubly perplexed. The intellectual history question, "Why didn't we know?" stumps us in another way, one best phrased as: "What happened to what was *once known*?" That other historical narrative—the intellectual history—requires us to compare how Gene Gauntier was figured *in her day* in relation to how the first historical accounts of U.S. motion pictures written between 1914 and 1975 referenced her. For if in 1914 she was "equal owner of the enterprise" (Gene Gauntier Feature Players), we want to know why she was gradually demoted in 1926 to synopsis writer for *Ben Hur* (1907), in 1938 to "daredevil actress," in 1962 to a "gifted leading woman" who also wrote screen adaptations of classic literature, and finally in 1975 to one of the "first screen scenarists."[17]

It is tempting to say, in answer to the intellectual history "what happened" question, that they were "forgotten" by later critics. But here the language of forgetting implies memory lapse or benign neglect, and thus erases the struggle over inclusion and exclusion. A more political approach might think in terms of knowledge apportionment, a rationing of the women credited in the industry story of triumphant corporatization. Or, this is a case of what could be called the *unequal distribution of narrative wealth*, a relegation of a larger portion of credit to men to which women demurred. Gene Gauntier exemplifies this deference in her unqualified promotion of director Sidney

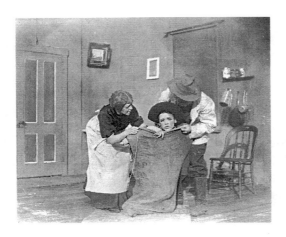

Gene Gauntier, actress/writer/producer/director, *Further Adventures of the Girl Spy* (1910). Courtesy Margaret Herrick Library, Academy of Motion Picture Arts & Sciences. Beverly Hills, California.

The Olcott-Gauntier Unit, Kalem Company on location, Jacksonville, Florida, circa 1910. Courtesy Margaret Herrick Library, Academy of Motion Picture Arts & Sciences. Beverly Hills, California.

Olcott. Yet while Gauntier's 1928 memoir advances the reputation of her former partner, Olcott, the understatement of her own claim is belied by the grandiosity of the title "Blazing the Trail," which encourages us to see her experience at Kalem, 1907–1912, as the work of founding an industry. And further, as we will see, there remains the irrefutable testimony of her onscreen bravado, still there in the extant film titles in which she plays Nan, the cross-dressing girl spy.[18]

FROM "NO WOMAN IN 1925" TO THE SILENT-ERA HEYDAY OF WOMEN

In retrospect, we may be startled to find that, in the 1970s, feminism's "story" was the same as that of the film industry histories: *There were no women.* The story was of course differently inflected, developed in feminist academic circles as a "loss" narrative to the effect that, although there had been women such as Alice Guy Blaché and Lois Weber who had worked in the silent-era U.S. film industry, in the year 1925, no woman directed a single motion picture.[19] The strength of the "no woman in 1925" assertion was that it was empirically—as well as theoretically—stunning, confirming the feminist principle of women's symbolic exclusion. Thus "no woman in 1925" could merge with the implicit "no women" narrative of the 1970s. Thirty years later, however, another narrative is supplanting the "no women" version of motion picture industry history. Scholars researching the silent-era U.S. film industry are now revising a narrative that could be called the silent-era "heyday of women" version that complements what Mark Cooper summarizes as from "cottage industry to corporation" (2010, 124). This narrative is strong on the careers of the serial queens who are discovered anew and valued for their bodily transfiguration. For example, in the last decade some of the most exciting new scholarship has looked at the careers of the silent-era serial queens such as Helen Holmes, Pearl White, Ruth Roland, and Grace Cunard.[20] These studies convince us that if we are looking for the onscreen expression of female fortitude, ingenuity, and bodily transgressiveness, it is to be found here.[21] Gene Gauntier emerges

What Happened to Women in the Silent U.S. Film Industry?

as a theoretical paradigm in the moment that we learn that her cross-dressing girl spy films inspired the female daredevil series and serials that followed.[22]

Remarkably, the discovery of physical daredevilry combined with economic savvy in the case of those actresses who produced and sometimes directed now works as an antidote to the 1970s feminist analysis of erasure and victimization. Rather like the way reception studies in the 1980s countered the abstraction of psychoanalytic spectator positioning with empirical viewers, the sensational melodrama serial queen counters the abstract anti-image strategy advanced by an earlier feminism. Further, these new studies ride in on the discovery of pre-1915 cinema as itself an antithetical exception to the economic and aesthetic monolith it would become.[23] The field has thus been prepared for a new narrative about women, one that demonstrates aspiration and attainment as well as partnership with men in innovating an industry. Not surprisingly, then, scholars face the expectation that another narrative will finally offer a comprehensive explanation and that it will do so by means of new evidence as well as a fresh interpretation. But even as contemporary scholars may agree that women who were empowered were at some point no longer in charge, they do not, however, unanimously point to a single decisive event.

The dilemma posed by how to say what happened is further evident in the different terms that scholars now use to dramatize the end of what we are calling the heyday. Taken together, they are an indication of multiple forces at work. Thus, for example, one scholar writes that the Universal Company "banished" women directors (Cooper 2010, 1); another says that at First National, women producers were led to "abandon their companies" (Neely 2010, 22); and a third describes how the United States, relative to other early film industries, saw the "swift expulsion" of women (Mahar 2006, 2). These authors all pose some variant of the "what happened" question yet characterize the moment without the benefit of the unequivocal empirical evidence we might ultimately want.[24] Dampening our empirical hopes in one move, Karen Mahar discourages investment in the expectation that an undiscovered document might settle the matter. "There was no memo circulated to studio heads asking them to eliminate women filmmakers in the 1920s," she says (2006, 7).

WHAT ANSWER DO WE NOW WANT?

It is not, then, as though women were working one day and let go the next. Thus, my title *Pink-Slipped* is an intended irony. If there is no confirming memo to be found, what then? If there is no document, we are challenged to think in terms of multiple and disparate developments, to think instead about the kind of evidence we want to use to stimulate an imagination about "what *might* have happened."[25] In the difference between "what might have happened" and "what happened" there is space to accommodate a scenario to fit the contemporary moment, which means that the question is effectively turned on us: "What kind of an answer do we *now* want?" We have already seen how the empirical but also theoretical "no woman in 1925" told feminists what they wanted to know in the

1970s. Only now can we see this formulation as unable to imagine the conditions of possibility for women between 1907 and 1925, one consequence of which was that women editors and writers who continued to work past 1925 into the sound era were overlooked.[26]

If today the field anticipates a new historiographic position for women producers, we want that position to accommodate a variety of work histories as well as personal situations, recovering the significance of these producers in their time without, however, exaggerating it.[27] Major work remains ahead on the meanings of "producer" in the first decade. Catherine Carr's *Art of Photoplay Writing* refers to the "Director, who produces the picture," (1914, 22), indicating that one source of our difficulty is linguistic. If "to produce" is synonymous with "to make," the word can encompass a wider range of work activities than any other occupational term. This terminological confusion has the advantage of signaling not only that the earliest "producers" took on a range of jobs but, as I will argue in chapter 7, that the chaos of the set meant job fluidity.[28] While we want to illuminate a pattern, we remain as cautious about overestimating as much as underestimating the relative influence of these women, as I said in the introduction. A major breakthrough in this regard has been Karen Mahar's work on early Hollywood, which gives us a set of frames for women's careers, looking at new chances for women beginning around 1907 and following some of them to the height of their power in the industry. Using the "star name company" as one indicator of their attempt to exert more creative control, Mahar maps two high points for such companies, 1911 to 1915 and 1916 to 1923 (2006, ch. 2 and 6). Within these parameters, scholars can establish that women were there in the industry in influence as well as in numbers in the first two decades.[29] In the first phase, Marion Leonard is as historically significant as Florence Lawrence, often

Marion Leonard, actress/producer,
Gem Motion Picture Company.
Courtesy Margaret Herrick Library,
Academy of Arts & Sciences. Beverly
Hills, California.

cited as the first motion picture star, but, as we now know, also founder, in 1912, of the Victor Company.[30] In 1911, Leonard and her director husband, Stanner E. V. Taylor, left Biograph to set up Gem Motion Picture Company, the first of two companies they would start, the second named Mar-Leon, capitalizing on Leonard's star recognition. Further confirming the pattern, Helen Gardner left the New York City studios of the Vitagraph Company in 1911 and started Helen Gardner Picture Players in Tappan-on-Hudson, New York. In the second phase, 1916–1923, independent female producers benefited from the exhibitors' war, which gave them a distribution outlet and a connection to uncommitted theaters for their motion pictures with financing through exhibitor companies, the most important of which, for them, was First National. Thus, in 1917 alone, at least nine actresses working in Hollywood were involved in attempts to start independent companies: Bessie Barriscale, Lule Warrenton, Alla Nazimova, Olga Petrova, Anita Stewart, Norma Talmadge, Constance Talmadge, Lois Weber, and Clara Kimball Young.[31]

Even more significantly, in the 1916–1923 period, writer June Mathis rose to prominence as a Metro Pictures executive producer, a case to which we will return in chapter 8. Veteran screenwriter Eve Unsell started a screenplay consulting company, and writers Marion Fairfax and Lillian Case Russell started companies to produce feature films, as did writer-actress Leah Baird.[32] Most undertook these challenges with the significant help of men (Barriscale, the Talmadges, Weber, Young, Russell, Baird), although some took on the burden entirely without them, such as Western genre star Texas Guinan and widows Mrs. Sidney Drew and Dorothy Davenport Reid.[33]

Olga Petrova, actress/producer, Petrova Pictures. Courtesy Margaret Herrick Library, Academy of Arts & Sciences. Beverly Hills, California.

CHAPTER 1

Alla Nazimova, actress/producer,
Camille (Nazimova Productions,
Metro Pictures Corp., 1921).
Courtesy Margaret Herrick Library,
Academy of Arts & Sciences. Beverly
Hills, California.

Companion to Mahar's "star name company" research is Wendy Holliday's definitive study of scenario writers in which she explores the hypothesis that over 50 percent of the silent cinema scenarios were written by women. Although this estimate has been recently challenged, as discussed in the introduction, the very controversy stimulates ongoing research.[34] Also recently, scholars have added outsiders like Chinese American Marion E. Wong, who founded the Oakland, California, Mandarin Film Company,

Vitagraph Company reunion, December 22, 1926, at the home of Norma Talmadge that included male as well as female players. Back row: Leah Baird, Flora Finch, Ann Brody, Anne Shaeffer, Anita Stewart; front row: Mabel Normand, Norma Talmadge, Constance Talmadge, Florence Turner. Seven of these nine women started "star name companies." Courtesy Margaret Herrick Library, Academy of Motion Picture Arts and Sciences. Beverly Hills, California.

writing, directing, and producing the extant film *The Curse of the Quon Gwon* (1916) and casting herself as the villainess (Lau 2013). Mexican American actress Beatriz Michelina founded Beatriz Michelina Features, producing motion pictures in San Rafael, California, between 1917 and 1919, and African Americans Tressie Souders and Maria P. Williams both started companies in Kansas City, Missouri.[35] Given this cumulative research and in the light of my argument that the field has been prepared for a new paradigm, one expects that the preferred figuration of the story of women as industry "trailblazers" would now need to emphasize not their absence but their demise as relative to (as well as a condition of) their very rise, the two together accentuating the reversal. This is achieved in the move from the narrative of what could be called "no woman in 1925" to the narrative of the ascendance that for most was "over by 1925."[36]

OVER BY 1925:
THE POLITICAL ECONOMY EXPLANATION

The "over by 1925" story has other advantages over "no women in 1925," reinforcing Mahar's two phases that in turn correspond with recently established U.S. film industry history coordinates. If the first, 1911–1915, has the features of the transitional cinema moment (Keil 2001), the second, 1916–1923, reinforces the story of the independents' challenge to Adolph Zukor's monopoly strategy.[37] Thus the "over by 1925" corporatization story stands a good chance of acceptance as part of "the history," helping the field to shift focus from American film industry history as studio system history to the study of opposition to the studio system. Certainly the well-documented and widely accepted financial changes taking place as fly-by-night enterprises became big business support the "over by 1925" narrative. And, finally, it is well established that within the industry, the director-unit system gave way to the central-producer system as it became the studio system, with more oversight and supervision, or the constraining "new conditions" that Gene Gauntier began to experience around 1912–1915 (Smith 1924, 102).[38]

Thus if we were to offer only one answer to the question, "What had happened by 1925?" the answer "finance capital," referencing Marxist economic theory and the commodity production it grasps, would likely satisfy most motion picture film scholars. Case closed. "Finance capital" leads us back to the bank investment that the studio moguls were able to secure in the 1920s and opens up a monopoly capital approach to U.S. industrial culture over the cinema century. Summing up the pro-business boosterism of the moment, Terry Ramsaye, commissioned by *Photoplay* in the 1920s to write the first comprehensive U.S. motion picture industry history, exclaimed: "Every element of the creative side of the industry is being brought under central manufacturing control" (1986, 833).

We could, however, object that the "over by 1925" women's story achieves plausibility because as a "failure narrative," it is just a retelling of the familiar studio success story from another viewpoint. If we follow this logic, however, the only way to challenge the "winner take all" approach to narrative history would be to *not* write the underside, that is, to refuse to narrate the story of financial and personal losses. Of course, we could just write accounts of these careers as triumphs, however temporary, downplaying loss and hardship, as is so often done. Certainly this is the favored model, the "trials and tribulations" structure of biographical writing, and it will continue to be popular (Beauchamp 1997). But, finally, the extreme alternative, a feminist refusal to narrate, especially given the amount of new evidence, is unacceptable. After all, if telling begets knowing, *not telling* obviates any hope of our ever knowing more. There is, however, a stunning alternative option, one that Monica Dall'Asta proposes in her theoretical work on Italian silent-era female producers. Noting the unusual number of failed women's companies in both the United States and Europe, particularly those that managed to make only one film, she suggests that we look at these cases as serial and coincidental. But further, she wants to see another principle applied to women such as Georgette Leblanc in France and Eleonora Duse in Italy who attempted projects in which they defied the strictures of age in casting themselves against norms. In Dall'Asta's terms, their failure is "exceptional" because of the audacity of their challenge to gender assumptions. For us, she says, "exceptional failures," even "beautiful failures," have more ultimate value than any success (2010b, 46–47). We have yet to test the productivity of the concept of the "beautiful failure" on the U.S. cases of "unwept and unhonored" figures, but the possibilities are there in each example of a woman who wished herself beyond her station and strategized ways to mount productions for a world of motion picture viewers. In its magnanimity as a concept, the "successful failure," since it is references projects that were dreamed but never realized, allows us to answer our question with an imagination of what might have been, what didn't happen but could have, and even *would* have happened if only something else had come to fruition or not stood in the way.[39]

There is one more difficulty with the "over by 1925" narrative, one dramatized by the problematic of what I call the "successful failure" which reminds us of feminist theory's powerful analysis of gender hierarchies and the ideology of women's place. Inevitably, we wonder how to position workplace gender discrimination in the narrative, and we still want to know how gender was a factor, even though at this late date in the history of feminist thought we have learned that neither political economy nor sociology is adequate to the task. But conversely, gender alone cannot be made to explain every conceivable sociopolitical outcome. Fortunately, Mark Garrett Cooper gives us a theoretical way around a predictable "gender answer" to the question "what happened?" as he takes up the case of the women working at Universal Film Manufacturing Company where, between 1916 and 1919, more women worked as directors than at any other company. In addition to the prolific Lois Weber, this directing group included Grace Cunard, Ruth Stonehouse, Lule Warrenton, Cleo Madison, Ruth Ann Baldwin, Ida May Park, and Eugenie Magnus Ingleton. But Cooper challenges an established premise of cultural historiography. Provocatively, he asks why the industry should be necessarily understood as a "read out" of the culture and further proposes a critical strategy. If we take the workings of sexism to be a "puzzle," he argues, we have effectively countered patriarchal culture, turning on it by "[depriv-ing] it of its sense of inevitability" (2010, xxi). We should be "puzzled" rather than certain about the operations of sexism, following Cooper, advancing an approach that rather than using gender bias as a one-stop explanation forces us to think about insti-tutions as complex by definition. A feminist analysis, it would seem, both explains too much and explains too little, and, if too little, Cooper calls our attention to patterns for which gender in and of itself cannot provide a complete rationale. In other words, an understanding of gender discrimination in the culture does not adequately explain either why women at Universal were once promoted or why they were no longer pro-moted.[40] So we might then say that another problem with any new "over by 1925" story is that while it may be dramatic, it is just too easy to tell.[41] It is easy to tell as both an industrial development and a feminist gender parable. Paradoxically, "over by 1925" both encourages and begs off simple answers to the "what happened?" question.

We are not wrong to think in terms of social and economic cause and effect, which allows us to say, for instance, that in the early 1920s consolidation and control within the studio produced a constraint on options for the writer who wanted to direct or the star actress who attempted to start a "name company." Yet the explanation in terms of finance capital doesn't help us enough with the *lived* aspect of social and economic events, that is, with the equally pressing "what happened *to them*?" which translates the consequences of economic relations as gender relations into an emotional register. Both Mahar and Neely stress the male-female partnership dimension, with Mahar noting how many career ends coincided with the termination of personal relationships (2006, 8). Neely concludes that in these relations the men, whether business partners or husbands, were finally more "ambitious" than women (2010, 28).

Perhaps the lived aspect of these changes is captured in a scene that star actress Mae Murray narrates in her unpublished "Life Stories." At a meeting that most likely took place in 1921, she and her husband, director Robert Z. Leonard, sit with the inves-tors, "men from Detroit," as she calls them, who have agreed to her conditions. These conditions, in addition to her salary, are a percentage of sales, unlimited budgets, script approval, and choice of director for the company she says she will call Tiffany Productions after the famous jewelers.[42] "You can run the company just as you like," they say. Then they ask if she has thought about distribution. "'Had we thought of this very practical angle of our business?' The men from Detroit wanted to know. I told them I believed we will [*sic*] do much better if we waited and did not arrange a release first. . . . The men looked at me as if they thought I had gone to [*sic*] far afield of their conventional business methods. 'You said I could have my way, carry out my own ideas, so this is my decision!'" (Murray n.d., 41–42).[43]

HOW CAN WE SAY WHAT HAPPENED?

The overview in the last section gives me pause. Evidence that during the first two decades women were more highly placed in the U.S. motion picture industry than at any time in the following century pressures us to narrate a growing body of empirical information. Yet I hesitate. I hesitate because to write a narrative of failure is to rewrite the dominant narrative of success. I hesitate because I *know* that I don't know exactly what happened, and I hesitate because the evidence is so irrefutable and consequently the reversal of the historical narrative so striking. How can anyone write knowing what we now know about how much we did not know earlier? How can anyone write yet another narrative? The answer, I am arguing, is not to write another narrative that "corrects" earlier accounts.[44] We revise the historical record at our peril, knowing that it will be revised again and yet again, long after this moment of film reassessment. Taking the long view, ours would then need to be a dual project, starting from before we knew and framing what we now know more critically. In refining an approach, we might take our cue from Joan Scott's "double-edged analytic tool." As feminists, she says, our tougher assignment is to go beyond revising the record to the "production of new knowledge through reflection on the processes by which knowledge is and has been produced" (1999, 9–10). Today, then, with so much evidence surfacing, when we are expected to say "what happened," feminist critical tradition asks *how* we know this (if in fact we do) and encourages us to stand back.

Standing back, we can see problems with the "What happened to them?" question, and some will note how it invokes the historicism that was resoundingly rejected by 1970s film theory. This is the historicism Walter Benjamin critiqued in his answer to followers of philosopher of history Leopold von Ranke: "To articulate the past historically does not mean to recognize it 'the way it really was'" (Ranke 1970, 257). We cannot possibly know "what really happened," and not only because we weren't there through the highs and lows of the 1911–1923 period. Even the key figures did not know "what was happening" at the time, although of course we can argue that we are asking far too much of them when we assume a historical perspective, given the myopia of every historical juncture. But in regard to the demise of women in the silent film industry, it is striking how more than one writer continued to champion women's careers even *after* they were no longer working in significant numbers (Gebhart 1923; Gilliams 1923). Some fan magazine and women's magazine articles published in the early 1920s give the impression that there were still opportunities for women, and, looking now at the irrefutable drop in numbers as evidenced by motion picture credits, we can only wonder why these writers did not know "what *had already* happened." There is a chasm between not knowing what events had taken place and the inability to explain events, however, and in this regard consider the 1925 fan magazine article, "Why Are There No Women Directors?" which observes that "For some reason or other, they do not seem to be doing it now."[45] Here, "for some reason or other," not knowing for want of an explanation, is revealing not only in its blind-sidedness but, before feminism, for the admitted incomprehensibility of certain historical conditions.

If they did not know and we cannot know, then how can we proceed to tell? Perhaps the significance of new research on women producers is as it effectively creates a new historical reality, giving existence to events that have never been so "real" as they are today, events that have been and continue to be "realized" in our retrospective telling. Or, as Hayden White would put it, "events are real because they are remembered, not because they occurred" (1987, 20). To the degree that the evidence now shows otherwise, historical narrative productively imagines another historical reality. In 1973, however, these historical events were unnarratable because unimaginable. By unimaginable, I mean both that feminism could not imagine these figures and that they were inconceivable relative to realities already imaged into existence. Clearly, evidence alone is not sufficient to overturn prevailing narratives. Although historiographic method places great store in evidence, accumulated evidence does not signify so powerfully as when it is backed by the newest knowledge paradigm but also as it is positioned in time, that is, as it is narrativized. As Geoff Roberts has put it, "historical knowing" is traditionally a "narrative mode of knowing" (2001, 1), which is to say that telling and knowing are intertwined in such a way that to tell is to know.

Let us suppose finally that "What happened to them?" is compelling because it incorporates so many questions, only the most obvious of which is "What events took place?" A final variant of "what happened?" is "where did they go next?" emphasizing the consequences of what had already happened, although leaving narrative historiography intact.[46] And if we are theoretically adventuresome enough we can imagine what might have happened to the historical figures whose careers now exemplify "successful failure." There is, finally, another theoretical alternative to these questions within questions, perhaps the only approach that accommodates the problem of how it is that the once unimaginable historical scenario can become accepted historical narrative. This approach treats "What happened to them?" as rhetorical, as a strategy that postpones a definitive answer while it foregrounds the epistemological stakes for feminist theory as well as political economy. This would mean that the "answer" was in the title to this chapter all along: What happened to the women in the silent U.S. film industry? Well, what happened?

CHAPTER 1

2

WHERE WAS ANTONIA DICKSON?

The Peculiarity of Historical Time

"All the kingdoms of the world, with their wealth of color, outline and sound, shall be brought into the elastic scope of individual requirement at the wave of the nineteenth-century wand" (2000, 33). Who wrote this? *History of the Kinetograph, Kinetoscope and Kineto-Phonograph* was published as a pamphlet in 1895 under the names W. K. L. Dickson and Antonia Dickson.[1] Perhaps because the writing style is unusually poetic for a scientific tract it was singled out in the 1890s for its "florid" prose. Later, in the 1960s, a film historian attributed the wording to Dickson's sister Antonia, contrasting the style with the brother's "soberer writings."[2] A recent historian, more sympathetic toward Antonia, sees a coauthored effort (Spehr 2008). If coauthored, who wrote which parts? While an earlier moment assumed that Thomas Edison's accomplished assistant William Kennedy Laurie Dickson wrote the technical descriptions, leaving elaboration and poeticization to his sister, today we might argue that, since she had already published an essay on the telephone and later lectured in musicology, Antonia had the potential of her scientific genius brother (Dickson 1892).[3] For our purposes, however, Antonia's Victorian prose style and the question of her technological knowledge will have another function. They serve as an entrée into the problem of how to *locate* ourselves relative to the women who helped to found the global growth moving image industry in the first two decades of the twentieth century. These would be women like French Canadian Marie de Kerstrat who, with her son in 1904, started the Historiograph Company in Montreal.[4] Such an intriguing finding might encourage us to write a "history" of the Historiograph Company.

ANTONIA DICKSON AND
HISTORY OF THE KINETOGRAPH

The historian is always looking for something to find, but our job is to remember to locate the historian. What follows, then, is neither a "history of" Antonia Dickson nor another "history of" the kinetoscope, but rather notes toward more theoretical caution. To better understand the philosophical conundra ahead, let us try a riddle: "What exists at the same time that it does not exist?" Answer: the historical past.[5] Now let us use this riddle in relation to what could have been a typical Second Wave feminist research project, noting four possible answers to our riddle. One of the first answers to the question of how the past can be said to "exist" in the present is quite simply this: the past is referenced in a contemporary time. A second is that the past persists in legacies and traditions, a third is that it persists in objects or relics. Fourth, and corollary to a concomitant preservationism is the familiar idea that the past, through the remarkable skills of the historian restorer, can be "brought back," even to "live again," as we have just noted. Thus the question "Who was Antonia Isabella Eugéne Dickson?" cues a generation schooled in feminist historiography to anticipate a narrative that brings back or *restores* to us the talented and well-educated Victorian woman. In that narrative, she will be "restored to life" even if that is impossible. *Who* then will be restored to us? Perhaps a woman who could have been as great a scientist as her brother, William Kennedy Laurie, the man who, working for Thomas Edison, was instrumental in the invention of the American kinetograph, prototype for the Lumière cinematograph and forerunner of projected motion pictures.[6] In this restorative approach, the one the reader may be expecting, we would follow feminist art historians in the 1970s who brought back Artemisia Gentileschi, the Italian Baroque painter taught by her father (Pollock 1999, Ch. 6). Like the long-overlooked Italian painter, Antonia Dickson is the perfect feminist subject *from* one and *for* another historical moment. A classically trained concert pianist, she was a child prodigy in Europe and continued to give recitals as well as lectures on music after moving to the United States with her mother, sister, and brother. She remained unmarried and lived with her brother whom they called Laurie and his childless wife, a domestic situation that has led to speculation that the two women were lesbians (Spehr 2008, 14, 53). Antonia, a valued contributor to *Cassier's Magazine*, who in addition to the 1895 *History of the Kinetograph, Kinetoscope, and Kineto-phonograph* also coauthored a biography of Thomas Edison with her brother.[7]

Over a century later, Antonia Lant brings Antonia Dickson to our attention for the intriguing ideas at the end of *Life and Inventions of Thomas Edison* (1894). Lant suggests that Dickson's sister provides a germ of feminist theoretical thinking in the coauthored biography's reference to "new forms of social and political life" that augered new relations between the sexes (as quoted in Lant 2006, 6).[8] Undoubtedly, Antonia Dickson is a model historical subject, a possible progenitor for feminists. Yet I wonder. I am not completely convinced. Does one forge ahead today to write a new historical narrative

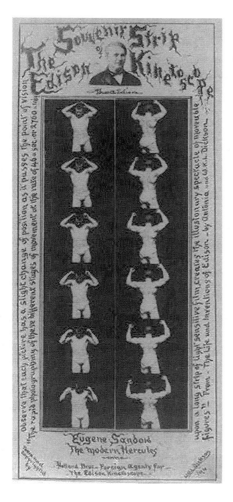

Souvenir card advertising, Edison Kinetoscope, featuring Eugene Sandow (1894). Courtesy U.S. Library of Congress. Washington, D.C.

that "finds" Antonia Dickson as a forgotten ancestor for women and technology? Given that there is ample evidence of Dickson's intellectual investment in the invention that would become motion pictures we want to know what is required to make such a case stick. We want to know exactly what is entailed in any effort to "locate" her as a nascent historian and theorist of technology.[9] I am hesitant to take this direction because of our two daunting "location" questions—the "location" of the historian as well as the "location" of the historical subject thought to have been "found" and subsequently "restored" to the present. So to pose our problem: "*Where was* Antonia Dickson when feminist film scholars had no knowledge of her?"

Antonia Dickson comes to our attention within a new historical moment. She appears not within the Second Wave feminist 1970s but at the beginning of the following century, *after* the big feminist wave. As argued in the introduction, today is *post-post-feminist*, giving us something like three feminisms—feminism past, feminism now, and feminism "to be," all implicated in the current critique of feminism. Today we find in the "post-post" an "after" afterward that defines a moment that knows that the feminist revolution has been incomplete and that promoting women does not in and of itself guarantee social transformation. In addition, over the past several decades feminism has often been of two minds about the social situation of women in the nineteenth and twentieth centuries. They were not only victims but may themselves have been victim-izers, as Adrienne Rich scandalously pointed out.[10] Since feminism must be strategic above all, what do we most need to "find" these early industry women to have been? Feminism's sometimes two-mindedness sees women as both powerful and powerless as well as progressive and reactionary, ahead of and behind their times. Here, then, is the place to acknowledge how much of a stretch it is for feminism to be all things to all women across class and culture. Undoubtedly, the use of the category *women* to hold both singularity and diversity remains a conceptual challenge, but one that animates this study. These then are the contradictions of feminism itself that interest the post-post critique, and to the degree that a contradiction is figured as a paradox, these are the intriguing paradoxes of feminism.[11]

Two post-postfeminist positions especially urge our attention. First, the consensus that the term *women* has been categorically overburdened and, second, the sense that gender analysis has less potency than it did when it first disturbed established disciplines nearly forty years ago.[12] But just when we thought that *gender* had completely lost its capacity to provoke, we face new categorical trouble: *gender* as separable from *sexuality* in the category *transgender* (Valentine 2007, 4). Unanticipated demands are thus placed on both categories—"women" and "gender." Feminist theory is further called upon to *relocate* the feminist present, a relocation that reevaluates the transnational status of women worldwide relative to feminism's hoped-for future.[13] Sara Ahmed thus asks us to face these daunting questions: "What can we do? Or where can we go? What kind of future might we imagine for feminism? Does feminism have a future?" (2004, 183). Here, where we introduce the "future" and begin to relate it to what in the following chapters I refer to as a qualified *feminist utopianism*, is where feminism is at a crossroad.

So why continue against these odds? Why undertake another project centered on "women"? If we continue, one might infer from this that we are intrigued by unan-swerability and on that basis choose to follow Scott's post-structuralist lead. If this is the case, let us make it even more difficult for ourselves. Let us ask why we would continue to undertake historiographic work along the lines of deconstructive historians like Carolyn Steedman, who, taking a critical approach, have conceptualized "history" itself as an impossibility.[14] Or follow Jacques Rancière who, although not aligned with deconstruction, concurs that "history" is impossible while finding productivity in its impossibility: "It is the science that becomes singular only by playing on its own condi-tion of impossibility, by ceaselessly transforming it into a condition of possibility, but also by marking anew, as furtively, as discreetly as can be, the line of the impossible" (Rancière 1994, 75). But since *impossibility*, in current usage, is as much an empirical conclusion as it is a theoretical move, we are still without guidance as to how to proceed because from an empirical standpoint it sounds slightly ridiculous to ask about the parameters of an impossible research project. To frame this differently, we have begun to stage the presumed incommensurability of theoretical and historiographic approaches when we pose the unanswerability of "gender" along with the "impossibility" of "history."[15] Assuming that I have prepared the reader adequately, it is now time to take a long detour to demonstrate why *history*, the very term, should cause us as much difficulty as it does.

THE REMARKABLE AMBIGUITIES OF HISTORY

If we take seriously the invitation to grapple with the historiographic conditions of impossibility, something will begin to trouble us. When the historian says that she or he is researching "history" in order to write "history" we assume that the referent is the same. In truth, we have no way of knowing for sure whether it is or not. What exactly is meant here by "history"? The double meaning of the term *history* is a depth probe pointing to the degree of philosophical difficulty beneath. Within basic theory of history sources the doubleness of "history" is foundational: *history*, the term, signifies both the *object* of study and the *study* of the object. Strangely, the object and the study of it go by the same name in the Romance languages, an observation made by key theorists, often as though the point had never been made before.[16] One finds this insight as early as Martin Heidegger's *Being and Time* where the ambiguity of the term *history* is a point of entry into what he calls the "vulgar" or, better, the "popular" understanding of his all-important term *Da-sein* (1996, 346).[17] New utility may be found in Heidegger's concern with popular usage, that is, with fallback notions indispensable to us in everyday discourse.[18]

Pointing to the philosophical puzzle ahead is Heidegger's observation not only that "history," as in "the history of history," is oddly doubled, but that other meanings of "history" are ambiguous as well. Here, on top of the two-pronged "history of history" is a second problem of doubleness, perhaps just as prevalent—the popular understanding of "history" as synonymous with "the past." The rest of this usage is the effortlessness with which we say things like "here today, gone tomorrow," "that was then, this is now," not to mention "you're history." Following Heidegger's thought, if we subscribe to "history" as synonymous with "the past" we can mean both that "the past" is "no longer objectively present" *or* that, while still present, it has no "effect" on the present. It may be present as a legacy, but may still be "long gone" and although persistent in the present considered "out of date." And yet, the opposite can hold in which case "history" as "the past" is not dismissed but continues to have an effect, captured in the riddle about the past that I posed: "What 'does and doesn't exist'"? It may then be that a legacy, as, for instance, human slavery, is held over into a present that struggles to throw off that past-as-history, or when ancient religious orthodoxies persist into a modern present.[19] Heidegger marvels at how "the past" which does not belong to our time, can still, as he sees it, be "objectively present 'now.'" This, he observes, is a "remarkable ambiguity." And yet, his example of the past-as-history still "objectively present" seems a deceptively easy way into the problem. I say this because for Heidegger, the "past" as "objectively present" is exemplified by the Greek temple remains in which a "bit of the past" is "present," that "present" synonymous here with the material reality that remains "now" (1996, 346–347).

Fortunately, the Greek temple remains bring home my point, which is this: the vernacular uses of the term *history*, of such interest to philosophy, will go their own oblivious way. What to the philosopher's mind is unusually ambiguous is not, of course, a problem for history tourists visiting the Parthenon, and, for that matter, for museum curators and perhaps some traditional historians as well. Indeed, the objectively present temporal persistence of the relic is so taken for granted that there seems little point in making a point of it. After all, common sense would have us agreeing that what is "here and now" is what is "real." Philosophy might, however, contend that the ruin is fascinating because it has succeeded in being *both* objectively present as "real" *and* "past." Still, popular understandings of "history" are under review here because, as we will see, they constitute the scaffolding for the sleight of hand in the professional historian's traditional practice. And yet, the tourist's very fascination is a sign that today we may all be inexplicably moved by a felt "presence" of the past; the very term *presence* is now offered by Eelco Runia as another theoretical angle on our enigma (2014, 104).

The history tourist's awe as well as the historian's sleight of hand is undoubtedly enabled by something else, something that enlarges as it shrinks an idea of history: it is both everything and every day. Commenting on this ubiquity, Elizabeth Deeds Ermarth explains how it works as conventional assumption: "Historical conventions function for us as basic tools of thought; it is difficult even to think about personal or collective projects without them. First this happened, and then that, therefore something. It seems as 'natural' as breathing, despite the fact that historical explanation is the ultimate artifice and is anything but natural" (2007, 51). She continues: "The commonsense idea is this: that history is a condition, a medium, something almost indistinguishable from time itself. This is quite a different idea of history from that of a written record. 'History' in this expanded sense stands for everything that has ever happened and will ever happen, whether we know it or not, whether we record it or not" (ibid., 54). To be both having-been-recorded and having-been-unrecorded, to be both written and unwritten? How is this possible? One wonders how the practicing historian can promise to scrupulously deliver any of this "everything" unless, of course, history-as-everything is accepted by incredulous readers or viewers. It is all in the framing, says Reinhart Koselleck, without missing the irony that the perspective of the historian is the privileged point of view on absolutely everything: "In practice, the object of history is everything or nothing, for history can declare just about anything to be a historical object by the way in which it formulates its questions. Nothing escapes the historical perspective" (2002, 4). But wait. If "history" is everything, what is there to differentiate it from anything else?

Interestingly, the critique of traditional historiography that asks when and what is "history" has focused relatively little on the claim to everythingness. The new philosophy has made more of an investment in challenging claims to "objectivity" and in pointing out what has been most denied—the historian's reliance on narrative form in the effort to deliver the past to the present. Ermarth, in her assessment, goes on, noting that "decades after Hayden White's *Metahistory*, it is still taboo in the discipline to suggest that historical writing is not basically objective: that its methods are fundamentally literary . . . or that historical writing functions to produce a 'reality-effect.'" (2007, 53). It is now forty years since that influential book, in which time White has continued, followed by others, to urge attention to the literary aspect of historical writing, accounting for much of the impact of the "discursive" or "linguistic turn" in the field of history.[20] That the ambiguity of "history" relies upon the self-effacement of narrative structure, however, is well established in fields already transformed by post-structuralism, as noted in the introduction.[21]

The field of film and media studies might well claim exemption given that narrative form has already been critiqued, no more thoroughly than in feminist film theory.[22] Now it would be a real boon to my project if such a critique were behind us because narrative keeps entering from the wings every time I attempt to give another problem center stage.[23] Thus, although the new philosophy of history has hammered away at the narrative history tradition, the literariness of written *narrative film and cinema history* has escaped scrutiny within the field.[24] If there was a problem, it was not literariness but linearity, an issue inspiring David Bordwell and Kristin Thompson to ask quizzically: "What would a nonlinear history of American silent film look like"? (1983, 5). Within film and media studies, narrative history still has not been submitted to the tough critique that classical narrative fiction film once endured.

Actually, all historical tellings should be in dispute. Why? For one reason, no narrative of past events can hope to reconstitute those events. Further, the claim that any single telling is *the* history would seem to subscribe to a "correspondence theory of truth."[25] One might turn this question around, however, and ask why any historian would knowingly conceive of any narrative of past events that did *not* correspond with those events. What would be the point of constructing an account of what transpired that does not correspond at all? What could justify studying events that "never happened" as though they had, although we do study the *construction* of events that *could not have* or did not happen as genres of imaginative fiction or as subjunctive "what if" histories.[26] There are, as well, fictions that intersect with real historical events, which makes the case for studying J. R. R. Tolkien's *Lord of the Rings* as the 1916 Battle of the Somme, Tolkien's initiation into World War I (Leconte 2016, SR10). But fictionalization takes us too far afield since the issue here is really what the philosophy of history sometimes calls "adequation" (Ricoeur 2004, 279–280). And it is this impossible goal—to discover and to convey what "really" happened that encourages historical truth-as-correspondence and its close companion "fidelity" in which historical accounts are judged by their "trueness to" an original moment. The implications of inevitable noncorrespondence, however, extend further, even bringing us face to face with the possibility that the unknowable past is also a meaningless past.[27] Still, behind noncorrespondence is the more compelling and elusive problem of temporal structuration. Thus my idea of proposing the "peculiarity" of time's structure juxtaposed with time as linear, this structural oddity introduced by theories of *historical time*, the concept to which I next turn.

WHAT IS HISTORICAL TIME?

When Reinhart Koselleck asks "What is historical time?" he cautions that historians themselves have difficulties with the question, especially if they start from the premise that history is a proper science (2004, 1). All theorists of history do not follow him in his interest as, for example, F. R. Ankersmit, who takes the position that historical time it is just a cultural construct.[28] Taking Ankersmit's point in the other direction, however, one can argue that if historical time *is* cultural this is all the more reason to think about it. In the following, what I call the *historical time paradigm* will have its greatest utility for the silent era and *its* own "modern" moment, which is not our moment. Here, I acknowledge Hans Ulrich Gumbrecht, who thinks that this older paradigm may no longer describe our present (2004, 120). Yet, as we will see, our present time is implicated as the time that motion picture inventors and entrepreneurs anticipated. Further, we need to grasp the *historical time paradigm* if we are to argue that it no longer applies, just as we would want to know what is meant by the modern if our time is thought to be postmodern. So, rather than abandoning historical time as outdated, I take up its elaboration relative to theories of history.

But what is usually meant by *historical time*? We know we are in new territory when our first guess as to what the term means turns out to be wrong. Those new to the concept might venture that any "history" and "time" relation must have to do with evidence. But no, Koselleck says, our evidentiary sources never directly indicate "historical time" (2004, 1). Still, we may be inclined to think of evidence marked by time passage. After all, the scientific processes used for "dating" documents are well established; the composition of paper is analyzed to reveal the decade in which it was manufactured; a motion picture film print is "dated" by examining the edge numbers indicating the film stock used by a studio. What theorists of history mean by historical time, however, has little to do with dating or periodization. Thinking about historical time involves not so much knowing dates as thinking about the temporal modalities by which we live, what Paul Ricoeur saw as "moments of the historical operation" (2004, 293) or as Heidegger preferred, "temporal ecstasies" (1996, 308–321).[29]

These "moments" are the dimensions that we reference with only three terms—present, past, and future. Yet if delimited by just these terms the problematic of *historical time* appears deceptively simple. How, one might ask, can any of us hope to grasp the complexity of "lived" time with only three terms? Especially for theorists of history, the arrangement or "location" of the past relative to the present, or the past relative to the future, is not at all given but is always unresolved and highly paradoxical.[30] No, our sources do not help here. Our sources can never tell us how they will be retrospectively positioned in the future. Nor do they tell us "when" or "if" they will become or already have become or "once were" and no longer are or ever will be considered "historical." In Koselleck, what is and is not "historical" is under review as a matter of how we invest and arrange events-in-time relative to one another. Here, we enter Heidegger's legacy as seen in the way the three modalities, past, present, and future, constitute what Keith Tribe, citing David Carr, calls a "hermeneutic circle" (Tribe 2004, xi).[31] We might then think the constant turnover of the modalities as an interpretative schema, a relation of continual rereading. Thinking these relations as circular is not really new, however, given that historians *do* use one mode to grasp another. Following Koselleck, though, we think of this schema as setting up a relational pattern. Thus, for instance, our "present" present "interprets" Antonia and W. K. L. Dickson's present, a "former" present, as "the past," and relative to the Dicksons' present, our contemporary moment is their "former future."[32] Alternatively, although we do not directly know their time in its own present we *do* know what was once the "future" for the Dicksons' century because we are that future. For Koselleck, the end of the nineteenth century could be understood as a present facing forward toward what was to come (2004, 3–4).[33]

Now consider what these reread modes do to the eerie question attributable to Antonia, the literary stylist, in 1895: "What is the future of the kinetograph?" (Dickson and Dickson 2000, 52).[34] From the vantage of the "former" present of 1895, the kinetograph had a number of "futures," which in the Heideggerian sense, would be the "possibilities and prospects" envisioned at that time (Carr 1987, 198). If in Heideggerian terms human history is a study of the possibilities ahead, including study of the past as it has conceived of its futures, this approach interprets Dickson's question as expectant. We could, however, go two ways with this approach to historical aspiration—first to consider what *wasn't* yet imagined or second to ask how the degree of openness to future possibilities might be assessed. Taking the first option may be less interesting as it might interpret the "former" present of 1895 in relation to the "future" that W. K. L. and Antonia Dickson could not then have imagined—the machines that would immediately succeed the kinetograph and the kinetoscope: first, the Lumière cinematograph and then the Edison Vitascope.[35] When in 1897 this photographic image of her was taken, Antonia might, for example, have said that her brother's company's superior Bioscope system had become the future of the earlier kinetograph.[36] But Koselleck is interested in the second option—the study of historical changes in conceptions of the future and not the difference between what was imagined for the future and the later realization or failure to realize what had been projected forward. Taking a long view from the late eighteenth century, Koselleck sees a reading forward such that we increasingly interpret our world by looking ahead to the future rather than back to the past.

Antonia Dickson, Edison National Historic Site. Courtesy U.S. Dept. of the Interior, National Park Service. West Orange, New Jersey.

In Koselleck's approach, what is important in the 1895 question "What is the future of the kinetograph?" is the implication of an imaginable future in which anything may be possible. For the Dicksons, it was not so much that the kinetograph had a future as that it *was the future*. Today, of course, we can confirm their confidence in that future. Not only can we assuredly say that such a statement is based on the evidence of W. K. L. Dickson and Thomas Edison's technological invention. But historians of technology can confirm that, in the years after 1895, when Antonia Dickson asked this question, moving picture machines based on the kinetoscope prototype proliferated.[37] Then again, it should be clarified that while there was no future for the short-lived kinetoscope, as such, there *was* a future for the *aspirations* of that first apparatus.

We have veered somewhat from Koselleck's concern with *historical time*. Still, the philosophy of history is interested in these other issues—those concerning the configurations given to forms as well as events, shapes that they can *only* have in their aftermath. Philosopher of history Arthur C. Danto thus expresses the lag and the handover: "The present takes its form from the future, and, by the time it has that form, it is past" (2007, 297). To instrumentalize this principle for technological history, we might say that the kinetograph later took its form from the future cinematograph; the cinematograph took its form from the institution of cinema that followed it; cinema now takes its form from digital cinema, the form it has by virtue of the form that it no longer has—motion photographic cinema.[38] One could keep going with this principle and consider in this regard that the present digital incarnation of motion picture film, looking back, has given form to the "photochemical," Thomas Elsaesser's example of "retroactive causality" in which the later technology "reconfigures" the earlier (2004, 91). Or more broadly applicable is Rick Altman's theory of the social and historical contingencies brought to bear on how representational technologies are defined, his "crisis historiography" approach.[39]

Now there may be doubters, and of course one could object that at least one key component of the cinema apparatus—the light sensitive negative film strip exposed, printed, and run through a motion-effect projecting machine—already had and will always have a scientifically established existence in its photochemical composition. Following this line of thought, the pre-digital moving image celluloid strip *could not* become "photochemical" only later in the digital present since scientifically it *always had* a photochemical base. The issue is not, however, the scientificity of the "photo-chemical" but one of the ways in which the existing object is post-constituted as "what it is," opening up a means of thinking about the relation between a technological past, its present, and its future. Laura Mulvey's observation that for us today, new technologies refract old cinema through another prism goes to this point as well (2004b, 1292). So, too, the analysis that in 1927 sound cinema, the "talkies," produced the earlier cinema as "voiceless," establishing that the silent cinema's future determined its form (Gaudreault 2011, 11; Chion 2009, 7). Although one could object that silent film was technologically *what it always was*—without sound. Thus it is that cinema, a technological apparatus, an institution, an aesthetic and an era, is still shifting while its future, that is, our present, decides *what it is that it was*. So, too, is the case with the enterprising women featured in Chapter 1, women for whom we will decide *who it was that they were*, which can only be *who they are for us*. Clearly, I am recruiting Altman's "crisis historiography" theory of technological change for the study of early industrial women, the reasoning being that if we see useful technologies as "social" how could we not see "social" beings as categorically "named" one way then another. "Who is Antonia Dickson for us?" is in this regard thus not unlike the question "What is cinema?"

While theories of *historical time* don't directly address the problem of technological change there is something useful in the way that the paradigm encourages another angle on the ontological. Let us say that we are looking for a way around asking "what is cinema?" or declaring "what cinema is" or posing the somewhat improved "what *was* cinema?" or even "*when* was cinema 'cinema?'"[40] So in the move away from any once-and-for-all ontology of the thing, the "what is it" question, we have instead the consideration of *when* it was thought to have been *what* and *when* it may be something else again.[41] Here Danto offers, in addition to a philosophical orientation to historical form, a metaphor for the difficulty of *when*. Let us say, for instance, that we want to know how in the "present" present we should begin to position ourselves before we begin researching and writing or recording, that is, how, given the question of location-in-time, to approach a "former present" and to situate ourselves relative to the future present-to-be. The reader may be able to see where the pressure for a methodological solution is brought to bear if I pose the problem as what I call the historian's *location-in-time quandary*, developed in Chapters 5 and 6. Hopefully the example of "*when* was cinema 'cinema?'" makes clear what is meant by the historian's temporal quandary, since the answer to *when?* will depend on *when* the question is asked, that is, on his or her location relative to the two other modes, although in order to understand why the quandary we need another concept. So I borrow from Danto the idea that the modalities are "asymmetrical."[42] I would take this further to propose the *location-in-time-quandary* as consequence of the *asymmetry* of past and future in which one wonders what to do given that from here we know neither the past as it "was" nor the future as it "will be."

If *historical time* is an *asymmetrical* structure that is always out of alignment, try as we might, we will never get the ever-askew modes to line up. One mode will always be passing into the other, one accessible and the others not. Danto's "asymmetry" theorizes the lived disjunctures of "then" and "now," an imbalance that puts ordinary people as well as researchers in a constant state of temporal uncertainty, a condition to be developed in Chapter 5 relative to what I call the *dramatized dilemmas of historical time*. As a starting point, we might now complicate the *asymmetries* of the composite form of these modes, as in the following derived from Deleuze (1994, ch. 2), with indebtedness to Koselleck:[43]

Past = Former Present (and Former Future) which anticipated a Future

"Present" Present = Former Future (once anticipated) now passing, becoming a Past for a Future Present

Future = Future Present (or Future "to be" Present)

Now consider what this chart suggests about historical inquiry and the temporal quandary we find ourselves in when researching past events, given that three moving modes, now modified by each other, structure how we dare to order and analyze. And I do mean "dare" in deference to the precariousness of historical knowledge, always "of" one moment that is "for" another one. For Deleuze, this disjunction of modes is caught in Hamlet's complaint that "time is out of joint" (1994, 88).[44] Not only is there structural disjuncture but we could say that the ordering of time exhibits an inequitable distribution of the modes. And worse, it is not only that events cannot be made to line up but that as a consequence they elude empirical capture. Deleuze goes on: "It matters little whether or not the event itself occurs, or whether the act has been performed or not: past, present and future are not distributed according to this empirical criterion" (89). Neither can the empirical help us with how the past and present can also, in the Deleuzian sense, be felt to *coexist* (Deleuze 1994, 81–82; Cohen 2006, 246–247).[45]

Reconsider then the question from Chapter 1, "What happened to women in the silent U.S. film industry?" While in the 1920s the answer to this question was a lament, in the 1970s the empirical response was silence, and in the last decade, with research resumed, the answer was "finance capital," the corporatization of entertainment. This economic analysis, as I intimated, is derived from positions in academic ascendence, one more reason why any attempt to answer in the present a question about "the past" always entails some intellectual risk, and why at the end of Chapter 1 I dodged conclusiveness. Now let's ask again the "what happened" question to foreground the always *asymmetrical* arrangement of modes: "*Where* was Antonia Dickson when feminism had no knowledge of her?" If the whereabouts of Antonia Dickson is a matter of her "not having been" brought into existence by a feminism past, then the issue is "where was she?" relative to one feminism or another. Strategically we have turned a "what happened" empirical question into a more disjunctive "where was" question.[46] This consideration of past feminisms then opens up onto the future as in: "*Where* is feminism going?" Then, to borrow from Jacques Derrida on the ghost of Marxism, the question of "when and if" relative to the spectre's arrival, is one of the futural starting points. For feminism, as for Marxism, this is the question of "how it proceeds from the future"(1994, xix).

NARRATING THE FEMINIST 1970S

Addressing the problem of how to narrate the events of the feminist 1970s, Clare Hemmings provocatively argues the importance of "theories of history" for feminist as well as queer work that wants to assert that "all history takes place in the present" (2005, 118).[47] "[A]ll history takes place in the present?" What is meant here? That the present is as historical as the past? Or that nothing really "takes place" for us in the past since we can only give meaning to past occurrences in the present? Undoubtedly, the ambiguities of "history" enable Hemmings's statement for it tells us neither whether the referent is past events themselves nor the account of them. Nor do we know whether "history" here means "the past" or not. Maybe it does, maybe it doesn't.

Actually, because of the ambiguities of *history*, the term, Hemmings's statement efficiently introduces the historian's locational dilemma. Quickly, we are led to the crux of the matter of "where" former events occur. To say that they "take place" in the "now," as she asserts, is of course a "where" answer to what is thought to be a matter of "when." Further, the vernacular expression "here and now" covers up any apparent time-space illogic and wards off any literalism that might insist that the answer to "where?" cannot be "now" but must be either "here" or "there."[48] So *where are* the auspicious events of the life of Antonia Dickson if "all history takes place in the present"? In this theory, those events are surely not just elsewhere but are also here. We wonder, however, if the phrase "takes place" that encourages us to think "time" as "space" doesn't mean that we're just "staging" one historical moment within a later one, when, for example, today we make a statement as simple as "Antonia Dickson wrote the first history of the moving picture." Telescoping the two historical modalities, "then," with "now," has its special effect, however, since the point is that the political imperatives of feminism's project today drive the ways in which we "make" feminism's own historical past. As Hemmings justifies her effective relocation, the "past taking place in the present," it allows for feminists to engage "a politics of the present in the making of the past" (2005, 118), a provocation to challenge objective "history."

Hemmings's "politics of the present," useful as it is in foregrounding what's at stake, may, however, sidestep the battleground terrain of theories of history. While we might want to settle the question of how to "make" histories of women for the present by adhering to political goals, no scholar wants to be left vulnerable to the charge of "making things up." Remember, however, that "made up" is none other than the charge periodically leveled against theories of history aligned with the constructivism of post-structuralist thought. Now this criticism can't be completely avoided, and we need to have a ready answer to the charge of "fictionalizing" to which we are always subject if we take the position that historians reconstitute the past. However, following Hayden White, one would also want to point out the difference between the inevitably "fictive" aspect of historical reconstruction and just "making things up."[49] To be sure, the accusation of "making things up" is ideologically loaded, especially as it is deployed in defense of an idea of history as an objective science. But the "making things up" accusation can also be useful to us as it dramatizes the problem before us, and that is this: There is no other way of accessing events that took place in the historical past other than by reconstituting them in the present. Further, we *must* imagine what we can't imagine. "How else can any past, which by definition comprises events, processes, structures, and so forth, considered to be no longer perceivable, be represented in either consciousness or discourse except in an 'imaginary' way?" White asks. How else other than by imagining that past? Thus, it is that he further insists on the distinction between "real" events and "imagined" discourses as well as imaginary events and discourses realized (1987, 57). However, to say that we can only imagine is not an explanation of how historical representation works that can satisfy naysayers. And, if asked, our answer would not be so straightforward because the work of the historian is in one way the opposite of what it appears to be since it involves as much as or more making than finding. As Joan W. Scott has put it, "History is in the paradoxical position of constituting the objects it claims only to discover" (2004, 260). This is, then, the paradox of what I am calling the *constitutive discovery*, a contradictory concept that acknowledges constructivism yet seeks to avoid the controversies around that term (Scott 2011, 14). Luckily, *constitutive discovery* also raises the "where" question, sometimes posed as the prior "autonomy" of the historical, but a "prior" from which we are barred direct access. Usefully, Judith Butler tips us off that the only way of getting to that "where" is from here: "What is constructed is of necessity prior to construction, even as there appears no access to this prior moment except through construction" (2004, 186). In order to access the silent motion picture era, we need to *make* the events that precede our making of them such that it could be said of these events that they "happen" not once but again and even again.

There is much at stake for feminism and film in the polemic that "history takes place in the present" and that contemporary politics figure in feminist past-making

(Hemmings 2005, 118). Yet I propose that we take this formulation provisionally as an initiation into *historical time* and its theoretical problems. Although the following chapters explore the problematic relation between past, present, and future as modes of historical time, at this point I submit only this one question to the test: "Where was Antonia Dickson when we didn't know about her?" We seek to avoid the easiest answer, which would be to say that feminist media scholars in earlier decades would have known this "history" if they hadn't been focused elsewhere, that is, on theory (Slide 1977, 9).[50] This case is intriguing, as I have said, because of the marked discrepancy between the powerful impact of feminist film theory in the 1970s and 1980s and the underdevelopment of feminist film historiography within that period.

HAVING-BEEN-THERE BEFORE

I have introduced Antonia Dickson and wondered if we should take her up as a feminist historical topic, asked about the relation between her "past" and our "present," and hinted at the inadequacy of available paradigms for representing that relation. Using the occasion of the technological advent of the kinetograph, I have drawn together the historical world and the machine that delivers it, showing how the term *history* does double duty while I planted seeds of doubt about the ambiguous concept. Following Clare Hemmings, I have foregrounded an approach to the history of feminism as critical intervention and turned to *historical time* as a paradigm to suggest why no historical "telling" is easy. Indeed, *historical time* can be useful to us only as a paradigm. But having divulged the historian's secret, that, vis à vis the past, there really is no knowing, where do I go from here? Somewhere else. I am helped by the hermeneutic circularity (Carr 1987, 198) of the relation of the modes of historical time, always a rereading of a reading. Thus as the present rereads the past we see that as a field *we have been here before*, and if, following Deleuze, we posit *coexistence*, we are there now as well (1994, 81–82).

Before there was the anti-historicism of Althusserian Marxism. There was Louis Althusser's essay on *historical time* where he lambasted the "ideological obviousness of the continuity of time" and the "continuum of time that only needed to be punctuated and divided" (1979, 103).[51] Here is where we have been before so, understandably, we may be impatient. We have already learned by rote the political problem with "realism" and "linearity" as well as "continuity." What more is there to grasp? And what is the antidote to the continuum if not the nonlinear? Well, Althusser gave us two approaches to the problem of *historical time* and we took one. To explain the title of this chapter then let's consider Althusser on the antithesis of the ideological "continuum" of linear time. There he poses a "complex and peculiar temporality" that he contrasts with the linear "simplicity" of the "ideological continuum." And to Althusser that "peculiar temporality," so complicated in structure, is just "utterly paradoxical" (ibid.). Where have we heard something like this before? Well, it sounds rather like Heidegger, thirty years earlier in *Being and Time*, but, of course, with the addition of the concept of ideology (ibid. 101). So what I want to suggest, in case my reader hasn't already guessed, is that 1970s film theory picked up Althusser's critique of linearity but not his metaphor of the "peculiar" construction of *historical time*. But how to grasp its "peculiarity"? We come closer if we consider Danto's *asymmetry* of past and future as well as past and present. Then again, there is no grasping, really, and there may never be. For as Eelco Runia tells us: "We moderns . . . have disciplined and straightened time so thoroughly that it requires an enormous, almost Proustian effort to 'unthink' the linearity to which we have accustomed ourselves" (2014, 59). So here is the point: It is not to be against linearity but to be *for* seeing perplexing peculiarity in the temporal modes that order human events.

ANTONIA DICKSON AND THE ANTICIPATION OF THE FUTURE OF THE KINETOGRAPH

"And what is the future of the kinetograph?" wonder the Dicksons who then answer their question with a statement of enormous expectation:

> Ask rather, from what conceivable phase of the future it can be debarred. In the promotion of business interests, in the advancement of science, in the revelation of unguessed worlds, in its educational and re-creative powers, and in its ability to immortalize our fleeting but beloved associations, the kinetograph stands foremost among the creations of modern inventive genius. (2000, 52)

This may be one of the most wildly optimistic statements to be found in the nineteenth-century literature on invention. The Dicksons' optimism, of course, comes to us from a time when business, science, and education were not thought to be at odds and when the genius of Thomas Edison explained the marvel of the machine. This is the Edison Company before the brother fell out with the inventor and before the overreach of the Motion Picture Patents Company brought on a U.S. federal indictment for its monopoly practices. Here, then, is the aggrandizement of *human* achievement coupled with the hopes of mankind, pinned to an emerging technology. Even so, a century later, after two world wars and the unstoppable growth of technologized militarism, we may recoil at the apocalyptic imperialism of the Edison Company worldview.[52]

But what is this "modern" for the Dicksons? Today, it goes without saying that cinema was a "modern technology" and even that the early-twentieth-century "New Woman" was "the modern woman," but in neither case is this saying enough. Since earlier times that are not thought "modern" are no longer on our horizon, we are left wondering what times to measure "the modern" against.[53] We are rudderless without some relative idea of when the world entered the Modern Age, that time distinguished from Ancient and Middle Ages. Let us see how workable Koselleck's theorization might be. In Koselleck, while earlier times expected the end of the world that did not arrive, the Modern Age, in contrast, has been invested not in an end but in the opposite—in an idea of a future to come, as we have seen (2004, 3–4). One might guess that this future orientation would have something to do with ever-accelerating technological transformations, although futurity would be nothing wonderful if it were not coupled with the anticipation of changes for the better. At the social level, this would be upheavals in the gendered social order.

With so many modernities, however, it is difficult to know which one is relevant.[54] As a way around modernity's conceptual exhaustion, I prefer Koselleck's term *new times*, which has the advantage of relativity, encouraging us to think of 1895 and the following two decades as one "new time" among many "new times" or moments thought to be in advance—whether in morals or technologies—of a previous time.[55] This is especially seen in Koselleck's *neue Zeit* or the composite *Neuzeit* as like "Modernity," which, as developed from the eighteenth century, casts preceding years as "old" times (2004, 224–225). Important for us in later chapters will be the ways in which *neue Zeit* has been understood as the new that is "even better than what has gone before" (228). However, where Koselleck's formulation offers a most original feature is as he identifies a "relocation" of past and future from the eighteenth century onward. Or, consider that following the French Revolution, "new times" correlate with future expectations. As he says: "The more a time is experienced as a new temporality, as 'modernity,' the more that demands made of the future increase." So this approach, involving the study of the present as a formerly "anticipated" future, posits an orientation toward one's prospects, toward having goals and expecting them to be realized (3–4).[56]

To study the technological moment of silent pictures relative to Antonia Dickson's projection is to study one such "new time" as it deferred to a future; to define it by its expectation of things "even better." These would be times in anticipation of times to come, of improvement over old ways. That is, to study past expectations as they got caught up in technological promise. Now, we bring this back to the questions with which we began this chapter. For Antonia Dickson's present, cinema was the future of the kinetograph, although the cinema of our time is in Koselleck's terms, a "former future," that time that "once was" the future they anticipated. What, then, of digital cinema? For us, in the "present" present, the kinetograph is the "former" present and digital cinema our "former future." Now, try to think of the Dicksons' relation to the cinema century ahead, their much anticipated future, relative to our reception of digital cinema and networked technologies; think what expectations accompany the "digital turn." Yet something is definitely not the same. With a gesture toward Koselleck, Gumbrecht diagnoses a shift from the future as highly expected to the future as effectively out of reach. Furthermore, and quite strangely, Gumbrecht's now "inaccessible" future, he thinks, is accompanied by an obsession with the artifacts of the past (2004, 121).

For a moment we might be tempted to think we have in Koselleck's theory of history some more objective measure of changing times. However, he holds that there will always be more than one *historical time* and that therefore we now live or have lived according to different temporal structures at one and the same time.[57] Or, while at any one time, some may continue to live according to a sense that time is eternal, unchanged since antiquity, others may be facing toward a future (2004, 3–4). No, however, we are not handed a key in either Koselleck or in Gumbrecht's update of him that will help us to resolve the tension between "technoutopianism" and the "death of cinema" nostalgia of our times. In this relatively "peculiar" arrangement of times, there is no chronology and therefore no such thing as *anachronism*. If there is no chronology, there is no ancestry, and no "birth of cinema" either.[58]

Let us say that there is neither chronological development nor singular "birth of cinema." How, then, does this jibe with the commitment to archival film excavation? Undoubtedly, we do defer to the evidentiary testimony of "the films themselves" (Smoodin 2007, 11) as documents with the potential to challenge established theories and to testify to alternative accounts of industrial practices.[59] So what do we do with the extant archival films that prove how many women were credited in the silent era? Well, the films just may be a sticking point. After the 1978 Brighton Conference, one could say that the "films themselves" told a different story and that revision of that earlier official story of aesthetic evolution began by studying surviving films of the first decades.[60]

If we start with surviving artifacts, we are concerned with the evidence supporting a historical narrative that feminist researchers most want "to find." What, however, does the historian do if the existing evidence does *not* support a much desired new story? Today, the use of motion picture archival material to make a case for the significant contributions of women in the silent era defers to professional practice—claims are based on evidence, "the films themselves" count. Case closed. Yet it may be that given our political commitment to inserting women into an old narrative, the new feminist retelling of the "birth of cinema" has *gotten ahead of the evidence*. We may find ourselves in the position of claiming that a definitive motion picture film was produced in 1896 when no evidence to support a new much-wished-for "birth" narrative can be found. It may be that *no such film was made* in 1896. Such is the case to which I now turn.

3

MORE FICTIONS

Did Alice Guy Blaché Make
La Fée aux choux (*The Cabbage Fairy*)?

We do not know for certain that Alice Guy Blaché made a film titled *La Fée aux choux* in 1896 and yet we may state that she did. How can this be? Even today, even after we know with more certainty what films she did make, her own historical non-existence makes it difficult to introduce her case, the case of a figure whose career narrative has been radically revised over the century. Like Gene Gauntier, as we have seen, Guy Blaché has been variously characterized, demoted and promoted. Although missing entirely from the earliest French history (Coissac 1925), she was later described as an actress (Bardèche and Brasillich 1938) and titles she most likely produced were attributed to others (Sadoul 1948). More recently, however, her position as a Gaumont Company director-producer has been restored (Abel 1984, 1994; Williams 1992) and her Solax company presidency confirmed (Kozarski 2004, 118–141).[1] Still, she has only gradually been squeezed into silent-era overviews. Alison McMahan, the preeminent scholar of the work of Alice Guy Blaché, first asserted that this young Frenchwoman was responsible for directing or producing as many as one thousand short and feature films in the years 1896 to around 1920 (2002, xxvii). McMahan also tells us that not only did Guy Blaché direct, script, and produce the majority of Gaumont Company films made before 1905, but that, as head of production, she supervised the work of others. After marrying and emigrating to the United States in 1907, between 1910 and 1914 she owned and ran her own studio, the Solax Company, opening a plant in Fort Lee, New Jersey, in 1912 (McMahan 2009a, 48–50).

It remains to be seen, however, whether Alice Guy Blaché's historical status can be elevated, even after the recent rediscovery, restoration, and retrospective exhibition of surviving motion picture film prints. Today, her place in the world film history narrative is still not assured although feminist scholars have been claiming her for the origins of cinema for several decades.[2] Significantly, this claim has been based on written accounts that linked Guy Blaché with the short film she herself referred to in her memoirs as *La Fée aux choux/The Cabbage Fairy*. Based on this one reference, publications in recent decades have variously credited Alice Guy Blaché with having made the "first film with a plot" (Foster 1995, 161), the "first scripted fiction film ever" (Kuhn 1990, 184), the first film that "tells a story" (Quart 1988, 18), and with having been "the first director of a narrative film" as well as "starring in the first narrative film" (Acker (2011a, 9). One encyclopedia references her as the "first woman director and possibly the first director of either sex to bring a story-film to the screen" (Katz 1979, 319). Another hedges its bets: "According to an 1899 document, a 'terrace' was set aside for shooting scenes, and Gaumont's private secretary, Alice Guy, seems to have been the first to make films there" (Crafton 2005, 265). Admittedly, the majority of these statements were made *before* the discovery of an actual film that might confirm how early she had made a film or *what* to call what it was that she had made—a story film, a fiction film, or a scripted film. But relative to the "first fiction" issue, the actual film print discovery posed an unanticipated problem. The newly discovered film, scholars concurred, did not exactly fit the category of "fiction." Neither could it be mistaken for a "story film" but was more like a one-shot *actualité*. The discovery raised new questions, such as how, in the absence of any extant film, could scholars even *know* what kind of film she had first made? How other than because of striking evidence of some kind?

Production still, *Sage-femme de première classe/First-Class Midwife* (Gaumont, 1902) in 1977 captioned: "Alice Guy Blaché with Yvonne and Germaine Serand, the players in her first film, *La Fée aux choux*." Courtesy Anthony Slide.

Yet this is a case that also makes us rethink what evidence constitutes "evidence." For in the absence of any film, one piece of evidence had cinched the many "first fiction" assertions. While no extant film evidenced Alice's fiction, a single photographic still *did* evidence that film. Or, rather, that still photo encouraged *the idea of* such an early film (McMahan 2002, 22). Consider how a surviving photograph might even foster a "first fiction film" myth, especially if, as published in 1977, it bore the following caption: "Alice Guy Blaché with Yvonne and Germaine Serand, the players in her first film, *La Fée aux choux*," (Slide 1977, 17). Then ask what scholars should do if they were to find a discrepancy between this photograph and the one-shot film discovered on a reel in Sweden twenty years later.

THE DISCOVERY: WHICH FILM IS HER *LA FÉE AUX CHOUX*?

In the late 1990s, a 35mm reel of short films attributed to the Gaumont Company was discovered in the Swedish Film Archive in Stockholm. The reel of seventeen titles had been purchased by Emil Sieurin, a Swedish engineer, along with a Gaumont device that worked as a projector and a camera (McMahan 2002, 20). On that reel, spliced in among the *actualités* and short comedies, was a one-minute one-shot film featuring a fairy character framed full length in a long white dress. In this short minute, the fairy, dancing among large painted cabbages against an artificial garden backdrop finds three "babies" among the rows. The first two are "real" squirming babies, which she holds up to the camera then places ceremoniously in the foreground. The third, a stiff doll, she returns to its place behind the cabbage. Around 1996, scholars "identified" this print as *La Fée aux choux*, attributed it to Alice Guy Blaché, and estimated that it had been made somewhere between 1897 and 1900.[3] As a consequence of this discovery, for over a decade now, the Swedish Archive print has consequently stood, especially to feminists, as Alice Guy Blaché's "first film."

The Swedish discovery has stood as a "first film" in the absence of any earlier film. Curiously, in the intervening years, in every way this film has become *La Fée aux choux* for feminist scholars, and this situation is understandable given that it was found on an early Gaumont company reel and that it *almost* fits Guy Blaché's own description— almost but not exactly. That the film depicts a fairy among cabbages no viewer would dispute. A closer consideration of the evidence, however, suggests that the Swedish Archive film may *not* be a print of that "first film." Where does this leave us? If the extant one-shot film is *not*, in fact, a print of young Alice's earliest effort we may still want to know whether it is another version of that "first film" or whether it is a film made by others and later attributed to her. Here is the problem. Much as we might want it to be, the Swedish one-shot is *not* the film that Alice Guy Blaché describes in her published memoirs. But neither does the Swedish print resemble the film she refers to as *La Fée aux choux* in two other places—in a 1964 interview with French film historian Victor

Bachy and in a taped interview appearing in a Canadian television broadcast.[4] How can scholars who attributed her with a "first fiction film" have gotten it so wrong for so long—if in fact they did?

For one thing, most available sources point to the existence of a film titled *La Fée aux choux,* and the most compelling of these sources has been Alice Guy Blaché herself. In her memoir she describes how, as Léon Gaumont's secretary, she had asked permission to "write one or two little scenes and have a few friends perform in them" (Slide 1996b, 26–27). She recalls working with cameraman Anatole Thiberville who set up a camera next to the Gaumont photographic laboratories in Belleville. She then describes a production scene that might have been an amateur theatrical: "As actors: my friends, a screaming baby, an anxious mother leaping to and fro into the camera focus, and my first film *La Fée Aux choux* was born" (ibid., 28). In the Canadian television interview material, she more precisely describes the story her friends enacted: "It was about two lovers who wanted to have a baby." Two lovers? The Swedish Archive cabbage film only features one fairy and no other characters. In other words, *there are no lovers looking for a baby in this film.* We are not completely out of luck, however. There is another possible extant film that does conform to Alice's recollections, although the problem is that this film has a different title and is dated relatively late. That other film, however, is not titled *La Fée aux choux* but is instead titled *Sage-femme de première classe,* usually translated as *First-Class Midwife,* and is now dated 1902. It is *this* film, not the Swedish Archive film, that depicts a young couple buying a baby from a fairy. But the title of this film as well as the 1902 date are also at issue, as we will see.

The 35mm print titled *Sage-femme de première classe,* held in the Cinémathèque française, might then actually "be" the film that Guy Blaché continued to describe and to refer to as *La Fée aux choux.* In the French archive film a fairy undeniably pulls babies from behind cabbages. But can this be *that* film? On close comparison, the premises of the two extant films, our two contenders, do not match up; while the one features the fairy *showing* babies to the camera, the other has her *selling* babies to a couple. In the three-character, two-shot French archive film, a couple approach the cabbage fairy in her garden booth as though to inquire about babies; then, the fairy submits babies to the approval of the young couple. In the one-shot Swedish film, the fairy only holds up babies to the camera. Further, in the two films the babies as opposed to dolls are presented in the opposite order. While in the Swedish Archive print the first two babies appear to be "real" babies and the third a doll, in the Cinémathèque française print titled *Sage-femme,* the fairy shows the couple three dolls in the outer garden, none of which they select. Entering the door to the back garden marked "Réserve," the couple is offered several more babies from the live supply and they enthusiastically select the squirming sixth.[5] Most notably, in *Sage-femme,* we see that the young Alice in trousers and a hat plays the male character who, once the female character indicates that she is satisfied with the choice, finally pays the fairy for the baby.

Based on this analysis of two prints, we may now want to reconsider the widely circulated production still captioned *La Fée aux choux* referred to earlier (page 52). Comparing the Cinémathèque française film with the production still, we see that the mise-en-scène of the film now titled *Sage-femme de première classe* matches that photograph in her 1996 memoir now captioned: "Alice Guy (center) with the stars of her first film, *La Fée aux choux*, Yvonne and Germaine Serand" (Slide 1996b, 84). The three female actresses costumed as the fairy and the couple stand against a painted garden fence between two fancifully painted wooden cabbages. But where and when was this caption added to the photograph? Was Alice's daughter-in-law Simone Blaché the later source of the title? While this photographic still may once have stood as evidence that the woman known then as Alice Guy made a film about a fairy, today, however, it does not help us to confirm *which* of the two extant cabbage fairy films is *the* cabbage fairy film to which she continually referred in both her memoir and the television interview; and it is the film *to which she referred* that is the film we seek. As we will see in a moment, there is much at stake in the correct "identification" of the Swedish discovery and therefore some pressure to get the hard evidence to line up with Guy Blaché's version of events. But the evidence cannot be made to line up, for in all three of her accounts of the making of her first film Alice Guy Blaché never once mentioned a film in which *one* fairy finds babies among the cabbages as we see in the Swedish Archive print. Neither does she confess to having given her cabbage fairy film another title—least of all one using the term *midwife*, especially, it would seem, given the sensitivities of the times.

Suspecting how much is on the line here, no less than the French version of the emergence of the *cinématographe* machine and the story film, we need to ask about the official position. Where has the French film history establishment stood on the place of Alice Guy Blaché? Decades before the 1996 Swedish Film Archive discovery at least one French film historian, Georges Sadoul, referred to two of her earliest films with different titles (1946). Aware of this, Victor Bachy, in his 1964 interview, pressed Guy Blaché on the enigma of the two films, both referenced in Sadoul's 1946 history. Bachy pointedly asked her if there had not been two films, since Sadoul mentions two titles although he gives them one date—1902.[6] Bachy unequivocally asked her which of the two extant films with cabbages is *the* cabbage fairy film. Yet, in the interview, Guy Blaché evaded Bachy's question and, on first consideration, it might seem from her answer that it was more important to her to distance herself from the title "Sage-femme de première classe" than to respond to his question. Thus ignoring "Are they really two distinct films?" she responded instead to the "midwife" reference. After deflecting Bachy's question by raising the scandal of the term *midwife*, she quickly cut off this line of questioning: "The story of a midwife? At that moment in time, I would never have dared speak of such a thing. *La Fée aux choux*—that is a part of history" (Bachy 1985, 32, as translated in Simon 2009, 10).[7]

A "part of history"? Notice the conflation of our two histories. While we might first assume that Guy Blaché refers to the textbook side of "history," she just as easily means "history" as past events. In the same interview with Victor Bachy she said: "We and the kids made our first film, *La Fée aux choux*." Asked the date by Bachy, she replied: "It dates back to 1896. People had never seen anything like it" (Bachy 1985, 38, as translated in Simon 2009, 7–8). This year, of course, resonates because of the longstanding commitment to December 28, 1895, date of the Lumière Brothers Paris public exhibition of their *cinématographe*. And if we accept Alison McMahan's assertion that the film was made *before* May, 1896, this would indeed be a milestone—a mere four months after that inaugural date (2002, 10).[8] The 1896 date is quite remarkable, all the more so because no historical overview of the field has ever inserted Alice Guy Blaché here in the kind of definitive chronology one expects to find in a textbook. Let's consider for a moment what could so disturb the officially established narrative of invention. From McMahan's chronology one could conclude that two years after she had begun working as Gaumont's secretary, Alice was suddenly thrust into the center of internationally significant technological developments. Just consider then what could be claimed if indeed *the secretary* had in 1896 made a story film, no matter how short, only four months after the inaugural public moment of the cinematograph. Further consider the trouble that this causes for the French official version if she had made such a cabbage fairy film so soon after the Lumière premiere of their comic story *Le Jardinier* (1895), later titled *Arroseur et arosé*, and the same month that Georges Méliès is thought to have made his first story film.[9] Especially considering the "narrative cinema" that this phenomenon would later become, the scene of the making of a film she called *La Fée aux choux*, is of enormous consequence.[10]

But the chronology in published sources fluctuates too much for us to ignore. The Whitney Museum catalog timeline places the making of a story film closer to an earlier event in which Léon Gaumont and Alice Guy are in attendance at the earlier Lumière *cinématographe* demonstration—the March 22, 1895, at the Société d'encouragement á l'industrie nationale.[11] After this 1895 date, the Whitney timeline lists: "Guy persuades Gaumont to let her use the Gaumont camera to direct a story film" (McMahan 2009b, 125). But when? Immediately afterward? That year? This timeline allows a year for the new Gaumont company to assess the challenges that *chronophotographe*, their competing system, faced before the company could finally start production and enough time for Alice to begin to imagine better films. If the Whitney timeline is to be believed, however, she now "writes, produces, directs" *La Fée aux choux* not four months after the December 1895 public screening but around a year after the March 1895 scientific meeting screening (ibid.). Yet we are still unsure of the chronology, and the memoirs, written between 1941 and 1953, rather than clearing up the issue of what happened in 1896, are themselves a source of further confusion. There, Alice Guy Blaché recalls the

Lumière invitation to the Société d'encouragement á l'industrie nationale, extended to herself as well as to Gaumont, as well as their attendance at that March 22, 1895, meeting. But then this momentous event is run together with the next one. "A few days later," she writes, "the first Lumière movie was given its first showing in the basement of the Grand Café, 14 boulevard des Capucines," a sentence clarified by memoir editor Slide who has inserted "[on December 28, 1895]" (1996b, 26). Perhaps in retrospect, the events of nine months, between the scientific community and the public screenings, got telescoped and became "a few days." Perhaps not.

For some scholars, Alice Guy Blaché's unconfirmed assertion of precedence disqualifies her for premiere pioneer status. This is the status that would put her on a par with the Lumière Brothers and Georges Méliès and would no doubt effect a radical revision of the story of a breakthrough invention. But rather than disqualification, any uncertainty about the French contribution could potentially have the reverse effect. This dilemma of dates, rather than diminishing, could expand the magnitude of importance of the 1996 Swedish Archive discovery and all of the issues that flood from it. If nothing else, that discovery feeds the imagination. A "what if?" fiction, after all, may be as valuable in this regard as definitive proof. More to the point here is the question as to why today we would want to assert that the young Alice Guy made a film she called *La Fée aux choux* as early as 1896 when, as of this moment, absolutely no evidence that she did has been found. Let's not deny the motivation to upend the men-first gender hierarchy as well as to challenge the established order of things.[12] Quite possibly, however, feminism's case is advanced by merely asking the questions that keep the controversy alive. To ask where to place Alice Guy Blaché in the historical scheme of things is to upend that scheme itself. And what if she did attempt to insert herself in the historical narrative of invention? As Kim Tomadjoglou rereads the memoirs, the former secretary strategically places herself in the scene, especially as she describes how Georges Demenÿ, who had assisted Ètienne Jules Marey, presented his own camera, the phonoscope, to Gaumont. And more importantly, from her intimate vantage, Guy Blaché saw something other than singular genius at work, concluding in her memoirs that the *cinématographe* was the "synthesis of innumerable labors and discoveries" (as quoted in Tomadjoglou 2009, 103). Opening the door to multiple contributions and accounts, Alice encourages a reconsideration of all of the "birth of cinema" claims.

And yet a more contingent, imaginative approach such as this does not necessarily solve the uncertainties that turn all attempts at a chronology into puzzles. Organizers of the Whitney Museum retrospective, aware of the dangling question as to what happened in 1896, have walked a fine line. In the accompanying Whitney publication, Alison McMahan states of Guy Blaché that she "filmed her first version of *La Fée aux choux* (*The Cabbage Fairy*; fig. 13) by her own account in 1896." But here the recourse to Guy Blaché as a source is the opposite of the mystification I detail above. Rather, relying on Guy Blaché as source turns her fuzzy memory into statement of fact. Co-organizer Joan Simon also defers to Guy Blaché's recollections, writing: "And so, at the age of twenty-three, by her own account, Alice Guy made her first film, *La Fée aux choux* (*The Cabbage Fairy*; fig. 13)" (2009, 5). But think about this strategy again. While the phrase "by her own account" pays homage to the legend, it privileges Guy Blaché's version at the expense of historiographic dilemma, leading the organizers to resort to a stop-gap solution to the problem of verification. For example, the figure 13 in the Whitney exhibition catalog is a frame enlargement from the Swedish Archive print with the following caption: "*La Fée aux choux* (Gaumont 1900). According to Alice Guy, this was her first film, made in 1896. The Gaumont catalog lists its date as 1900" (Simon 2009b, 28). We have, then, a contradiction between the Whitney catalog text and the Whitney photo credit. How can the frame enlargement from the uncredited, unverified film *be* the 1896 *La Fée aux choux* that Alice Guy Blaché later recalled having made when she was Alice Guy? How can we be certain that the Swedish Archive print is "her" film when there is no evidence that the film she described in interviews is this particular film? While the Whitney picture credit says that the Swedish Archive print *is La Fée aux choux*, the Whitney extant film list gives two separate titles even though only one print, the Swedish Archive one, is understood as extant: "*La Fée aux choux* (Gaumont 1900)" and "[*La Fée aux choux, ou La naissance des enfants*]. Alice Guy Blaché noted in interviews and her writings that she

Frame enlargement, *La Fée aux choux, ou La naissance des enfants* (Gaumont, 1900). Collection Musée Gaumont. Paris, France.

made this film in 1896" (Simon 2009a, 139). *This* film? How could she have made "this" film in 1896 when the frame enlargement from it gives the date of production as 1900? *Was* it "this film" that she referenced? In other words, even with this level of caution, the confusion produced by extant prints with multiple titles is reproduced everywhere. The reasoning seems to be that if she *said* that she had made a film she called *La Fée aux choux*, she must have made it. But did she make "this" extant film? Again, the question keeps returning because what we are calling the Swedish Archive cabbage fairy film, now dated 1900, *may* have been a film that she made even if it is not *the* film that Guy Blaché continually described. Or, it is quite possible, as we need to consider, that she didn't make this one-shot film at all.

The discrepancy between Alice Guy Blaché's "own account" and the extant film evidence leaves the door open to any number of other explanations, even, as I am saying, the possibility that the young Alice Guy did not "make" the one-shot Swedish Archive cabbage fairy film. Indeed, the confusion of dates invites further research but also encourages the expectation that other versions of events will be advanced or even that other film prints will be discovered. Most recently, Maurice Giannati, after a new review of records in the Gaumont Company archives, concludes that Alice Guy Blaché could not possibly have made the Swedish archive print. Giannati presents evidence that the earlier of the two extant film prints cannot be attributed to Guy Blaché following a company records search where he finds that both of the films in question had once been titled *La naissance des enfants*, although while one was later titled *La Fée aux choux* in 1901, the other was titled *Sage-femme de première classe* in 1903. This evidence can be interpreted to mean that not only would the Swedish Film Archive print *not* be Alice Guy Blaché's "first film" but that *that* print may not have originally been titled *La Fée aux choux*. Or, to think of it another way, the one-shot film, originally titled *La naissance des enfants* became *La Fée aux choux* two times—first, when retitled in 1901 and, by default, at its rediscovery in the late 1990s. What does Giannati's research change? The Swedish Archive film that may not have been first titled *La Fée aux choux* but may have originally been titled *La naissance des enfants* is today titled *La Fée aux choux* but dated 1900, most likely following the first published Gaumont catalog. However, it is not as though the existence of this alternate, possibly not original, title is complete news to scholars. Indeed, French film historian Francis Lacassin had decades earlier put the *naissance des enfants* or "birth of infants" title forward in his filmography, there as *La Fée aux choux, ou La naissance des enfants*, and estimated that it was made in 1900, again based on its placement in that particular Gaumont catalog. In the preface to his filmography, Lacassin explains that the title grew from the list Guy Blaché gave him at the time of his 1963 interview with her. Yet he cautions that this list enumerates a small fraction of her output (Slide 1996b, 143). Here, Lacassin also opens up the second issue that follows from the question of the 1896 date because it is not only her place in the pantheon of "firsts" that is at stake.

Also at stake here is the account we give of an industry developing, a form evolving, and an authorial "hand" creeping into a mechanical process, raising attendant issues that will be developed further in Chapter 4.[13] Following from the question of what happened in 1896 is also that of when it was that Alice Guy became head of fiction film production at Gaumont, a position she held until in Spring 1907, when she married Herbert Blaché and resigned in order to move to Cleveland with him (McMahan 2009b, 126). Lacassin, unable to rectify the making of her first film with the beginning of Gaumont fiction film production and the erection of a studio, concludes that she must have been mistaken and mixed events up in her mind: "Alice Guy, betrayed by her memory, is in contradiction of herself in affirming that she inaugurated the production of fictional films at Gaumont. Either she did not, which is highly improbable, or else she did and *La Fée aux choux* is not her first film."[14] Lacassin further reasons that Alice Guy could not have been made production head in both 1897 and 1902.[15] Although either date would have been prefatory to Gaumont's commitment to fiction filmmaking, the later date is closer to that of the new studio construction.[16]

The question of the Swedish Archive cabbage fairy film remains, and the mysteries of that film print abound, inviting a number of explanations, each of which can be seen to have advantages over the others. Giannati's conclusion that the young Alice Guy did not make this film allows us to wonder if it didn't exemplify the works that she herself called "brief and repetitious," those uninteresting "demonstration films" that she wanted to improve upon in her own story film (Slide 1996b, 26). To see the

Alice Guy Blaché, c. 1907. Courtesy Belgian Film Archive. Brussels, Belgium.

one-shot cabbage fairy film this way reminds us that Gaumont's early goal was only to make moving image examples to promote the sale of cameras. Further, the possibility that it could have been a "test film," as Joan Simon suggests (2009b, 10), allows the one-shot cabbage film to be the young Alice's idea. Alan Williams concurs, crediting her with the cabbage fairy concept (2009, 36). To his point, which supports a case for seeing a continuum of interests between the cabbage fairy and Alice Guy's later films, we could add the irrefutable photographic evidence of the wooden cabbage props. Are these fantastical vegetables the work of the "fan-painter" to whom Guy Blaché refers in her memoir as well as the Bachy interview? While the backdrop she recalls as the fan-painter's work differs in style in the two films, the wooden cabbages appear to be the same props in both films (Slide 1996b, 28; Bachy 1985, 38). Still, Williams's conclusion is closer to Lacassin's since he too thinks that the director's memoir evidences her "confusion" between the earlier and the later films. The "confusion" thesis is further strengthened by the fact that Williams has had the advantage of comparing extant film prints that Lacassin did not have available to him when he compiled the first filmography (Williams 2009, 36). Finally, however, because Williams thinks that 1900 is too late a date for the Swedish Archive print (36), he lends weight to the argument for the existence of other versions, Alison McMahan's implicit solution, and a point to which we will return (2009a, 49).

We are still in an empirical pickle, however. These interpretations, all based on viable evidence, do not uniformly confirm or deny that the extant one-shot film is "hers." Here is indeed a conundrum, and one I have confronted before. Knowing that Alice Guy Blaché's descriptions were at odds with the newly discovered Swedish Archive print, I earlier attempted to avoid the empirical "identification" problem. But perhaps *avoid* is the wrong word because the idea was to circumvent the problem by diverting attention away from it, the strategy being to change the subject, to attempt to make a case for seeing the Swedish cabbage fairy one-shot as the "first fiction film" by interrogating, in turn, the relevant concepts: "fiction," "narrative," and "first" (Gaines 2005). This exercise was one way around the dilemma of two extant film prints, neither of which support the factual statement: "Alice Guy made *La Fée aux choux* in 1896." My discussion created a diversion, if you will. In the end, while I was more invested in a theoretical "solution" to the problem of "fiction film," I was yet curious to find an empirical solution that only more archival evidence could satisfy. But can our empirical desires ever be fully satisfied? In the end, of course, just how far apart the theoretical is from the empirical may itself be immeasurable because these two approaches will never have to meet the same test. For while the one is measured in the effectiveness of the argument, the philosophical complexity, and the poetics of discourse, the other is decided in the meeting between claims and evidence, a meeting that might never take place. Then again, it could be said that empirical evidence can trump all inquiry, even that of a philosophical bent, although the critique of empiricism is a card that we still want to hold.[17] Since it would seem from this that the theoretical and the empirical hold each other in check, we will let them go their separate ways for the moment.

1896: WHAT HAPPENED ON THE TERRACE AT BELLEVILLE?

When we tried to pull apart the two sides of the term *history* in the last chapter we had difficulties. The ambiguity in the usage kept returning, effective as it has been at camouflaging the gap between later versions of events and those events as they transpired in their own time. Further, if traditional historical writing strives to be "true to" earlier events, the camouflage continues. Now, given the "truth effect" goal of much historical discourse, tightly tied to its historical referent, consider again the statement "Alice Guy made *La Fée aux choux* in 1896." But considering the other story, the contemporary one I am telling about the difficulties of extant print dating and identification, how do we now read this sentence? On first consideration, the newly informed reader may say that the statement is untrue or as-yet-unproven. On second thought, one wonders how any such statement of fact, nothing more than a linguistic entity anyway, as Roland Barthes argued (1986a, 138), can stand so convincingly, even as convincingly as motion photographic representation itself has stood. And here, even more problematically, the sentence that refers to the event comes into conflict with the films, the films that index the event of their making, because neither of these films can guarantee that a performance event took place in 1896. What we have instead of a proven statement of fact is a provocation that marks a site of factual contention. Certainly the statement "Alice Guy made *La Fée aux choux* in 1896" is a frontal assault on existing historical narratives about what happened in France in the late 1890s, as we have seen. In answer to such a challenge one might expect a strong defense of the reigning historical narrative in which the key event following the 1895 Lumière exhibition remains the Edison Company's exhibition of the kinetograph at Koster and Bial's Music Hall in New York on April 4, 1896. But no, not really, because in recent years the field trend has been not toward reinforcing but toward critiquing accounts of the invention of cinema and especially the nationalism that advances one "inaugural moment" over another, whether French or German or American.[18]

Recent critiques, as effective as they have been at challenging the established "birth of cinema" narrative, while shaking up old versions, however, have not discouraged either fans or film historians from continuing to revisit "births" or origins—to attempt to replace or to reaffirm the Paris scene at the Café Indien, December 28,1895. Nothing has really dislodged the basic assumptions behind historiographic method in the field. Although recently André Gaudreault has argued that a critical undercurrent challenging any "birth of cinema" project began with Jean-Louis Comolli's series of 1970s essays, suggesting that the disillusionment started even before the Brighton Conference of 1978 that inaugurated the "historical turn" in the field.[19] In calling all contemporary work concerned with the way historians think about their object of study "'post-Comolli' criticism," Gaudreault is in effect declaring that we have already rejected traditional historiography (2011, 12). Yet if this is the case, we should ask if Comolli's critical project is so foundational as to have become part of the critical woodwork. And was the replacement of the earliest historical narratives of Maurice Bardèche and Robert Brasillach, Georges Sadoul, and Terry Ramsaye *all* that was implied in the "historical turn" project? If not, why hasn't the "historical turn" then also "overturned" the narrative that does not include Alice Guy in 1896?

As we know, another great achievement of narrative history, in addition to its closure of, *as well as* production of, the gap between past and present, is its ability to shift our attention away from itself as constituting and onto its very own referent. This is the shift that so effectively encourages our belief in the autonomous existence of past events. Acting on such conviction, trained researchers assume both that historical events existed and that the burden is on them to describe those events precisely in order to bring them into present focus. Ordinary people recounting past events can be expected to make a similar assumption and consequently to treat the divergent double meanings of "history" as one, explained as the ambiguity of "history" in the last chapter. In this regard, Madame Blaché's remark to her interviewer, "La Fée aux choux—*that is a part of history*" [my italics], wonderfully exemplifies the ambiguity of *history*, the term (Bachy 1985, 32; as translated in Simon 2009b, 10). What obfuscation this statement (as translated) allows and what confusion it encourages! While the statement can suggest that she means that this inaugural making is now established as historical discourse, she is also relying on the other side of the meaning of history—on the events that she believes that she "really" instigated in 1896. She is thus thinking of these events as having happened, as verifiable by historians and consequently as comprising established "history." Because to be "part of history" is to assume that past events have passed over into a discourse of which they are now an integral part, a discourse that disappears as it asserts historical existence with "state of being" verbs like *was* and *is*, as in "La Fée aux choux?—*that is a part of history*." However, remember this. When Guy Blaché made this statement to Bachy in 1963, the making of *La Fée aux choux* was not at all "a part of" established French film history. Then what did she mean? Possibly, she assumed that what she remembered was the same as "what had happened." Thus, she may have taken *La Fée aux choux* and its making to be safe in the bank of the historical past. Once stored in that bank, her film and the events of its making could never be withdrawn, or so she thought.

We, however, are not satisfied with this, and we're asking what *really* happened in the making of *La Fée aux choux*, which is also to ask what film was made and in what year the making took place. In asking this, I echo the obsession of Chapter 1, "What happened to women in the early motion picture film industry?" a question I then deigned to answer there. But our want-to-know "what happened?" does not go away. Again, the emphasis on what "really" or "actually" happened is meant to call up an association with Leopold von Ranke, founder of nineteenth-century German "historism," whose phrase *wie es eigentlich gewesen* ("what actually happened") has become a touchstone for traditional historiographic approaches as well as their critique (Von Ranke 1973, 57).[20] Referenced by Walter Benjamin (1970, 257) and explicated by Hayden White (1973), the phrase has stood in for the scientific aspirations that empirical historiography cannot realize. Further, beginning in the 1970s in film theory, "what actually happened" could even characterize a "historicism" associated with naive realism.[21] If we consult thinkers in the "new philosophy of history" tradition on this, however, we get a more complicated picture and even a mediation between traditional historiography and critical theory. In defense of Leopold von Ranke, for example, Hans Kellner thinks that the ideal of the past "as it actually was" is from a contemporary point of view an "unfortunate choice of words," a choice that leaves Ranke's original project too vulnerable to easy dismissal.[22]

For feminism, here is what we want to achieve—perhaps the impossible, but at least an illustration of a paradox. We want to demonstrate that Alice's making of *La Fée aux choux* was an inaugural event that did happen (even if not in the way it has been said to have happened) *and* that this "making" once was, has been, and continues to be a constructed event. We are not then abandoning the constructivism of what I am calling Joan Scott's *constitutive discovery*, in which, to recall, the historian "constitutes" the very objects he or she claims to have "discovered" (2004, 260). But we still want to say *both* that Alice *did* make a film she called *La Fée aux choux* and that, if only constituted "after the fact," the event, now irretrievable, is therefore *nothing at all* other than what we make of it. How, to put it another way, do we admit the constructedness of the past event without also denying that the event took place? This is not the first time this kind of question has been asked in recent history, dramatized certainly by the phenomenon of "holocaust denial."[23] However, even given Paul Ricoeur's contention that, while things from the past may be "abolished," there is finally no making that such things "should not have been," this is no reassurance to the empiricist (2004, 280). And yet, I would contend that Alice's cabbage film may be less important as a case of conflicting evidence than one of the power of French institutional denial.

UNTHINKABLE EVENTS

The last chapter introduced the ambiguity of "history" as highly ideological, but the duality of the term "history" also opens up a method for thinking about subjugated knowledges from the world of women's work in earlier decades. Here, the key to that method is in the very ambiguous doubleness of history, the term. Where some see this ambiguity as obfuscation, Haitian anthropologist Michel-Rolf Trouillot sees a productive two-sidedness. Rather than "history" as a self-canceling "study of" and "object studied," he splits the term into "what happened" and "that which is said to have happened"(1995, 2). Diverging from the standard critique, he dares to "embrace" the ambiguity, as he says. That is, he wants to keep the difference between the two while acknowledging the "overlap" (23). Thus it is that Trouillot proposes a two-part approach he names *historicity one* ("what happened"), which is "intertwined" (25) with *historicity two* or ("that which is said to have happened") (29). Admittedly, this seems another response to the old question of narrative history, which we cannot seem to escape, but that question is here formulated with an especially Foucaultian feature—the *power* at the source of what it is that is "said to have happened." Quite beyond the way in which power enters to enable one story and to disqualify another, Trouillot insists on power as preceding events. So, following Trouillot, one sees why historicity one, "what happened," matters so much and is so important that it must be kept separate and the "boundary" between the two respected (13). Further, we grasp what is gained by demonstrating how historicity one is attached to historicity two, or what the imbrication of "what happened" with "that which was said to have happened" achieves. But most crucially for Trouillot, the division as well as the inextricability derive from a political imperative. Because for the anthropologist, the refusal to relinquish "what happened" is a radical stand on behalf of the success of a slave revolt. To insist on "what happened" is to counter the way that European written history denied the successful revolt that was the 1791–1804 Haitian Revolution (2, 13).[24] To insist on "what happened" is to confirm the events of the only successful eighteenth-century slave rebellion.

Am I comparing the making of *La Fée aux choux* to the Haitian revolutionary victory? Yes. In Trouillot's terms, young Alice's filmmaking has been an event constituted and reconstituted by power as well as an event prefaced and completed by power (28–29). In both cases, French establishment historians could not admit such incomprehensibilities to thought. Where the parallel is the most striking, then, is in what might be called French structural unthinkability. We have here nothing more nor less than two events that were totally unthinkable *in their time*. In the Haitian slave victory over their colonial masters and the company secretary's innovation with the representational technology that defined the twentieth century, we have two events prefaced by unthinkability.[25] Further, the very unthinkability of these events precedes and accompanies them as they were originally enacted. As Trouillot asserts about the Haitian slave revolt, the events leading up to it were "unthinkable before these events happened" (95). Additionally, this revolution was "unthinkable as it happened" (27).[26] Historical silence here begins with unthinkability which is why Trouillout wants to trace the inability to think or to say unthinkable things, to the source of prohibition— to power. The question for him then is not so much what "history" might be as much as a matter of "how history works." Or, quoting Foucault, it is not only a question of who wields power but one of "*how does it happen?*" Power may get there first, get there early, really, but getting there once is not enough because it must reenter the narrative of past events again and again (28).

If understood as a counter to the power that would assert that she "couldn't have" and that therefore she "didn't," Alice Guy Blaché's attempt to repeatedly reinsert herself into the story of invention over and over again begins to look different over the years.[27] She revises the story to fit the idea of authorial control while still downplaying what she was doing on the Belleville terrace, all the better to give the impression that she and her friends were totally unaware of the significance of their play. In her first published account, the memoir written between 1941 to 1953, Guy Blaché portrays the making as innocent and spontaneous:

> At Belleville, next to the photographic laboratories, I was given an unused terrace with an asphalt floor (which made it impossible to set up a real scene) and a shaky

glass ceiling, overlooking a vacant lot. It was in this place that I made my first efforts. A backdrop painted by a fan-painter (and fantasist) from the neighborhood made a vague decor, with rows of wooden cabbages cut out by a carpenter, costumes rented here and there around the Port Saint-Martin. As actors: my friends, a screaming baby, an anxious mother leaping to and fro into the camera focus, and my first film *La Fée Aux choux* was born. (Slide 1996a, 28)

After having put her story forward, however, she becomes exasperated with the keepers of the definitive versions, and, writing to Léon Gaumont in answer to his 1954 letter, she thanks him for the catalog he has sent and queries "But why has my poor *Fée au Choux* [sic] been placed in 1902? Incomprehensible mystery for me" (as quoted in Simon 2009b, 24). In her later 1964 version of the making of a film, friends are told that they will make a comedy, and she recalls to Victor Bachy that she said to them: "Listen, we're going to perform a comedy together." Then she proceeds to describe the scene somewhat differently, stressing that there was a rehearsal and placing the emphasis in this version less on spontaneity than on staged performance:

> I rented costumes and we rehearsed, we cut out cardboard cabbages, we found children to hide behind roses and all that. The story was what children were made to believe. . . . I got them all dressed up and we rehearsed our short scene. . . . Gaumont had a small house in Belleville where there was a garden with a cement platform; that's where I shot my first film. A sometime painter of women's fans did the backdrop. We and the kids made our first film, *La Fée aux choux*."

When asked the date of this event by Bachy, Guy Blaché replies: "It dates back to 1896. People had never seen anything like it" (Bachy 1985, 38, as translated in Simon 2009b, 7–8). Here she insists on the 1896 date whereas in the memoir pages she merely prefaces her description with the statement that "In 1896 unions did not exist" (Slide 1996b, 28,). But seven pages later, where she describes taking up the "errors" in his texts with Georges Sadoul, the first correction she lists is this: "*La Fée aux choux* dates from 1896." Between 1953 and 1964 there is further confusion on a number of details. While in the memoir a carpenter cuts out wooden cabbages, in the later interview the friends cut out the cabbages in cardboard, and, as Joan Simon has pointed out, Guy Blaché refers to babies found not behind cabbages but found behind roses (2009b, 7). Also telling is the difference between the Bachy interview and the memoir version in which her cameraman figures prominently. As she writes, it was "Anatole [Thiberville] and I," who "planted" the camera—"our first"—thus downplaying what she calls "my first efforts" (Slide 1996b, 28). Between the memoir and the 1964 interview, however, she has apparently learned to take more credit for herself, only later asserting that, at Belleville, as she says, "I shot my first film" (Bachy 1985, 38).

Alice Guy Blaché, we cannot fail to observe, occupies that most strange discursive position taken up by the historical actor-historian. Here she has stepped into a "being" as well as a "speaking" position as that actor who becomes his or her own historian, so to speak, and Trouillot has noticed such historical persons. As actors they may at first have "caused" events in the past but they are later "themselves involved in the narrative constructions." As he thinks, this "there" and then the "later" puts human beings on "both sides of the ambiguity," that functional ambiguity of the term "history." Thus straddling the divide, in Trouillot's terms, these persons are "doubly historical" (1995, 23–24). On second consideration, though, this "doubly historical" person can also disturb the distinction between the two historicities. The historical actor-historian could even take the emphasis off from the crucial distinction between "what happened" and "what was said to have happened," especially if that actor-historian can counter all other versions or "what was said to have," by testifying to "what really happened" by virtue of "having been there." Then consider the powerful agent who attempts to "make history" all the while that he or she is "making it" and who, as a consequence, actually succeeds in "making a history," here a contrast with Alice who belatedly asserts in the passive voice, "La Fée aux choux?—*that is a part of history.*" Although she may have been there at the "making" of events she comes to the story too late to construct the "birth narrative" of cinema.[28]

In 1896, it was "unthinkable" that a woman would make the first work of narrative film, that is, it was quite inconceivable *before* she had made it, *as* she was making it, and *long after* she may have made it. But it was not only that it was a *woman* making something that was so "unthinkable"; it was also *what it was* is that she had made. That is, it was also "narrative fiction film" that could not be thought as yet. Motion picture film as narrative fiction "had not yet been" in 1896 and it would not be until years later after it finally "was" and then even later after "it was said to have been." In the case of Guy Blaché, however, this making was not just inconceivable, it was also prohibitable on multiple counts—she was a woman, she was too young, and she held down a secretarial job that supported a widowed mother. As she recalls: "If the future development of motion pictures had been foreseen at this time, I should never have obtained his consent. My youth, my inexperience, my sex, all conspired against me" (Slide 1996b, 27). Permission granted on condition that her secretarial work was not interrupted, young Alice took time off from work, that is, time off without pay, and, as she tells us, the work week extended beyond six to seven days, the hours "unlimited" (Slide 1996b, 28). We wonder how she found the time. As a secretary, Alice Guy's duties also appear to have been so broad as to have included attendance with Léon Gaumont at the March 1895 scientific meeting, as we have seen, and in this capacity she witnessed

Alice Guy, Gaumont Co. secretary, c. 1894. Private collection.

the marvelous phenomenon. Later she recalled to Victor Bachy what she saw: "One of the brothers went downstairs, started turning the handle, and we began to see the Lumière factory in Lyons projected onto the sheet, people leaving and running. We were absolutely stunned" (1985, 37).[29]

THE ORIGINALITY OF HER REPETITION

In an interview in the *New Jersey Star*, August 8, 1914, Alice Guy Blaché recalls that they sold eighty prints of the cabbage fairy film, and that the film had to be remade two times because, as she says, the "prints disintegrated." Empirically, this tells scholars something important relative to an avenue they have already considered. Given the evidence of the two extant films, there is really only one option open to Guy Blaché scholars who want to invest in her version of events, and that option is to make room for yet another film, a hypothetical "earlier" film, or, as McMahan says, to "[leave] open the possibility that an earlier had been made" (2009a, 49). Historian of French film Alan Williams concurs, adding as well that the Gaumont company relied more on remaking than other companies because they had begun production using the 60mm Demenÿ camera format and subsequently had to remake all titles in the standard 35mm (2009, 36). There is as well the question of the necessity of remaking due to original print disintegration from multiple screenings.[30]

But this most empirical insistence on the existence of a motion picture film print becomes a fascinating theoretical problem at every turn. We see this immediately in the ambiguity of *copying* or *to copy*, an ambiguity that does not reveal whether lookalike films were duplicates of a company's own films or versions of films that other companies had made. In the heyday of copying, the young Alice Guy learned by doing or by copying, whichever, as did every other producer (MacMahan 2002, 23; Williams 2009, 36). By convention, the term *copying*, as we know, refers to both the attempt to completely remake as well as to reprint as occurs in the photographic laboratory process involving image production, ideally from a camera original negative. That both "to remake" and "to reprint" have come to be understood as forms of "copying" might at first engender confusion. But that is my point, one to be developed in the next chapter. Here I want to expose the nonsensical logic of the authentic print in which the cult of the original is upheld by a pejorative notion of having "only copied." Copying, whether undertaking a complete reproduction or just striking another print, let us now recall, was the order of the day at the inception of cinema. For example, as earlier mentioned, the later *L'arroseur aroseé* was a copy of the earlier *Le jardinier*, screened in the inaugural 1895 Lumière program at the Salon Indien. Louis Lumière had later copied *that* film as *L'arroseur arrosé*, probably in 1897, producing one of perhaps as many as ten other "copies" made by competing companies (Gaines 2006, 235). Georges Méliès, understanding a successful formula, also *made L'Arroseur arrosé*. Thus, not surprisingly for these years, even Alice GuyBlaché made *L'arroseur arrosé* (Gaumont 1898), producing what has been called an "exact copy" (McMahan 2002, 23, 253). My slippage from "copied" to "made" may not be obvious, so let me restate my point. It would be as technically and as grammatically correct to say that Alice Guy Blaché "made" *L'arroseur arrosé* as it would be to say that she "remade" it. The difficulty lies in any assertion that the film is produced the first time and reproduced the second since, in fact, it is "produced" a second or third time as much as it is produced the first (Gaines 2005, 2014b).[31] In addition, Guy Blaché made one of the many pillow fights as *Bataille d'oreillers* (Gaumont, 1899–1900) after the American Mutoscope *A Pillow Fight* (American Mutoscope, 1897) of which the Edison company produced at least two versions—*Seminary Girls/Scene in a Seminary* (Edison Mfg. Co., 1897) and *Pillow Fight* (Thomas A. Edison, 1897). Most likely, Alice's Gaumont version was after the Lumière's first film *Bataille d'oreillers* or *Bataille d'oreillers No. 2/Pillow Fight No. 2* (Lumière Co., 1897) which was photochemically duped in the United States by the notorious Siegmund Lubin who sold it as a Lubin company title (Gaines 2014b).

Thus, if remaking was the practice of the day, so was the laboratory reproduction of prints, that is, the production of positive prints struck from a camera original negative.[32] These practices make the assertion that either *L'arroseur arrosé* or *La Fée aux choux* is the first *anything* even more tenuous when we add to the question of "which remake" the question with which we began, that of "which print" it is that counts as the version that we want to consider "the first film." If *Le jardinier*, the title of the film screened in 1895 at the Salon Indien in Paris wore out, that is, disintegrated after countless screenings, could it not be that this too was the fate of the 60mm Gaumont film featuring cabbages and a fairy? That Alice Guy Blaché was inclined to remake the cabbage fairy idea is further substantiated by a third extant film, *Madame a des envies/Madame Has Her Cravings* (1906). In this later story film a woman whose pregnancy drives her to grab and gobble things up, gives birth in a garden represented by the same wooden cabbages we have seen in the two other extant prints.

Frame enlargement, *Madame a des envies* (1906). Collection Musée Gaumont. Paris, France.

CONCLUSION: WHERE DO FILMS COME FROM?

I continue to stand by the conclusion of an earlier article on *La Fée aux choux* in which I placed more emphasis on sexuality. Since Alice Guy herself is cross-dressing in *Sage-femme de première classe*, this film may invariably find its way into the queer film canon.[33] But my argument (Gaines 2004, 113–114) was that thinking about mechanical reproduction can have the effect of making human reproduction seem the strangest of all repetitions. Clearly I am influenced here by Andy Warhol's view of such reproduction about which he says: "When I look around today, the biggest anachronism I see is pregnancy. I just can't believe that people are still pregnant" (1975, 118). No pregnancy? Warhol's insight points to the transgression in mechanical repetition. Here is a vision of the world in which things are miraculously produced without either the insemination *of* or the gestation *within* the female body. Note that the cabbage patch euphemism that replaces biological pregnancy and childbirth substitutes for them a utopian wish—a vision of regeneration that, controlled by women, circumvents the old womb mode of reproduction. The wise cross-dressing midwife does not deliver the young couple's baby. She merely plucks the baby from the garden and sells it to them.

But Alice insists in the memoir that it was on that terrace in Belleville that "my first film *La Fée Aux choux* was born" (Slide 1996b, 28). Considering the cabbage fairy, in reference to mechanical reproduction, I previously argued that not knowing where films come from is like not knowing "where babies come from" (Gaines 2005, 1313). I was wrong because the analogy doesn't work so well given that in Western culture it would be hard to find any adult who still did not know the facts of biological reproduction. Yet the prevalent ideology of artistic expression has for a century suppressed the material conditions of mechanical mass reproduction.[34] We are not today so naive as to *not know* about how babies are "made," but as a culture we may be clueless about how films are made, especially if we believe that they come out of the psyches of originating auteur directors. From reading popular film criticism today, one might still conclude that motion picture films, if they are deemed "good," are unique works of innovation created by auteur directors and not the product of a technologized assembly line relying on computational wizardry and numerous creative workers. Although ironically, if mechanically, electronically, or computationally produced works are thought to be nothing more than rubber-stamped industrial products, we may be closer to grasping how the motion picture mode of production works, from performance before the camera to film print and today to digital video and internet links to streamed images.[35] If the mechanism of distribution and exhibition that includes the circulation first of motion picture film prints and now DVDs has been hidden from spectators, the process by which films were doubly reproduced—duplicated from masters or remade as other versions—has been just as mystified over the decades as the technicalities of human reproduction has historically been for children. Thus, for all of the answers to the question as to whether Alice Guy Blaché made *La Fée aux choux* that I have suggested, the most basic requires considering "where films come from," to which I turn in the next chapter.

4

OBJECT LESSONS

The Ideology of Historical Loss and Restoration

Where do motion picture films come from? What can the 35mm motion picture film print tell us about that? As insistently empirical as a fossil and as functionally specific as a nineteenth-century corset, the film print is not, however, so obviously an object. An atypical object, the extant film print is also an odd artwork, if "art" at all. Always one step away from realization, the film print has historically existed to-be-projected because technically a "print of the film" is not immediately a "film" to-be-seen in any viewable condition. Decades after its first exhibition, discovered in an archive, that print may continue to be "the film" in its new life as an artifactual object. But not for long. Because given recent technological changes in archival restoration practices, "a film" may no longer, materially speaking, be "film" at all. So what *is* the film in question if it is neither *a film* nor "film"? (Streible 2013). For us, this moment of ontological confusion occasions a reevaluation of the very "stuff" of the extant photochemical film object. Here the "what is it?" ontological question is caught up with the specificity of representational relations, the very relations to past events-in-time that make photographic media prized historical sources. As sources, let us then acknowledge the basis on which motion photographic prints have been awarded special *indexical privilege*, that is, how as indicative signs they are thought to confirm their referents.[1] But, further, I urge us to see such indexical privilege, linked to "pastness" and mirroring historiographic claims as encapsulating the method we are critiquing. Today, after the "digital turn," however, the *index* as evidence has increasingly less of an epistemological leg to stand on. What, then, is the consequence for historiography?

Some silent motion picture film prints have survived into the present as historical objects and although these film prints exist, the creative personnel who produced them and their worlds do not. While this distinction may seem obvious, it turns out to have been an all-consuming problem for the philosophy of history. Here is the problem of objects like Heidegger's extant antiquities that are "objectively present yet somehow past" as opposed to the more difficult category of "there-being," the no longer existing but not exactly "past" (1996, 348–349). This philosophical problem, as we will see by the end of the chapter, has relevance for the difference between silent-era filmmakers, their times, and the "objectively present" objects that survive them in the present. Undoubtedly "objectively present" film prints prod us to research the work histories of the women behind silent motion pictures worldwide. Yet what do all of these prints yield?

We may examine extant prints, as we have in the case of Alice Guy Blaché, in an attempt to prove "firstness," that is, to claim preeminence. But as we saw in the last chapter, the extant film print itself is no final proof of *the existence of past events* and therefore the surviving object alone *may not* put an end to questions about what actually happened behind or in front of the camera loaded with light-sensitive film stock.[2] An extant motion picture print, while it may be in structuralist terms a "document of its own making," may constitute incomplete evidence of events that took place at the scene of its own making. The print in question, may, however, yield evidence, but not of its "making" so much as of its chemical makeup. But this is no small thing. For in the very chemical composition of the archival film object we find another evidentiary universe, one that archivists refer to as the "internal history of the copy," a chronicle of the physical changes that a motion picture print has undergone (Cherchi Usai 2000, 147). So while the print may not necessarily guarantee historical knowledge of specific events that "happened" in time, as a photochemical object it may hold the key to *what happened to itself* over time. Here is where science takes over. From a scientific point of view, the print contains the secrets of its own production, and, from an archival standpoint, this is relevant to its restorability as an object.[3]

This chapter finds tension between the wholeness, the transformative promise of restoration, and irreparable "loss." Six "object lessons" revolve around several kinds of "loss": "loss" of image detail through decomposition, "loss" of past time, "loss" of virtue, and "loss" of connection effected by digitization, all "losses" dependent on the presumption of something once intact. Further, "historical loss" contrasts early motion picture industry female workers with the material objects they helped to produce, objects that, once "lost," reappear, now given a "second life" by archival restoration. Illustrating how archival rescue engenders new theoretical issues at the moment of the "digital turn," I offer a case study of the Amsterdam EYE Institute restoration of *Shoes* (1916), directed and written by Lois Weber.

OBJECT LESSON 1:
THE ARTIFACT AS HISTORICAL INDEX

As I began by saying, the motion picture film is somewhat of an oddity among art objects. Materially speaking, an archival film print is hundreds of feet of cellulose nitrate or cellulose acetate strips, wound around reels, canned, and shelved in temperature-controlled storage vaults.[4] Such a print, depending upon its age, may also be in various stages of decomposition. The film material in these cans, once so devalued that it was scrapped in bulk for the silver content in the emulsion, is, however, now national cultural treasure (Pierce 1997, 6). What is the new value of such films? Of course, their images are thought to hold visual testimony to the former existence of human and animal life, of landscape and architecture, of dramatic scene and artificial set. The film print object may even, as a consequence of its capacity to hold so much detail, be thought to "store history," that is, to retain moments *it has made* into "history" out of events before the camera.[5] But we will be less interested in stored events than in the way film prints evidence their own "historicity" as art form as well as celluloid material. Taking an archivist's approach to the film print as exemplifying what Philip Rosen calls methods of "modern historicity," we also find here the two fundamental elements of that approach: first the index, and second the ordered sequence that follows events (2001, 354). Inasmuch as the film print is a kind of index par excellence, it is taken to be indicative of changes, or alterations to itself, if you will. These changes in turn are often sequenced as two stories: first, the story of its own chemical compositional change over time, including its own use or abuse; and second, the story of its place in a stylistic development. Of these two stories, the print is more often consulted on the latter—the stylistic evolution of a medium or the "history" of itself as representative of an evolving form and a creatively constructed "work," a term taken up in the fifth object lesson here.[6]

Motion picture film restoration as institutional commitment conjoins an idea of the index with archival procedure. As we will see, the archivist approaches the motion picture film print with a technical concern about "historicity." For archivist Paolo Cherchi Usai, *historicity* is exemplified by "indexical indications on the face of the artifact" (2008, 207). Yet what is meant by "historicity" here?[7] We will want to ask about the renewed dedication to the indexical test that we hear in film archivists' discourse today, a discourse rather like something we have heard before, something akin to the "true to life" claim from the first decade when the Edison Wargraph Co. advertised: "Life motion, realism, photographed from nature so true to life as to force the observer to believe that they are viewing the reality and not the reproduction" (as quoted in Hampton 1970, 37). Here the synonymity of "realism" and "true to life" are symptomatic of the associations that arrived with motion photography, associations that only accumulated and permutated. Along with "truth claims" and the enabling phrase "real and true," there is, of course, the attempt to be faithfully "true to" an original, whether the real-world-as-original or the work of art. Whether "true to" life or "true to" the original, the issue is one of representational relations. But what, to review, is the problem here?

While for the last thirty years film theory has critiqued "reality and its reproduction" or "realistic reproduction," arguing that "realism" was an ideological effect of the moving image, now the terms "real" and "reproduction" appear in archival discourse as though to forget the warnings of the critique of realism (Gaines 1999). To connect that critique with archival discourse, consider how realist representation aspires to the achievement of that supreme restoration—the "restoration to life."[8] Then think how archival restoration is dedicated to the "real" materiality of the photochemical object and the historical "reality" of its production and exhibition. It must be objected, however, that these are not quite the same "real" at all, for a more notorious pair of "reals" also define the motion photographic object. I say "pair" because these two "reals"—one guaranteed by indexical connection and the other confirmed by iconic lookalikeness— underwrite each other. Therefore, due to the status of the film object as *both* iconic and indexical, the restorer defers to visual elements that produce the astounding "reality effect," that special attribute of "photorealism" codified as an aesthetic belonging to the image (Manovich 2001, 200–201).

Would that we could once and for all separate the epistemological from the aesthetic, or "truth claims" from stylistic "realism," since they stubbornly stick together. Yet, if we look back to Heidegger to the philosophical rumblings around the term *representation* that translated into aspects of deconstructionist antihistoricism, we find another angle on our problem of the recourse to so many "reals." There is a forgotten step, if you will, one that needs to be pinned to a moment, so think of it this way. There will have to have been a new "construction of *certainty*," one that Fredric Jameson, following Heidegger's reading of Nietzsche, finds to have enabled "truth as correctness" to appear as a feature of a new time (2002, 47). Following this insight, we can combine this expectation with the privileged connection between the photographic sign and the world it indicates, merging the two. Adding "truth" to photographic privilege, we come up with *indexical certainty*. For what does "history" as the discipline that aspires to be scientific most need other than certain proof?

The archivist's "real" has less to do with the illusion of "the real," the success of an aesthetic, and more to do with scientific certainty. Aligned with "truth as correctness," the archivist's commitment is to measurable object relations, archival science being as it is, reliant on chemistry and, more recently, computer science.[9] Now, following 1978, with the "historical turn" to "the films themselves," these odd objects, as never before, become measurable indicators among other rare documents. Archival prints verify exhibition and production events and are themselves to-be-verified by chemical test. After the "turn," with renewed dedication to archival work, the challenge comes most forcefully, comes along with a promise and a new set of concerns.[10] Finally, and as significantly, the film historian's source material is now raised a cultural notch as it enters the realm of cultural heritage formation in hopes of following the esteemed arts of sculpture and painting. Thus elevated, the motion picture film print, once only a copy, now becomes a unique work.[11]

As I said, the value of the archival film print is as singular source material available for analysis as a photochemical substance *and* a work-on-film. But its restoration today may be less its perfect reproduction than its total transformation, and this makes what it *will be* relative to *what it was* into something ontologically unanticipated. Not only may the print be restored to something that is ontologically unlike its original self, but it is restored by means of a transformational process *as never before*. So we want to know how this happens as well as what it is that we should call "the film" that is no longer photochemically "film" and therefore not really "a film" at all (despite its still being called a "film"). Following the idea that technological developments reconfigure earlier forms such that, for example, cellulose nitrate becomes rarified, we now see a series of revaluations (Smither 2002). But accompanying revaluation, the arrival of digital technology delivers a new "uncertainty" since we are now deprived of the "certainty" of the film as the indexical carrier (Mulvey 2004b, 1292). And indeed, if we were to say what is finally at stake in any attachment to the indexical it would have to be the certainty or proof of existence that it has historically offered, which is why I see archivists and historians wanting *indexical certainty*, to coin this redundancy.[12]

Now the historian's investment is predicated on the conviction that the artifact has an inviolate evidentiary relation to the historical past to which it once belonged, which makes it, as primary source, a key to knowing that past. Here, however, is where the logic of modern historicity starts to unravel and Rosen pushes us to see what we can no longer dismiss. What we cannot deny is that the artifact is but a tiny piece relative to the rest of the past. Indeed, it is given inordinate significance relative to its fractional portion. How strange that the primary source document, only a remnant, but *the very remnant*, can come to stand in for the entirety of the whole to which it once belonged (2001, 117). Even more illogically, the artifact that stands for the whole that it cannot completely "be" also promises to help reconstitute that whole, to bring back the missing world from which it came. Where is such an impossibility institutionalized but in the methodological traditions of historiographic reliance on sources? Here, then, is the parallel between the historian's methodology and the archivist's work, for, as Rosen goes on, the goals of preservationism are dedicated to the "aesthetics of reconstructed totalities" (131).

In this first object lesson, I have asked how the artifactual object, thought to prove past existence, stands for the whole of which it is only a part. Of course there is no bringing back the missing world, either by restoration of the archival object or by means of written "history."[13] And yet, how strong is the cultural desire that there be no lapse, nothing left out or lost. Let us not pass up the chance to remark as well on a companion object lesson. This is the lesson of the incremental "loss" of detail on the image that may be read as "loss" of connection to the historical past. Yet the lamentable "loss" has still more ideological work to do, and here no more so than in the very lesson of the film whose restoration is our case study. Quite serendipitously, Lois Weber's *Shoes* is a domestic melodrama whose moral centers on the young girl whose wrong choice results in the "loss" of her virtue.

OBJECT LESSON 2: THE YOUNG GIRL'S MORAL LESSON

Shoes (Universal, 1916) gives us a narrative of the choice made by the shopgirl Eva Meyers who "falls" from innocence, seduced not only by a heartless rake but by the gleaming object of consumer culture—a pair of shiny high button shoes in a store window.[14] Testimony to widely shared belief, Eva's moral failure echoes that historical "loss" with which we are concerned here, drawing as it does on the same cultural assumptions to produce the "loss" of virtue that cannot be restored. Culturally, such loss is felt when one mode of *historical time* turns into the next, past to present, sometimes a turn away from the old where aberration from tradition is a "fall" downward. One can thus see how a moral lapse borrows the structure of *historical time*, explained in Chapter 2 as the relative arrangement of past, present, and future. This is the structure that we will begin to translate into melodrama's terms, terms of the distribution of justice that borrow the temporal lockstep march forward that allows "no going back," no return to earlier events, no restoration to the fullness of the past. How remarkable that so many uses can be found for the ideology of historical "loss" premised on *historical time* as resolutely irreversible, as we will see in the next chapter. So it is that as in *Shoes* the drama of "virtue forever despoiled" leans heavily on irredeemable "loss," historical studies "from below" also rely on such a "gone forever" claim, confirming our suspicion of how well this lament works as an argument. Carolyn Steedman explains how effectively "loss" works as a rhetoric in women's history: "A sense of that which is lost, never to be recovered completely, has been one of the most powerful rhetorical devices of modern women's history" (1992, 164). What sympathies are aroused by exclaiming, "She is 'lost' to history!"

Now consider how this idea of "loss" organizes the most elementary level of meaning-making, seen in the difference between a presignifying reality *before* and *after* its rendering as words or images, privileging an original reality and associating it with the authentic and "the true." It is as though, says Elizabeth Cowie, a complete reality is thought to have existed "*before* its fall into mediation, interpretation, narration, and presentation" (2011, 20). She asks us to question why in the conversion of events into signs, the presignifying complete "real" gets cast as something it "no longer" is any more. We begin to suspect that the problem is the ideology of "no longer" when the conversion of photochemical signs into digital signs is similarly lamented. Why, we want to know, are digital tools considered such a threat to photochemical signs, those forms considered so altered by digitization? Here is the yearning for a reality intact, "before the fall," prefatory to distortion and disconnection, or the worst "loss"—complete eradication. Whether "loss" of virtue or of detail, definition, or information or of connection to the events of the past, this *ideology of historical loss* is of course predicated on an idea of an intact earlier time, a "former" present or a virtue intact that has been violated. Now consider how *Shoes* itself functions as a restoration allegory. Eva's "fall" from innocence is recapitulated in the deterioration of the very nitrate material of the once pristine film print that supports the *Shoes* narrative, marred now by bacterial erosion of the image.

OBJECT LESSON 3: LOST TIME AND DISAPPEARING SIGNS

In the following chapter, taking up *Shoes* as domestic melodrama, I return to our cultural familiarity with historical "loss" as in close proximity to melodrama's worry over "that which is no longer," whether lost virtue or lost family ties, lost worlds or ways of being. Thinking about these losses, we cannot help but note how much traditional history needs the idea of "loss." And yet the recurrent metaphor "lost to history" misleads. How exactly is it that a person, object, or event can be "lost" to "history"? Or for that matter "hidden from history"? It is time we noticed the mixed metaphor of "history" as both unseeing and repressing. How strange that it that both does the hiding by "repression" or "exclusion" and can't see what is "hidden" from it, as in the old "unseen by history" cliché. Further problems arise if we think of "history" as the same as "the past" as in the vernacular expression "and the rest is history" where "history" is "past time" *and* its story. Throughout, I follow theorist of history Keith Jenkins for whom "the past" and "history," are, as he says, "ages and miles apart" (1991, 7). And what are the consequences of the conflation of the two? When we don't separate the two but think "history" as synonymous with "the past," we always come up with "loss" thinks Steedman, which is why she argues that we might better acknowledge our emotional investment in the "romance of history," which she associates with holding out the "hope" that that which is long gone, "irretrievably lost, which is past time, can be brought back" (1992, 42).[15] Consider then what historical discourse achieves politically by both indicating how much has been "lost" *and* by stepping in to restore to wholeness. For if the "lost" cannot finally be "brought back," something at least compensatory must be achieved. Something must be done. Here is what is political: from historical "loss" and its concomitant "forgetting" in histories "from below," those of African Americans, Asian Americans, and the lower classes, something else is now at work. Researching and writing "lost" stories enacts something like *restoration as restitution*. That is, historical telling becomes symbolic *restitution* for acts of exclusion, obliteration, exploitation—*reparation*, really, for what had happened in the past.

Without negating a politics of *restitution*, however, let's admit how much the lament "lost to" or "unseen by" history is just so much common sense wisdom. Yet historiography as a method of research, writing or image making still depends upon this commonsensical idea of "past time" as "lost time." That long gap between past and present, which an idea of "lost past" as "lost time" keeps before us, is not ancient wisdom, however, but recent accommodation. Rosen, who suspects that this very historical "loss" is just one more dubious feature of "modern historicity," argues that the historian's primary sources only have their "evidentiary authority" because of the particular organization of time that has come to prevail after the Enlightenment. That is, post-Enlightenment, time is ordered in such a way that the past is not fixed but continues to recede (2001, 117). Thus the weary "passage of time" metaphor puts the past further and further from the present, and, we should add, produces as it recedes an "irretrievability," hence scarcity, and then, finally, almost without our noticing, institutes venerability and value. Variations on this popular idea of historical loss as the past moving out of sight and out of reach are plentiful, enriched by clichés like the "distant past." Further, the past is not only receding in a long shot but eroding in close-up as in "ravages of time," readable on aging objects and human faces. No, wait, some will say. All this about the "loss of the past" is self-evident and "just the way that it is." After all, reclamation of the "lost past" is a goal everywhere espoused. Yet we have reason to be dubious, especially when, as we have seen, the "passage of time" that puts events further and further away from us is equated with "loss of the real." So consider the most recent recruitment of the "historical past = loss of the real" equation on behalf of the analogical object as resistance to digital media conversion. Apropos of the "past = lost" equation, David Rodowick wants to know why we find historicity "only on the side of the analog" but *not* on the side of the digital. To align the analog with human history and to figure the digital as its antithesis is an ideological response to the appearance of new technologies, Rodowick thinks. And that ideology makes a familiar case on behalf "the real" as something that we are in danger of losing. By now we may also have lost count of the many losses that must be countered, accompanied by multiple recourses to "the real," each, Rodowick argues, "equally imaginary" (2007, 5). We will continue to persist with this question as to exactly how it is that "historicity" is thought to be on the side of the photochemical-indexical as opposed to the digital, and how the digital, thought to be "historyless," after failing reality tests, becomes subject to the charge of being "made up."[16] Ideology of "loss" aside, at every juncture in the historiographic project we *do* face disappearing signs. As archivists rightly remind us, photochemically registered "signs of life" are everywhere disappearing—especially on decomposing image frames at rates that threaten to make entire archival image-objects disappear.[17] The question of comparative processes now comes to a head, however, in the restoration project where the motion picture film print becomes the theater in which the meeting between photochemical and computational is made dramatic, played out as the last

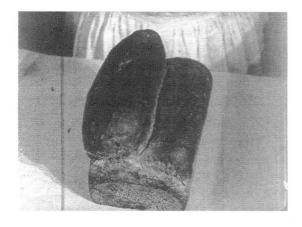

Frame enlargement, *Bread* (Universal Pictures, 1916), Ida May Park, director. Courtesy Library of Congress. Washington, D.C.

gasp of a feared-to-be-lost "real." Here, then, the *ideology of historical loss* takes on a new role in this most recent drama involving the feared "loss" of connection to "the real." But this is a drama in which the only means of "rescue" for the motion picture film print, its only hope, is in its digital conversion by means of the same processes thought to obliterate its material objecthood. Indeed, this seems a cruel irony. The motion picture film print object is rescued by turning it into something other than an object. This something into which the print is converted is not, however, identifiably *there* in the same way, and although not immaterial not exactly material either, at least not material in any way we have known before.[18]

OBJECT LESSON 4:
THE LIVES OF PRINTS: DECOMPOSITION

Among the nitrate film print collections that the Academy of Motion Picture Arts and Sciences accepted were those belonging to Lois Weber and Will Rogers. While the Rogers family rescued prints from the UCLA Archive vaults where they were stored and preserved with the help of the Museum of Modern Art, the majority of Weber's films were left at UCLA. Although in 1970 the American Film Institute agreed to preserve the academy holdings, the project was postponed until 1981 by which time it was too late. Lois Weber's films had decomposed to the point that they could not be restored (Slide 1992, 15–16).[19] Fortunately, despite this massive loss, all prints of Lois Weber films had not yet decomposed. Remarkably, a 35mm film print of *Shoes* (1916), written, directed, and produced by Lois Weber, did not completely deteriorate in the Amsterdam Filmmuseum where it had been stored. In 1990, the print was first preserved with Dutch language intertitles and in 2008, after an effort was made to locate missing sections of a still-incomplete print, the extant material underwent restoration, this second time using digital "tools." Today, then, postrestoration, *Shoes* could be said to now be part digital, part photochemical. So we could claim that this new form both *is* and *is not* the motion picture film print form that it once had when in 1916 it was released by Universal Pictures. But, then, we wouldn't want to insist on the singular of "form" for a number of reasons, the first being the way in which the motion picture print, as I have said, is such an odd artifact, a queer work of industrial art among artworks, its ontology a defiance of art object conventionality. As both the source material for multiple copies and itself a copy among copies of itself, the print is to-be-copied and later to-be-projected: in the first case like a plaster cast mold from which copies are made and in the second like the inserted player piano roll that requires both the piano and its human operator in order to facilitate the production of music.[20] Of course the motion picture print has historically existed to-be-exhibited, more exactly, as I began by saying, to-be-projected on a screen and to-be-seen as advertised at its theatrical release. A film title was never singular at the time of release since print multiples were struck and screened in more than one venue, effecting in the first decade a newly re-markable same-film-seen-everywhere phenomenon as Charles Musser has noted (2009, 64). Multiple prints of the title *Shoes* were threaded through projectors during the U.S. exhibition run and some were also shipped to Europe and the Far East.[21] In 1916, at least one print of *Shoes* was distributed in Japan in a short window when Universal Pictures was attempting to set up an exchange in Tokyo.[22] If, after this run, prints were shipped back to Universal in Los Angeles, they may have been stored on the studio lot only to be later junked in 1948 when the company disposed of its remaining silent film library (Pierce 2007, 128). Most American prints, deemed economically worthless at the tail end of their runs, were not sent back to the United States and consequently may still survive in foreign film archives although they may not be intact. Only a portion, or less, a fragment, may now be left after the decomposition of one or more reels, as was the case with the print of *Shoes* found in the Komiko collection in Tokyo. The mate-rial life of the print, however, has never been part of the central narrative of motion picture film history even while print quality has become a cinephillic obsession and a marketing tool.[23] Taking seriously the lives of prints could take us far afield from traditional humanities concerns since this would entail studying laboratory processes as well as the machinery of film distribution, that is, booking film titles and "shipping" cans containing celluloid strips wound around metal reels. The very wide distribution of multiple prints in the first decades of the century helps to keep alive a classic film title, critically acclaimed at its release and exhibited worldwide.[24] Then there are the exceptions—those titles canonized despite originally weak public response.[25] In such exceptional cases, the myth of "having been seen" may be generated later by word of mouth, published writings, and even the imagination of exhibition events that never took place. Let us remember that for nearly a century, with the exception of archival schools, exhibition events, and retrospective festivals, archival objects were segregated from the sphere of cultural criticism. Extant prints existed in one realm and the criticism on "the work" in another. Over the century, film prints were increasingly divorced from the very "work" that these prints continued to shore up in public discourse and shared memory.

In recent years, as a consequence of the more exacting technological requirements of DVD production, archival print quality has become a major concern of national archives (Horak 2007). But reviewing national holdings is also where we encounter fortuitous accidents. For instance, the survival of a print may produce a title as a candidate for canonization that was never publicly exhibited, as is the case with Elvira Giallanella's antiwar film *Humanity/Umanità* (1919).[26] Or, a random 35mm film print becomes a rare archival object when all other prints have deteriorated and it gets a second chance as an artifact considered valuable enough to restore, at which point that print becomes the "original" for another generation of copies.[27] Such is the case with the original print material, source material from which more copies of *Shoes* can now be made. *Shoes* is then all of the following: the film original material, the archival object, "the work," and, as we will see, one copy as well as all of the copies of the material that constitutes "the film."

OBJECT LESSON 5:
OBJECTLESSNESS AND MIXED ONTOLOGIES

In conversation with other archivists about the future of film restoration, Michael Loebenstein speculates about the ontology of data-derived signs that make up what we have heretofore thought of as "works of art." If one assumes that there is no "master negative" to begin with and that new digital processes allow entering the digital stream at any point, it would seem, he thinks, that something stable has disappeared. "What is done away with?" he asks, then answers: "The whole notion that something is a 'work'—one manifestation of a certain point in time—is done away with completely" (Cherchi Usai et al. 2008, 207). Yes, of course. The *notion* is "done away with" or is under pressure. And yet, nothing so drastic really happens, this being a *notion*. Then again, something else is more likely to happen—the notion of "the work," like the notion of "the original," may later be put back again, and even more insistently. For example, critical discourse can easily refer to the title *Shoes* as the same film "work" even after it has been recovered by means of a combination of digital and analog procedures and embodied in multiple forms. We only need to count to learn that *Shoes* is more multiple than singular. Thus, to see *Shoes* as multiple we could say that Lois Weber's *Shoes* is embodied not only in two copies of the restored digital intermediate, or uncompressed DPX files, but also in a 35mm black-and-white motion picture film printed on negative stock and a 35mm positive projection print. If we count the five-reel (1,150 meter) 1990 Dutch language nitrate and positive projection print versions, that would total six "copies."[28] But why include the DPX files in this list of copies? After all, the uncompressed digital intermediates are technically computer files containing code and as such are not available to the eye. Archivist Giovanna Fossati thinks that the digital intermediate could be called a "virtual artifact" in that it has existence although it is not tied to either the hard drive or to the digital tape that supports it. Although not a physical "copy," it can be "copied" by means of migration without quality loss (2009, 122). The digital *Shoes* thus stored is then a "copy" that is not a copy although it does have some features of the copy. Here, then, is the digital defiance of the copy-original paradigm on which aesthetic theory has historically relied. If there is no quality diminution and effectively no differentiation between copy and original, it must be said that *they are the same thing*. If they are the same thing, an old aesthetic hierarchy is threatened with collapse, as we will see.

Let us recount these iterations that comprise "the work," that constitute it without exactly embodying it. Since we can no longer argue that there is no "work" except when that "work" solidifies in the form of an object, what is it that we now have—if not a "work"? It would appear that if, with the "virtual artifact," the "work" is files containing code, we have a contradictory "objectless" work. From this, it would seem that digitization *has* succeeded in canceling the notion of "the work," in which case Loebenstein is right—there really is no more singular "work."[29] This cancelation, however, may be too much to hope for if we look back at the fate of Walter Benjamin's "authentic" photographic print, which, like "objectless" work, was an ontological impossibility, that is, until museums and collectors invented the "authenticity" that elevated machine-made photographic works.[30] As Fossati spells out the ramifications of the original-copy logic: if the digital copy is "identical to its original," then *every* copy can also have "authenticity" (2009, 122). If this is the case, then we have a third ontological impossibility—the "authentic digital copy." Most likely, however, as in the case of Benjamin's no longer nonsensical "authentic" photographic print, there *will no longer be* nonsensical objectless works because, over time, the contradictoriness of the concept will become tolerated. In the meantime, however, "the work" has undoubtedly more work to do as it coordinates and covers up disparate processes.

So to describe the restoration procedures in *Shoes*: in the so-called analogical stage, the tinting was "simulated" onto the 35mm projection film print by the Desmet method. In conversion, the film was digitized by an Oxberry scanner at a 2K resolution (2,048 pixels wide × 1,556 pixels high) in the Haghefilm laboratory.[31] Considering these two technological processes, one could argue that *Shoes* as a "work" is now embodied by two ontologically incompatible somethings; but, not to worry, these somethings are made commensurable as they have been used to produce what we take to be a single restored "work." This would mean, however, that the resulting restoration now exists *not* as an ontologically "pure" motion picture film but as an ontologically "mixed" entity. My preference would be to treat the digital-photochemical restoration as ontologically mixed if for no other reason than that the very idea of *ontological mixture* can throw a monkey wrench into any "what is it?" line of inquiry. How can something be ontologically two things at once? If nothing else, here is the chance to "call the question" relative to such apparent ontological impossibilities, to review the objectless work, the original photographic print, and the authentic digital copy.[32] However, there is yet another solution to the problem of "what is it?" in the analog-to-digital transition moment. This would be to consider that restoration takes place in two distinct "realms" or "domains." This approach has the advantage of calling attention to protocols and even to technological possibilities in what is envisioned as a new unprecedented representational world. But here I stop to wonder how to foreground our own human participation in the constitution of things. To say that part of the restoration took place in the "domain" of the digital and another part in the photochemical analogical "domain" is to put off a showdown that may then never come. Without a reckoning, things will continue to appear to be "what they are" and we will lose sight of why we have historically needed them to be this or that.

Already in the digital so-called "realm," a conceptual conversion has taken place and archivists refer to photochemical image aspects as "information," perhaps still indexical signs but more importantly "data" to-be-scanned or data missing but hopefully recoverable. And here in data recovery is also where the digital process appears most miraculous. Portions of frames where "information" is missing are restored by extrapolation from adjacent frames where the image is more complete. Scanned, digitally cleaned, and rerecorded on film, such "information" restoration is like growing missing limbs from existing ones by means of DNA harvesting. Indeed, replaced portions are described as "cloned," and archivists invariably ask whether digital restoration alters the "genetics" of the work (Fossati 2009, 85; Cherchi Usai et al. 2008, 113). So we now want to know what ideological work is done by these genetics metaphors that are today found at the juncture between the dystopic and the utopic.

OBJECT LESSON 6: HISTORYLESSNESS

The DNA metaphor, if it appears on the dystopic side of the debates, contributes to the current climate of "crisis." And thus the crisis rhetoric swells to encompass many kinds of perceived losses. In addition to "objectlessness," among the concerns expressed in archival discourse are sourcelessness, authorlessness, and distinctionlessness, all further testimony to the *ideology of historical loss*, actually, as one might expect, symptomatic of concern about divergence from dependable points of reference. Consider then whether the problem here is "change" read as "loss" and whether such worries are not an entirely predictable response to a situation in which the procedural status quo has been upended. From all accounts it is clear that film archivists face a magnitudinal challenge to established protocols. But our concern is less changes in archival practice than the more formidable "lessness" of "historylessness." As Michael

Loebenstein summarizes the crisis: "Nothing is historical anymore, since data doesn't age, decompose, gradually change" (Cherchi Usai et al. 2008, 195). Aligning "nothing historical" with the disappearance of the "work" effected by the fluctuation of every element, he interprets this new capacity for digital alteration as a challenge to what we have been calling *indexical certainty*: "You could make changes to something on a weekly basis. So, in a way, historicity is done away with" (ibid., 207). Traditional assumptions about the goals and means of film restoration, it would seem, no longer hold in the digital realm. So what have we here? There might be a thousand ways in which "historicity is done away with" if by "historicity" we mean a quality of being "historical" or the guarantee of authenticity or decompositional change, readable and therefore mappable on a time line. However, these would be only a few kinds of "historicity" among a "variety of historicities" (Rosen 2001, 7), all having little to do with the usual relation between written historiography and events of the past.[33] Again, to the archivist, "historicity" may have to do with the "internal history of the copy" (Cherchi Usai 2000, 147), as we will next see. But in Loebenstein's worry about "historicity" as something obliterated—"done away with"—we come at our problem from the other side—"historylessness," not "historicity." So what if, following Loebenstein, we consider "historicity" from this other angle, that is, if we consider the state of things thought to be "historyless." We wonder if "no longer historical" then means the state of constant changeability in contrast with "historicity" as measurable change in the chemical makeup or physical condition of the film print. Certainly archivists' concerns are centered on photochemical film as a special materiality, yet one also suspects that the current discussion is only to a degree about the apparent immateriality of the digital.

As Paolo Cherchi Usai characterizes the digital, it is even more ontologically strange than the film medium and for him, the "peculiarity" of digital technology has to do *not* with its inability to register so much as with its capacity to cover up its own transformations. For Cherchi Usai, as for Loebenstein, its oddity *is* in "historylessness," that is, "no history" as another kind of "no longer," closer perhaps to "no longer readable" as a historical object, with the digital seen as almost sinister in its "intrinsic ability to conceal [the] historicity of [the] process." Cherchi Usai goes on, with reference to the internal "historicity" of the digital image: "You may find out that it happened, but you don't know when" (Cherchi Usai et al. 2008, 207). This unreadableness contrasts with the readable "historicity" on the face of the photochemical image that evidences signs of compositional change to-be-read, ideally yielding one of the historian's favorite measures—chronology. The internal "historicity," Cherchi Usai's "what happened" to the film, points toward the "history of the film print," or, as he confirms, the "history of the image" that can be read in the pattern of decay (2000, 147). Here, an example might be the way archivists read the pattern on the four hundred and thirty-five Universal prints that survived after burial in the hoarfrost in Dawson's City, Yukon. These silent-era film prints all register the chemical reactions to freezing and thawing. Light and humidity produced the distinctive imprint of a visible "melting" of the emulsion on the reel edges.[34]

Strip of images, *Bread* (Universal Pictures, 1916).
Courtesy Library of Congress. Washington, D.C.

SHOES (LOIS WEBER, UNIVERSAL PICTURES, 1916): THE CONTINUITY "MISTAKE"

If we understand film archivists' concerns with "historicity," it may translate into something as small as a scratch in the emulsion or as large as a sequence or cutting order. Or, as we will finally see, this "historicity" has to do with the difficulty of erasing raindrops on a window pane in a photographic shot. And, to remind us, why does digital restoration fail the archivist's "historicity" test? Cherchi Usai wonders skeptically: "But if digital technology tends to erase the 'historicity' as indexical indications on the face of the artifact, this is fundamentally a wrong tool for our job, which is the job of protecting and promoting historicity, insofar as history matters to a curator—which may or may not be the case in the future?" (2008, 207). Entirely "wrong" for the job? But the archivist's commitment to what Cherchi Usai calls "promoting historicity" (ibid.) is often tested, arising at multiple junctures in the restoration process. So in our case let us narrow our investigation to one issue: "to correct or not to correct," and if to correct, to intervene digitally or analogically or not at all, because in the name of respect for "historicity" as authenticity, the archivist may of course do nothing at all to the image. In this instance *Shoes* presents us with an unforeseen test of concern for "historicity," that is, authenticity measured by "indexical indications" (ibid.). Here is what tests commitments to "historicity": an apparent error in the original material, one revealed in a close frame analysis comparing the use of an "incorrect" as well as a hypothetically "correct" insert shot.[35] Consider, then, the order of these close-up shots from *Shoes* where we find a violation of the rule of narrative continuity, a rule in place by 1917; here, it's an editing convention ensuring spatial as well as temporal coherence (Bordwell, Staiger, Thompson 1985, 194–195).[36] Technically, we're considering a continuity error found in the 35mm film original.[37]

One can grasp what is meant by a continuity error in a comparison between three shots: the establishing shot of the sunny street (page 86), the close up of the pair of high button shoes toward which her eyes will be directed, a second establishing shot from later in the film, during the rain, and the close-up of the object of Eva's longing, the same pair of new shoes in the window (page 87). Here is the error: the identical close-up of the shoes in the window is an insert in two different scenes, one early and the other later in

Frame enlargement, *Shoes* (Universal, 1916), store window, medium shot, sunny street. Courtesy EYE Institute. Amsterdam, the Netherlands.

CHAPTER 4

Frame enlargement, *Shoes* (Lois Weber, Universal, 1916), rainy window, closeup. Courtesy EYE Institute. Amsterdam, the Netherlands.

the film. The first establishing shot of Eva shows a sunny street, a sequence appearing before her resolve (like the soles of her shoes) becomes worn down. The film needs to establish that it is her final exasperation with poverty, not her first wish for new shoes, that causes her to succumb to the pressures of her male seducer. The narrative takes the character from longing to despair and finally to a "night of sin." Eva sees the new shoes in two close-up inserts but in two different frames of mind—first in the context of pure wish and second relative to the desperate need that leads her to relinquish her innocence. The second use of the close-up is importantly contrasted with the image of Eva's own soggy and tattered shoes, ruined in the downpour. But something is wrong in the cutting order. *The same rain-specked store window close-up has been cut in twice.* The rainy store window close-up has been used in the earlier scene in which no rain falls. In the extant print, the "wrong" insert resulting in a continuity error produces a "wrong" meaning. In this scene, as cut, Eva sees the wished-for shoes through the rain-spattered store window pane on a sunny day, but the rain-marked image belongs to a later point in the narrative when, after days of rain, her shoes are now ruined and she has become desperate.

What does the restorer do? This editing error cannot be rectified by re-cutting the film to insert the "correct" close-up of the high-button shoes as seen through a clear pane of glass because such a close-up, not found in the extant original footage, *may never have been shot.* Or the film was reedited at some point. Is there a digital solution? A hypothetical "digital tools" solution to this problem of the need for two different insert shots—a sunny as well as rainy one—might be the erasure of the raindrops to produce a clear store window pane. Is this achievable? We already know that among the miracles of digital intervention is the capacity to "clone" portions of one frame in order to reconstruct another. Here, however, is a restoration problem that can't be solved with such extrapolation and although digital "cleaning" to eliminate scratches is standard, the erasure of portions of an image is not as yet possible in the Desmet digital application.[38] The inverse of the additive cloning, the subtraction of some portions while leaving other portions intact, is currently beyond the capabilities of the software. The raindrops cannot be digitally erased from the frame to produce the sunny-day store window close-up insert.

I must quickly confess that this *Shoes* "mistake" is a nonproblem because the stated policy of the EYE Institute is neither to change nor to add to the motion picture print copy-in-question. Although later stage reediting is acceptable, if the need arises to replace a missing element, this is allowable only when evidence supports the likelihood that the element *had been there* in earlier versions. Considering this policy, the archivist's decision not to change the original edit of *Shoes* or to digitally alter these frames is understandable. However, if we were to begin to put Cherchi Usai's promotion of "historicity" (Cherchi Usai et al. 2008, 207) to the test, think how many other places we would need to look for evidence of threat. Because the "loss of historicity" is everywhere—even digital cleaning, for example, may eliminate scratches in the emulsion that indicate how the 35mm original was projected, effecting the "erasure" of exhibition history as indicated indexically. And a digital correction that could "fix" the narrative mistake still risks the loss of other "historicities" to which we will now turn. The one flawed continuity sequence is not only an "indexical indication" on and of the artifact (ibid.). As a document of the film's making, the editing mistake indicates on-location production as well as postproduction events; or, the continuity error in the print of *Shoes* is an index of the production conditions for this low-budget film. The error indicates that Lois Weber might have cut corners on her shoot of only twenty days between April 1 and April 20, 1916.[39]

REAL-BEFORE-THE-CAMERA TO REAL MATERIALITY

In causality's terms, the raindrop that hit the store window registered as light that touched the sensitive emulsion on the film loaded into the magazine of the 35mm motion picture camera on a rainy day on Lois Weber's street location shoot in 1916. Considering the raindrop as it hit the window, we are chronologically *before* the question of the "historicity of the artifact." That is to say that even before the original "work" there was something else, a preceding something, one with which documentary film theory has been especially concerned. This theory has strived to wrap itself around the problem of how to feature the profilmic event, prefatory to shooting, but without offering indexical guarantees or deferring to the existence of anything said to be "real."[40] But in the archivist's discourse, the question of the reality of the event-before-the-camera, in front of and prefatory to it, becomes irrelevant. *That* so-called "reality" gives way to another reality—the material reality of the photochemical storage medium. Or, better, the indexicality of the profilmic event becomes subsumed into the materiality of the medium.

The archival film then could, if it wanted to, claim a double indexicality—one that looks outward and another that faces inward—a surviving photorealist object thought to carry (as the raindrops) an indexical connection to the event-before-the-camera *and* indexically marked by decomposition—the archivist's indexicality *internal* to the image makeup. But in the restoration mode, the photo-indexical sign of something that was "once there" merges with the real materiality of the photochemical medium, that very odd object strip, and, you will recall, likely only one of many supports for "the work." Remarkable then is how the archivist's objection to the digital is made *not* on behalf of the real-before-the-camera, now become medium, but on behalf of the integrity of that mediated stuff itself—the motion photographic analogical material.

Something else is relevant to this pair of indexicalities that we might not necessarily notice: Lois Weber's location shoot. The image of Emma (played by actress Mary MacLaren), looking into the store window—the staged event once before-the-camera—calls us back to Lois Weber's 1915 street location and from there to the auteur director's shot choice, her composition-in-the-frame, and to her screen direction to McLaren. Yes, of course, the director may also be thought to have been "there," and her "intentions" may be later brought back as a guide to restoration, a reference relevant to the specificity of the medium, as Fossati tells us (2009, 126). But restoration, however much it would defer to auteur's intent, especially given Fossati's "film as art" paradigm (ibid., 231), can potentially undermine the premise of authorial singularity. For restoration now opens up space for an additional creative agent, one besides Lois Weber. Today, especially given digital capabilities, the space of agency now shifts from the original 1915 scene of production to the contemporary archival laboratory. The capacity to digitally erase and then to duplicate frames in order to make the insert shot of the window without the raindrops, a shot that was likely *never* taken in 1915, places the restorer in a new position—a creative one—analogous to that of postproduction editor or on-location director. In cases that call for archival decision making, Fossati thinks, restoration becomes more like filmmaking itself. The restorer is now like the filmmaker-as-artist, especially given the computer capability to circumvent the photo-indexical stage, to make a "realistic image from scratch" or to completely recreate the "image that was there and is now gone" (ibid., 141). In our hypothetical case of *Shoes*, such digital re-creation could produce an image that although it most likely never existed, probably *should have*.

WHERE WAS LOIS WEBER?: THE MIXED ONTOLOGY OF FILM AUTHORSHIP

Do these new powers foretell the digital restorer as an auteur?[41] The objections to auteur theory on the basis of the incompatibility between human and machine now seem distant. Elaborating on this, Serge Daney considered that the way in which the *politique* was most "scandalous" was as it attempted to "instill subjectivity within a system of production and communication that seems intrinsically incapable of accepting it."[42] Few have raised objections to auteurism on this basis—that the human is at odds with the mechanical. Who has noticed that the human-machine mixture is yet another kind of ontological incompatability? Others, although they noticed the incompatability, still contributed to the cult of the auteur. André Bazin, for one, marveled at the "automatic" function of the process: "For the first time, an image of the outside world takes shape automatically, without creative human intervention, following a strict determinism" (2009, 7). Bazin even went so far as to claim that the absence of the human in the photograph explained its success: "All art is founded on human agency, but in photography alone can we celebrate its absence" (ibid.).[43] How strange to find a celebration of the absence of the human from the critic who so championed auteur directors Orson Welles, William Wyler, and Roberto Rossellini as human agency personified. Looking back, we might marvel at the way in which, over the cinema century, an "authorial imaginary" took hold and overrode objections that cinema was mechanical, all in an effort to elevate "film as art."[44] This other ontological incompatibility, that between the human and the machine, has been easily wished away by means of a periodically renewed commitment to human creativity.[45]

The jury may still be out on the question of the authorial "hand" within the digital imaging process, although there is nothing to prevent the invention of new forms of authorial agency as well as ownership claims.[46] Certainly archival restoration has reopened the door to intentionality as a measure and perhaps a check on archival decision making in which the once existing auteur-maker becomes a guide in the process. But that process can also be thought of in such a way that the authorial position comes unraveled. So if we follow William J. Mitchell's argument that digital imaging has changed the effective "rules" of image making, we can entertain his idea that, as he says, the difference between "camera processes and the intentional process of the artist can no longer be drawn so confidently" (1992, 31). Today, when we are finally in a position to program the machine's own creative contribution, *its* stylistic expressivity, we ask whether the computer age has reinflected "machine-made" such that it will never again be a term of denigration. Now, in rethinking these processes, we have occasion to revisit the apportionment of artistry, leading us to wonder if, over the cinema century, the difference was stacked in favor of the human artist over the machine. After all, the artist has been credited with processes that belong to the camera or to laboratory equipment and even to computer code.

One might say, listening to some archivists, that the "digital turn" is the occasion for a belated recognition of motion photography as an "art of reproduction" despite the legacy of usage that dismissed "reproductive art" as a contradictory concept.[47] For Alex Horwath this brings Walter Benjamin into archivists' debates and reminds us of what the " film as art" paradigm has disallowed. For one, "film as art" cannot recognize the group input of creative personnel that characterizes "industrial cinema."[48] In considering such circumstances of production, Horwath says that the "touch of the artist" is problematic, and, he goes on: "If we think of film as a form that often has many authors, and whose actual author is the producer of the company which has released the work into the world, whose stamp are we talking about?" Inevitably, however, the culture will again override the tendency of the machine as Horwath reminds us happened after Benjamin. There have always been ways, he thinks, of "introducing uniqueness, originality, authenticity into reproductive media" (Cherchi Usai et al. 2008, 111). If there have been ways of inserting "uniqueness, originality, authenticity," then of course there would be ways of adding "historicity" or "authorship" to the digitally produced form.

To repeat this statement as a question: If "the human" as auteur director could be so successfully inserted into the mechanical process, why can't "historicity" be inserted anywhere into the digital processing of the image? Of course the digital requires neither body *before* the camera nor body *behind* it. It admits no author-person, admits nobody, really. Indeed the digital is understood as "bodyless." And what kind of mixed ontology is the part analog, part digital, compared with that other mixture—of the mechanical motion photographic with the authorial hand and the human psyche? Over the cinema century, the measurable contribution of the mechanical and the chemical, as well as the materiality of bodies, objects, and landscapes before-the-camera were systematically downplayed in favor of the immeasurable contribution of the auteur-maker, even as authorial intent has been discredited in some humanities circles.[49]

But we are looking for Lois Weber. We started by asking what, if anything, the extant print of *Shoes* could tell us about its "making" as well as its makeup.[50] It may be that *Shoes* writer-director-producer Weber intended to save production costs by not insisting that her crew reshoot the store window close-up on a sunny day. But what of the editor who cut the film? We want to know why one "hand" would be credited but no others.[51] So here is the relevant question for us: Is Lois Weber on the side of the photochemical or on the side of the digital? An auteur theory–inclined answer might be that she is part of the pro-filmic event, and consequently that her "hand" intervened in the filming, directing the action in the scene, and that her conception was realized in the editing. This approach might then treat the erroneous close-ups version as something like the "director's cut" of *Shoes*. Here, Weber is on the side of the photochemical. Even to digitally erase the raindrops from one close-up to produce a second close-up without raindrops, because that is what she *must have* intended, is to defer to the auteur. The problem is that either a photochemical purism or a digital erasure "correction" actually returns Weber to where she *may never have been*. It may not, after all, have been her decision to save production costs by cutting the rain-spattered window insert into the sunny-day sequence. She may have taken the advice of one of her three cinematographers: King D. Fray, Stephen S. Norton, or Allen Siegler (*Shoes* press kit, 2017, 18–21). Thus, Weber, on the side of the photochemical, is not in such a secure authorial place after all. And surely, on the other side, digital erasure will in the future be credited *not* to a director such as Weber but to the digital Desmet system itself, as some new media theorists might predict.[52] Consider this: if Lois Weber is aligned with the photochemical, is her causality on a par with that of the raindrop itself, the raindrop that "caused" its photographic image? Or perhaps Weber-as-auteur has been later "inserted," rather like "authenticity" was historically added to the photograph in an attempt to elevate it.

Finally, there is the parallel between film restoration as combining image fragments and narrative piecing as restoration of the biographical lives of directors. After all, scholars continue to reassemble Lois Weber's filmmaking career in the foreign representational realm of the written sign—that representationally sketchy sign that has even less of a chance of ever corresponding point-to-point with the events of her illustrious career than the film medium has of registering a raindrop. Yet the myth of realist representation keeps such historiographic efforts alive. We have not really solved the problem even if we try to align the writer-director-producer with the extant print of the film she "authorized" (to the degree that she did) and use her intentions as a guide (Fossati 2009, 126). Effectively, "historicity" as indication on the archival print, inscribed on its photochemical source material, encourages us to borrow the print's apparent indexicality, transferring that perceived "real life" advantage to historical persons involved in the making of "the work." In the end, however, this indicator may be less a guarantee than a pointer—the index as the adverbial "this" or "that," as in "This is Lois's photograph."[53]

Above all, we must insist that Lois Weber belongs to an order of being significantly *unlike* that of either her photograph or that of the motion picture archival print, both of which survive into the present. If we were to draw a distinction between the no-longer-being Lois Weber and "her" film *Shoes*, on the side of Lois Weber we have nothing and on the other side, that of the extant archival object, we have something. In Heidegger's terms, we have the "no longer objectively present" Weber and the object that although

Lois Weber, actress/writer/director/producer. Private collection.

CHAPTER 4

it might have "belonged" to "former events" is now "objectively present" as well as past (1996, 347). Lois Weber as an entity is so radically "no longer" that to speak of her as though we know what she meant by her actions is quite presumptuous on our part. Nevertheless, the historian pieces together existing artifacts in an attempt to reconstitute life events "as they were" as well as to try to devise a persona that matches the one that the historical figure may have "imagined herself" as inhabiting.[54]

The goal of the traditional historian is to make that which is irretrievable and unknowable known to the present, so let us not take such unknowability lightly. And in this regard, Paul Ricoeur offers perhaps the only position that those who "come after" can safely claim relative to historical loss, and this when he says that nonexistence in the present does not necessarily mean nonexistence in the past; even if we cannot say *what* they once were, our saying cannot negate *that* they were. It is finally for the philosophy of history a problem of existence; thus, the only viable counter to historical "loss" would be to paraphrase Paul Ricoeur from the last chapter (2004, 280) to the effect that all that we can confidently say is that no one can now "make it be" that there never was a Lois Weber.

So now to bring together the "no longer there" and the "never there." We still want to know why the digital "never-having-been-there" gets little or no respect and the photographic analogical "having-been-there" gets so much more. Clearly the no-longer existence of the once-existing past matters in a theory of history that informs historiographic practice. But there also must be a way to acknowledge digital referential nonexistence instead of discrediting it. After the "digital turn" and relative to Heidegger's *Da-sien* as a "there-being" that although no longer existing is not exactly past but is "*having been there*," we end up in yet-to-be-charted philosophical waters (1996, 348–349). At least, the "never-having-been" existence of a world relative to the digital image that creates it should not be held against the image that so successfully simulates photorealism.

RESTORATION TO WHAT IT HAD NEVER BEEN

In the future we *will see* perfect impressions of the photochemical now without the necessity of the original object and its imprint on light-sensitive film stock. Or, digital erasure will make it appear that something "had-never-been" at all. Taken to extremes, the hypothetical digital erasure of the raindrops in the close-up frame from *Shoes* could be seen as a "reaching back in time" in order to make it appear that something had happened in 1916 that never did happen—that Lois Weber's crew had shot two different store window close-ups on different days. The erasure that would "correct" the print of *Shoes* would then restore it to what? The film may be restored to what it had never been or, to what it wasn't. Here is the definitive statement about the enterprise of all historical representation as restoration, a statement that stands as a refutation of fidelity and correspondence-as-truth. Like the archival object restored to what it "had never been," the narrated events of the historical past are an account of *what never did happen*, at least *not in that way*. Even a restoration to a condition as close as possible to "what it had been" is still restoration to "what it never was."

To review: Today, we insist on the singular "work" when there is no one form of it, refer to motion picture "film footage" when there was no film stock used in the making, claim that something is an "original" when it is an *original copy*, and speak of the "film" when what now exists is a hybrid product of photochemical *as well as* computational processes.[55] So we may wonder if we should not also take the digital form of "the work" to be an object when there may be no object, as is the case if we start from the non-object prework existence of data on a computer hard drive. Perhaps it is something like loyalty to what we call the analog that, standing in for lost connection, keeps the old ideology of realism, companion to the *ideology of historical loss*, alive. While the critique of realism may have taught an entire generation to suspect truth claims and to relinquish the vain hope of ever coming face to face with "the real," in archival discourse, "the real" returns, but by another door—now as measurable "historicity" on the face of the film print. Not "true to life," but a second kind of "true to," this historicity-as-reality is deferential to an "objectively present" materiality. Let's call it what it is. The archivist's historicity-as-indexicality, especially as it espouses fidelity to an original, comes close to the function of "the real" that Heidegger critiqued in historicism. For it was not only that the "thesis of *realism*," as he called it, was committed to the need for "proof" of the world's reality. It was that this realism was "capable of proof" (1996, 192).

5
THE MELODRAMA THEORY OF HISTORICAL TIME

As we have seen, the "where-in-time" question of historical location, the past relative to the present as the future waits, concerns the philosophy of history. But this "where" would not be a philosophical issue were it not, as we have seen, part of a problem of existence that is almost beyond comprehension. And yet we must admit that the difficulties posed by the *historical time* dynamic are close to home and that temporal imbalances are all too familiar. The structure theorized by historians has its "lived" aspect, experienced as anxieties, taken up here as the *everyday uncertainties of historical time*. Think of the anxieties expressed as "What will become of me?" Then consider our adaptations to temporal uncertainties—procrastination, nostalgia, or worry. Sometimes these uncertainties are caused by the disjuncture of the shifting modes of time and at others exacerbated by the inexorability of events-in-time following the historian's causality map: "First this happened, and then that, therefore something" (Ermarth 2007, 51).[1] Against an idea of time as a measurement, French historian Marc Bloch once posed *historical time* as a "concrete and living reality with an irreversible onward rush" (1953, 27). Let us then call Bloch's one-way "onward rush" the *irreversible* problem associated with the linear model of time. Then, we can conjoin the *irreversible* with the *asymmetrical* problem, shorthand for Louis Althusser's "peculiarities" of historical time, the absent and present never together.[2] While, in the philosophy of history, these two metaphors may be in competition, in the case of human beings, any metaphor will do. Time, it is said, "flies," "slips away," "runs out," and we are apt to be "stuck" in it. Or, we just throw up our hands, agreeing with Hamlet that time is "out of joint."

As for melodrama, here is where we see *location-in-time* structures shaping the most lowly of dramatic forms standing behind the very ideological scheme of things represented. Thus, while many would dismiss popular melodrama as formulaic I choose to think of it as *schematic*. *Shoes* (Lois Weber, Universal, U.S., 1916), as a melodrama of virtue despoiled, relies on a *moral scheme*. The pattern is familiar—a woman's sexual past can ruin her wished-for future, a morality belonging to the silent era that remembered the Victorian theater. Yet codes of Victorian conduct reprised through the silent era were newly opposed by social forces that loosened the protections around young women. Contrarily, new working women like Eva were protected yet exposed; toughened yet defenseless. Old codes were under revision.

Why *schematic*? Adding the terms *scheme* or *schematic* to *moral* insures that we pay attention to the structure of the work. We might, for example, consider how the recurring "loss of innocence" schematized as narrative structure complements the ideological scheme of things that organize events-in-time.[3] Over time, while the woman is "ruined," the man becomes "worldly" and "experienced." Or, as one Australian melodrama was advertised: "The WOMAN SUFFERS—while the man goes free!"[4] Thinking *scheme* as structure thus keeps questions of formal scaffolding always before us when we ask how melodramas such as *The Woman Suffers* (Australia, 1918) deliver life's teachings as "genre lessons." Melodrama is both generic and more than genre, however. Following Christine Gledhill, I take melodrama to be larger than one genre, and in her terms, an overarching culture-based "mode" that "generates" genres (2000, 227; 2014, 18). These would be genres like that of the domestic melodrama exemplified by *Shoes* and the other silent-era titles from which I draw to propose *the melodrama theory of historical time*.

Recall from the last chapter the narrative of *Shoes*, which concerns the shopgirl Eva torn between the need she has for the money to buy a new pair of shoes and the value of the sexual purity she trades for needed cash. Such a dramatic dilemma has temporal implications that align with the way we have been discussing *historical time*. Although I began with the "lived" aspect of this temporality, we are more likely to find what we're looking for in the dramatized. Of course the "lived" is regularly opposed to the dramatized and the latter dismissed as improbable and far-fetched. But such dismissal fails to see the mysterious ways in which "lived" and "dramatized" are reciprocal. Assuming reciprocity, my approach is to take melodramatic devices as a means of studying everyday adaptations to the problem of *historical time*. Let us then refer to melodrama's *dramatized dilemmas of historical time*. Here is the enactment of predicaments that follow from situations encapsulated in our two metaphors: the *asymmetrical* imbalance of the three modes and the *irreversibile* momentum of events-in-time.

Think of this as an exercise in triangulation: melodrama's fictional devices, the theory of *historical time* relevant to historiography, and our "lived" experience of the three modes of time. In the following, I move between these three angles, but the primary goal of this chapter is to revitalize *historical time*.[5] Melodrama, the mode, is thus recruited here to repurpose *historical time*, a concept thought outdated by some but of certain value for studying the culture of a century ago.[6] Throughout, I have urged the development of "theories of history," but, rather than turning exclusively to philosophy in this chapter, I propose to look closer to home to film melodrama theory as it has evolved from the 1970s as especially applicable to silent-era moving pictures.

Let us first take a moment to think about the "lived" aspect of *historical time* to see what humans make of it. After all, it is we who "endow" events with temporal structures, says Keith Tribe (2004, xi). Witness how we give structure to time in clichés like "here today, gone tomorrow" that express the one-way direction of time. Then consider how we invest narrative structures with the capacity to order what the philosophy of history refers to as the "asymmetry" of the modes of time (Danto 2007, 170). In narrative structure, borrowed from daily life, the present and the past are never together and the future is out of reach. The past returns to "haunt" the present and consequently to threaten the future; the present in turn "forgets" the past. The professional historian may be as perplexed as the rest of us, for *historical time* is nothing measurable like the minutes of clock time. But while the historian deals with the dilemmas of temporal imbalance and irreversibility by writing *around* them, melodrama *uses* them to its own hyperbolic ends.

In *Shoes*, melodrama's genre lesson borrows the *uncertainties of historical time* to posit the consequences of a wrong choice and to frame Eva's worry: "What will happen *tomorrow* if I do this *today*?" Such a dilemma is so often posed in time's terms that we scarcely notice the creaking of the well-worn dramatic setup. The tale *is* a time telling, all the better to illustrate Eva's difficult decision and to represent her mistake as having *irreversible* consequences—the forfeiture of her innocence. Undoubtedly, Peter Brooks's "recognition" of the "sign of virtue and innocence" (1985, 28), a key aspect of one of silent film melodrama's favorite *moral schemes*, is in narrative play here. In Brooks, there is a narrative "struggle" to bring about "recognition" of the virtue that may be hidden, imperceptible to the community. Virtue needs to be visibly proven. Virtue needs to be seen, and, paradoxically, villainy provides the opportunity for the public recognition of virtue. Think here of *Shoes* where Eva's seducer has this odd function—to prove that she is an innocent victim. What am I adding to basic melodrama theory here? Reinforcement by means of a deeper structure. The goal of "making the world morally legible" (43), in which endangered innocence must be "seen for what it is," gets a boost from the *dramatized dilemmas of historical time*. Here, I see something even more harrowing than the "inexorable deadlines that force a race against the clock" (31). Of course the melodrama of the fallen woman depends on the principle of *irreversibility* (there is no undoing) but the drama makes everything harder by insisting on the absolutely impossible—the return to what "once was." Here, to recall, is the strategic power of the "space of innocence" in melodrama theory (29). As Linda Williams, following Brooks, proposes, "*melodrama begins and wants to end all in a 'space of innocence'*" (2001, 28). Melodrama wants the impossible. Against "there is no going back," it insists on recognition as reversal, all the better to ostentatiously award victory to the victimized in the most spectacular but improbable manner.

Think here of Anna Moore's rescue on the ice floe in *Way Down East* (D. W. Griffith, 1920), to which I will shortly turn. If an attempt to return to the beginning meets with such huge resistance, with difficulties and crises along the way, think what stubborn absolutes innocence is up against. Melodrama, of course, needs absolutes and what is more absolute than the givens of *historical time*? Further, thinking of *historical time* alerts us to how things get even worse for the innocent. For the fallen woman, "there is no going back," but, what is worse, for her there is no future.[7] The import of Eva's vacillation thus cannot be found in the present moment of choice alone because a wrong decision will have consequences for her future, that is, "for life." We can now amend from the last chapter the "loss" of virginity analogized with historical "loss." For here, from the vantage of theories of *historical time*, there is in addition to "loss," a horrible "gain," especially if one considers the persistence of "the past" in the present, to recall from Chapter 2. Conventionally, it is the woman more than the man for whom the past persists. She, not he, is ostracized for having "a past," that is, a *sexual past*. Fear of acquiring a *sexual past* weighs heavier on the young female character who, paradoxically in her "loss" of innocence, gains this ineradicable "past." In society's terms, what the sexually experienced woman acquires is a bad reputation, that dark "past" that cannot be outlived or "lived down." Once "ruined" she will forever be "having been" ruined.[8] She cannot return as an innocent to the "space of innocence" (Brooks 1985, 29).

Once the young woman has "lost" her innocence and gained "a past," her past and her future are forever at odds. The philosophical past and future that we have been considering translates into a scenario played out as one of the most worrisome *uncertainties of historical time*, as ruled by an older moral code and as heard in the outburst: "Will my future be ruined?" Consider then the end title card of *Shoes* that begins: "Life goes on, even though cruel." which calls up historical time's structure of *irreversibility* in melodrama's sternest terms—"no more" or "never again." In the end title, we see how *Shoes* makes didactic use of the irreconcilability of past and future, mapped as the impossibility of a return to the beginning no matter how much the character might wish that she could.

Here the epilogue deploys the reformer's "it did not happen in vain" voice. The voice of melodrama can rescue Eva's unfortunate mistake by making a genre lesson out of her wrong choice. How does the film propose to effect this moral rescue? She will be a warning to other young girls: "Then her sad story will not have been for nothing." For Eva, there is no redemptive reversal, no return to things as they were. In lieu of a return, Eva's sad story is retold as what *should not have been*. Although, unlike Anna Moore, Eva is not retrieved at the edge of the precipice, her situation can still be sympathetically rescued. Her story will be a watchword for young female viewers. In the silent era, there is a future and it is in the social reform that will save vulnerable women (Balides 2002; Stamp 2015, 101–118).

EVERYDAY UNCERTAINTIES AND HISTORICAL TIME

So let us return to the root paradox that every historian encounters when he or she engages in research and writing or other representational arts. To state that paradox again but differently than it was stated in Chapter 2: the past isn't there at the same time that it is. Here I propose that we enter the philosophical paradoxes of historical time by way of the means we use to negotiate its unevenness in our daily encounters. This temporal *asymmetry* produces troubles stemming from the difference between "that which is" today and that which "had been" yesterday, between the undoubtedly "now is" and the uncertain "will be"—differentials that humans try to navigate in words and acts. The constant replacement of one time with another produces what I have been calling *everyday uncertainties of historical time*, consequences of the shifting between modes of historical time. We are daily made aware that yesterday cannot continue into today, that a single second marks the difference between what "is" and "was," and that the future, always "to be," is held out as "the possible" that may or may not "be" when we arrive there. Consequently, we face situational predicaments *in* and *of* time. Life choices as to whether to give or to take, to speak or to remain silent, to leave or to stay, are culturally calculated within historical time's proscribed frames. Clearly, then, it is not so simple as this time or that one. Recall from Chapter 2 how the philosophers of history, from Heidegger to contemporary theorists of history, have considered this phenomenon, treated by Reinhart Koselleck not only as the challenge of "historical time," but of "times" (2004, 1–2). In this plurality of "times," we can also wonder if *historical time* does not stand for an irregular inequality of times: the present definitively "there" but always passing into another time, the future never to be arrived at, and the past left behind but neither to be either escaped from nor returned to.

Basic to *historical time* in contemporary theories of history are Heidegger's three temporal "ecstasies"—the past, present, and future (1996, 308–321), or, as we have also been calling them, "modes of time." Further recall from Chapter 2 the way that the past, present, and future are in circular "hermeneutical" relation such that we invariably understand each one in terms of the others (Carr 1987, 198). Add to this Koselleck's formulation of the present as the very time that was "once anticipated," a feature of the new temporality of the modern moment (2004, 2). Especially relevant, the previously anticipated present is for him a "former future," or, more exactly, any given present was once a future.[9] Koselleck's "former future," the present, is a facing ahead in expectation of another future, what I call the future "to be" to distinguish it from the "former future." We always forget, of course, that the "present" present was a once-wished-for future, a "former future" that the present can no longer be. Here is the inevitable relationship that Gilles Deleuze seized upon in his paradox of the *coexistence* of past and present: it is the new present that makes the "past" what it is and that past remains contemporaneous with the "present" that it once was.[10]

Why has philosophy been so interested in *historical time*? Philosophy finds in the everyday phenomenon of "one time replacing another time" an ideal degree of impossibility, or, rather, infinite impossibilities, exemplifying one generic aspect of philosophical writing, which John Frow sees as just as rule-bound as any other genre of writing. If clearly rule-bound, we ask, why is it so difficult to learn the rules of philosophical discourse? According to Frow, philosophical writing is difficult because by convention it finds no solution to the question that it poses, even reframing that question in such a way that it stays ever open (2006, 87–92). Contrast philosophy's interminability with the traditional discipline of history, dedicated to conclusive scientific proof and resolution. While philosophical discourse on the problem of *historical time* keeps itself going by asking how the past "persists" when what was "now" is no longer "now," historiographic practice is stopped in its tracks by such questions (White 1999, 2–3). Where traditional history asks "What happened then?" the philosophy of history asks "How can one write knowingly about that which no longer exists?" In contemporary philosophy of history circles, no one would assert knowingly that an event took place in exactly the way that we say that it did. Conversely, such absolute certainty is expected of historians.

In contrast, melodrama translates what philosophy takes up as the problem of existence into dramatic confrontations, famously its oppositional absolutes, as we will see. This is not to say that there have been no attempts to consider melodrama's worldview in more philosophical terms. Peter Brooks has compared literary melodrama with deconstruction in the way that it, too, tackles the problem of things not lining up with their meanings (1985, 66–67; Gledhill 1987, 33). Thus melodrama, in its own way, dramatizes the way in which words "cannot say" what must be said. What critics most often observe, however, is the way moving picture melodrama cleverly manages for viewers and readers the irresolvable difficulties that stem from the structural defects in social life—the difference between that which is "said to be" and "what is."[11] This is the difference so often lived out as the consequence of social inequities. It is argued that the raw material of melodrama, the material that it works into drama, is drawn from the set of socially fraught situations historically specific to a given culture.[12] In *Shoes*, the new working girl exchanges the value of her sexual innocence for the price of an immediate necessity—the shoes she requires to walk to work. As a worker, she now functions outside the family and, since she is now the breadwinner, she forfeits traditional family protections. Only after she has made her bad bargain does her lazy father get a job—too late to save her.

The dramatization of the rawest social material may borrow temporal disjuncture or *asymmetry* for emphasis. The characters just miss opportunities, arrive too soon or return too late, appear at the wrong time or surprisingly just the right time. Narrative complications here draw their power and definition from everyday "lived" time in which one moment impinges on the next. Where daily life sees anxiety-producing doubt (Will I ever be the same again?) and philosophy sees the "paradox of co-existence" (Deleuze 1994, 81) (the past that "once was" as an old present haunting the new present), melodrama, as I am arguing, sees crises and their consequences-in-time. This is quite the opposite of certainty, then, and especially as melodrama has favored the powerless, the mode can be said to have a worldview that assumes that we are at the mercy of villainy beyond our control, and thus the one-way temporal "march" may both "be" and represent heartless forces.

NO EVENT CAN BE REPEATED

With its narrative rendering of human longing for what *once was* and will *never be again* and worries about what *will be* (what lies ahead) melodrama specializes in the reenactment of the kinds of difficulties that stem from living in societies at odds with themselves.[13] Life's scenarios are charted along familiar temporal lines: One's hands are "tied by time" when an unbearable injustice cannot be rectified because "there is no going back" to change conditions in the "former" present. Technically, the boundaries between the three modes of time cannot be breached, and although melodrama by and large reinforces these time obstacles, as we will see, it also devises ways around them. Characters register their frustration with these constraints—ranting against the course of events, resigning themselves to "what's over," or struggling to keep "alive," as it is said, a hope for the future that they had before in a "former" present. An injustice, shown as the effect of an unbending law, might be represented in historical time's terms, narrativized as "no return" or responded to as hopelessness given a future always out of reach, a future passed on from one "former" present to another and seemingly "never to be."

So, too, the historian grapples with the stubbornness of *historical time* exemplified by the event that, once over, cannot come again later as the same event that it was, no matter how much this may be wished. Even Annales School founder Ferdinand Braudel chafes against unidirectionality, referring to "historical time, so imperious because it is irreversible" (1980, 48). Certainly the consequences of unrepeatability are *felt* as irreversibility, but also the temporal rule of "one day at a time" means that there is no leaping around "in time," as we say; there is neither skipping forward nor retracing our steps backward. "It is not only because events, once transpired, cannot be repeated that past and future cannot be reconciled," Koselleck reflects (2004, 38). If not only this, why else? For one thing, consider the unbridgeable separateness of past and future realms, neither directly accessible from the other. Where theories of history may posit past and future as irreconcilable (the past and future as never together), moving image melodrama leads viewers through imagined events to their uncertain outcomes, from one moment, one "now" to the next "now," never properly resolving familial issues because never able to revisit events and actions nor to access what may be ahead. The caring mother who has killed her child to save it cannot return to "the time before" in Minna Canth's play adapted as *Anna-Liisa* (Finland, 1922). Or, if the much maligned false epilogue is resorted to, the wrong or illogical narrative outcome may fail to resolve irreconcilable class or race difference or states of being (alive as opposed to dead).

Think here of Laura Mulvey's observation that film melodrama narrative leaves a dusty "cloud of over-determined irreconcilables" in its wake at its conclusion (1987, 76). The drama may try to oppose "money" with "love," for instance, but in theory the end will leave some element dangling. Think here of the magnitudinal conflicts between victim and the victimizer, colonized and the colonizer, powerless and the powerful that cannot be resolved in one drama. Following Thomas Elsaesser's more recent formulation, melodrama speaks to the conditions of social injustice that have persisted long after the Enlightenment raised the expectation of equality, liberty, and fraternity (2014, 32). Thus, it could be argued that for over three hundred years melodrama has worked to rectify and reverse, to ameliorate and absolve, as part of the therapeutic work it does for the lesser among us. The mode offers scenarios of loss and retrieval, fall and restitution, failure and triumph, that is, melodramatizations of the exercise of power and its demise, often consequence *of* as well as exaggerated *by* the brutal *irreversibility* of events-in-time. A fortune squandered cannot be reclaimed, one is never young after one is old, and, as in *Shoes*, a woman's forfeited virtue cannot be returned to her. Or, in all of the variants of Mrs. Henry Wood's *East Lynne*, once the heroine has renounced motherhood she can never again be a mother to her own children, although she will try to find a way.[14] But narrative unrepeatability can be scaled down, seen merely as the difference between moments, as, for instance, in so many "recognition" scenes when identities are restored in an instant.[15] The swift "turn" of events has no time for the philosophical. However, in our case, the philosophical implications of *historical time* can be drawn out, which is to say that melodrama can be found to engage with the fallout from Koselleck's irreconcilability of past and future (2004, 38).

THE "NOWS" THAT CAN NEVER MEET

Now, splitting up our two metaphors, *irreversibility* and *asymmetry*, we see that philosophy has more interest in the latter. We detect this in Heidegger's dismissal of what he calls "vulgar" time as nothing more than a "succession of nows," a sequence as in the "course of time." He thinks therefore that the too easy *now-time* of the clock functions to cover over other structures (1996, 386–388). If *now-time* cannot fathom the phenomenon of constantly disappearing "nows," neither can it fully indicate the profound adjustment humans make in an effort to accommodate what we have been treating perhaps too summarily as the *asymmetry* of historical time. To get a better sense of the antithesis of the too easy "succession of nows" let's turn to Edmund Husserl's explication of Heidegger's three "ecstasies." Here is one of the original philosophical configurations of the *asymmetry* problem: "The now as actually present now is the givenness of the present of the temporal position. When the phenomenon recedes into the past, the now receives the characteristic of being a past now; but it remains the same now, except that it stands before me as past in relation to the currently actual and temporally new now" (1991, 68). To rephrase this without ironing it out too much: Once past, the "now" remains the same "now," but that "now" has also a past status relative to the "new now" that has succeeded it. The goal of the historian may be to retrieve or to know the "now" as it was when it *was* a "now" but for him or her that "now" cannot be other than a "past now" because inevitably that "now" is only that relative to another succeeding "now," or the "temporally new now." In Husserl, this "past now" may "remain the same now," but only philosophically because, it could be argued, while it may be the "same now," it is what it is *only* relative to this other "now," the new one. I would add that since the first "now" is only a "past now" because of the succeeding "now," these two "nows," the past and the new one, are forever separated. They are the "nows" that *can never ever meet.*

Recall here melodrama's investment in oppositional absolutes, polarized forces-at-odds, such as "life" pitted against "death."[16] Next, we want to know what melodrama does with the temporal conundra that Husserl renders in philosophy's terms. Of course it is not that melodrama devises anything so new, because it already depends upon novelistic time, the time that has historically strived to approximate the birth-to-death trajectory of human life.[17] Moving picture melodrama, perfecting the novelistic, invents its own devices for representing temporal change-over-time *and* forces-at-odds. Let's look at how this melodrama deals with the problem of the "past now," in its dramatic terms, the "once was," that former "now" to which characters cannot return in the present "now." We have already seen in *Shoes* (1916) how Eva's "past now" mistake cannot be undone and she can't return to the "now" of her former innocence, unless, of course, another ending pronounces that the "past now" *did not happen. Shoes* has the option of altering story order, and in a "new now" present, canceling the "past now" of Eva's downfall by revealing that it was the "now that never happened"—"only a dream." As easily, a mistaken account of a "past now" event may mean that the "past now" *stays the same.* In the latter case, to which we now turn, two "nows" are temporarily placed at apparent odds. Husserl's question of the "actual and temporally new now" is especially relevant since the "now" that has become "past now" is tested with the problem of the presumed dead who did not die (the "now" remaining the same). Thus we see the "past now" put in conflict with the present one in which the character is reported dead. In the return from the supposed dead, the "past now" must be reconciled with the present "now" that it could not have known and can never really meet.

A compact example of "nows that never meet" is Lois Weber's *The Rosary* (Universal, U.S., 1913), an early domestic melodrama short featuring the problem of the romantic couple separated by war, the consequences of which render their reunion after the war impossible. The American Civil War calls the soldier suitor to battle and after he is severely injured and taken to the hospital tent, he is declared dead. He is not, however, dead. He is not really dead. But he is dead to his fiancée for whom the news of his survival comes *after* the news of his death and therefore comes "too late." As a consequence of the news that he is dead, she enters a convent, which is where he sees her from afar in the end, an end that confirms in historical time's terms that the "past now" is *the same* even relative to the "new now." The soldier was only wounded in the past but is alive in the present.

Frame enlargement, *The Rosary* (Rex Motion Picture Co., US, 1913), Lois Weber, writer/director. Courtesy Library of Congress. Washington, D.C.

Consider in more detail the narrative of *The Rosary* reconfigured to explore Husserl's problematic, from the "now" of the first courtship scene to the "now" of the soldier's hospitalization, the "now" of her receipt of the news of his death, the "now" of his miraculous recovery, and finally the "new now" in which he returns to find her lost to him because of her vow. To test Husserl's thesis, first consider the point at which the "new now" has succeeded the earlier ones, the moment in which all of the "nows" are made "past nows" by their successors ("new nows"). This is the narrative point at which the soldier returns. It would seem at first, confirming Husserl, that at the soldier's return those "before now" events *do remain the same.* The soldier left for battle, he was injured, and he was declared dead. No event is changed. Except that, in another respect, the events *don't* remain the same, at least not as they are received and interpreted by the characters. Each "now" has a new status relative to a succeeding "now," plus these "nows" have been reordered and reinterpreted, melodramatized, really, by means of narrative structuration. Such a structuring option is of course an old theatrical stage and literary device—the "return" of the lost character.

Recall Roland Barthes's analysis of sequenced time, which he thinks has "very little connection with real time." It is, of course, so much artifice given that "suspense" is a "game with structure," a withholding of events designed to produce "anxiety and pleasure" (1977b, 119). *The Rosary* narrative "holds back" the news of the "past now" recovery event from the fiancée. That missing event, the soldier's complete recovery, is held in abeyance in the game so that it may be later "put back" into the plot order of narrative events. Here, the *everyday uncertainties of time* that cry "Will he return?" are dramatically manipulated. Although without much finesse, in *The Rosary* the soldier's recovery is kept from his fiancée just as the scene of her vow is withheld from the viewer. Since, in 1912, filmmakers were only learning how to manipulate time by means of crosscutting, it's not surprising that Lois Weber's *The Rosary* doesn't use the device.[18] For viewers of that film, however, events represented as the present "now" take on a sad meaning because the characters cannot get back to the "past now," the innocent same "now" in which the soldier *was alive.* That is, he was alive in one "now" before the later "now" in which the fiancée and her mother find his death announcement in the newspaper. We lament that these two "nows" were unable to meet.

Something more is yet needed to bring this problem to bear on the practice of historiography to which end I would add two insights from the philosophy of history. First, to paraphrase Hayden White, the "reality" of the past event is not in its occurrence but in its recollection (1987, 20). But White's observation actually circumvents the *historical time* problematic in its commitment to critiquing traditional historiography. Granted, this theory yields another explanation as to the power of a "new now" recollection over a "past now" so-called "reality," which compliments Husserl's temporal relativity problem. But we want to keep the modes of time in play. So let's secondly consider how the "hermeneutic relation" of the modes (Carr 1987, 198) could as easily produce incorrect as correct interpretation. One could say in this regard that the soldier's fiancée's present misinterpretation of a past event had as its consequence a wrong choice—her religious vow. Or, if any of these "before nows" could have been repeated (reversed and corrected), the tragic event of her vow could have been averted. Events in the "now," following Husserl, stay the same. But in retrospect one might argue that the "now" in which the suitor is "taken for dead" in the hospital tent or the "now" in which his fiancée receives the news of his death are "nows" that *never should have happened.* After all, you will argue, he didn't really die in the hospital and she received news of an event that never happened. Except, to emphasize interpretation, *that terrible event as much as did.* She read the *news* of his death, which she interpreted to mean that he was dead. To her he was dead.

THE PARADOXICAL AND PECULIAR STRUCTURE AGAIN

A thousand times we have critiqued narrative form for its aid to teleology, it's tendency to illusionism, even its gendering effect, and none of this is in dispute here. While the powerful efficiency of narrative causality has been basic to the critique of narrative, we may not, however, always recall the historical trajectory that brought us to that position. Recall the reference in Chapter 2 to Althusser's attack on "*continuous and homogenous* time" and his expression of exasperation with its antithesis, the phenomenon we are trying to pin down here, that "complex and peculiar temporality" that he found so "utterly paradoxical" (1979, 103). Now let us consider Althusser's formulation in which the "presence of one level is the absence of another." The "there" of the one that depends on the "not-there" of the other produces, in effect, the "past now" relative to the "new now" or produces the paradoxical "coexistence of a 'presence' and absences" (1979, 99–106). Let us not, however, dismiss this insight as a throwback to post-structuralism, especially since we are testing a 1970s theory in the present of this writing, staging in effect the very coexistence it posits, as I argued in Chapter 2. So, following Althusser, I change course so that we are no longer only *against* narrative continuity as we were in the 1970s but rather, more importantly, *for* seeing the structure of *historical time* as puzzlingly peculiar. And what are the temporal devices that moving image melodrama uses in its attempt to harness for its purposes the stubborn separateness but also the "entanglement" (Ricoeur 1985, 63) of these modes of time? As I mentioned, melodrama deploys to its advantage special editing devices as in the crosscut sequence, involving what was called the "cut back," an edit that takes us "back" to another scene that might be behind (as in a chase) or before, as in an earlier moment.[19] Finally, as we will see, silent cinema also perfected the special time-defying device of the narrative coincidence.

Now I want to turn to the dead center of my question about what film melodrama can tell historians about the peculiarity of *historical time* as well as how formal conventions work "against time" in the fictional world as so many races and split-second maneuvers. Because one of melodrama's favorite devices, the narrative coincidence, uses, to maximum effect, the edge of difference between our modes of time. A critical work we already have on this, Linda Williams's discussion of *Way Down East* (D. W. Griffith, U.S., 1920), analyzes the time of the cinematic crosscut, the patterned alternation of shots to represent simultaneous time but disparate spaces. To review, Williams sees the ice floe last-minute crosscut rescue at the edge of the icy falls as the outcome of a battle with time. In the race against the "river of time" Anna Moore's rescuer (Richard Barthelmess) is shown by means of the cutback, intervening "against time" in an attempt to "turn back" the *irreversible*. Unwed mother Anna Moore (Lillian Gish) is thus saved from the harsh New England judgment. But, Williams thinks, Anna's rescue marks a more momentous victory—"time is defeated" (2001, 31). She goes on: "But if we have lost our "connection to the lost time of innocence," it might be because "what is lost is time itself " (32). Let's review how *historical time* gets associated with "loss."

First, I reiterate the importance of the "irreversibility of time" (ibid., 31) and, indeed, acknowledge Williams as my original inspiration. Yet we want to know more about how time is "lost" or how crosscutting can be said to "defeat time." Williams confirms that it is "melodrama's larger impulse to reverse time, to return to the time of origins and space of innocence" and thus the engrossing question of the crosscut alternation: "will we ever get back to the time before it is too late" (35)? In arguing, as Williams does, that "what is lost is time itself," what must be implied is the equation "the past = lost time." Here, as in *The Rosary*, the past "now" is *the time that cannot come again*. Not ever. Hence, that time is said to be "lost." Recall, from Chapter 4, Carolyn Steedman's "rhetoric of loss" that attaches itself to past time (1992, 164).

But the "defeat of time" is a little more tricky because viewers are, in fact, tricked. What counts in the crosscut rescue is how past and present are made to seem coincident (two incidents at once) in their convergence, an editing trick that overrides the rules of events-in-time. Note, however, that the crosscut overrides not one but two impossibilities: First, two or more distant spaces, alternated and represented as occurring at *one and the same time* (effecting "simultaneity") are made to converge. Second, separate modes of time are made to converge in the "all at once" of the rescue. Now, considering these two impossibilities, there is even a confusion between "time" and "space," the one standing in for the other. Anna Moore is barely saved from sure death on the icy river by the coincidental intervention of her rescuer in a *space*—the precipitous edge of the falls that stands in for a *time*—the edge of difference between one second and another. The trick works on the viewer who is given to see only alternating spaces but made to

Production still, *Way Down East* (D. W. Griffith, 1920). Courtesy
Museum of Modern Art. New York, New York.

"feel" a play with time. How would the viewer know that he or she had been tricked?
After all, the long establishing shot, suggested here by Griffith's still photograph of the
river location, is withheld. Strangely, we are even, by means of the cutting, Williams
thinks, made to "feel" time as "too fast" and "too slow" (33). Let's pause a moment to
notice all of the apparent inconsistencies here. In the confusion of the rush to save, the
coincidence can represent "same time" *and* "back in time." Further, it is not so clear
whether the intervention "in time" works to *stop time* or to get just *ahead of time* (as
in the "nick of time" moment).

And we are assuming that "time" here means events-in-time, following one influential explanation as to why we cry. Tears come, thinks Steve Neale, in response to seeing
events over time as *irreversible*. Here, then, is the pathos-producing realization that
events-in-time cannot be reversed (Neale 1986, 8; Gaines 2018). But also because, to
add Althusser's deeper insight to the long gone "space of innocence" problem (Brooks
1985, 29), there is the pathos of the levels "never together"—the paradoxical absence
of the one time depending on the presence of the other (1969, 99–106). Innocent time
can never come again because past and future, by definition, can never be together.

COINCIDENCE AND CHANCE TIME

What theater critic Eric Bentley called "outrageous coincidence" (1964, 201) is, as we know, much maligned as the most preposterous of melodrama's store of devices by the measure of cultural probability. The narrative coincidence marks the moment in which forces fail by a hair or succeed by a second. Forces at odds locked in a battle may come to a head at the coincidence, all the better to teach. Think here of Williams's observation about *Way Down East* that the ice floe rescue coincidence "stages" virtue or "justice over all" when moral foundations are at issue (2001, 10). With so very much at stake, justice no less, one might well ask if there is some risk here in the recourse to the broadest device. One might further wonder if this outrageous divergence from plausibility might make dubious its utility for a *melodrama theory of historical time*. But no, it is quite the opposite. To work, the *dramatized dilemmas of historical time* must be decidedly unambiguous, with no nuance tolerated. The complex device works as melodramatic rhetoric—a temporal coincidence staging "astonishment" is an argument on behalf of the innocent.[20] Spectators may be startled to witness how this device can achieve so much by swift realignment of forces: recognition, reform, and the rectification of wrongs. Although Eva in *Shoes* is judged to be a sad case by a preachy title card, Anna Moore is flamboyantly proven innocent by a sensational *historical time*–defying rescue. And what is more rhetorically effective than a genre convention reinforced by the workings of *historical time*? The coincidence achieves its amazement because it has re-jigged the Althusserian peculiarity of the "never together," the "now" (presence) that marks the "before now" (absence), the "there" that depends upon the "not there." The staged coincidence does what philosophy cannot do so succinctly. It acknowledges while it defies the separation of levels to stage the "felt" "coexistence of a 'presence' and absences" (1979, 104). For what does "coincidence" do other than double the number of "nows," both in succession and together *at one time*? In other words, the coincidence "defeats time" by overriding *historical time*, and, in the rescue of the innocent, even creates the illusion that Koselleck's most separate of modes, past and future, are "reconciled" (2004, 38). Anna Moore and her rescuer will have a "future."

There remains the question of the illogic of what scholars acknowledge as the "unmotivated" aspect of coincidence by which is meant that there is little or no narrative preparation for the coincidental event.[21] Although Ben Singer heralds the coincidence as melodrama's distinctive device (2001, 46), this device that fascinates today was in the silent era thought to be a crutch to avoid, and screenwriting manuals warned scenarists to refrain from using the coincidence. The rule was that if the coincidence had to be used it should appear early rather than late in the story (Bordwell 1982, 4). If the coincidence came too late it had the potential to disrupt since, rather like the epilogue, it could be seen to "resolve" narrative issues too belatedly and therefore too starkly. Returning to our critique of traditional historiography, it is, however, only insofar as we subscribe to the narrative logic of narrative history that a coincidence is problematically "unmotivated," that is, unjustified given events that have gone before. What is indeed threatened by coincidence is the logic of traditional historical causality wherein the earlier event is borne out in the later one.

The now discredited "What comes before explains what comes after" lends itself to what we could call a paternity theory of historical change in which the sins of the fathers are "visited upon the children," or even that the "seeds of destruction" lie within all of us. In the domestic family melodrama, we see this paternity theory of narrative born out in the dissolute son who follows in his father's narrative steps to ruin, as well as in the mulatta, child of racial mixture, whose life narrative is determined by blood. We should not be surprised then to find something like a family melodrama theory of history based on causal chain-linkages underwriting major works of history. Consider how one popular narrative history finds the source of the 1917 Russian Revolution in Empress Alexandra's overprotection of the hemophiliac heir, Alexi. As a consequence of the Empress's obsession with the safety of her son, the Romanovs lost touch with the Russian people, or an overprotective mother *caused* the Russian Revolution (Massie 1967, vi).

This question of historical causality leads me to venture an early hypothesis about the device of narrative coincidence: it is the accident that is no accident. In other words, the accident, the seemingly random, is in melodrama's fictions not the *least* planned but the *most*, making it a carefully *rigged occurrence*. But for our purposes, the better question to ask is when exactly the coincidence is *felt as* a coincidence, that is, when are two or three instants felt *at once*, at the impossible "one and the same time." This question of "when felt" requires me to add to this hypothesis a corollary: since the coincidence or *rigged occurrence* triggers unexpected future consequences (there being no such thing as unexpected past events), it is relatively more forward-looking in its orientation toward events hoped-for or dreaded. Or, given a dreaded empty or an uncertain future, the coincidence unites the estranged and benefits the characters for whom there appeared to be no hope, rewarding them with another time, an annexed extra time—effectively giving them "a future."[22]

Having said that the rigged narrative event adjusts outcomes, that is, controls the future, we must also see that there is a strict limit on its temporality. For "chance" itself can belong *only* to the time of the present. This limit does not mean, however, that the "now" ever stands completely alone. As Husserl's translator puts it, "The now is not a thing capable of independent existence." since "past and "future" always accompany it (Brough 1991, xxvii). The "chance" occurrence intervenes in the present to abruptly change the course of events and thus to alter outcomes, to either secure or to threaten hopes, the "best laid plans" for future happiness, often threatening and securing within the same motion picture. For example, in *Strike* (Alice Guy Blaché, Solax, U.S., 1912), the fire that accidentally breaks out in the living room threatens the union leader's happy home, and the boss's arrival with his car, "just in time" rescues the worker's wife and child, securing a future for them. While we cannot overlook the politics of using the boss's car to save the worker's family as a way of proving the union's grievances unwarranted, we still have the basic structure of one time hinging on another. Or, another way of configuring this is to think "just in time" as attempting the impossible "one and the same time," that wished-for alignment of the modes of time, which although "never together" cannot help but impinge upon one another, confirming that no "now" is ever left completely alone.

In one of the few theorizations of devices for rendering events-in-time Mikael Bakhtin advances "adventure-time" or "chance time," and although his literary example is the ancient Greek romance, its relevance for modern popular genre structure is easily established (1981, 92–96). First, to identify the generic logic operative here, we need to acknowledge the logic of "sheer chance," popularly known as "anything can happen." Thus, if "anything can happen," what may be surprising is that with Bakhtin's chance event there is no rule as to *when* that event can burst on the scene. This means that in Bakhtinian theory the coincidence *can* come at any time, "early" or "late," contrary to the advice of early screenwriting manuals (Bordwell 1982, 4). Further, crucial meetings can be either *not* missed or missed "failures to meet," both completely contingent (Bakhtin 1981, 95). Now here is what is important for us. In this either/or of the "chance" intrusion we see a completely unsystematic unpredictability at work. Then, not so surprisingly and relevant to our fascination with *historical time*, we learn that "chance" was an anomaly to the historicists. We may be able to guess

Alice Guy Blaché directing *My Madonna* (Solax, 1915). Courtesy Ft. Lee Library. Ft. Lee, New Jersey.

why nineteenth-century historicism, as Koselleck tells us, discounted the workings of fortune or "chance." Invested as historicism was in reading "history" as a plan, it could not admit to the unplanned "chance" event (2004, ch. 8). Bakhtinian "adventuristic 'chance time,'" in contrast, is disruptive of any plan or projection, in effect fully *expecting* "irrational forces" to "intervene" in the course and direction of fictionalized human events (1981, 94). So it is that we learn something valuable about history and time from a popular narrative device rather than from professional historians. What we learn is to expect to find chance happenings that cannot be made to follow from earlier events and that even elude feminist analysis.

At this point I need to rescue the reader. While I am finding in melodrama an acute awareness of the hard task of negotiating past-present-future as well as grasping the relativity of the modes, I began this chapter with the promise to address the implications for our historical research, writing, and moving image making focused on the women who turned deeply felt life experiences into moving pictures. What, if anything, do we owe those historical actors whose "time" it is feared we may color? For us, as I have been arguing, the first difficulty we encounter, even before that of finding the words or images, is where to position *ourselves* in the relative modes of historical time. Here, indeed, is the historian's *location-in-time quandary*. It is, of course, the issue of the vantage from which we select evidence if the present from which we represent "the past" is no longer the future it "once was." What follows from this is the intertwinement of our time and theirs—especially if we think of our present as not just any "former future" but as *their* "former future," that is, the time ahead that they once anticipated.

From the preoccupations of everyday life, the conundra of philosophy, and the dramatic dilemmas of moving picture melodrama, however, I want to derive something else, something quite different from all of these approaches to a hard, if not the hardest, problem of existence (because the hardest to bear). I would state it this way: the present cannot exactly know either the past or the future, no matter how hard we try to align these modes of time in the present, to try not to fail to remember, to try to anticipate, and even to attempt to predict (Koselleck 2002, 133–136). Translated into historiographic method, the discrepant modes plague us at the research and writing stages. At every juncture, the problematic of *historical time* enters—when, in "the before now" (Jenkins) an event *was* what it was, when in the present we say *that it was* (which might or might not have been the case), and later, long after, when the event will inevitably be *said to have been* something else again even while it might remain the same. Whatever happened then both *does* and *doesn't* depend on what we say happened, *does* if we are constructivists and *doesn't* if we see historical events as autonomous or independent of our rearrangement of them. Since theorists of history do not necessarily agree that past events have an existence independent of our later configuration of them, I will continue to defer this question. However, despite their divergence on the question of the autonomy of the past, the theorists in question might at least agree to this: we can't get back there again.[23]

6

ARE THEY "JUST LIKE US"?

What if our current historical work says more about *us* than it does about them? As contemporary feminist historians, we try to describe the work lives of Alice Guy Blaché, Germaine Dulac, Dorothy Arzner, Elvira Notari, Asta Nielsen, and Lois Weber, adhering to sources from their time. A century later, scholars scrupulously research their careers, and current readers take our descriptive studies to be accurate depictions of the lives of these women as they were in their moment. These readers, we assume, want to know more about women in the silent era. They read about historical women in order to learn about *those* women but not about contemporary women. Right? Yet it is possible that contemporary accounts of silent-era filmmakers may not describe those historical women very well at all and in "representing" these women today we say more about our contemporary selves than we do about historical selves. What is the problem here? For traditional historians, contemporary preoccupations violate traditional conventions of historical representation and hence the prohibition against what we might call "tainting." It may, however, be that concern about "tainting" is but another aspect of the scientific aspirations of history, the discipline, since such a worry goes hand in hand with commitment to objectivity. Thus, we have this variation on objectivity cast as the historian's great challenge—to study historical figures "in their own terms." In feminist historical studies of women, however, to think that we could study them purely in "their own terms" (which by implication means not "in our terms") seems quite impossible. For if we begin from the premise that the present is itself historical (in its own way), the charge of tainting—fear of "our" ostensible contamination of "them"—makes no sense.[1] We cannot extricate ourselves from our time any more than they could have from theirs. So a study that aims to portray historical others "in their own terms" has set an unrealizable goal.

Let's consider this. Given her inextricability from her own time, the contemporary historian faces the apparent unavoidability of her subjects sounding "just like us," a phrase I borrow from Joan W. Scott (1996a, 3). There is, however, little feminist commentary on the "like us" historical effect, if we could call it that, perhaps because the vulnerabilities of historical studies are too exposed here. To even call attention to a "like us" effect is to reveal the worry that the present might *already* have contaminated accounts of the past. The need for historical quarantine becomes understandable if one sees the historian's job as sealing off past events to protect them—but from what? Admittedly, the contamination metaphor is an exaggeration since the issue is actually more that of the impinging present, the present and its assumptions that we can neither exactly "see" nor really "get out of"—although Hayden White would have us try (2007, 225). Of course, assumptions being assumptions, they escape us, especially in those categories of what is thought to be human nature such as "what women want" or "what men will do." Here, however, facing the historian's predicament—whether to find them to be "us" or "not us"—we face again the philosophical concern as to where to *locate* the historian in the cycling of modes that we are calling the historical time structure.

I have been arguing that this disjuncture of times so beyond our control produces for the researcher something like a historical *location-in-time quandary*, effect of the everyday uncertainties of where we are relative to past and future. Here, the researcher will worry about how to say "what happened" in the past because of the relativity of modes: Does one speak "as a" contemporary from the vantage of one's moment, or not "as a" contemporary but rather "as a" historically unspecified neutral observer of past events?[2] If one can claim to be writing "as a" female or "as a" male, foregrounding one's gender, why wouldn't one write "as a" twenty-first-century historian, thus situated? Since in literary studies one is expected to write "as a" contemporary literary critic or "as a" present-centered novelist, or if a documentary moving image maker "as a" social agent engaged with today's issues, the prohibition against "presentism" would appear to belong mostly to traditional historical representation. This is not, however, to say that even traditionalists don't ignore this old rule, inserting personal anecdotes and framing their process. Foregrounding the critical present is especially vital to the new philosophy of history where writers *do* flesh out themselves as contemporary historians, ideally with the kind of pedagogical impact achieved by Carolyn Steedman with the confession that she mistakenly assumed the existence of a rag rug in a working-class British home in 1840, an error revealed by further research (2002, 112–141).[3] Although Steedman's mistake could easily be read as a cautionary tale for researchers, we can also take it to be illustrative of the kind of slip into present-centered all-knowingness that worries theorists of history.[4] And yet, it is not just that coloration by present assumptions is unavoidable or that the historical writer is effectively guessing when he or she attempts to reconstitute past scenes. It is also that the entire historiographic project is unsettled by its own commitments. And, to review, what would these be?

One questionable commitment is simply that one time must purport to know another. Philip Rosen, weighing in on this problem he calls "historiographic positionality," finds the modern historian to be on especially shaky ground. It is not only that time is seen to be *both* all-present and unidirectional, he says, but that "consequently the continual production of significant differences between pasts and presents, necessarily makes the historian's logic a slippery or fuzzy one" (2001, 119).[5] Here the trouble is the historian's commitment to knowing "all that happened for all time." We see something of Rosen's "significant differences" problem in the historian's convention of finding a figure to be "ahead of her time" or belonging to the "wrong time," but at the same time historically specified and defined by an era. And here is the fuzzy logic. Of this figure we might ask how she can be said to be defined by an era to which she doesn't belong. As a technological visionary, Antonia Dickson cannot logically be both "of her time" in the late nineteenth century and "ahead of her time."

The historical writer faces our *location-in-time quandary* in which he or she must research and write from a present position of relative "knowing" but "about" an unreachable "past" position, and, especially if a feminist, "for" an unknowable future position. This is not, however, to say that such a *quandary* is negative. On the contrary, there are rich theoretical possibilities here if we see the connection between the three temporalized locations or modes as always in play, against the pressure to judge events as relatively retrograde or advanced. Here is where that comparison leads. While in historical discourse it is a given that the present is in the position of experiential authority, that position, I would argue, also allows the present to bestow ultimate authority on the historical past, which then becomes a final arbiter. Paradoxically, however, the contemporary moment may be under ideological pressure to demonstrate progress over the past at the same time that this present is deferential to its authority. In this dubious past-present comparison, the present then looks backward, both superior to (given progress) and inferior to the venerable past.

ON FEMINISTS LOOKING FOR FEMINISTS

Something like this historical *location-in-time quandary* is, of course, endemic to historical research and writing as well as to historical moving image making. The historian may struggle to accurately represent the "past," but given the pressure to compare must claim that a phenomenon is both different from and similar to the present from which he or she writes or otherwise represents that "past." These difficulties are dramatized in the construction of genealogies or legacies.[6] Any historical family tree drawn up after the fact may easily be faulted for making connections that are obviously designed to shore up a pedigree for the present. Yet consider how seldom one encounters criticism of a major historiographic effort on the basis of how it may have slanted past events to make them pertinent to the present, especially since "relevancy" and "timeliness" may also be a basis for critical praise. One striking exception is the recent criticism of the Second Wave academic feminist classic *The Madwoman in the Attic* on the grounds that it is skewed to the present of its 1970s writing. Forty years after publication, the book that "rediscovered" the great nineteenth-century English-language female fiction writers comes under scrutiny for its too close adherence to the feminism of its time. From the vantage of a later literature "after" feminism Rita Felski turns the "just like us" question back on the authors of *The Madwoman in the Attic*. In Sandra Gilbert and Susan Gubar's literary history, Felski now hears *not* the voice of the nineteenth-century writers but the voice of Second Wave feminist literary criticism. Gilbert and Gubar, she concludes, returned to Charlotte Brontë's *Jane Eyre* and Charlotte Perkins Gilman's "The Yellow Wallpaper" only to find women other than those who were the objects of their study. As Felski argues, these feminist critics sought to find not writers in "their time" but sought to find themselves. That is, Gilbert and Gubar found not Victorians but figures fashioned after 1970s feminist ideals. Consequently, *The Madwoman in the Attic* tells us as much as or more about the 1970s as it does about the 1870s. That these female writers were depicted as "seething rebels rather than moral guardians" or "maimed victims of patriarchy rather than prim and censorious foremothers" is a tip-off, Felski argues. And what would be the purpose of this remodeling? Why other than to aid in the construction of a genealogical legacy? Finding earlier writers to be "seething rebels" and "maimed victims" served Gilbert and Gubar's purpose of making their own necessary "precursors," Felski thinks. The authors found the Victorians to be "very much after their own heart" (2003, 66). There we have it, at the deepest level of cultural assumption. Gilbert and Gubar's Victorians are sympathetic echoes of the authors' moment, nineteenth-century writers who suffer in 1970s terms and exhibit 1970s sensibilities. So, let's return to my opening question about what readers expect to find in historical works, that is, whether readers would have turned to *The Madwoman in the Attic* to find writers "in their own time" or not. Why, we wonder, would 1970s feminists have found in these Victorian writers so much similarity rather than strangeness, similarity that encouraged them to feel a perfect affinity with *them*.

Affinity with *them*? The ambiguous use of the pronoun "them" is intentional and parallels the question with which I began this chapter when I asked what readers and viewers expect to learn about "past" women from historical accounts. It is all in the wording, because one could easily argue that 1970s readers were most interested in feminist-victims who found ways to refuse victimization, thus hoping to find those who predated them to be "like them." And looking back, it might seem that 1970s literary and art history scholars as well as feminist film scholars *did* prefer to "find" feminist precursors.[7] Indicative of the wide interdisciplinary influence of feminist literary history, early on, feminists working on motion picture film culture considered the film and literature parallel but concluded that there were no equivalents to British novelists such as Jane Austen or George Eliot in the early motion picture industries.[8] The irony of this position is that if these feminists had been looking for precursors they might have found *no women* at all, which, strictly speaking, is what they did. In the absence of evidence of either extant films or female makers, they opted to study, as they said, the more theoretically productive "absence" of women (Doane, Mellencamp, and Williams 1983, 7). On a purely empirical basis then the "no women" position appears to be unassailable. At that time, there were no women in the early film industry like the great British writers "to be found," as we say. And yet, today we know that they were "there to be found." Further, the comparison that these film scholars make with the position of literary historians implies that if there *had been* female equivalents in the first decade of film, an empirical direction might have been taken. This position—that they weren't there but that if they had been there they would have been studied—is elaborated in E. Ann Kaplan's argument about what could be called the missing tradition. Kaplan goes so far as to hypothesize a legacy that was thought not to exist, suggesting that if there *had been* women scenario writers and directors between the 1910s and 1940s they might have produced films comparable to the literary fiction of Olive Higgins Prouty, author of the 1923 novel *Stella Dallas* (1987, 133).[9] The implication again is that in the 1970s feminist film scholars *would have* studied those films, would have, that is, if they had been made. As we know now, however, many women wrote original screenplays or adapted women's fiction, most notably Frances Marion who adapted the earlier version of Prouty as *Stella Dallas* (dir. Henry King, 1925).[10] The reader may conclude the obvious—that the theoretical "absence" of women, shoring up the empirical "no women" position, guaranteed for a time that no films would be found.

The other problem with the "no women" presumption, companion to Gilbert and Gubar's discovery of the literary foremothers they sought to find, is that it is no wonder that no "women in film" were found since the search was for ideal women but not for all women. To return to the 1970s feminism and film comparison with literary studies, let us say that since few, if any, ideal feminist examples could be "found" in the early film industries, for all intents and purposes there were "no women." Women, however, were everywhere on screen from the first decade, as I have been arguing, and were furthermore impossible to miss in retrospective silent-era screenings, beginning with the first women's film festivals in Europe and the United States[11] Although motion picture actresses were plentiful, feminists in the 1970s were by and large more interested in "finding" film directors and sometimes screenwriters than in enumerating more actresses.[12] The possibility that actresses might also have been writers seems not to have been explored.[13] Neither was there much interest in lower-level women's jobs filled by extra girls, script girls, lab workers, and stenographers, whose situation I take up in the following chapter. Stimulated by the first retrospective women's film festivals, the 1970s stirred a demand for larger-than-life women who were in charge of things and whose different vision might have been realized on screen. Put another way, the 1970s implicitly prioritized the study of historical women "approved" or preferred by feminism.[14] When we contrast the 1970s with the 1990s, however, we see a pattern that makes one wonder how first "not finding" and later "finding" so many women could *both* be self-fulfilling prophesies.

Let us return to the question about silent-era female filmmakers with which I began, but now ask it with some incredulity. How could they possibly sound like *us* when the traditional goal of research remains that of understanding historical subjects "in their own terms"? One wonders how, given this disciplinary tenant, the 1970s could produce so very many studies of feminist literary and art historical progenitors. Feminist studies at the time were, by definition, excavations of overlooked female talent and, looking back to Linda Nochlin's question, "Why have there been no great women artists?" (1973), one finds that the first studies that answered the question featured accomplished and talented women, again, *some* women but not others. Today, we can finally ask if the authors of these studies were not themselves striving to be understood as similarly gifted and successful and, quite possibly, worried that they might also end up unrecognized "in their own time." This may be one more "like us" tendency. So now let's ask what may sound like a naive question about feminists writing about female historical subjects. And why *wouldn't* they sound like us? Why should we expect anything other than that the "now" in which we research would come to bear in mysterious ways on the "before now"?[15] Our "times," after all, will evidence themselves in ways quite beyond our control.

There is then finally no putting off dealing with the present as historical, especially as we cannot "absent" it from the later moment in which absent events are represented as "having happened" one way as opposed to another. Here, then, we confront the implications that follow from seeing the historical worker in his or her present as determining what are taken to be the significant events of the past, again Joan W. Scott's paradox in which the historian creates that which he or she intends only to "discover" (2004, 260). Thus, part of our notion of *constitutive discovery* will need to expand to deal with the historian's historical location approached by means of the *location-in-time quandary* and the concomitant confusion *between* historical modes or times *at* their conjuncture. For whose time do we interpret the events of their time? We return to the companion to this quandary, the question posed in Chapter 2 of how in the "present" present we locate ourselves and how the absent past becomes "presentified" as we now begin to write "It was . . ." or "They were. . . ."[16]

THE DIFFERENT SAMENESS OF THEM

Relevant here is Scott's "sameness versus difference" conundrum (1996, 3–4), that sticking point for feminists, and following her lead let us cast this problem in terms of feminist historical research. That is to ask, to begin with, "For whom do we search"? Do we search for those "like us" or for those "not like us"? Of course some of the distinction originates in the question as to whether we take *women* to be singular or collective, an issue raised here from the outset. The conundrum previews the difficulty faced when we try to fit empirically researched, diversely situated historical women into "women," the feminist gender category. Recall from the introduction that in Scott's analysis the issue as to whether "woman" is socially diverse or singular remains an "unanswerable" question (2008a). Neither, she also says, has it ever been established whether the category of *women* preexists its contemporary usage or whether it has been recently produced (1996a, 4). Certainly, Scott goes on, the historical past contributes examples of "endless variation," and if we are looking for empirical examples of gender inequality they are everywhere to be excavated (1996b, 159). Examples may be endless, but we still proceed with feminist political caution. Merely raising the question of "women" risks returning "womanness" to the "essence" so resoundingly critiqued, and this project is no exception (Dall'Asta 2010b). If the trap of essentialism is a risk, so too is the political fallout that can follow from claiming "we" in solidarity with others categorically unlike ourselves, including historical others, so radically unlike us in their abject nonexistence. And what would be the special abjection of the historical other?[17] If we start with the category of "insignificance" that Carolyn Steedman has rescued, we have taken only one step (1992, 164–165). Why? Because even the concept of women's "historical insignificance" cannot hope to contain, let alone fathom, all of the no-longer-existing women of every class and race category worldwide. Here, considering such no-longer-existing others, this second trap, this "we," is especially treacherous, appearing as a generous all-encompassing gesture—the ambition to study women in world perspective. Further, the "we are all women" aspiration risks a split over who is to speak about whom, potentially giving rise to dissent in which the generous gesture backfires. As Judith Butler has pointed out, the "we" claimed in unified solidarity can contribute to the factionalization that "we" as a unifier is intended to dissolve (2006, 199). In attempting to encompass, feminism risks splitting the world into the divisions that it can't then obliterate, even if obliteration is the goal.

What then of historical others as also "like" or "unlike" us? Recall the early Black feminist claim to the category of what might be called "doubly other" as the "other of the other" (Wallace 1990, 227), which called for situating Black women relative to Black men, a politically strategic reclamation of theories of otherness. In such terms, Black women excavated from the historical past could also be conceived as "triply othered," that is, *also* "othered" by the present-centered present. To continue this line of inquiry, surely historians of women, male as well as female historians, are not immune to the kind of critique to which the old anthropological "us vs. them" paradigm has been submitted in recent decades.[18] No contemporary feminist will miss the well-worn issue of "identity" lurking in the question of "us" or "not us," and that paradigm does not exactly go away after women who no longer exist become objects of historical study. So, in the spirit of this long-standing feminist internal critique, we might consider how to theorize the unequal power relation between the historian and his or her historical subject. Thus, in addition to a *location-in-time-quandary*, or the dilemma of the historical present that wants to know the past for the unknowable future, the historian wonders how to speak "for" those almost beyond abjection—those who no longer exist.

CHAPTER 6

Here, however, is where women's history wants to be an exception. If I correctly read Joan W. Scott, source of the phrase "just like us" (1996a, 3), she is obliquely addressing an issue for historiographic method that I began by exaggerating as the unwanted contamination of the past by the present. Following Scott in this position means translating the powerful but fraught "sameness versus difference conundrum" into a research agenda that takes on a double burden—the historically "like" *and* the historically "unlike." But here it would appear that "just like" goes to the "sameness" side of the opposition in which all women, no matter how different, are still "women." The historically "like," however, is not so easily seen as one might assume, especially since "like us" can stubbornly stick to "identity" or "personhood," those notions of the self also indicative of the shared historical moment of writing or image-making. What are we in danger of missing here? We might fail to see that gendering historical subjects as male or female reveals our own moment, even as today transgender troubles old gender categories, and identity as a basis for politics is discredited.[19] Someday we may even come to see how merely looking to the historical past for "persons" not only mirrors our moment but reveals a retrograde tendency to the genealogical.[20] But, to repeat, women's history sometimes appears to claim exemption from these issues.

This is where Scott's feminism appears to claim immunity, and not only from identity politics but from disciplinary tradition. In a move that goes decidedly against longstanding disciplinary claims to objectivity Scott argues that the commitment to finding feminist precursors means that we *do* comb the historical record in search of those similar figures whose "actions set precedents for our own" (1996a, 3). Invariably these figures are seen to be fundamentally "just like us," she says. Let us then ask our naive question a second time but from another angle and with new emphasis: "*Why* would they sound just like us?" After all, since we have rejected objectivity and embraced the "relativity" of every cultural moment, we can acknowledge that our historical location contributes to every *constitutive discovery*. But Scott goes one step further in answer to this kind of question. It is not only that sounding "like us" is unavoidable. It is that for her the historically biased historian is fundamental, even the basis of a feminist historiography. Thus seeing ourselves in historical subjects, she argues, is "preferred hermeneutic practice." Really? The explanation she gives is somewhere to be found in a contemporary yearning for meaning—for feminist meaning, that is. Scott goes on in an astounding passage to say of our relation to the historical subjects we research that these subjects have meaning "for us" not because of who they were but insofar as they are found to be "just like us": "They have to be just like us if the comparisons and precedents are to be meaningful" (1996a, 3). They would at the least need to be considered persons with gender identities, one would assume. Beyond that, however, would historical figures need to be understood as having similar, as the saying goes, "hopes and dreams"? If women, do we assume that historical figures have our same "wishes about gender relations," to use German feminist Frigga Haug's phrase (1992, 66).

To test Scott's assertion, consider the converse. That is, what if historical figures *do not* sound "like us"? If they did not sound "like us," then contemporary readers might find them meaningless and therefore irrelevant. Figures from the distant historical past like Cleopatra or Catherine the Great might remain inaccessible if popular historians did not shape them after recognizable selves and did not suggest, albeit without offering much proof, that these figures had unconstrained sexual appetites in the most contemporary sense.[21] Following this line of thought, the entire project of women's history might fail to ignite interest if readers or viewers could not find familiarity in historical figures. We are now on the other side of the unavoidable "like us" problem in which historical figures *must* be recognizable and where we might find ourselves asking: But what is there to criticize in the historical past made relevant for a new moment? The broad sweep can be exhilarating. Yet the very ambition of many popularizing historians should make us dubious. What, after all, does Scott's "just like us" give contemporary historians the license to do? Or does "just like us" merely acknowledge what we cannot help but do, given the stubbornness of our time-bound conceptions, again, about "what women want," "what men will do," and "what people are like."

Thinking through Deleuze, Sande Cohen interrupts here with the contrast between two historians. One historian starts from the premise of what is most recognizable and the other takes up an uncomfortable past as one "that few in the present can live with." The first historian approaches the past as "pre-known," finding nothing there but the already realized. The risk of such "pre- knowing," Cohen thinks, is that it makes readers of historical works "indifferent," "an indifference reiterated every time we are given a past that we already know, a past that confirms 'we're just like them,' 'they're just like us,' 'we're all the same.'" If not quite "like us," the equally unacceptable antithesis is that they become "exotic creatures, always 'more and less' like and unlike us" (2006, 239).

Now the project of feminist historical recovery is not what is in dispute here, and indeed this is the place to remark on a venerable legacy that is now several decades old. However, we still must ask if Scott's "just like us" position might in some respects be contradictory. On the one hand, feminist historians override the "too much like us" prohibition against present-centered knowledge, finding historical figures to be "just like us"; on the other hand, these historians are expected to know what they themselves cannot experientially know in order to elucidate the lives of others so "unlike" themselves. Here we need to acknowledge the "unlike" or "not us" part of Scott's equation, which places the burden on feminist researchers to seek out and study the "least like." Feminist historians, then, are expected, in her terms, to "recover" lives with special attention to those women "unlike us," that is, women whose "difference from 'us' need[s] to be acknowledged and explained" (1996a, 3). So historical women, admittedly different, thus retrieved, can't be seen to be *exactly* "like us" after all. They can't be seen to be so much "like us" because their unfamiliarity *requires our explanation.* Is this the case? If we start from the project of women researching women, one would then assume that historical women must be "found" to be different in their very sameness. But of course this is not really saying anything and only restates the paradox of the "different same." Worse, we may be methodologically stuck, not knowing what percentage of them should be interpreted as "just like us" and what part "unlike us." Neither is it a small matter as to who we decide to include in our sample as not at all "us."

ON HISTORICAL OTHERS

Where, then, do we locate cultural as well as historical others and how do we determine what to foreground in representing past events, especially if there is no escaping the cultural shape of the "present" present? To reiterate—some aspect of the "like us" historical effect may be unavoidable, although having said this we would still insist that no historical phenomenon is really reducible to "like-not like." And yet, since scholars continue to wrap historical figures in contemporary concerns, more vigilance is required, putting us on theoretical alert, so to speak. To take only one precautionary step, in the historical present we can begin to think about what could be called our strange historical linkages with them and their time, opening up theoretical territory that thinks historically about the historical present. Then, to take a step further we can acknowledge invisible assumptions and try to name the preoccupations of our moment. Or, rather, we might consider how today's studies carry contemporary resonances. Tony Slide wonders if Alice Guy Blaché's director-producer husband Herbert hasn't been overlooked as a consequence of the focus on his prolific wife (2012a).[22] Tami Williams discovers Germaine Dulac as a French feminist moderate (2014) and Judith Mayne sees Dorothy Arzner as a lesbian filmmaker who made Hollywood industry films unlike those made by men (1994); Kay Armatage claims director-producer Nell Shipman as ordinary (2003); Heide Schlüpmann finds a critical edge in Asta Nielsen's performance (2010, 110–122), and Shelly Stamp finds Lois Weber setting up her own studio as an "emancipation" from major studio "hierarchies" (2015, 142–147).

I wonder whether this critical move has gone too long unnamed although perhaps it is figured in E. H. Carr's concept of historical "reciprocity" (1964, 35). Yet since the exchange may never be as even as Carr's term suggests we need to at least try to name features of what I'm calling the "like us" proclivity. In addition to the popular historians' *re-familiarization of the historical past* there is of course the commitment to political issues mirrored in topics. Undoubtedly targeted research areas reveal how today we project the historical world as needing enlargement. Thus, today, scholars would concur that more research is needed on another five historical subjects whose careers have gone relatively unclaimed in the field: Mexican American Beatriz Michelena whose Beatriz Michelina Features produced *The Flame of Hellgate* (1920), Chinese American Marion E. Wong who wrote, directed, produced, and acted in *The Curse of the Quon Gwon* (1916), Japanese American Tsuro Aoki who also worked with her husband actor/producer Sessue Hayakawa and African American Drusilla Dunjee-Huston, who wrote a never-produced screenplay, and Maria P. Williams who with her husband started a company to produce films for African American audiences.[23] Defending this particular selection reveals our preoccupation with hyphenated identities, immigration, and minority populations. Actually, we have no option other than to recruit objects of study that resonate in the present and what the contemporary moment selects as its echo is a rough measure of how "different" or how "same" we need their "different sameness" to be. At such a juncture, we can be critically pulled in empirical and theoretical directions at once, effectively stumped by the problematic of historical location—the "for" whom and "from" what temporal standpoint, with the injunction to proceed with caution, following Judith Butler (2006, 199). This is then our location relative to the critique of power differentials, *after* three decades of asking who speaks for whom, *after* identity politics, and *after* the so-called post-1970s impasse, a dead end feminists associate with the prohibition against representing women on screen.[24] While Scott's inevitability of "just like us" can assuage political guilt as we attempt to speak and to imagine *for* historical others, there also lingers the doubt that our research is adequate to their lives. In the end, we may worry that they will be found to be nothing more than *what they are for us*. In one remarkable acknowledgement of the way the historian experiences the sense of becoming unmoored, Linda Orr says this about historian-subject relations: "Every writer should leave space to show how undefinable and traumatic her or his objects of study are, before rushing in to explain them. Every work of history needs a moment of uncertainty, a moment given over to the disarray, or rather, the still point of uncertainty" (1990, 160).

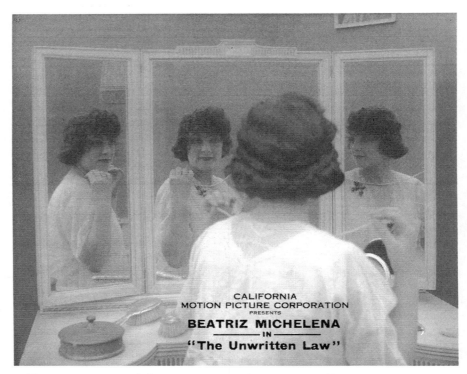

Publicity still, Beatriz Michelena, *Unwritten Law* (1916). Private collection.

CHAPTER 6

Marion E. Wong, actress/writer/director/ producer, Mandarin Film Co., 1916. Private collection.

Tsuro Aoki, actress/producer. Courtesy Billy Rose Theatre Division, New York Public Library for the Performing Arts. New York, New York.

Book frontispiece, Maria P. Williams and Jesse L. Williams, *My Work and Public Sentiment*. Burton Publishing, 1916.

Would that "uncertainty" had more legitimacy or that it could even claim half as much theoretical importance as deconstruction's "impossibility" or "instability." We have arrived at the kind of uncertainty-producing juncture to which Orr refers, a moment when we want to know "how" or "if at all" we can get beyond the present, a *location-in-time quandary* to be sure. Must we "find" them always analogous to us, the "different sameness" question so easily yielding to Scott's inevitable "just like us"? Because from this position it would seem that no matter how exhaustive the research or how analytical the method, historians will never be able to divorce themselves from perspectives in vogue or take off their present-centered glasses. But the present-centeredness in "just like us" may not necessarily be a negative to be overcome as traditionalists might want us to think, as a review of the theories of history literature suggests. First, the question is not new as R. G. Collingworth's interest in the historian's "empathy" relative to historical subjects reminds us.[25] Second, in one of the more provocative recent statements of the problem, Keith Jenkins argues that the method of trying to know a past divorced from the present is not only "logically impossible" but is clearly "anti-historical." For Jenkins, "historical consciousness" requires more than "knowing" events and figures from "the before now" as they would have been known then, but needs also knowing "as historians now do, looking back." Because, as Jenkins sees it, the very contemporary assumptions that we cannot relinquish are what enables historical thinking (2003, 39–40). In short, if contemporary perspectives facilitate a historical consciousness, we could not have that consciousness at all if our analysis didn't also have contemporary currency.[26]

Of course we would not want to overlook the shape that the current moment gives to historical material, and we might even try to imagine how strange that shape will look in ensuing years. While one can't fail to see the humor in Felski's caricature of Victorian writers as 1970s "seething rebels, " the historical aspect of her analysis is not just in the study of Gilbert and Gubar but also in the very moment within which readers "now" grasp the point of her feminist caricature of feminism (2003, 66). Felski's own "after" feminist literary critical moment and its assumptions, following Jenkins, are themselves precisely historical and only in the way our present historical conscious-ness can know. Continuing this line of thought, it is not so much that the present day "colors" an analysis of past events. Rather, it is that every "now" is historical in its own characteristic way. Some will no doubt object that, in this conceptualization, we have negated the entire project of historical research, writing, and image making. To get some perspective on this conundrum there is nothing better than Jenkins's own way out of the futility of knowing the "the past" in terms other than those of the present. Taking the position that we can "now live without histories," he recommends that although we may still live in time, in a moment, a better goal would be to attempt to live "outside of histories" (2009a, 15–16).[27]

"HISTORIES OF THE PRESENT" FOR THE PRESENT

Leaving Jenkins's provocation aside, let us consider the productivity in Foucauld-ian "histories of the present," the point of departure for this chapter. First, we might acknowledge that foregrounding the historical present gives justification to aspects of Scott's "just like us," making it less easy to dismiss approaches to "nowness" and relieving us of the charge of "presentism." And why? Because if our goal is the present, especially if the past and the future have been "relocated," to remind us of Koselleck's point (2004, 4), we need to unlearn the equation "history equals the past" and its cor-ollary in which "history" is therefore never the present. But the point is not so much the substitution of the historian's object of study, the "present" for "the past," as it is "critique." Borrowing here from Hayden White, the point of "historicizing" the present is to gain critical distance on that present, to which end we use the historical past, that past brought back into being for this very purpose. For White, "historicization" of the present is seen as a means of "restoring events to their presents, to their living relations with their conditions of possibility." That is not all, as he goes on: "But more: it means treating the present as well as the past as history . . . but also as something to be gotten out of " (2007, 225), as I began by noting. This idea of the present as "something to be gotten out of," or on which we need to achieve critical distance, puts the past in the position of "foil." But only the past? While popular thought may be undecided about whether to prefer the "good old times" or to pass judgment on too much "living in the past," effectively alternating "foils," one would expect the professional historian to have resolved the question of the ultimate destination of his or her research. So perhaps here we can appreciate how Scott herself resolves the destination question, which is to argue that historical subjects need to be "meaningful" for the present (1996a, 3). She goes on: "The object of critical history-writing is the present, though its materials come from the archives of the past" (2007, 35). The past brought back to critically "historicize" the present makes the present historical as an object of study insofar as it is the rationale *for* that study? But that cannot be all, as we will see momentarily.

But first, some knotty methodological issues follow from this position, and should empirical worries arise about the failure to "get it right," let us remind ourselves that we are not dealing with either events or persons to whom we can finally be "true," or lost objects like motion picture films that will ever be the same as they were at the time of their release. Rather, to use Koselleck's phrase, our written historical representation "lives on the fiction of actuality," which is all we have since the past for all that it was is now so radically gone. He goes on to say that although we would not want to be arbitrary and do adhere to sources, those sources do not finally "prescribe what may be said" (2004, 111). It is, after all, up to us to bring the past into the existence it can no longer have. How is this to be done and what would be the point, if any, of primary and secondary texts, or sources, references, and citation?

TEXTUAL EXISTENCE AS THE ONLY EXISTENCE

Taking a position that some find extreme and others may find difficult to dismiss, Keith Jenkins argues that "history" refers not to past worlds but only to other texts. As he puts it, "only texts matter historically," and this means that they matter more than "what actually happened" (2003, 42). Note the shade of difference here between Jenkins's theory and Trouillot's, the latter cleaving to the "autonomy" (1995, 6) of the past event and holding out for a configuration of events that can't just be "said to have happened," as discussed in Chapter 3. For Trouillot, "autonomy" not only defers to but reserves something for the discovery of evidence that could counter the official story motivated by powerful interests. Counter interests, of course, may invest in these events as well as in their subsequent tellings, ones often based on new evidence pertinent to those events. With the exception of the stress on the duality of two historicities—"what happened" and "what was said to have happened" (1995, 2, 29), Trouillot's theory may perhaps be too easily accommodated to traditional approaches, that is, his theory of history can fit into the conventional position that "history" is always being revised (or historicity two is always subject to adjustment). But if historicity two is always under revision, what becomes of "what actually happened," the past events of historicity one? Do past events remain pristinely *the same*, to apply Husserl here (1991, 68)? Yet how can we possibly know whether or not "what happened" has changed if we have no access to the events of historicity one? So it would seem that Trouillot's theory of history runs up against the proverbial "untold" event. This "untold" event can be the telling event, evidence of which may surface to threaten the entire enterprise of "the history of," that is, the direction of the "told" events with their contemporary ramifications mapped. And yet, if historical evidence, misplaced or buried, remains unnarrativized, it would be just as though "nothing happened" in the past. Our example of this would be that if past events were to go unnarrativized women simply would not have been instrumental in the making of the U.S. film industry. So again, if we follow Jenkins, written texts trump whatever it was that "actually happened" by *presenting* "what it is that actually happened" *as if* these events had actually taken place in the past.

But no, some will insist, written historical texts are valid only if they have been scrupulously researched and rely on verifiably genuine documents that refer to objects and events that "really" existed in the past. Texts cannot just assert by presenting some documents. Or can they? We know well that the traditional historian's achievement is assessed by the criteria of evidentiary accuracy whether drawn from oral testimony or moving image footage or census record. In this empirical tradition, the goal is to access that historical "past" to which sources testify, and to hold that past as the ultimate arbiter of the various and often conflicting accounts of it. Jenkins, however, answers this prevailing position with his deconstructionist one, countering the historical "past" as the final authority with what so convincingly stands as that history—*other texts of history*. And this is how it works. The historian, he says, compares the ostensible "past" not with an "evanescent unrecorded, unrecalled realm." He or she compares that "past" *not* with events themselves but rather sets them up "against other accounts of it." In the end, Jenkins maintains, "accuracy" is measured not against "the past" but against other published texts in the field (1991, 14). Accounts of the past thus validate and insure other accounts.

We would not, however, want to imply when we say that events and persons have only textual existence that this kind of existence is not real existence. For all intents and purposes, in the force field of film and cinema history scholarship, textual existence *is* existence and all that there is really. Textual representation is the only way *into* former existences as well as the only way out. Usefully, the power of textual existence supplies one more answer to my persistent question: "Where was Antonia Dickson?" After all, she was not "there" for the field until she began to be referenced in publications and brought to our attention in reprinted excerpts from her "Wonders of the Kinetoscope" (1895) (Lant 2006, 405–410). And *where* did we find her so recently? In those reprinted texts. A more curious case is that of Lois Weber, who, understood in this manner, can be seen as moving in and out of textual existence, beginning with the assessment of her career during her lifetime. Shelley Stamp tells us that from the point of view of Weber's own time, the writer-director-producer was not completely erased, but that as a version of her career spread from the 1910s into the 1920s, *she* changed in print. She was "written out" at the same time that she was "written in" all over again (2010b, 359, 380; 2015, 282–283). Lois Weber then presents us with one of the more interesting disappearances during a lifetime, disappearances both textual as well as beyond-the-text in which the severity of a career setback caused the director to go to into seclusion as one contemporary commentator describes it (Williamson 1927, 226–231). And, again in our contemporary moment, Weber has been "written out" once more, as Stamp tells us, subsumed in one recent history into the description of the "brief vogue" of early Hollywood women filmmakers (2010b, 359, 380). The subsuming of Lois Weber becomes that much more egregious when we acknowledge textual existence. This is because while we may indeed be concerned about Weber's historical existence in the past the *only* existence that she can now have is a textual one.

Let us return to the question from Chapter 2, "Where was Antonia Dickson when we had no knowledge of her?" to consider the corollary to what I have been calling *constitutive discovery*. Consider what the *constitutive discovery* does when it brings historical events and persons into existence. My initial "where was" question should now look somewhat different. Why did the field between 1975 and 1990 believe that entrepreneurial women in the early national film industries *did not exist*? Where was Elvira Notari before Guiliana Bruno's study of the Italian director-producer? Although it took almost another decade for feminist film theory to take up Bruno's theoretical historiography, her *constitutive discovery* established the existence of Elvira Notari. That discovery has further constituted more Dora Films titles produced by Notari's Neopolitan company like the recently restored *A' santanotte* (1921). Notari now exists for us in the present, constituted first by Bruno's account followed by that of other scholars but also by Notari's extant silent film melodramas seen again by contemporary audiences (Tomodjoglou 2013). These are the audiences for whom "Elvira Notari" now exists, but only insofar as she is brought into *coexistence* with the historian. Legitimating this position Bruno says of Notari, "In a way, I *desire* the author: I need her figure . . . as she needs mine" (1993, 240). Elaborating this theoretical move, Monica Dall'Asta, speaking of Elvira Giallanella and her lost *Umanità/Humankind* (1919), refers to a two-way "relation of constellation" in which contemporary feminists bring such earlier work into an existence that it would not otherwise have had. Thus it is that as historians we are "constellated" with these historical subjects (Dall'Asta and Gaines 2015, 19).[28]

HISTORICAL COINCIDENCE

To justify bringing them into our age, we need to "find" them relevant to it and thus in equal proportions find "us" as well as "them" in their lives and their work. But, of course, the ideas they used to make sense of events in their lives would be made out of whatever was "conceptually available" to them—just as ours must be.[29] Conceptual "unavailablity" means that Olga Petrova, actress-producer, before "gender distinction" became available as a concept, would claim about male directors that "the idea of their sex didn't occur to me" (1996, 107). So their concerns both were and weren't the same as ours, and cannot now be the "same" as ours except that they *now* appear to be, which confirms an impossible temporal construction if there ever was one, given that our age was then "not yet." No, "not yet," and still, is this not to relapse into "time marches on"? What, then, if we were to think of historical times as "superimposed" (Koselleck 2004) or, following Tani Barlow, see historical events as "cumulative" rather than "continuous" (2004a, 3). Or as "copresent," as Jacques Rancière proposes when he says, "It's over two centuries now since history has designated not the narrative of things past, but a mode of copresence, a way of thinking and experiencing the co-belonging of experiences and inter-expressivity of the forms and signs that give them shape" (2006, 176). So no, increasingly, the past is not exactly nonexistent and there is certainly no denying our imbrication with it in ways beyond the genealogical. If, for instance, today we use the concept "gender discrimination" to make sense of their erratic employment, is this not a case of co-belongingness, their experience of "gender discrimination" inextricable from our contemporary one, our concept constituting *their* experience and their experience ours as well? This is especially the case if today we superimpose women in the early U.S. industry over women who are passed over today for plumb directing jobs in favor of men, a pattern that may rise to the level of discriminatory hiring practices, the basis for a recent California appeal to state and federal government.[30] What was then an inexplicable pattern is today a set of illegal practices.

Now, with such *historical relations of coincidence* in mind, let us return to one of Joan Scott's knottiest of paradoxes as explicated by Victoria Hesford and Lisa Diedrich, who claim the term "feminist historian/theorist" (2014, 107). We have now made these early figures historically coincident with us, and here is where a theory of history helps us think about the *historical relations* we have had and are having with archival materials as remnants of the historical past. As motion photography has had documentary relations with the real historical world, so researchers establish *historical relations* with that world through archival materials. As an alternative, Eelco Runia proposes our metonymic connection to all historical phenomena, whether war monument or museum object or random photograph. But it is not just that the phenomenal fragment "stands" as the part for the rest of it. Runia is less interested in the reconstruction of historical wholes than in the means by which an architectural scene or historical object or its display can strike us, and even be felt to "know us" before we could "know it." In the historical presentation of "absence," there occurs a "transfer of presence," he thinks, offering a theory as to how the past unsettlingly persists (for us) (2014, 83). So one way he thinks historical reality is as it is "absently present" (ibid., 80).

Perhaps now, with the critique of realism behind us, we can follow Runia's position and rather than urging that the field come face to face with the failure of representationalism, might now marvel at how some cultural texts as well as material objects are *felt* to bring us closer to what we call "historical reality." We would then be powerfully touched as well as constituted by past figures, given our "mutual constitution" (Hesford and Diedrich 2014, 107). Now, having gone overboard to state the case for

Germaine Dulac, director/writer/critic. Courtesy Bibliothèque du Film, Cinémathèque Française. Paris, France.

our *constitutive discovery* of them, I need to argue the reverse to get at mutuality. In reverse, it is *we* who are constituted by Germaine Dulac, sitting at the table with so many important French men, wearing a tuxedo cut just like a man's. And if "they constitute us" could we not also, again following Runia, propose a reverse *recognition*?[31] Now look to see how this photograph "recognizes us" in it. The row of men turn toward us as though to ask what we are doing here at this exclusive dinner. We know that the photograph "knows" because Germaine sits there among them, right where we would be.

Recruiting them for the paradigms we need in the present we produce them as theoretically coincident with us. Thus we are constituted by Dorothy Arzner, living a double life as a lesbian and feature film director in Golden Age Hollywood. Even better, Arzner is now in a mutually constituting relation with her Chinese American lesbian double, director/producer Esther Eng; who Louisa Wei's documentary tells us was notoriously promiscuous in the Hong Kong years.[32] But again, who are we? I wonder who we would be without them. Today, then, we take into account not one but at least three points of historical reference, so it is no wonder that we experience a *location-in-time* conundrum. But the quandary, rather than a reason for paralysis, might be integrated into our work, aware as we are of the unlike modes of historical time while under pressure from the historical present to deliver a meaningful analysis of past events. Thus, for whom am I writing, situated *when*, about *what was*, and from *which* historical location? To ask this is to begin to admit the historical present into this very study, the first step of which is to acknowledge the following: the moment within which this sentence is today being written *is itself as historical* as the moment belonging to these silent film era historical subjects.

Dorothy Arzner, editor/director. Courtesy
British Film Institute. London, England.

Esther Eng, director/producer. Courtesy James
Wong and Sally Eng.

The "are they us" question in which women are made historically comparable yields
an approach developed by "historians of difference" whose basic method can be analogy. To relinquish this powerful method may be to ask too much of contemporary
feminist historians whose work lies ahead in "pasts" yet to be fused with new presents.
Further, who are we to denounce the power of matched things, of finding resemblance
between ourselves and earlier others? There is a symmetrical "eloquence of the same"
that remains irresistible, or perhaps a politics of "she too": "She too" was burdened
with family responsibilities, "she too" was unacknowledged in her time, and "she too"
could not get the job for which she was qualified.

7

WORKING IN THE DREAM FACTORY

There is no denying that 'the question, "What happened to women in the silent film industry?" is biased toward figures of visible achievement like June Mathis, Lois Weber and Frances Marion, and, before them, Alice Guy Blaché and Gene Gauntier. To some degree, this can be explained by academic conventions in which new research builds on top of existing research, layer upon layer. Our recurring "What happened to them?" question, after all, features influential women at the top, the drop-off in *their* numbers, and *their* disappearance in the U.S. industry by 1925. But only these women. Lower-level workers have not been the measure of women in the industry, even though one could argue that they were holding it up from the silent era on. The irony here is that when we consider workers at the bottom of the pay scale, their numbers skew the premise that in the silent era there were "more women" than today and then gradually "no women." For female workers *did* remain. They remained if they were working as "stenographers" in the office or "joiners" in the editing room, as they had been since the first decade. In numbers, lower-level female workers stayed while "top" women writers, producers, and directors were phased out. Admittedly, these lower-level worker now make our original "What happened to them?" query seem elite and narrow. But adding these workers to our consideration in the current moment, just when digital tools and networked connections are revolutionizing research methods, seems politically fitting.

Clearly, this expansion reverses the premises with which we began as we shift from women who "rose to the top" to women who "stayed at the bottom," so to speak.

Closer examination also reveals the two groups as physically proximate, the differences between them often blurry. Beginning in the mid-1910s, for instance, lower-level workers were to be found everywhere surrounding the "top" women, defined as those whose profiles were circulated by publicity departments. But because the profiled women were elevated by the first historical researchers, these "top" (but not entirely representative) women were singled out, for instance, by Anthony Slide who started to discover women's names in silent-era film credits around 1972 (1996a, v). Accordingly, these credited and profiled women came to constitute "women in early Hollywood." These select few were not, however, the only moths attracted to the Hollywood light as Hilary Halett demonstrates in her recent study of the female migration to Los Angeles during this period (2013).

A day at work in the dream factory was not the same for all of the women who held jobs there. Some workers could barely glimpse the lives that others lived, those others who wrote scenarios with potential box office appeal and who received large salaries. Aware of how unusual these salaries were, screenwriter Clara Beranger commented on the phenomenon when she compared her position with that of women in other industries where the same successful writers might have found themselves in "purely clerical" positions (1919, 662). But Beranger did not comment on the difference between highly paid and lower paid women in the same film company. Within a studio, job status defined women relationally, and in the writing departments some worked over others. One woman working as a secretary "for" another was paid significantly less, as surviving records show. Anzia Yezierska later recalled her secretary's complaint that she was making $25 per week, $10 less than she had made in her Iowa home town. But Yezierska is also painfully aware that she is making $200 per week to assist in writing the screen adaptation of her book, *Hungry Hearts*, and that she had received $10,000 for the rights (1925, 647). These hierarchical work relations further produced a double eclipse so that just as men obscured powerful women, highly paid women eclipsed less powerful women. In this comparative respect, occupations as categories are predictive, telling us that "what happened" to one group of women *was not* necessarily "what happened" to other groups but was consistent within each group, confirming Joan W. Scott's observation that "worker" is more categorically airtight than "gender" (1999, 285–286). Within the category *worker* we are in addition looking for breakdowns, categories within the category. Remarkably relevant then is the case of studio secretary Valeria Belletti whose letters from Hollywood written between 1925 and 1928 to her childhood friend Irma Prina in New Jersey function as a historical index (Beauchamp 2006, 1–6). Valeria's letters are further a narrative guide to relative work status, one measure of which is difference in the pay she earned in her two jobs—first as executive secretary to Samuel Goldwyn and later as a temporary secretarial worker. More striking, however, is the discrepancy between her salary and that of powerful screenwriter Frances Marion. As we will see, Valeria raises for us the delicate issue as to why some did climb to the top and others didn't, as well as why, in 1928, a woman might choose marriage over work. She also dramatizes a tension between old and new research methodologies where numbers may now rival narrative accounts, as we will see when we consider Metro Pictures and Paramount Pictures DeMille unit payroll records.

Historical references to secretarial-level work are most abundant in the context of scenario department work. Exemplary is Catherine Carr's 1914 *Art of Photoplay Writing*, where she details the labors involved in photoplay selection: "First it is delivered to the Scenario Department, where it is duly opened and cataloged by an under clerk. It then reaches the professional reader (if the company is a large one), and if thought to contain merit, is finally placed upon the Editor's desk, where it has its final reading and the decision is made to either retain it or return it. If the decision is favorable an offer is made at once. If the reverse, it is returned with a polite note of regret as unavailable" (21). That the clerk, stenographer, and reader jobs were predominantly held by women is also confirmed by the photographic evidence of these office spaces. Even celebrity photographs may show clerical support women like the one taking dictation from Cecil B. DeMille's head writer Jeanie Macpherson.[1] Further, payroll records from the 1920s indicate an army of women in script department stenographer jobs whose work entailed retyping drafts for highly paid screenwriters like Josephine Lovett and Alice Duer Miller for much lower pay.[2] Another point of indexical entry into our "what happened" mystery, then, must also be silent-era studio payroll records; these records are a key to the order of a work world in the 1920s toward the end of the heyday of women, a clue to the relation of top to bottom and bottom to the top of the scale of pay and influence.

Throughout we have been taking the long view of the problem of how to say "what happened" to women in the early industry, looking at both their ascendance and their demise. We still want to know more about the conditions of work before these jobs were

Jeanie MacPherson, screenwriter. Courtesy Harold B. Lee Library, Brigham Young University. Provo, Utah.

defined, conditions that may or may not have led to more opportunities for women in this emerging enterprise.[3] Here, 1920s payroll information confirms the correlation between job classification and women's weekly pay. In addition, the very existence of payroll records may indeed be one more sign of the "new conditions" Gene Gauntier is quoted as having said she could not work under, perhaps evident to her as early as 1915 (Smith 1924, 102). The office—itself a product of the new studio efficiency—had to be maintained by more efficiency workers. Thus, more women as stenographers, accountants, payroll clerks, and executive secretaries were needed to support the new management system that would eventually squeeze out women at the top.[4]

Looking back, however, although we see a proliferation of jobs, we find little evidence of stable labor in descriptions of the very first efforts to make moving pictures. While there may have been plenty of "work" in the first decade there were few delimited "occupations." Not only do we find few occupations as yet, but what jobs did appear were by no means industrial jobs. In 1909, Mabel Rhea Dennison in *The Nickelodeon* wrote optimistically that "Women's chances of making a living have been increased by the rise of the biograph machines" (19). However, this article might best be taken to mean that, before 1910, it was assumed that women would be needed only on screen. In other words, this was a vision of work as stand-ins, in effect, women "working" at playing women. Only later in the second decade did journalists note the fuller range of new jobs that were no longer just actress or "extra" jobs (Slide 2012b; McKenna 2008, ch. 3). By 1924, however, the variety of occupations was clear, and Myrtle Gebhart in *Picture-Play Magazine* gives more detail about this work, explaining that a film joiner is a "splicer" and that, in addition to working as a librarian, a woman might be employed as a "research worker" and further that women were numerous not only in the millinery but in the drapery department (102, 119). Yet, how strange it is that fan magazines would become this interested in skilled jobs for women in 1924, by which time women in occupations such as director had largely disappeared and they no longer headed up writing departments as scenario editors as they had a few years earlier.[5]

THE "THEY WERE THERE" THESIS

Considering the power and the influence of women in the early business, scholars have recently expanded beyond the "woman director" to consider female exhibitors and newspaper women (Mahar and Fuller-Seeley 2013; Abel 2016) and, as we have already seen in Chapter 1, women who promoted themselves as "producers." This reevaluation also returns us to other jobs in the office and on the set. Let us say, following Antonia Lant, that the "woman director" serves as a barometer of what was achievable (2006, 562). Immediately, this raises the question as to *when* to see the "female director" (among male directors) as an indicator that women could and did move up because she appears to be a phenomenon of the nascent studio before it was a system. First, however, we need to try to imagine how *before* that system there might have been no strict gender system—or *that* was all that there was. To put it another way, existing gender hierarchies were not so rigid because as yet there was nothing at stake in making moving pictures, but men were still the bosses. We know from Chapter 3 that Alice Guy most likely took time off from work to put on a play in front of a camera, which her boss would have considered nothing more than amateur theatricals with friends. Here, Alan Williams reminds us that Blaché writes in her memoirs that she had permission to do this because no one had any inkling of how "big" this business would eventually become (1992, 55). Fortuitously, Alice, even as the secretary, was also there at the first Lumière screenings in March, 1895, again, because no one imagined the significance of the occasion. Or, "they were there" at the beginning because no one knew for certain what it would become, although, as we have seen, Antonia Dickson, sister of the inventor, articulated dreams of worlds transformed. If in the very first years it was the secretary who slipped in early, later it was also the actress. And yet a word of warning here: In France as well as in the United States, it was still the woman who was the secretary. Thus, Alice could make her film because filmmaking was itself almost as inconsequential as the female secretary.

From this broader consideration of the "woman director," from the time when there was no such thing, really, a new hypothesis emerges. Let us call this the "they were there" thesis, one conjecture advanced to explain, in part, why more women in the United States were more highly placed in the earliest years than in the following decades. That hypothesis is this: women became directors as well as scenario writers because "they were there" on the set.[6] They were *already* on the set, ready and willing to step in to do anything that was required right from the start when there were no real jobs for them other than that of secretary and actress. However, when we ask further about who, other than the publicized few, were "there" and "which women did what," the project becomes more multidimensional and we begin to question the focus on female directors. From a contemporary point of view, of course, female directors—considered since the 1970s as exceptions to the workplace rule—have been important for the way in which they overturned historical assumptions about women in the 1910s and early 1920s as relatively powerless.[7] But now that we are there on the set, what does a closer look reveal? It reveals not only more women but, in the first decade, a corollary to the "they were there" thesis—relative job fluidity.

This closer look shows much more job "doubling up" and worker versatility than one might have assumed, given the interests of studio industry history in recent years. However, Terry Ramsaye, in his 1926 history, describes how the earliest actors were recruited to do anything and everything.[8] An earlier generation of film industry scholars, however, still did not carry this point forward. It would be Karen Mahar who recently reclaimed the theatrical term "doubling in brass," or doing more than one job, for her study of women in early Hollywood.[9] As relevant here is the evidence that early jobs were also hierarchically in flux. Ramsaye tells us that Florence Turner, who in 1910 became the Vitagraph Girl, was first paid $18 per week if she worked as wardrobe mistress and $5 a week if she acted (1986, 442–443). Vitagraph founder J. Stuart Blackton, in a memoir, recalls how many other kinds of work they relied on Florence Turner to do: "In addition to acting she was cashier, paid off the extras, served lunch to Albert and me (and tea at 4:30) superintended all make up and in a pinch helped back muslin on scenery flats."[10] Directors had not yet been promoted over writers as Gene Gauntier tells us in "Blazing the Trail," her memoir that begins around 1907 at the Kalem Company when, as she tells us, writers made more money than directors.[11] Epes W. Sargent observed how, at the Edison company, all of the players were writing scenarios (1914, 199). Even Mary Pickford, as an actress at the Biograph Company, tried writing. In 1910, she wrote from New York to the Selig Company: "Kindly return my script if you have no use for it."[12] Given these examples, the "they were there" thesis appears to support the idea that women were willing to do more kinds of work. While this variation on the job fluidity corollary requires further research, we can say that women exemplified early work "doubling." It was not just Mary Pickford. From the beginning, many actresses also wrote scenarios, suggesting the need for the term *actress-writer*.[13]

Further support for "they were there" and they did "any and every kind of work," comes from Lois Weber but with a twist in which business has priorities other than maintaining gender hierarchies. In 1928, she looked back in the first of a two-part *San Diego Evening Tribune* series where she recalls: "Personally, I grew up with the business when everybody was so busy learning their particular branch of a new industry that no one had time to notice whether or not a woman was gaining a foothold. Results at the box office were all that counted" (3).[14] But, Weber argues, *women can do it*, and did do it. While we might not want to argue for anything like gender-blindness or even a utopian space of gender equality, the idea that in the early years "no one had time to notice" whether or not it was a woman rising in the ranks because all that mattered was box office success suggests an uncomfortable irony. That is, that the commercial "success" of the new enterprise to which women workers had contributed attracted the attention of investors who pressed for the very stabilization that contributed to the later demise of women like Weber. Thus we could ask *when* it is that the gendered order of things is or is not at odds with box office "bottom line." Years after Weber's assertion that box office results were "all that counted," Mark Cooper argues in his study of Universal Women, the studio where women were more likely to direct, that gender discrimination does not completely explain why women were no longer promoted there after 1917 (2010, xxi).[15] Or, as I argued earlier, there is a danger that feminist analysis explains too little by explaining too much; that is, if gender discrimination is expected to account for everything that happened to women, we miss historically specific contradictions. Because, as in the case of Lois Weber, gender could be discounted, and yet gender counted—why other than because she was a woman would Weber have been made into such a cause célèbre?[16]

That because "they were there," got a "foot in the door," and volunteered to do whatever was needed, does not, however, constitute *the* narrative of "what happened to them." No, "they were there doing whatever job" is still a hypothesis, one that in my earlier account is supported by only a small cross-section of sources—two early motion picture film industry histories and one recent one, a city newspaper article, a trade press article, a published memoir, an oral history, and two primary documents deposited in archives—a letter and an unpublished memoir. Other sources could underwrite other hypotheses, for instance, that men dominated in numbers and influence, even from the start. Although the job fluidity hypothesis goes to an idea of possibilities for women, the apparently "ungendered" status of some (although not all) early moving picture work does not yet help us posit what factors contributed to the gradual "gendering" of jobs, the premise on which scholars have largely relied to explain what "happened" to women. So where do we supplement the job flexibility hypothesis with an analysis of the arbitrariness of power that translates into what today is understood to be gender bias in hiring and promotion? For this, we need interlocking hypotheses. For example, to the thesis that women were "there on the set," we would add that the work they did, although perhaps not *yet* dominated by one gender or the other, was still subject to conventional gender typage even as gender privilege was temporarily breaking down in the silent era just before corporatization. This premise is most dramatically exemplified by the work of writing and the organization of the scenario department.

HOW WOMEN WERE ADVANCED DOING "WOMEN'S WORK"

To the hypothesis that "they were there" with a "foot in the door" and even that gender "didn't always matter," as Weber's recollection suggests, let us then add the hypothesis that gender "mattered." Gender did and didn't matter. Karen Mahar might concur, warning as she does about what she calls the "empty field" approach in which we assume that in this new venture jobs were as yet "ungendered" (2006, 5). These companies were in the process of organization so that by 1912 the Vitagraph Company premises were cordoned into the all-male "projecting machine" shop and all-female "wardrobe department" and "joining room."[17]

We thus can't avoid the issue of what kind of work after the turn of the nineteenth century was considered to be "women's work." This question comes to a head when we single out the scenario department, which presents historians with a counterintuitive case: the idea that women were especially fitted to clerical work served first to advance women in the new industry and later to protect some jobs in the scenario department after 1925. In her recent study, Erin Hill explains how women were newly imagined as specially adapted to clerical work and, in the studio as well as on the set, were early associated with paperwork and typewriters.

Vitagraph Company advertisement, *Moving Picture World* (1912). Courtesy Bison Archives.
Hollywood, California.

Unidentified typist on set of *The Love Flower* (1920). Courtesy Museum of Modern Art. New York, New York.

In her analysis, this association produced a kind of cover for the women who continued to work at writing, research, and story-related tasks into the silent era when female directors and producers were phased out (2016, 20, 51). But the typewriter is both a clue and an issue. For established writers, there is a disassociation with the typewriter. Publicity stills of top writers often posed them with a pencil as Hope Loring is here, or lounging at home as Frances Marion, who was noted for writing in bed on yellow pads (Beauchamp 1997, 53, 79).

Hope Loring, screenwriter. Courtesy Margaret Herrick Library, Academy of Motion Picture Arts & Sciences. Beverly Hills, California.

Frances Marion, screenwriter. Private collection.

Anita Loos professed that she never did learn how to use a typewriter (Brownlow 1968, 313). For these women, there were stenographers employed to do their typing, although relative to the men on the set, the woman is always the one at the typewriter as Sarah Y. Mason is seen here.

This stenographer/writer division of labor does not, however, discount Wendy Holliday's powerful observation in her study of silent-era screenwriters. Paradoxically, she says, women "rose to power and prominence doing 'women's work'" (1995, 134). Still, however, we need to posit that the tiresome drudgery of scenario reading, editing, and sorting, along with writing, was from the beginning taken up largely by women, thus their doing that work reinforced that it was after all, "women's work." Holliday's principle is thus best supported by the number of female scenario editors, a top job

Sarah Y. Mason, screenwriter, on set of *Bound in Morocco* (1918). Courtesy Margaret Herrick Library, Academy of Motion Picture Arts & Sciences. Beverly Hills, California.

whose numbers are significant.[18] Scenario editor was a job that entailed not only reading piles of scripts but overseeing an entire staff of writers, part-time readers, and freelance writers. In a 1917 essay Louella Parsons, scenario editor at Chicago's Essanay Company, describes the tediousness of evaluating so many scenarios since they received about six hundred per week, the majority of which she found "absolutely worthless" (117). But lest we discount these submitted stories the way scenario editors, as well as the first historians, did, let us not forget that so many scenarios indicate yet another worker—the anonymous one who mailed in stories on the encouragement of fan magazines. This was the woman who succumbed to the dream of stardom accessible through writing and may even have enrolled in the popular photoplay correspondence schools that Anne Morey has studied (2003). Despite the volume of attempts, research reveals only one early scenario submitter other than Anita Loos who subsequently made a career of screenwriting—Agnes Christine Johnson. And we have this on the evidence of the thank-you letter she wrote in 1914 to Albert Smith for her first check from the Vitagraph Company, which she received when she was only sixteen.[19]

Today, we can support with more numbers Holliday's premise that women rose in a new workplace doing "women's work" in the U.S. silent era (1995, 134). A few such notable and prolific screenwriters as Bradley King and Virginia Van Upp began as clerical workers.[20] Then there is the case of June Mathis, who combined writing with executive producing, and those like Lois Weber, who began as actresses and would later write as well as direct and produce. But to add to scenario editors, the largest group specialized in writing, their numbers were based on counting film credits.[21] Period

Agnes Christine Johnston, screenwriter. Courtesy Margaret Herrick Library, Academy of Motion Picture Arts & Sciences. Beverly Hills, California.

sources fill out the profile of the working writer as female, but we can also argue that screenwriting was as often ambiguously gender-coded, especially if writing was seen as cerebral labor and top paid writers were distanced from writing machines. Yet, the very defense that female screenwriters themselves made of their special gifts puts writing back in the column of "women's work." Screenwriting called for "expertise" in emotionality. they claimed, and, further, Clara Beranger once asserted, women were just better at screenwriting than men (1918, 1128). Now, considering the range of labor from affective to menial associated with writing for the screen, let's rethink the implications of Anthony Slide's more recent gender breakdown. Slide's recount of silent-era feature screenwriting credits, between 1911 and 1920, lists women as 20 percent of screenwriters and, between 1921 and 1930, women as 25 percent, thus estimating men at 80 percent and 75 percent, respectively (2012a, 114).[22] We must then conclude from these percentages something rather remarkable—that Slide's majority of male scenario writers in the silent era were also doing "women's work."

While the contemporary insight that male writers for the silent screen were doing "women's work" will come to fruition in the following chapters, I want to put back in play Slide's challenge to the assertion that over 50 percent of silent era screenwriters were women. For it may be more productive to argue instead that the number of women who wrote scenarios was statistically incalculable. Such an approach annexes anonymous writers, some of whom may have functioned as Holliday's "professional amateurs" (1995, 104), others of whom may have been, as we say, "complete amateurs." And here is thus one way to challenge Slide's dismissal of the 50 percent estimate. If we multiply Louella Parsons's scenario submission estimate of six hundred submissions per week times fifty weeks, we have thirty thousand scenarios per year submitted to one of several notable companies operating that year (1917, 117). Granted, we have no way of knowing whether a greater number of women than men sent in scripts, but it seems likely that women, more homebound and jobless than men at the time, would have accounted for the large majority (Casella 2017). We could just as well argue in addition that many more women than men *aspired* to be screenwriters, an idea taken up in the next chapter.

Anonymity as a research topic has the virtue of being almost unresearchable.[23] By this I mean that since there is often "no knowing" who they were, empirical certainty is thwarted from the start, keeping questions open Further, the unknowability of the unnamed appeals to the skeptic in me who would challenge both the auteur director as single-handedly "making" the moving picture film and the human agent as "making" historical events. Although "bottom-up" anonymous history is now well established, humanist accounts of the past remain skewed toward *nameable* persons as historical agents. While the historical studies of the lives of the *unnameable*, like slave populations, is now highly valued, research on the anonymous first motion picture workers is not equally respected. This is despite the ease with which it may be established that in the United States before published credits around 1910, the overwhelming majority of creative workers—actors, writers, directors, editors, and producers—were effectively anonymous workers (Bowser 1990, 108; Gaines 2012a). What, then of physical plant workers, laboratory workers, technicians, carpenters, painters, and office workers? Historical spectators, equally if not even more anonymous, have received more attention than anonymous motion picture workers. In the absence of *nameable* workers or spectators, the historian must extrapolate from the one to the many others and such is the function here of Valeria Belletti, the historical spectator as well as the secretarial worker who harbored a secret dream of writing for the screen.

VALERIA BELLETTI: FROM EXECUTIVE SECRETARY TO TEMP WORKER

Valeria Belletti, the New Jersey daughter of Italian immigrants took her first important job in 1925 as executive secretary to Samuel Goldwyn. When head writer Francis Marion was making $10,000 per continuity that she wrote, Valeria was making $40 per week, a good salary for secretarial work (Beauchamp 2006, 17, 83). However, after a six-month vacation trip to Europe, Valeria returned to Los Angeles looking for less demanding work. Because Valeria's letters to her friend Irma Prina survive we know something of her own view of her rising and falling economic situation over a four-year period. Historian Cari Beauchamp extrapolates from those letters to place Valeria historically in proximate relation to the ferment in the industry and writes the following:

> Without necessarily realizing it, Valeria had witnessed a major shift in the business of filmmaking. During its first few decades, the doors were wide open to women and they flourished, not just as actresses, but as directors and writers. Lois Weber, Cleo Madison, Gene Gauntier, and dozens of other women were successful and prolific directors. Before 1925, almost half of all films were written by women.[24] Yet as banks and Wall Street began to invest and studios became major economic forces, the work became more respectable and better paid; men wanted the jobs. Some of the early pioneers, particularly writers such as Frances Marion, Anita Loos, and Jeanie Macpherson and the editors Margaret Booth, Blanche Sewell, and Anne Bauchens continued to be in demand, but by 1930, they were the exception and no longer the rule. (2006, 205–206)

Although the estimation that 50 percent of the Hollywood screenplays were written by women is challenged by Slide (2012a), as I just noted, this narrative of ascendancy and disappearance due to economic change has become the accepted explanation as to "what happened" to powerful women. Here, again, is the "over by 1925" paradigm referenced in Chapter 1. Useful for us, Beauchamp's decision to tell the shift from Valeria's point of view deftly moves us to the underside of the story and asks us to think how to explain why one woman and not another got ahead or why the huge discrepancy between Frances Marion's and Valeria's pay. As Beauchamp narrates Valeria's situation: "While she worked in Hollywood, Valeria had her share of role models and occasionally exhibited signs of real ambition. At various points she expressed hopes of becoming a script girl or a screenwriter. She was 'thrilled' when Frances Marion took her under her wing, but while Valeria took advantage of other opportunities when they presented themselves, perhaps she was too intimidated to follow through on Frances's offers" (2006, 206). What happened to Valeria? Beauchamp interprets the letters, a retrospective analysis that factors in Valeria's wish to be married and her decision to marry Tony in 1928 (196, 206–207).[25] Few would challenge the explanation that "perhaps she was too intimidated" with "intimidation" a code word for social class difference as a "felt difference" attributable to some subjects of historical study. Valeria writes to Irma about Frances Marion that "she has read so much that I feel positively stupid in her presence," and wonders why the screenwriter invites her to lunch (Beauhamp 2006, 18) Yet, this kind of foregone conclusion—that some will and some will not rise above their social station—is actually antithetical to the story of women in early Hollywood as historical "exceptions to the rule," the old rule of gender and social situation handicap. That has been the story of some few succeeding, a story that leaves out so many, as I began by noting. Yet, in other ways, as part of a new generation of working "girls" Valeria, too, is an exception. Just by working, she defies the restricted-options-for-women rule of an earlier historical time. But let us count the kinds of factors that first allowed Valeria to take these studio jobs and that later encouraged her to marry. Then we will stand back to assess the evidentiary terrain.

Let us pick up Valeria's work history from the DeMille payroll records. In addition to taking freelance typing work after her return from Italy in 1927, Valeria began work again in the Cecil B. DeMille Paramount unit. She writes to Irma in November, 1927, that she started there at $30 per week in the script and scenario department taking dictation from writers (2006, 166–167). The April 14, 1928, DeMille payroll, however, lists Valeria as making $5 per week as secretary to scenario writers, not $30 per week, a discrepancy to which we will return. The same week's payroll further lists the top paid writer as Jeanie Macpherson at $1,000 per week, just above Beulah Marie Flebbe, who was making $600.[26] Of course, class opportunity can explain such pay gaps, and we know that moving pictures attracted women from a range of backgrounds—from the smallest towns as well as from the metropolitan East Coast. Thus, we have an easy contrast between Ivy League–educated Beulah Marie Dix Flebbe, who graduated with honors from Radcliffe College (Holliday 2013a) and Valeria, child of Italian immigrants from West New York, New Jersey, who left high school early to take a secretarial job in Manhattan (Beauchamp 2006, 3–4).

With this background in mind, in the following I want to recruit Valeria's pay numbers and studio payroll information as they raise the question as to what this data can really "tell" us. In Chapter 1 I began to raise the question of "how to tell," especially given disillusionment in some circles with the narrated weaving of sources. There, I suggested how traditional narrative film industry history, biased toward success, needed a challenge, and even wondered if we should face that challenge with the refusal to tell

Beulah Marie Dix Flebbe, screenwriter, in her home office. Courtesy Billy Rose Theatre Division, New York Public Library. New York, New York.

Beulah Marie Dix Flebbe, screenwriter, with husband George at home. Courtesy Billy Rose Theatre Division, New York Public Library. New York, New York.

anything at all. With so much new evidence, however, we also need to consider innovative ways to configure that information; since it is increasingly accepted that there can be no *one* master account of events, we will still want to explore more approaches without succumbing to the false hope that yet another story will come closer. It would perhaps be better to embrace historical research as an interminable, never-ending project. For, as Vivian Sobchack says of the historian's exercise, it is "always writing itself over and writing over itself" anyway (2000, 313). Companion to frustrating interminability is the promising inexhaustibility of approaches, which justifies more experimentation with our findings. Thus it is that I have come to wonder about the difference between telling and counting as ways of grasping new knowledge. Whatever humanists think of data-driven research, one wouldn't want to deny that computation yields better "counts" and that counting boosts the authority of historiographic endeavors. Yet in the following I also reflect on some of the drawbacks of digital humanities approaches.[27] More precisely, the phenomenon alluded to, what Steve F. Anderson discusses as "database histories," are decidedly not narrative accounts but rather collections of "infinitely retrievable fragments" (2011, 122).

The title of two book chapters by German media theorist Wolfgang Ernst, "Telling versus Counting," sets up the dichotomy I want to mine for any utility that can be found, especially as it may point toward technological transformations of archival research practices. In his introduction to Ernst, Finnish scholar Jussi Parrika predicts that the field of media archaeology will move in what he calls a "technomathematical direction" (2013, 5), a move that represents more of a direct challenge to traditional narrative discourse than one might first guess. As our point of departure, let's take the summary of the years in question, cited earlier. Then to review, recall that earlier chapters described the traditional historian's training as in how to smooth out the remnants of the past deposited in archives as well as how to make inferences from pieces, extrapolating and generalizing from the part to the whole as these parts are used to make new story knowledge. This would be story knowledge like that of "what happened to women workers in the silent era," women who were employed at so many levels. So the parts from which the whole is generalized might be studio payrolls, here exemplified by two extant records, those of the DeMille unit at Paramount Pictures and those of Metro Pictures as it became Metro/Goldwyn/Mayer. What, however, if we were to ask our original question, but our answer was confined to payroll data? What would we have then? Or, as importantly, what would we *not* have?

What we *would* have if we had only payroll data are lists. These columns of names and numbers may be likened to those historiographic structures that Ernst calls to mind—the chronicle and the annals. From the listlike structure, chronicled knowledge, as it were, we analogize our own case—the studio payroll as list—from which we then segue to the online database drop-down menu list of silent-era film worker occupation terms. In the latter, we would then make a distinction between 1) data *inputted* by researchers, and 2) data *generated* by means of algorithmic tasks or operational sequences performed by the computer (Ernst 2013, 150). Then, as to the matter of what kind of data is called up by search functions, our example is "keyworded" lists of occupation terms and lists of names organized by occupation. In the drop-down menu, for example, scenario writer, accountant, director, wardrobe mistress, and camera operator, are some of the terms comprising the computer-generated occupations list.[28]

There will be upheavals, as Ernst sees it, in any shift from "telling to counting." In such a move we would relinquish two basics upon which the traditional historian is completely reliant: storytelling and the archive as storage, each of which we will deal with in turn. Significantly, it is in the list that Ernst thinks storytelling meets its most significant challenge. And why? Here, in the list, we find another order, an order other than a story order, and if in the digital realm, an *ordering* of data. In our case, the archival payroll, there is an order recognizable as a list of names, occupations, and pay rates. Ernst goes on to say that there are other ways in which such data ordering challenges narrative discourse. First, the mere existence of lists, in our case, of weekly pay rates and occupations, raises the possibility of order "without stories," or, we might say, here we have data *ordered* but not yet storied (2013, 150). This first challenge, I would argue, is quite familiar to many historians, especially if they admit to being initially stumped by raw data in their research. Think here of the first encounter with what, after Roland Barthes's critique (1986b, 132), we might call the "chastity" of data, configured in our case as the 1920s weekly studio payrolls—typed, carbon copied, and filed or placed in binders. The archival researcher may be surprised to find numbers that *do not* confirm his or her working hypotheses as well as numbers that *do* support premises about, for example, gender-typing and job classification. But what numbers do not give us are immediate answers to our most perplexing questions like, for instance, "What really happened to them?" How then does the researcher proceed?

Consider the standard procedure in which historical writers use narrative form to interpret numbers and categories that, technically, can only tell "what," how many, and how much. Numbers as numbers do not exactly "speak for themselves," and drawing inferences from them is not only part of *constitutive discovery* but also entails conjecture. What, for example, does the historian do with the following data: Metro Pictures payroll lists for July 2, 1921, under the job category "janitor" a Mrs. H. Peterson, the same term under which employees with six male names are listed.[29] Four years later, after the company is now Metro/Goldwyn/Mayer, the name Mrs. H. Peterson is now listed as "janitress" making $21/week and Lulu Evans, also listed as "janitress," is making $1 a week less.[30] The historian might conjecture that the $1 difference in pay is due to the seniority of Lulu's fellow worker who has been with the company at least four years. Further, the term "janitress" could be interpreted as signifying that these workers with female names are assigned work different from that of the more numerous "janitors" with male names. Beyond this gender interpretation, columns of names, job categories, compensation amounts in dollars listed week after week, could support hypotheses about changes in the gender breakdown of occupations as Metro Pictures expands to become Metro/Goldwyn Mayer. But each of these interpretive moves is a constituting claim placed on numbers, numbers which now stand for the question of gender, job, and pay rate over four years of company changes. However, as soon as we begin to ask these numbers to index what was happening to this motion picture company between 1921 and 1925, we are narrativizing the data. Then how to keep what is effectively *narrative interpretation* out of the study of payroll numbers? Even a phrase like "expands to become" implies a progress-over-time explanation of change. But suspicious as we may be of narrative accounts, focus on numbers does not necessarily guarantee more precise access to the historical "what" (leaving off the "happened" in "what happened" because of its narrative implications). So how do we methodologically escape narrativization?

To get outside narrativization, we might start to think of data as abstractly patterned. Today, as processed data, lists can be infinitely reconfigured and visualized to give graphic emphasis to a numerical ratio. Further, the interrogation of the digital archive raises the question as to the new "destination" of material, its placement in an access point where that data can be used repeatedly, exemplifying what Lev Manovich calls the "permanent extendability" of the digital (2013, 156). Another way of putting this would be to say that once digitized and uploaded, historical data may be programmatically reconstituted and lengthened again and again. And if it is all in the ordering, following Ernst, we need to ask how reordering and continual reprocessing impacts the old standard of "conclusive" results, which may give way to the infinity of configurations to which I referred. Beyond the relinquishment of an idea of "conclusive" and an adaptation to interminability, we should also be prepared to be surprised by keyword search results. To give one example, the somewhat larger number of women associated with the occupation "producer" as opposed to "director" in the U.S. case may surprise silent-era historians. For example, computation of the Women Film Pioneers' "occupations" data yields an unpredicted set of figures. To date, the count shows somewhat more women categorized as "producer" as compared to those who assumed a "director" function at least once in the silent era.[31] The point is that while the field may remain focused on a key paradigm—the female director— the data points us in another direction.

Abstract data patterning, lists, tabulation, and visualization, however, do not themselves yield a clue as to why Ernst should be so interested in orders other than narrative order. Acknowledging the function of his argument as a polemic, here is what Ernst thinks making stories out of data tends to do to that data. Story structure, he argues, has a tendency to "deflect attention from data." But, we ask, deflect attention from data to what? Ernst thinks that attention is drawn away from data and directed instead toward "structures of consciousness" (2013, 151). So does toward "consciousness" mean toward human actors, we want to know. Suddenly, it may look to the interpretative narrative historian, especially one writing a biographical study, as though his or her reliable methodology has been turned upside down and that the end goal is no longer the meaning of human historical events. The goal would not be inferences about life choices drawn from numbers like weekly pay but *the numbers themselves*. And what for Ernst is the problem with consciousness and its structuration? Let's now think the question of numbers versus consciousness relative to historian Cari Beauchamp's interpretation of Valeria Belletti's career choices, the explanation that she "occasionally showed signs of real ambition," but "*perhaps she was too intimidated to follow through on Frances's offers*" (2006, 206 [my emphasis]). Valeria wrote to Irma that she was interested in writing, that she loved to write, and that she was even encouraged by accomplished screenwriter Frances Marion. In a series of letters to Irma in 1925 while she is working as Samuel Goldwyn's executive secretary, Valeria details how she has become invested in the screenplay for *Stella Dallas* (1925) while Frances Marion is working on it; then Valeria describes the disappointment she shared with, as she refers to her, Miss Marion, after the screening of the first cut. Valeria writes to Irma that after taking notes in the dark projection room during the screening, she returns home to eat dinner alone and "felt so blue I cried until I came to my senses" (2006, 61, 73–74). She shares the screenwriter's disappointment with that first cut. Later, she works with

Frances Marion, director Henry King, and a title writer to retitle the film (80). But finally, Valeria married in 1928, the year for which we have the DeMille payroll records, and she continued to work in some capacity after she married Tony but eventually stopped in 1929 before she had her first child (2006. 207). Yes the phrase "*perhaps she was too intimidated* to follow through on Frances's offer," shifting our attention to "structures of consciousness," does divert us from payroll data. Consciousness or state of mind (including feelings of "intimidation") rushes in to take over all of the explanatory work. Let us say then, just for the sake of argument, that Valeria's "intimidation" too easily answers the question as to why she didn't follow through on her interest in screenwriting, and that, following Ernst, the story of her life can "deflect attention" from numbers. But why would we look at numbers at all when the historian's analysis of her fearful feelings of inadequacy relative to highly paid female screenwriters (for which, read class injury) offers such an apparently plausible explanation for Valeria's failure to try screenwriting as a career? Turning back to the DeMille payroll data from April 17, 1928, however, we find in the numbers as well as in the relation between numbers, a connection that, shall we say, is "telling."

Now one *could* say that the DeMille payroll as unnarrativized data pops out when we try to fit it into the existing Valeria story. We can't help but calculate the difference between Valeria's $40 a week, which she has told Irma she was paid first as Samuel Goldwyn's secretary in 1925, and the $5 she is listed as earning on the DeMille payroll the week of April 17, 1928, as part-time secretary employed after the making of *The Godless Girl* (1928), for which Jeanie Macpherson had the screenwriting credit.[32] To schematize this relation let's borrow a comparison used to represent contemporary economic inequality in the United States that figures executive pay as a multiple of workers' earnings. That is, let's represent Valeria's pay as a ratio.[33] In 1928, DeMille, the producer, was making five hundred times what Valeria Belletti, the temporary worker made, and star screenwriter Jeanie Macpherson making two hundred times Valeria's wages.[34] Given this dramatic pay differential, we begin to suspect that the $5 per week is telling in several ways, and that it even has the potential to trouble Beauchamp's overarching narrative. For the DeMille payroll data doesn't exactly support the historical narrative in which "the doors were wide open to women" (2006, 206). Rather, Valeria's pay differential between 1925 and 1928 as a microcosm of that data suggests that the "wide open" doors actually "opened and closed," then opened to some but not others, and then "opened and closed" again, a pattern describing freelance and part-time writers and actors as well as secretaries in the 1920s labor pool, as we will next see.

Beauchamp's historical placement of Valeria Belletti's letters further reminds us of the layoffs during the first six months of 1928 due to the technological transition to sound that year (2006, 193). But 1928 was not necessarily an exception. As significantly, layoffs were regular, whether because studios used them to avoid taxes some months of the year or some other reason.[35] Recall that Valeria wrote to Irma in November, 1927, that her work in the script and scenario department is "temporary work, so I may be laid off any time"(167). This is also the letter in which she claims to have started in the DeMille department at $30 per week—$10 less than she made as Goldwyn's secretary. Today, however, we have the payroll data from 1928 that lists Valeria Belletti as making only $5 per week.[36] Was a $35-per-week pay cut after her job change too much to admit to her friend?

The first casualties of employment irregularity were, of course, workers who were not on contract, certainly those innumerable freelance writers, but also temporary clerical workers, as Valeria's case tells us. When Richard Kozarski argues that the freelance market, while strong in 1915, effectively collapsed after World War I (1990, 105, 108), we may assume that he is referring to writers. But during and after the war, it was not only writers but actors who, as the old stock companies were broken up, became irregular workers, adding to more total job uncertainty. As was the case with the Vitagraph Company breakup in 1916, full-time jobs became part-time. As *Variety* reported, Vitagraph actors and writers were "dismissed" as part of the new "jobbing system," in which talent was hired only for each film as it went into production.[37] In his history of the Vitagraph Company, Anthony Slide tells us that some of those stock company members who were laid off were writer Leah Baird, comedienne Flora Finch, and Mr. and Mrs. Sidney Drew (1987, 58). All of these former Vitagraph employees went on to form their own companies, exemplifying Karen Mahar's second period of independent producing companies, 1916–1923 (2006, 166–170; Kozarski 1990, 69–77). Chapter 1 refers to the two companies Flora Finch started between 1916 and 1920. Leah Baird Productions, formed with her writer-producer husband Arthur F. Beck,

Leah Baird, screenwriter, Leah Baird Productions, 1921–1927. Courtesy Margaret Herrick Library, Academy of Motion Picture Arts & Sciences. Beverly Hills, California.

continued between 1921 and 1927 and Mr. and Mrs. Sidney Drew Comedies, 1917–1919 until Sidney's death. After her husband died, the former Lucille McVey continued alone as Mrs. Sidney Drew Comedies for a year and then directed *Cousin Kate* (1921) back at Vitagraph.[38] But in contrast with Mrs. Drew, countless others were unable to turn layoffs into a chance to start a company.

The previous paragraph begins with the question of irregular employment in general, but it then abandons the question of office workers in the middle and ends with the solution to unemployment available only to those writers and actors who might have had the capital, connections, and public recognition to start up again outside the studios. Here is a familiar labor history hierarchy further exemplified by industry historian Benjamin Hampton, who, for the year 1921, divides the labor force into "important people" and those who were innumerable, as in too many to count as well as too insignificant to be counted. These "important" employees were "stars, leading men and women, character actors, small-part players, directors, camera men, art directors, and others drawing high salaries" (ibid.). The unnameable others seem like hordes on the set of DeMille's *The Ten Commandments* (1923) following Hampton's characterization and estimate. If "important people" were the two to three thousand workers the studios employed in Los Angeles out of forty to fifty thousand people

Mr. and Mrs. Sidney Drew.
Courtesy Museum of Modern
Art. New York, New York.

total, these others were, as he puts it, an "indeterminate number of extras" in addition to those men and women who "received occasional employment" (1970, 295). A low estimate would be a ratio of one "important" employee to twenty "temporary" workers, although the terms "indeterminate" and "occasional" should further encourage our skepticism of Hampton's estimated numbers. While Hampton's numbers may be unreliable, his breakdown, however, reminds us that basic to studio corporatization was the organization of labor into pools. While we might want to stress the specter of unemployment for women, bunching together higher paid workers with those at the lower end in order to make a point about layoffs can also make the lower-end clerical pool to which Valeria Belletti belonged completely disappear.[39] To emphasize, it is the crucial missing category, that of the unemployed, that helps us to see the similarity between typist and writer, to return to my earlier point.

Also, as the reader can see here, I have not resisted the temptation to try to construct a fuller narrative explanation around Beauchamp's version of the heyday of women that while discernible in 1923 was, as I proposed in Chapter 1, "over by 1925." But I am not done yet with the payroll evidence of Valeria's $5 a week paycheck. We do not want to give short shrift to payroll data, the utility of which we have only just begun to explore. So what if we grant that numbers *are* telling in some ways and that there is rhetorical power as well as knowledge efficiency to be found in numbers? We assume that Ernst is interested in numbers containing significant information based on an order that is *not a story order*. Additionally, Ernst wants us to remember that "To tell as a transitive verb means 'to count things.'" In other words, more simply, "to tell is to count." It would then seem that if "to tell is to count" there could be both counting without telling *and* counting that is, after all, also "telling." But is this not a case of conceptually "having one's cake and eating it too"? Let's see. What Ernst finally wants us to consider is how, as he puts it, "telling gets liberated from the narrative grip" (2013, 149). One may yet be dubious of this critique of narrative on behalf of counting. Accustomed to the humanist disdain for quantifiability, we may be unprepared to consider what "liberation" might achieve for numbers suddenly freed of their service to narrative explanation. Or this may be less a case for setting numbers "free to be numbers" than an old argument for rationality over irrationality, certainty over uncertainty. Let's look more closely at what Ernst thinks can happen when data, whether as clusters of comparable units like rates of pay or chronological lists or some other ordering is narrativized. Ernst goes further. Data, put into narrative form becomes, horror of horrors, "subjected to romance" (ibid., 150–151). Romance? If we were to narrativize the telltale data number that is Valeria's weekly pay rate at the bottom of the scale in 1928, we might have much more than a political point about gender and social class inequality. In Ernst's terms, we would have a melodramatization of data. And that is so bad?

Since this characterization is admittedly an exaggeration of Ernst, let us allow him to be more precise as he casts what he calls "romance" in structural terms. To quote him, romanticization is "where causality and the foregrounding/backgrounding of events are expressed through . . narrative subordination" (ibid., 151). Clearly, we have narrative subordination in a hypothetical sentence such as the following: "Many women took advantage of the opportunity afforded them because they were there at the founding of a growth industry, although some, like secretary Valeria Belletti, finally failed to do so." Even if historian Beauchamp wants to frame her story from Valeria's point of view by saying that she "had witnessed a major shift in the business of filmmaking" (2006, 205), Goldwyn's executive secretary who ended up a temporary worker is subordinated in our "although some" clause. Undoubtedly, publication of Valeria's letters gives significance to her life and her working conditions, but in the end she is a mere speck in the larger story that we call "modern history" and is no more than a subplot in "women's film history." As for causality, one can commend Beauchamp for placing Valeria's work in the context of economic developments, in which layoffs as well as losses of creative opportunity are consequences of the investment of major banks in the U.S. industry.[40] Valeria, however, also represents an approach that we have not as yet taken to the "what happened to them" problem. She opens up the sociopsychological territory of women's historical choices that, in the end, may always elude *both* the empiricist's quantification and the narrative historian's interpretation. Valeria's letters to Irma can be read as indicating that she chose to become a wife, but, before she was married, she also chose to buy a bungalow in Hollywood with the money that she had saved (2006, 182). Here, historian Beauchamp represents the viewpoint of the contemporary professional woman who laments the limited options of marriage as opposed to career in those times.[41] In Beauchamp's analysis of Valeria's situation, "She was also obviously aware of the tenuous nature of her position at the studio and that made the idea of marriage all the more attractive." Now while the vicissitudes of Valeria's work, narrated in her letters and confirmed by the payroll numbers, can be seen to support the historian's interpretation, here is where I want to step back from these methodologies. Even with access to valuable primary sources, the historian's interpretation still creates an exquisite illusion of totality out of the nearly nothing that is the archived residue of a life. Without a doubt, the payroll numbers are "telling." Yet while there can be attempts to "tell" there is finally "no telling" why Valeria left her stenographer job when she did.

Thus it is that the issue of Valeria's life options and choices introduces one more aspect of enumeration, one hovering in the background of historiographic projects. If we grant the theoretical importance of the "overdetermination" of historical events as a check on the tendency to write single-causality accounts, we may still be counting choices that are also "no choice." "Overdetermination," that neo-Marxist borrowing from Freud in which the constitution of consciousness is extrapolated to problems of historical analysis, insists on multiple causes as a means off-putting in check the tendency to find "one" determinant, whether individual choice or singular event (Althusser 1970, 87–128). But the ways in which "overdetermination" is also no solution is as important as its methodological challenge. Not only is there the danger that two few causal factors are considered, but there is the problem of their total number. In the end, there is no end to them. Linda Orr thus reflects on the same problem with which Marx, as well as historian of the French Revolution, Jules Michelet, wrestled: "Anyone or everyone can direct history in terms of his or her own desire. But remember that some other, unknown power also controls that desire, both its expression and its results. On the one hand, history is determined by us, and on the other, history is overdetermined and thus undeterminable" (1990, 153). Conceptual limitations aside, what of the practical limitations of taking multiple determination seriously? Consider what form an attempt at an *enumeration* of historical determinations of a single event might look like if not an incredibly long list, only beginning with the organization of labor in the workplace according to the needs of capital, expanding to enumerate the ways in which women were necessary as well as expendable as workers in the industrialization of photoplay making. Left off such a list, however, would be women's life choices and their internalization of events as triumphs or setbacks.

THE ARCHIVE: FROM STORAGE TO TRANSMISSION

It may be clear from my comparison between "counting" and "telling" as a means to historical knowledge that I am still weighing both methodological approaches as solutions to the problem of what to say "happened" to the women in the silent film industry. Yet the verdict is still out on "digital histories" as the critique of traditional history, and we have only just begun to tap the creative uses of data, including the myriad possibilities of programmed visualization. The data list may represent a challenge to or a check on the narrative means of making sense of historical fragments, which, historians may concur, is never an easy task (Lovink 2013, 196). Then, as soon as we raise the question of fragments, we have raised the problem of forms, formats, order, and storage spaces. Adjacent to the problem of the list is then the issue of the archivization of data or of whatever it is that is kept, a "what" that determines *how* that "what" goes in, gets processed, and is taken out.

While Ernst's more controversial challenge is to storytelling, he also stirs up thought about the storage function of the archive, given the gigantic capacities of the internet. In an interview conducted in 2003, he describes the ways in which he sees the archive as transformed, especially in a transition from inaccessible to instantly available. In contrast with the old archive as boxed up, vaulted, and hidden away, he wants to consider the archival function of digitized records online as "no longer forgotten," no longer unaccessed, and no longer the "final destination of the document"(Lovink/Ernst 2013, 193). And his prediction? The earlier notion of the archive will "dissolve into electronic circuits and data flow." The "dissolution" of that musty space, as Ernst envisions, signals the end of the archival function as defined by storage conditions (ibid., 202). The internet as space for the relay of data represents the great shift from finite storage to infinite transmission. But what replaces that space is enough unlike what it has been for centuries that the continued use of the term "archive" can seem absurd.

Ernst, following Foucault, wants to see the archive as a "discontinuity."[42] And yet, the archive as a "discontinuity" and therefore the antithesis of "narrative closure" may now be too predictable a point.[43] More problematic, even Ernst's insight about archival "discontinuity" is lost if we don't know whether by "archive" is meant the traditional "archive" or the online "archive," the difference between the two starkly contrasted in the theorization of the digital archival.[44] What media archaeology that follows Ernst and Foucault most usefully takes up is the logic of informatics and the hardware that supports the multimedia retainer, the *arché* of source codes focused on storage and rereading functions (Lovink 2013, 196). That is, this archaeology aims to study what are basically algorithmic tasks or computer operations (Ernst 2013, 150).

Here is where I begin to think about the disjuncture between computer operations, the material now archived on and offline by the Women Film Pioneers Project, and the historical women that it is meant to document.[45] The project began in 1993 with lists of women's names to which were added xeroxes of articles from *Moving Picture World*, death certificates, and glossy photographic stills, which have morphed into digital scans and pdf files, databased and indexed to other databases. Refiled and re-ordered countless times over more than twenty years, the archive, if one could call it that, is in constant disorder and need of reordering. Further, after sifting through paper files or exploring its online links, no one could argue that this depository bears very much relation to what "happened" to these women although that is what we pretend. Reassuring then for us, Ernst insists that there is "no place more deconstructive than archives," and explains that this is because there is no "coherent" relation *among* the documents there; neither do they neatly add up. Instead, he sees them as to-be-ordered in that, as he says, they "wait to be reconfigured, again and again" (Lovink 2013, 194). Yet archives don't exactly deconstruct themselves. In his chapter on digital humanities in his book *Data Love*, Roberto Simanowski has this to say about the future of uncertainty: "It remains to be seen to what extent the other privileged forms of presentation in digital media—visualizations, animations, interactions—can be employed not only for the sake of illustration and simplification but so as to create ambiguity and deconstruction" (2016, 86). Finally, if "deconstructive," the archive is both completely metaphorical as Derrida and Foucault have maintained and at the same time a "very real, very material network of power over memory" (Lovink 2013, 195).[46] Thinking of power, here is where we are vigilant about data, first raw and now processed, because power has already entered the project at so many points. But power? What academic assumptions, after all, structure the metadata requisite to every keyworded knowledge search?

Of course there is the power to think of minor historical figures as "not having been there." They just "weren't there," we say. Foucaultian approaches, however, will always be interested in what is "sayable and thinkable," Ernst urges (Lovink 2013, 195). Certainly any archive that stores and now itself transmits as-yet-unnarrativized information can promote the study of previously "disqualified knowledges" as challenge to the powerfully established (Foucault 1980, 82–83). And what has been more powerfully set in stone than the idea that "there were no women" in the silent-era U.S. film industries. Clearly, information about the range of occupations held by women at the high as well as at the low end in the early film industries was "disqualified" by the first historians. But my concern now is with the way in which research on entrepreneurial women may continue to "disqualify" the work of the less "qualified." How, for instance, can I get into the drop-down menu the information that "janitress" was a studio occupation in 1928 if the search menu is algorithmically programmed to constitute the occupations list only from the terms "recognized" in the narrativized text? Given the way that key-words are programmed on the Women Film Pioneers site, the term "janitress" cannot be made to show up in the drop-down menu of silent-era motion picture occupations. This is unless, of course, Metro/Goldwyn/Mayer "janitresses" Mrs. H. Peterson and Lulu Evans are made part of the story "told" in the online text.

8

THE WORLD EXPORT OF
"THE VOICE OF THE HOME"

I n 1925, former Metro Pictures executive producer June Mathis credited women with
the worldwide commercial success of American films:

> Women in Europe are more or less kept in the background; the man is the mouth-
> piece of the family; at home and abroad. While here, a woman pokes her nose into
> nearly everything, and makes herself heard. So even when the man who does not, or
> will not acknowledge that there is such a thing as a woman's viewpoint that is pos-
> sibly commercial, it's bound to creep in, anyway, through the voice of the home; and
> perhaps it is this same thing—this same magic something—that has made American
> films supreme in the world's market.[1]

Motion picture studio historians concur that between 1914 and 1917 the United States
achieved world market dominance as a consequence of World War I.[2] Alice Guy Blaché,
the French immigrant, observed that the World War I decimation of the European
industry gave the "advantage" to the Americans (Slide 1996b, 69). Assessing the moment, she goes on to describe the story industry from the vantage of her Solax studio in
New Jersey: "This was the epoch of the melodrama" (70). Outside of Mathis, however,
no other source from the period has suggested that women played any special part in
this economic coup.[3] As we have seen, documents from the 1910s and 1920s point to
women's contributions at all levels. The case for women as influential has now been
made, and yet that case stops short of Mathis's unprecedented assertion. Look again
at the enormity of her claim that the woman's point of view produced the superiority
of American over European films. She answers the charge that the women's point of

view didn't sell by contending the opposite—that this viewpoint produced Hollywood's commercial supremacy. By implication, it was via women that "the voice of the home" slipped into American films and it was this "voice," or what she calls this "magic some-thing," that insured popularity with audiences worldwide.

Granted, Hollywood's hallmark hyperbole is at work in this solicited essay, "The Feminine Mind in Picture Making." Hyperbole aside, however, the heresy of such a claim in the context of U.S. studio history demands that we attend to it.[4] So let us say that we take June Mathis at her word. Then what do we do? We might first be tempted to think that evidence in support of this statement might be found. Such a strategy assumes that empirical evidence has the power to change the going narrative. But even in academic circles it is never a matter of proving one narrative to be "true" and another "false." Rather, it is a matter of where new findings line up on the battlefield of compet-ing paradigms. So rather than thinking as the empirical historian who looks to find supporting evidence, let's take the long view: *What is the point of historical research?* Thus far, we have registered skepticism and challenged the idea that past events can be restored to the present. We have interrogated the term *history* and asked about the location of the present day historian relative to the events of the past. Where does this leave the vital work of historical research? Even while promoting June Mathis's state-ment as evidence to support a new paradigm, our position remains a claim. To make things more difficult for ourselves, let's just admit that it is not possible to empirically confirm or disprove our "voice of the home" thesis. But, once more, why, given the difficulties, does the historian look for countervailing or supporting evidence in the first place?

WHAT IS THE POINT OF HISTORICAL RESEARCH?

As Joan W. Scott summarizes Foucauldian "history-as-critique," it entails an analysis whose political goal is to expose the "that-which-is" by finding that what is established as "that which" has, in fact, "not always been" (2007, 28; 2009, 46). Actually, it may be that "history-as-critique" (2007, 28) is implicit in most academic work claiming the importance of historical specificity. After all, historical research by definition finds that every phenomenon was once something other than what it now appears to be. But we would not want to leave it at that. We would also want to consider what research to undertake given that some commitments to "that-which-is" are more entrenched than others. So there will be the question as to exactly what established knowledge we seek to confront. On this question, Scott herself says that Foucault represents a more fron-tal assault on knowledge than Foucauldians realize and even thinks that his challenge has yet to be taken up (2009, 46). But how assaultive do we dare to be? Foucault says of his "archaeology" that it would remove all stable reference points from the self and effectively "uproot its traditional foundations and relentlessly disrupt its pretended continuity" (2012, 88). Put to the political test, the goal of a historiography identifying as a Foucauldian "archaeology" is then to effect an epistemological *disruption* of the stability of the historical "going story." Here, the philosopher offers an incisive metaphor when he says that knowledge "is not made for understanding; it is made for cutting" (ibid.). Acknowledging the special challenge for Foucauldians given the complete absence of methodological proscription in his work, we may wonder what kind of research project is called for if the aim is to "cut up" the continuous and to disturb assumptions about how things "were" and "are." A rule of thumb, then, might be to study whatever produces the most turmoil.[5] Or, as Sande Cohen puts it, "What dangers can historiography elicit?" (2006, 254).

Really dangerous historiography might be the connection that Jacquelyn Dowd Hall made between rape and racial lynching that challenged 1980s feminism to reconceptualize the definition of violence against black as well as white women (1983, 331). What else is on this scale of conceptual disruption that can threaten epistemological comfort levels? Perhaps the evidence of the atrocities committed in King Leopold's nineteenth-century private war in the African Congo, in recent years exposed in narrative history texts but still unwelcome in the thought of many Belgians.[6] Here are dramatic cases of how historical research confronts the "that-which-is" of racial and national selfhood to unsettling ends. Yet, how many findings are potentially earth-shattering and who would want to give the impression that empirical discoveries have equally disturbing effects? Since these cases are weighted toward evidentiary proof, we wonder if there are other means of challenging the "that-which-is."

Consider then the case of feminist historiography where we know how much trouble research *categories* can stir up.[7] Let us not forget the capacity of "gender" as historical category to cause serious epistemological distress. No, Joan Scott insists, feminist history has not been about the documentation of women's lives and experiences. If there was a reason for researching the past, it was not to gather more evidence that would prove gender inequality or women's resilience; rather, she says, the goal was to "destabilize the present," to take up the challenge of making "the unthinkable thought." Her example, right under our noses, is the way that "gender," formerly "unthinkable" and once a historiographic blind spot, has been invited into thought; in recent decades *gender*, the category, has become an accepted part of historiographic methodology (2006, 393). "Gender," no longer unthinkable, is now everywhere thought.[8]

Today, after research that began in the Academy of Motion Picture Arts and Sciences Library forty years ago, Shelley Stamp confirms the early findings of Anthony Side and Sharon Smith and challenges the field with her conclusion that in the silent-era, U.S. motion picture culture was "shaped primarily by women." She describes how "women sat at its heart" at multiple levels and found ways to "insert themselves."[9] Stamp might have been describing June Mathis who was well positioned to speak with authority not only about women's contributions but about the female audiences to whom she gave the "gift" of Rudolph Valentino.[10] Mathis, who began screenwriting in 1915, was, by 1918, head writer at Metro Pictures.[11] Having risen through the studio system as a writer and scenario editor, she ended her career as a highly paid producer.[12] Although

June Mathis, screenwriter/producer. Courtesy Billy Rose Theatre Division, New York Public Library. New York, New York.

by June of 1925 Mathis had been fired at Metro-Goldwyn-Mayer by Louis B. Mayer who took over her *Ben-Hur* project, she was still working in the industry.[13] While Mathis's credentials are not at issue nor is her vantage in dispute, her statement newly brought to light will not necessarily overturn the established U.S. studio history narrative. Not alone, that is. It doesn't work that way. In considering the potential of June Mathis's "voice of the home" export thesis to "destabilize" a field, more important than calculating the number of creative workers would be assessing the historical juncture at which her thesis is brought forward. And why? A new paradigm at such odds with

June Mathis, scenario editor, Metro Pictures group picture, Cahuenga Blvd. Studio, Hollywood, c. 1922. Courtesy Margaret Herrick Library, Academy of Motion Pictures Arts & Sciences. Beverly Hills, California.

reigning paradigms will invariably meet with indifference or resistance. But then recall how "gender," formerly "unthinkable," is now an accepted analytical category (Scott 2006, 293). Since in the field of film and media studies, "gender" is already a powerful theoretical engine as well as research category, one might imagine the ease of "thinkability" encouraging serious consideration of Mathis's assertion. And yet, "thinkability" in and of itself may be insufficient. The "voice of the home" thesis threatens to disrupt too much institutionalized knowledge.

It would be easier to discount the "voice of the home" export thesis than to exhaustively follow through on its implications where the issues it raises are in play. For the thesis impinges upon so many areas—film industry studies, including the politics of global film exhibition, film form, or style history and genre theory as well as feminist gender theory. One imagines from the very number of approaches how much wreckage could be produced by this idea. However, let us not forget the widening feminist media circles where Mathis is already a flash point rather than an assault, and where the export of the "voice of the home" supplements ongoing research and emerging theoretical positions. Here the "voice of the home" thesis stands as a *harbinger* of a field-transforming theory.

While June Mathis's overblown rhetoric may encourage some to dismiss her statement, the very audacity of it commands our attention. Written by a powerful industry insider with an estimated one hundred and fourteen feature film writing credits, her statement stands as a direct challenge to the 1970s feminist "no women" hypothesis, which we have already put in check.[14] Now, nearing the end of this book, the reader can see how current research points to the number as well as the influence of women and therefore how the "no women" presumption does not bear out in the U.S. case. Here then is our theoretical point of disruption: women's new aspirations in the decades after the turn of the nineteenth century. In the silent era, as I have been arguing, *they were there* on the set. But such unprecedented "chances" that women claimed by virtue of their being there can't account for the way some "leaped at" these chances. Or, "chances" alone doesn't explain enough. If new jobs for women comprise one-half of the equation, the other half is how women aspired to these positions, investing their dearest hopes in the opportunities that fell to them in the first two decades. The theoretical goal, then, is to place women solidly at the historical advent of cinema as key indicators of a larger change. So, in this chapter, I want to go somewhat further to propose that some women caught the contagious expectations of the times even though theirs was a qualified *"expectation" against all expectation*, given that there were certainly no expectations that women would write, produce, or direct motion picture films.

COMPETING PARADIGMS

What are the paradigms in competition here? What have we been saying was exported? Studio historians and historians of style have, since the 1970s, held that the industry exported classical Hollywood narrative film. The seminal case for this is Kristin Thompson's study of the U.S. film export business in which she says that the rise of Hollywood cinema to world market dominance during WWI "has meant that for an astonishingly long period—from the mid-teens to the present, with no end in sight—a large number of films screened in most countries have been of one type: the classical Hollywood narrative film in continuity style" (1985, ix).[15] In this paradigm what was exported was a style, variously referenced later as "continuity style" and, more prominently, "classicism."[16] Now, add to Thompson's account the 1970s feminist film theory paradigm—the classical narrative as a male-gendered form—and we link the economic to a "gendered" subjectivity. Over the past decades, however, several new developments have challenged the classical paradigm, which held sway for so long, and the studio history and feminist theory that converged there took different directions.[17] Our question brings "gender" and "industry" back together again for purposes of historical rereading.

Let us say, for the sake of argument, that what was exported *was* the "voice of the home" and that it was the contribution of women that gave shape to Hollywood genre films. What was inconceivable by 1970s Anglo-American feminist film theorists now becomes conceivable.[18] Clearly, the "voice of the home" is the polar opposite of the 1970s position that Hollywood narrative structure negated women on screen and in the audience, a negation built into the editing style.[19] That this negation was then exported to the world seems not to have been a major issue in the 1970s. In June Mathis's essay, we find the starkest antithesis of the feminist film theory that proposed the looking structure of classical narrative patriarchal cinema as gendered "male" as opposed to "female." Now consider the stakes involved. If we were to follow Mathis we would then, reversing course, have to say that as a field *we were wrong*. How wrong were we? Given the huge theoretical investment in feminist film theory's voyeuristic "male gaze," we would have to say that we were very wrong.[20] We would then have to say that, in the silent era, Hollywood exported *not* an exclusively male but a female-gendered narrative structure as well as stories that women wrote to draw in male—and especially female—audiences.[21] June Mathis divulges the best kept secret of Hollywood success, one hushed up by the women who worked there.[22]

But we are going too fast. The "about face" in which women become a silent-era powerhouse, however startling to anyone encountering it for the first time, needs qualification.[23] For the shifting within the field that has prepared the theoretical ground for a reversal has been incremental and we would credit breakthroughs along the way, which, only when taken together, effect damage to reigning paradigms. Consider then these recent developments: the "cinema of attractions" found to be prefatory to narrative cinema, silent cinema research on female spectatorship, the rediscovery of American serial queens, and the concept of a "first global vernacular," which addresses global export-import.[24] Finally, there is feminist film melodrama theory, which now challenges the dominance of narrative understood as classical. For us, this last development will be the most pertinent for I take the "voice of the home" to be the resonance of melodrama as transgeneric mode, which means that even male genres—the western, the action thriller, and the gangster film—are structural melodramas organized around the woman's viewpoint.[25] This is why, as we will see, it would be a mistake to claim melodrama as a "woman's genre," most importantly because of the legacy of melodrama that predates motion pictures.[26]

The melodrama challenge to the dominance of classical Hollywood cinema has been slower to gain adherents and although it still has a distance to go, the implications are the farthest reaching.[27] That challenge, coming from feminist film melodrama theory where the project of unseating "classical narrative" is ongoing, reveals new theoretical options.[28] Both Linda Williams and Christine Gledhill counter Hollywood's "classicism" as the common denominator with the idea that melodrama is more foundational. Williams, displacing classicism, argues that melodrama, not classical narrative, is the "dominant form" (2001, 23; 2012, 528).[29] This is not the first time that this idea has been proposed, however. Suggesting the glacial pace at which paradigms move, it has been over thirty years since Michael Walker wrote that "Melodrama is arguably the most important generic root of the American cinema" (1982, 2). A decade later, E. Ann Kaplan asked that we consider the possibility that all Hollywood genres are melodrama.[30] We already know from Chapter 5 about melodrama as rhetorical power, about its obsession with innocence and its special cinematic devices that engage the viewer's senses on behalf of goodness. With its partiality to victims, melodrama takes the woman's sympathetic "point of view." Any case for seeing the irresistible "voice of the home" as the resonance of melodrama, however, needs to penetrate a density at once economic, aesthetic, and affective.

WOMEN AS GENRE: AFFECTIVE LABOR AND EMOTIONAL MERCHANDISE

What, then, constitutes this thicket between the affective labor of so many female screenwriters and producers and the elusive "something" that worked so magically— that reached the heart through the "voice" or the *melos*, an aesthetic on the analogy with music?[31] June Mathis insists on a connection between this resonating "something" and the "felt" attributes of the home. Here is the home by which we mean that space of belonging but also of detachment, "to which" one returns or "from which" one may be expelled. Silent-era female writers, aligning themselves with domestic affairs, when asked about women's special contributions responded with the refrain of "emotional expertise." Writer Clara Beranger, for one, is quoted as saying, "The heart throb, the human interest note, child life, domestic scenes and even the eternal triangle is more ably handled by women than men because of the thorough understanding our sex has of these matters" (1918, 1128). Such conventionalized gender associations are there as early as Alice Guy Blaché; recall that, in 1914, she claimed to be "an authority on emotions" (1996, 140). One might see from these formulations that "home" equated with the special sensibility of the "woman's viewpoint." It would be where "feeling" was what mattered most and would tip the scales for the unfortunate as well as magically reverse the order of things.

But a word of caution. Just as we aren't classifying melodrama as a "woman's genre" we wouldn't want such comments to return us to the idea of a "female aesthetic" that would essentialize the "something" that had slipped into these exported films.[32] The search for a relation between a stylistic and a gendered expressivity long ago hit a wall.[33] So now that writers such as Beranger and Mathis have been identified, let us say that we want to avoid the variant of the "female aesthetic" that I call *gender intentionality*. To come up with *gender intent*, I have modified the authorial intentionality that takes individuals to be agents whose personal input can be detected in the "work."[34] If *intentionality* has historically referred to authorial intent, here intent is put back on critics. By *gender intentionality*, I mean the critic's intention to find gender as exclusively explanatory. To put this another way: while we can say that it *does* matter who produced the work we wouldn't advocate tracing creative decisions back to gender alone—or to persons for that matter.[35] There is anther way through these critical trouble spots and that is to flesh out Richard Dyer's return to Raymond Williams's "structures of feeling" (1977, 132). Here we find an embrace of the socially shared as the basis of genre. Dyer sees all of us as connected to such "affective frameworks past and present, that we inherit and pass on" (2007, 180). Whether these silent-era female writers were aware of it or not, they were sharing conventions of theatrical and literary melodrama as well as "affective frameworks" at large in the culture, *a culture that includes men.*

Now the theoretical move that circumvents the cul-de-sac of intent and essentialism and takes us through the density of affective structures has been there all along, and that is this: *gender is a genre.* Certainly by now there should be no resistance to the interchangeability of our two critical categories, "women," and "genre," since the grasp of "women" as generic is one of the great successes of feminist film and literary theory. Now we ask "What is the genius of the artist compared with the genius of genre?" (Gaines 2012b, 17–18). At its most elegant, the case for the generic is laid out in Laura Berlant's study of women's sentimental literary fiction that names femininity as a "genre" because of its "deep affinities to the genres associated with femininity," however tautological this sounds (2008, ix). Berlant's starting point in genre is "affective expectation" (ibid., 3–4), a "feeling structure" that binds audiences to popular genres. Thus, genre theory, with its foundation in conventionality, familiarity, and formula is deployed to explain that other category, the one that feminism has fought so hard to define as categorical. Berlant describes the comfort that women come to expect from a genrelike structure: "To call an identity like a sexual identity a genre is to think about it as something repeated, detailed, and stretched while retaining its intelligibility, its capacity to remain readable or audible across the field of all its variations. For femininity to be a genre like an aesthetic one means that it is a structure of conventional expectations that people rely on to provide certain kinds of affective intensities and

Dorothy Farnum, screenwriter. Courtesy Margaret Herrick Library, Academy of Motion Picture Arts & Sciences. Beverly Hills, California.

assurances" (ibid.). What, after all, is more conventionalized than the social expectations of women—not only within but among cultures? In custom and tradition, like gender, like genre.

In addition, we have in June Mathis's "voice-of-the-home"–infused product something with the appealing exchange value of "love commodities" (ibid., 3), a concept helping us to cement the connection between industry and affect. Of course that "something" was "magically" elusive because as a "felt something" it was "just felt." Even the writing process was considered a "feeling process" and an experiential commonality between female audience and female writer was everywhere assumed.[36] One of the more suggestive descriptions of affect thus crafted is attributed to screenwriter Dorothy Farnum: "You must think with your heart and feel with your head. When I write my scenes I try hard to progress not from one thought to another, but from one feeling to another. For the majority of people want to have their hearts excited and their minds let alone when they come into the world of low lights and soft music of a motion-picture theater" (1926, C29). That same year, Terry Ramsaye confirmed in his history of film that what was for sale was the emotional commodity: "The only actual merchandise is the emotional experience wrapped up and delivered to the occupants of the seats. Because of the tenuous and intangible character of the goods no saturation point is in sight for the industry" (1986, 832). If "emotional experience" is the "merchandise," we

CHAPTER 8

need look no further for support for Mathis's analysis than here where it is married to Ramsaye's economic forecast.

GENDER ASSIGNMENT: WHY NOT MEN?

Slipped into Mathis's statement is also acknowledgment of the intransigence of the obstacles women faced, seen, for instance, in her reference to the "man who does not, or will not acknowledge that there is such a thing as a woman's viewpoint that is possibly commercial" (1925, 115). Mathis's observation that men couldn't see the commercial value of women's contribution is a rare expression of frustration. In print, these women seldom identified men as a problem and, although Mathis had just been fired by Louis B. Mayer, she is not accusative.[37] This is not to say that there is no evidence of antagonism between men and women or between actress-producers and the moguls who helped to underwrite companies that bore the actresses' names. Clara Kimball Young's legal battles with Lewis J. Selznick and Anita Stewart's with Louis B. Mayer were only the most public.[38] Battles with moguls aside, we would be missing the forest of industry men for the trees of some unusual women if we follow too strictly Slide's assertion that "in the silent era women might be said to have virtually controlled the industry"(1977, 9). While he is counting powerful female actresses and writers, Slide's statement does not take into account the "family mode of production," and it risks discounting male-female writing and producing teams like Josephine Lovett and John S. Robertson, Sarah Y. Mason and Victor Heerman.[39] Here, however, I want to use the documentary evidence of so many women from the first two decades differently. That evidence I take to be the source of fresh theoretical ideas that help to circumvent biographical *gender intentionality*. There are too many women to discount and as yet not sufficient evidence of what they contributed to make the case that they were "in control" of the industry—except, perhaps, in this secret way.

If we take "women" to be a "genre" or categorical "fiction," as Ann Snitow has suggested (1996, 517), then "women" is neither biologically nor sociologically guaranteed. On the contrary, with "women" as with "genre," we are dealing with cultural connotation, narrative situation, and iconic figuration, that is, sets of conventions *into which men too can step*. This would even be why, if creative personnel as well as critics, students, and audiences, female or male, "make and remake" popular genre films (Gledhill 2000, 241), they also make and remake "women," *that other genre*. While real historical women may have laid claim to June Mathis's "voice of the home," so irrepressible that "it's bound to creep in" (1925, 115), male directors, actors, and screenwriters would also have helped to develop that "voice," or stepped into the conventions that then became automatic. And thus, carrying over from Chapter 7, if we take Wendy Holliday's insight to its logical conclusion, all writers, male and female, as well as all actors, can be seen as doing "women's work" (1995, 134; Gaines 2016, 275–276). Here, then, is a somewhat disturbing idea whose time is yet to come. To say that so many of the early cinema

Josephine Lovett, screenwriter. Courtesy Margaret Herrick
Library, Academy of Motion Picture Arts & Sciences.
Beverly Hills, California.

pioneers, male as well as female, were doing "women's work" is to stir up historiographic trouble.

If men, too, then why "women" at all? Thus far, I have been patient with the claims made by silent-era writers and directors that women had the gender edge, June Mathis's statement notwithstanding. However, it would be a mistake to think that the moral positions or the sensibilities espoused in popular motion pictures "belong" exclusively to women and never to men. Christine Gledhill, while confirming that melodrama is "deeply caught up in the gendering of western popular culture," warns against any simple equation between melodrama and either male or female gender—at any historical point (2000, 226). There is a better course—to find values located in conventions rather than inscribed in persons gendered one way or another, opening the door to seeing "female" values as historically *assigned* to women rather than to men. Since, in another ordering of world cultures, these values might well have been awarded to men, we cannot help but envision their gender *reassignment*.[40] This is especially because *someone* needs to take on the emotional labor of "feeling more," and we're right to keep asking why women are always tasked with it. German Marxist feminist Frigga Haug's analysis of women's daydreams, not so surprisingly, finds them embracing virtues *as-*

Production still, *The Single Standard* (MGM, 1929), Josephine Lovett, screenwriter, from a story by Adela Rogers St. Johns. Courtesy Margaret Herrick Library, Academy of Motion Picture Arts & Sciences. Beverly Hills, California.

signed to them by tradition. But Haug goes further to argue that concerns associated with women turn out to be the social salvation of the culture. As she suggests, the vows "to protect, conserve, love, and rescue life" are commitments to what the society most needs (1992, 70).[41] So to enlarge the "woman's viewpoint" in an effort to explain its apparent success, let's start by taking the view from the home, the vantage of the heart, as nothing more nor less than the "legitimation" of feelings (Gledhill 1987, 34). Now we might just glimpse the irresistibility of moving pictures when we think what it is that "feelings," thus magnified and substantiated, achieve for the "world export."

One gender or another must supply the affective requisites associated with the heart, and if not women, who? Then think what women achieve for us all by assuming the work of amelioration and harmonization, those tasks taken up by women in this period, just after World War I.[42] But we can't stop there because those women themselves didn't. Beyond this ameliorative work, there would be the transformative apocalyptic millennialism as articulated in the conclusion to Marguerite Bertsch's *How to Write for Moving Pictures*. How much more could be attributed to the new moving image machine than the production of miracles envisioned as the utopianism of a better world?: "For centuries we have dreamed of a millennium. Great minds have planned and tried to put into practice their schemes for a Utopia, a land of love and harmony" (1917, 272)[43] Moving pictures were expected to achieve all of this?

We are now in a better position to argue that "woman," functioning as "genre" was crucial to the makeup of this emotional merchandise. But the "woman's viewpoint" in and of itself does not seem adequate to the claim to "something" so very "magical," so powerful and so spreadable over so much of the modern world. To what can we attribute this "something or other" that was thought to have been so unnameable yet so formulaically reproducible? June Mathis is claiming an American monopoly on this "something," but in the decade leading up to her statement, German observers of silent cinema began to predict the astonishing powers of the technologically new, even in "newness" itself. Because part of the "magic" of the "something" was the technological miraculousness of its delivery.

THE "MAGIC SOMETHING" AND THE "WORLD-IMPROVING DREAM"

We might not yet agree on what to call whatever it was that Hollywood exported when in 1917 it took over the world market, whether melodrama, or classical Hollywood narrative style, or the "first global vernacular," in Miriam Hansen's terms (2000a, 12).[44] However, we may agree to see an overlap between key theories of history and German theories of mass culture.[45] This overlap we will need as we ground women's aspirations in a theory of modern times attached to theories of the popular, the utopian, and the economic. June Mathis's capitalist bravado trumpets works of mass culture succeeding in their appeal but ventures no explanation for this other than "appealingness." For help with a theory of the "something," I turn to German Marxist Ernst Bloch, notable for having suggested that mass culture's appeal was in the hope it held out to the world's wishing audiences.[46] Like Mathis's "magic something," Bloch's "hope" is a thesis under review here, repositioned in light of women's work, but also marking the historical connection between silent cinema and theories of mass culture and modernity.[47] Recall from Chapter 2 Reinhart Koselleck's conviction that the modern notion of history posits the future vis-à-vis the past as relationally "relocated" (2004, 4), entailing an "inversion in the horizon of expectations" (12). Here, we align his "modern time" that privileges the future with an orientation to what has been exhaustively discussed as "the utopian." This realignment I undertake on the authority of Fredric Jameson who urges that "What we really need is a wholesale displacement of the thematics of modernity by the desire called Utopia" (2002, 215). In a moment, we will see what justifies such a "displacement" as it helps our "voice" or "magic something" to echo beyond June Mathis to wider political and philosophical debates. Here is where we want to attach a theory of history to the hermeneutics of how "modernity" or "utopia" as historical orientation finds expression in cultural forms.[48]

Ernst Bloch's Frankfurt School–aligned philosophy of hope adds to the final parts of our theoretical equation such concepts as "world-improving dreams" (1995, 91) as well as the orientation toward "wanting to have better" (99) but also such special "expectant emotions" as are found in the wish for change (74).[49] As importantly, Bloch theorizes the "doubleness" in the works of mass culture—the genuine utopian and its deceptive opposite, both given popular expression on the theory that without the "utopian" mass culture could never appeal (Jameson 1971, 144).[50] And what do we have in June Mathis's assessment of the U.S. film industry post–World War I but a public admission of the doubleness of the Hollywood product? Hers is an expression of the capitalist optimism of market supremacy, that brashness tempered with a secret ingredient slipped in undetected, noisy cheer at odds with a quietly genuine "something." Neither can one miss in Mathis the obtuseness of an American capitalist optimism that cannot see beyond its nose to the worlds into which it exported emotional merchandise. Vitagraph company cofounder Stuart Blackton, himself British, noted this proclivity when he defined the American film by its "optimism and happiness" (1926, 3). But *two* kinds of optimism? Two kinds of hope? First, the flashy optimism around the capitalist success that apportioned good to some but not others, an irresistible optimism that, as Bloch admitted, sometimes worked. Second, the "authentic" optimism Bloch sees in a yearning for "better" and the hope for "the good" that capitalism promised but finally failed to deliver. On the face of it, Mathis's is as unmitigated an expression of capitalist optimism as we will find in this moment in which women too were cultural colonizers. Here, they enthusiastically join the competition for global market dominance—although disputing the prize by claiming success as their own—going behind the backs of the men who were, by 1925, running the industry after having eased women out. Mathis disputed the prize, but in their lifetimes, none of these women were credited with this economic achievement. Yet what do we see here, saving the day, but this resilient, undeterred mix of optimisms, the maintenance of which, I would contend following Berlant, was part of women's job in the early industry (2008, 174). After all, they were working in the dream factory, and that work entailed fitting the happiest end to every narrative whether it fit or not. This is why such structural doubleness stands revealed in Mathis as the subterfuge that has gone on within the factory.

And what would their optimism have to do with utopianism? Let's not forget to ask why the future always wins out in Frankfurt School theory. It is a uniquely political utopianism, Bloch's signature "anticipatory consciousness," understood as the turning toward the possible in the "not-yet" (1995, 113). Significantly, he insists that the anticipatory, the looking ahead and expecting better, is to be found in ordinary lives and given expression in the products of mass culture, although in these products hopes are raised and that is the end of that. But we also need Bloch for something else. With all of the interest in wonders and technological marvels, amid classifications of emotions and explorations of the expansive terrain of the wish, one finds embedded in Bloch an eccentric but decidedly Marxist theory of history. In Bloch, we find a theory of *historical time* in his insistence on an overriding orientation toward "betterment" (1995, 144). Bloch's forward-looking is dialectically indicated in the opposite backwardness, the negative in the positive, but it can yet, hope beyond hope, win out over the opposition to expectation. So let us ask why we need Bloch's mélange of insights drawn from the lives of the lowly attuned to the special lure of mass culture products and elaborated as a philosophy of wishing for the future. Answer: Why other than because, in Marx, the "whole of history" *includes* the future.

Now let's bring Bloch together with Koselleck, the latter adding to the former a reinforcement of the future orientation in "new times," helping us to see in the silent cinema "dream-factory" (1995, 407, 410) a profound expression of expectations attached to the future. Here, Koselleck contributes to Bloch more historical precision—insurance, if you will—that "hope" does not devolve into an ahistorical human tendency. Rather, "hope" belongs to one "new time" felt to be ahead of an older time.[51] For Bloch's theory of the anticipatory describes a time that saw itself as technologically modern and increasingly turned toward a future to come, that key stage in the expansion of industrial capitalism. In other words, Koselleck, from a post–World War II vantage, tightens up Bloch whose project began at the end of World War I.[52] Koselleck brings out the theory of history that lurks in Bloch but also helps to situate the market triumph of June Mathis's dream factory product.[53]

As important for us is also Ernst Bloch's convergence with German feminist Heide Schlüpmann around the figure of Asta Nielsen. Both Bloch, beginning to write his "Spirit of Utopia" in 1918 (1995, 157), and Schlüpmann, looking back at the German silent film industry 1908–1914, draw inspiration from Nielsen whose eloquence Bloch saw in the "flicker of the eyelid" (1995, 405) and whose power Schlüpmann sees in the actress's command of so many aspects of production. To be specific, Nielsen's 1911 contract with the Projektions AG Union (PAGU) gave her, in Schlüpmann's terms, "unprecedented" independence as an actress as well as a share of the profits. The subjects of these new feature films were selected by Nielsen and director Urban Gad, who made thirty-four films together under these contractual conditions (2012, 44–47). Asta Nielsen thus becomes a vision of what Schlüpmann thinks *might have been* possible and what in silent-era Europe was still possible, but only before World War I. This, too, is Bloch's theme: "A *good* dream-factory, a camera of dreams which are critically inspiring, overhauling according to a humanistic plan, would have had, had and undoubtedly has other possibilities—and this within reality itself" (Bloch 1995, 410). But, more dialectically, the "dream-factory" full of possibilities tends also to be "more of a dizzy swindle" (407). The theorist of the future must find that better time augured in yearning for change, and it is to the wishful Bloch attributes "world-improving" dreams (91). Our problem remains: how to find the "world-improving" in that "magic something," a something so empty that it could stand for absolutely anything or, just as possibly, nothing at all.

"Utopia" is the final word in Schlüpmann's conclusion to the new translation of her German silent cinema book (2010, 220). But if Bloch's is a theory of *what can be*, Schlüpmann's is a theory of *what could have been*, where she postulates a possibility that she finds in this short window before the outbreak of World War I after which German cinema along with larger emancipatory movements were stopped by the war (218). Schlüpmann's theory equates women with the utopian because these films

Asta Nielsen, actress/producer. Courtesy Deutsche Kinemathek.
Berlin, Germany.

offer the successful "illusion" that woman is the "center of cinema" (67). She posits
that women *could have been* involved at the production end and even that a female
narrative perspective, glimpsed at this moment, might have been possible (94–95).
What Schlüpmann thinks had been facilitated was a "conjunction of actresses and
female audiences," a coming together in which the moving picture process takes place
(218–219).[54] What I earlier called a *feminist utopianist* hypothesis seems embodied in
Asta Nielsen, who is central in the historical story Schlüpmann wants to tell. As she
explains, the actress-producer was even able to negotiate a space in the Wilhelminian
film industry where she lost her work in 1914, refused to "surrender" after industry
changes, and continued under the new strictures (219).[55] Beyond Nielsen, this theory
of "woman-centeredness" might extend as well to Fern Andra, the American who
worked in Germany as an actress-producer, coincident with Nielsen, and who, in 1917,
started the Fern-Andra Company. In Germany, when men, recruited for the war, left

Asta Nielsen, actress/producer. Courtesy Filmarchiv Austria. Vienna, Austria.

the industry, women stepped in—a pattern we find throughout Europe.[56] So here is the theoretical-historical problem: if one woman, why not so many others?

Frankfurt School–derived *feminist utopianism* provides a kind of complete theory that envelops screenwriters, producers, directors, and actresses as well as spectators, a theory that also scoops up all straggling cinematic signifiers, from music to mise-en-scène to movement. Exemplifying this, Schlüpmann aligns the woman's narrative viewpoint with the highest expectations for the new industry that, in its first decade, held out so much possibility. That is, it held out possibili*ties*—plural—sometimes sensually "felt" and sometimes materialized as occupations for some although not for all.[57] Here, in the case of women, "possibilities" and aspirations linked to theories of history offer refinements to those theories. If the goal is to use a theory of history to locate a social phenomenon in time, we can also posit a theory of women's emancipatory expectations that met the technologically new.[58] What more must that theory contain? A theory of women and technological expectation in that newly modern moment would also contain the frustration of those newer hopes—the desperation as well as the aspiration, the setback as well as the triumph. For these women, that theory would also show what they were up against or what we are calling *"expectation" despite expectations*. For no one really expected that women could do what they had never done before. At that time, any expectation that they would help to found an industry would have been dismissed as nothing short of utopian, that is, "unrealizable," the other meaning of the word.

CHAPTER 8

Fern Andra, actress/producer. Courtesy Deutsche Kinemathek. Berlin, Germany.

NEW TIMES, NEW TECHNOLOGIES, "NEW WOMEN"

These were "new times," indicative of which is the sense of an anticipated future time as never before. The connection between women, modernity, and technology is now established in film and media theory, but the goal here, as stated earlier, is to ground gender in the span of technological history, using women's insertion at inception into the United States but also the European motion picture industry as a gauge. Let us state it outright. *There is no advent of motion pictures without women at the start*, and by this we mean women working *not only as actresses*. Too much emphasis on actresses ties women more tightly to social history and excludes them from the theory and history of technology. Of women filmmakers in early Hollywood, Karen Mahar says emphatically, "All could be considered New Women by virtue of their employment in the most modern of industries" (2006, 8). The approach to the "New Woman" at the turn of the nineteenth century, however, has been social history of custom and dress, manners and morals, which, not insignificantly, finds young women in public places and frames them more as consumers than as cultural producers.[59] The publicness of her body now well established, the "New Woman" needs to be revisited relative to her ideological function.[60] First, following Ben Singer, we want see new female mobility as *"required"* by capitalism's modern moment (2001, 262). Then we can ask what feminism in recent years has required of her. Finally, the "New Woman" is, in addition to a highly debated phenomenon, the historical writer's trope, as Hayden White would argue, his way of discouraging us from lining up empirical examples to fit a metaphor.[61] It remains for us to enlarge the theoretical space for women so that they help to conjoin the technological with the utopian, now standing in, following Jameson, for "modernity" (2002, 215). Already in Frankfurt School theory, utopian anticipation associated with freedom movements has been attached to the introduction of moving picture technology (Bloch 1995, 146). With this foundation, the theory gets a boost from women (who had more to gain from social change) as indicators of technological hope. Now figuring more women in the moving picture industry in the first two decades, we can argue that there is neither technology without utopianism nor utopianism without women.

Some will still call for empirical checks. So accustomed are we to looking for evidence of women's achievements that our first inclination is to seek to find those rare cases of historical women who ran the equipment that they were not expected to master. While there are those examples referenced later, they are too statistically insignificant to support empirical conclusiveness and, therefore, as I am suggesting, we take them to be *harbingers* of a feminism yet to come, a theory-in-progress. In the first decades of the last century, women and cameras, newly visible, stirred debate about women's capabilities. Public attention was focused on them as aberrations, but more importantly,

"'Cleo Madison's second to none!'
an assistant cameraman whispered to me. 'You ought to see 'em hop when they do what she don't want 'em to! There ain't a director on the lot that's got the flow of language or can exhibit the temperament she can when she gets good an' peeved.'" From the story by William M. Henry, in this issue.

Cleo Madison, director/screenwriter. *Photoplay* 1916.

as we will see, "women with cameras" was subject to expiration like the technologically new itself. For in the silent era, women were popularly aligned *not* with innovation but with novelty. Consider here the double novelty of women plus machines, exemplified by the significant number of directors photographed *next to* the 35mm motion picture camera as opposed to *behind* it.[62] Most were not themselves camera operators and the very few who *were* operators were explained by the gender extremes of the day.[63] In articles featuring these unusual women, the new and startling aspect of the camera rubs off on the woman herself. The female camera operator is a novelty because she is more interested in mechanical problems than in makeup and, for the times, even dressed oddly in puttees and clashing stripes and checks.[64] In the end, however, fan magazines vaunted women's technological capabilities only to lightheartedly dismiss them.[65]

Antonia Lant frames the issue of women's technological abilities, assumed to be innate, as a "debate" as to whether or not women were capable of undertaking the job of motion picture director (2006, 562). Although at the time one finds both sides articulated, today we may be surprised to find on the negative side one female director, Ida May Park, saying that women were *not* capable of managing the work entailed: "Is

Margery Ordway, camera-woman. *Photoplay* 1916.

directing a man's work?—I should say it is!" (as quoted in Denton 1918, 50).[66] On the positive side, director-producer Alice Guy Blaché speaks on behalf of women's new technological capabilities: "There is nothing connected with the staging of a motion picture that a woman cannot do as easily as a man, and there is no reason why she cannot completely master every technicality of the art." She goes on to mention how she acquired an education in photography from work in the Gaumont Company laboratory that continued, as she says, in "my own laboratory" in the Solax Studios (1914, 195). Emerging from research on these newly "modern" and technologically adept women are also examples of those who owned or managed motion picture theaters (Mahar and Fuller-Seely 2013). We can add to the list of unexpected occupations the Australian projectionist Mrs. Señora Spencer (Verhoeven 2013) and the Hungarian-Italian film distributor Frieda Kluge (Dall'Asta 2010a, 311–313). Then there are the female scientists who experimented with motion picture technologies, schooled in biology like Henderina Scott (Bethel 2013) and electrical engineering like Maude Adams (Jackson 2017). But to remind ourselves—the rationale for looking back to these exceptions is what? Of course they offer models to emulate and examples to disprove naysayers, to return us to the question of Antonia Dickson's genius. Yet all that we can confidently say of these women is that they are now part of our theoretical calculations. We can never know how many women wished to work so we seek to encompass them via their aspirations without, however, discounting their setbacks. In support of the *"expectation" despite expectations* thesis, what we can propose are the theoretical components of an implicit utopianism supporting the feeling that new worlds had "opened up" to women—for a time. Because the door "opened" only to close.[67]

Maude Adams, 1922. Courtesy Museum of Innovation and Science. Schenectady, New York.

A theory of women in the first decades of cinema needs to explain why there were so many more who aspired to be "producers" than we originally thought there had been, but also why the boom was so soon over. Looking back a century, what do we see of that utopianism linked to technological "wonders"? For one thing, we see how soon the surge is over. There is always a catch, given the expiration date on technological momentum. Tom Gunning confirms hopes pinned to a future "radically transformed by the implications of the device or practice," but, as he sees it, this is a utopianism concentrated just at the advent of motion pictures. There is a short window, he thinks, because the technology will soon devolve into second nature after having failed to deliver on its promise (2003, 56). And this devolution will impact some who rode in with it at its inception, newly positioned to benefit. For emerging groups, hopes for change are pinned more tightly to the technologically new, whether women or the proletarian class as in the revolutionary Soviet case. Considering Gunning on second nature we might say then that the technologically new, while promising much, guarantees no *place* in the imagined future. Thus to see the silent era as a novelty period prefacing corporate control is to predict that women with cameras along with powerful female producers would be "in" and then "out" again. One could even predict that women working visibly in the silent U.S. industry would disappear by 1925.

But this idea that women stepped into new opportunities and rose to the technological challenge, this *feminist utopianist* idea, where is it coming from and what groups—industrial or academic—does it serve? As I have been arguing, if a paradigm is at stake, what will ultimately matter is theoretical provocation. But I would add to that. A feminist paradigm must have the capacity to do double duty for us—to acknowledge the contradictions in the image of the early-twentieth-century working woman *as well as* the contradictions within feminist theory itself, especially if we need that theory to address the problem of conceptualizing two or more historical moments at once. And what has been more contradictory than feminism and film? This is where we celebrate women's creative triumphs and subversive potential *at the same time* recognizing oppression as evidenced in both screen representations and employment discrimination (Schlüpmann 1994, 83).[68]

We can just as well say about the career experiences of silent-era female producers what Ben Singer says about serial queen fictions: they evidenced a contradictory "empowerment and imperilment" (2001, 222).[69] That the energetic optimism of the serial queens, always under assault, might itself require special "protection" (Berlant 2008, 174) as well as constant renewal, occurs to us when we reencounter Ernst Bloch, who seems too sanguine about the political potential to be found—even just a crumb of it, really—in the anticipatory. To base a theory of change on wishfulness feels too fragile. Yet Bloch's "wish for a better world" has an uncanny likeness to the powerful fragility of what Lauren Berlant identifies in the "sentimental politics" (20–22) of nineteenth-century female novelists, exemplified by Harriet Beecher Stowe, author of *Uncle Tom's Cabin*. This is a world view too historically influential to dismiss.[70] Although on first encounter with nineteenth-century "sentimentalism" it seems counterintuitive that there could be so much strength in virtues and hopes; yet one need only recall the Christian reversal in which the weak inherit by virtue of their virtue.[71] For the dubious, Frigga Haug's use of Bloch's theory of hope comes with the caveat that while wishes may indicate a yearning for the better future, whatever desires embraced are surely products of social and historical circumstances, and if "wishes" are "mere wishes" they can be easily trivialized.[72]

Such reservations aside, the Frankfurt School validity of "the wish" has for decades justified serious consideration of ordinary lives. Here, we are extending this analysis to studying historical women in the capacity of purchasing their own homes, starting film companies, as well as thrilling to the serial queen's leap from bridges onto trains as Helen Holmes does in Episode 13 of *The Escape on the Fast Freight* (1915). The hopeful worldview is what allows us to put women on top, albeit precariously and temporarily.[73] So let us not abandon this dimension of Frankfurt School theory so soon. Recall that in the feminist theory of daydream-as-resistance where power relations are "gender relations," even erotic relations can place the powerless over the powerful (Haug 1992, 66). Still, in Frigga Haug's formulation, we see feminism's old sticking point—women are after all women. She sees "a strange contradiction: in all this reversal, this taking of power, this imagining of themselves as independent, free, important, secure and capable of managing the lives of others, women still pursue the fulfillment of traditional female values . . . they succeed in being nothing but women: they still rescue, protect, guard, conserve, love, devote, and abandon themselves . . ." (69). And because the yardstick of achievement used is male success, in order to be really excellent as women they need to be not just the women that they succeed in being; they need to be women who are *like men*. For in the silent-era industries, to be an exceptional woman was to *be like a man*, no questions asked. Or, as Shelley Stamp says unflinchingly of Lois Weber relative to directors who aimed for motion picture quality: "She was one of those men" (2015, 52). Here, the contradiction of feminism's double commitment meets the contradictory lived conditions that the historian strives to pinpoint. For Foucault, this is the key to historical specificity, given that, as he says: "Contradiction . . . functions throughout discourse, as the principle of its historicity" (1972, 151).

In a roundabout way, we are back to the question posed at the opening of this chapter: What is the point of historical research? If Foucauldian "history-as-critique" (Scott 2007, 38) is the political analysis of the ways in which societies are at odds with themselves, we can't overlook the inconsistency of the message to women at that juncture. The forces of change and the recalcitrance of tradition were on a collision course. So this means that we can't finally declare these women to be this or that, only one way such that aspirations cancel resignation or that futility wins over resilience. Further, since what happened to this woman or that woman *is* and *is not* what happened to all women, our paradox of sameness and difference rules against easy conclusion. How then do we theorize the juggling of accommodation and aspiration—a mechanism we find schematized not only in accounts of their lives but in the fictions that they produced and distributed?

Frame enlargements, Helen Holmes, actress/producer, *Conductor's Courtship* (Kalem, US, 1914). Private collection.

THE "VOICE OF THE HOME" THESIS
AND THE HAPPY END

Without question we use the same hermeneutic approach to the events of their lives as we do to their fictional works. Additionally, their lives have now been fictioned in ways that we most need these exceptions to be. Following Ben Singer's analysis of the intersection of the lives of young female audiences and the serial queen sensational melodramas featuring girls with their jobs on the line, we can propose a triangular theory of text, spectator, and creative producer (2001, Ch. 8). Here, the burden on the "voice of the home" as paradigm is to accommodate the aspirations of the producers who are viewers and viewers who are also producers of meaning. Most daunting of all, however, such a paradigm needs to stretch to encompass the rest of the world where imperialist overreach *projects* a commonality between peoples, or June Mathis' fantasy of one world enthralled by the "voice of the home." Again, what *was* the "something" that worked so magically in these exports?

Influential has been Miriam Hansen's argument that American cinema as an immigrant cinema, having passed the test of cultural amalgamation, had been readied for a diverse world audience.[74] As theorized, her concept of the "first world vernacular" has made room for local variation in 1930s China (2000a, 12) as well as Japan (2012). But the surprise case of U.S. export success, of which June Mathis was likely unaware, was the Marxist-Leninist revolutionary appropriation of serial queen fast-paced editing for montage aesthetics. We already know that the Soviets were taken with the "energy" of the sensational melodrama that Sergei Eisenstein adapted as Soviet Socialist montage-and-conflict in the 1920s.[75] But we are only now reconnecting serials starring Pearl White, Kathlyn Williams, and Cleo Madison with their Soviet admirers.[76] Granting the export of Hansen's mass culture "sensorium," we need to now ask about the scripting of what was "moving" in the picture.[77]

In this chapter, I have argued that the "voice of the home" is shorthand for melodrama, a cross-generic mode (Gledhill 2000, 227) and have suggested that we take this "voice" to be a code word for the resonance of certain conventions. Undoubtedly, emotions are structured and "voiced." Narrative features include opposing sides starkly drawn, feelings expressed on screen as outbursts or stimulated in the audience by cutting, and the swelling, hyperbolic enlargement of everything. "Voice" then reminds us that the "something" was conveyed in the performing as much as in the writing and further that, although largely wordless, this cinema was never silent as sound historians have long insisted.[78] Not only was there live musical accompaniment, but visual enrichments stood in for the sound not supplied by the image itself. So "voice" is a resonant expressivity reliant on, but not limited to, acoustic signs as carriers. From Chapter 5, also recall melodrama as offering dramatic *schemes* for showing up the difficulties that result from trying to live within deeply divided societies. Melodrama stages the intolerable pain of parental abandonment, the secrecy of illegitimacy, and the hurt of class hierarchy but also anxious hopes, as we will see in a moment. There would need to be the adjudication of wrongs, the amelioration of hurt, and finally the reward of suffering, tables turned, and victory awarded to the deserving (Berlant 2008, 34–35).

Thomas Slater's new analysis of screenplays written and cowritten by June Mathis follows Christine Gledhill's focus on the "innocent victim," the power of whose virtue is proven by the villain's assault against him or her. On the basis of finding so many passive but strong victims in screenplays credited to Mathis, Slater situates the screenwriter within the tradition of melodrama where women exert tremendous moral power (2002, 209–210). Here he relies on Gledhill's explanation that because "feeling" was inconsistent with the "ideology of masculinity," the "realm of 'feeling'" was assigned to women" (1987, 34, as cited in Slater, 210). Of even more significance, Slater's new reading of Mathis's treatment of Rudolph Valentino, informed by melodrama theory, contrasts with earlier readings of the matinee idol's appeal based on feminist gaze theory (Studlar 1996, 173) (Hansen 1991, 271–273).[79] Arguing that gaze theory ignores Mathis's contribution (2010, 114), Slater opens the door to rethinking Valentino in melodrama's terms, locating him as maleness reconceived as the consequence of World War I's "desecration of masculinity" (2010, 100.) His analysis of *The Four Horsemen of the Apocalypse* (Metro Pictures, 1919), Mathis's adaptation from the novel by Vicente Blasco Ibañez argues that the Valentino playboy character learns from the sacrifice of Marguerite (Alice Terry), his lover who devotes herself to her blinded husband after his war injury. Where Slater diverges most significantly from others, however, is in his conclusion that the heroic battlefront death of Julio Desnoyers (Rudolph Valentino) is a rescue from the excesses of patriarchy (2010, 112, 114). Valentino here, and even more strikingly in *Blood and Sand* (1922), pronounces the "failure of patriarchy" (2010, 102). Thus to the 1990s feminist claim to Valentino, followed by the queer claim (Anderson 2011, Ch. 3), is added the claim on behalf of the "sentimental politics" (Berlant 2008, 20–22) of motion picture film melodrama.[80] Or, June Mathis transferred the "woman's viewpoint" to Valentino to produce his "heartthrob" masculinity. *The Four Horsemen*, as Hilary Hallett now sees it in the light of that historical emergence of female sexuality, is a "passionate melodrama" (2018).

June Mathis, screenwriter/executive producer, *The Four Horsemen of the Apocalypse* (Metro Pictures Corp., 1921). Private collection.

There may be many positions and ideals aligned with the "woman's viewpoint," the vantage of the sympathetic heartfelt. But we are looking for the broadest affective orientations, for Mathis's "magic something" conventionalized across male as well as female genres and so irresistibly strong as to be a commercial "draw." This may be where the "home" space is abandoned and returned to, that return coincident with the *restoration of something feeling like "happiness."* Happiness as a goal, as we will see, requires some such familiar "leave-return" structure for its definition. Buoyed by an ideology of success and its rewards, the structure may even deliver happiness, nothing more than a feeling, really. But in the American case, happiness is much more now—is even an "achievement." From the instrumentalization of happiness, then, follows the question of goals and guarantees. But remember that we are talking about scripting. "Happiness" as strived for and *to be achieved* by characters suggests that it could be carefully crafted. So, going hand in hand with the ideological harmonization and resolution as women's values is the skill set that silent-era U.S. writers and directors developed in an attempt to deliver preferred feelings. In this respect, let's then ask: How does the industry worker achieve the "happy" in the practice of writing the "happy ending"? First, consider how difficult that work might have been, thinking of those many female scenario writers who wrestled with the narrative logic that might lead to outcomes that could not be ideologically tolerated at the time—the monster unleashed, the criminal unrepentant, the addict unreformed. These writers internalized a code, an amalgam of social custom and genre convention, a code we're calling "like woman, like genre." They were working in the dream factory, and more often than not, that work entailed fitting the "happy end" to every narrative whether the end fit so well or not, my earlier point to which I will return. Although I argue that structural doubleness stands revealed in Mathis as the subterfuge that went on within the factory, it is not that women were consciously planting oppositional time bombs in plots, the viewpoint having "crept in," as it were. Also, they themselves were torn, pulled two ways by tradition and liberation. Why wouldn't they assert their "authority on emotions" (Blaché 1996, 140) while deferring to men in everything else? And so the structure of the scenario, like the days of their lives, accommodated inconsistent positions. These writers, situated at the conjuncture of life and industry, doing "women's work," wrestled with story lines striving to placate gender strife.

To remind ourselves, melodrama is structurally tasked with the distribution of justice and the adjudication of warring positions. It is not as though an ideological message is just delivered, but rather that positions, impersonated as they are in the drama, step forward and become embroiled. Such dramatic situations for melodrama, arising out of perplexing social conundra, are played over and over until they sound like so many broken records. "Over and over," however, is not negative but rather explains why we can say with confidence that silent-era female writers drew so regularly from the well of Victorian theatrical and literary melodrama. Borrowing was the rule.[81] Parts of "The Colleen Bawn" by Irish playwright Dion Boucicault were recycled.[82] Victorian

Frame enlargement, Alla Nazimova in *Camille* (1921).
Courtesy Margaret Herrick Library, Academy of Motion
Picture Arts & Sciences. Beverly Hills, California.

novelist Mrs, Henry Wood's *East Lynne* (1861) was staged for decades.[83] Theater classic "Camille" by French playwright Alexander Dumas as well as contemporary women's issue novelist Olive Higgins Prouty were sources. Issues raised by the most well-known theatrical and literary melodramas that women rewrote for the screen include: "What kind of a man kills a poor wife in order to marry a rich one?" *The Colleen Bawn*—Gene Gauntier), "Can a prostitute be morally redeemed?" (*Camille*—Francis Marion, June Mathis, Olga Printzlau), "Can a mother abandon her children and still be a mother to them?" (*East Lynne*—Mary Murillo and Lenore Coffee).[84] Why can't marriage bridge the social class divide? (*Stella Dallas*—Frances Marion).[85] Since these are questions to which there are no good answers, what can be done?

Much has been made of the tendency in American melodrama to put the happiest ending on the narrative that relies on the rawest material drawn from social conditions. This material, staged as events that should logically take the story down the road to the worst, finally did not go there, and the worst was averted, however illogically. The last three of these examples, however, are noted for the endings of their sources in which sympathetic characters die and mother and child are estranged or separated by death. So, although early photoplaywrights *did* put "wrong" endings on stories, in effect, resolving the unresolvable—we need to add a caveat to this. There would be those contradictory positions that *were* unresolvable in life and that therefore stubbornly remained so in these narratives. One thinks, for example, of the mixed-race character whose tortuous identity conflict no narrative could resolve. Mathis herself confronted such a narrative dilemma in her adaptation of Edith Wheery's novel as *The Red Lantern* (1919).[86] Mathis and cowriter Albert Capellani organize the film around the vacillating allegiances of the Alla Nazimova character, Mahlee. As the illegitimate Chinese daughter of an upper-class British man, she forfeits her place within the white missionary culture when she joins the Boxer Rebellion against foreigners.[87] Following the novel, the writers end the problem of her doubleness without resolving it. Mahlee commits suicide in the end, an event made strange by the excessiveness of its staging.[88] But the "right" or ideologically logical unhappy ending calls our attention to its proximity to the illogically "wrong" happy ending. The "right" unhappy end acknowledges that there would be some social divides that could neither be broached nor denied. In the illogically "wrong happy" or "unhappy happy ending," the telltale last scenes register the incongruity between the conflict that has gone before and the outcome that doesn't follow as a consequence.[89] Some would say that such an ending has been "tacked on."

Commenting on the screenplay manual rule that earlier events *should* give rise to the ending, David Bordwell speculates that failure to achieve this might be the result of "lack of craft" or too many interfering "hands." In other words, so formulized was narrative causality that illogic should be chalked up to incompetence. He quotes Frances Marion's 1953 manual on how characters, even under difficult, presumably hopeless situations, must be rescued from circumstances in "a *logical* and dramatic way that brings them happiness" (1982, 2).[90] However, Marguerite Bertsch, in her 1917 screenwriting manual seems inconsistent on this issue, setting the writer opposite goals. Having warned against the "hackneyed" or "regulation ending," she defends the "happy end" as best for the broadest audience "made up of those who feel rather than think." So, she continues, "the happy ending, where it can be achieved, makes the appreciated finish" (1917, 259). Thus the position spelled out from inside the scenario office suggests that an unquestioned rule and a dramatic writing practice worked at cross purposes. For what Bertsch then coaches hopeful writers to do is to end with the *unpredictable* end that must also be *predictably* happy (ibid., 258).[91]

The trick, I think, was to use the *unpredictable* coincidence to produce narrative reversal. If nowhere else, this can be seen in the addiction narrative.[92] Repeatedly in the American story, the downhill path of the abusive alcoholic father is reversed by a chance event followed by his reform and family reunion, while in the European version, the road may veer downhill to the end.[93] To give one addiction narrative example, in Alice Guy Blaché's *The Roads That Lead Home* (Solax, 1912), the mother and child leave the gambling husband and find a better home. But that new home is with the husband's mother who earlier rejected the young mother. The mother has disguised herself as a servant in the household as a means of making a living for herself and her small daughter. The family is united by the father's *unpredictable* discovery, by coincidence, of a locket in a pawnshop window. Now wanting the home he had relinquished, the addict is cured. Given the powerful ideology that all roads in life "lead home" and that there is no other "place on earth" like the place "from which you came," viewers may be easily aligned with the "return" trajectory. In the addict's reform such as this, we find something of the "return" to a "space of innocence" as the "home," which in nineteenth-century melodrama is "where everything matters" (Williams 2012, 537;

see also Williams 2001, 28; Brooks 1985, 29). But the best place is also the worst. The home is the very seat of contradictions where one finds the greatest disparity within familial feelings, those between love and animosity or between caring and neglect—as in *The Roads That Lead Home*. We see the father at the gambling table, indifferent to the suffering of his wife who sits despondently at home. Held over in the tradition of twentieth-century female writers like Olive Higgins Prouty, author of *Stella Dallas*, home is where love, put to the affective test, can fail as well as succeed (Berlant 2008, 175). Home is where all hopes for happiness have been wisely or not so wisely invested. It is where the characters have "been" happy and where the hope is that they will be again—if only they can get back there.

That the "home" in American melodrama would all come down to "happiness," however, seems entirely too trite. I must contend here, however, that the question of happiness is more fraught and profound than we might think and best addressed as the *temporality of hope for happiness*. Already in Bloch we have seen hope for the future or "anticipatory consciousness" developed as a political philosophy (1995, 113). More recently, Sara Ahmed has explored the "futurity of happiness," especially as an implicit promise is held out. She notes as well the close proximity of the "nostalgic" and "promissory," backward- and forward-looking trajectories, which have something in common: for both, happiness is *always elsewhere*. It "once was" or still "could be," but never just "is." Happiness, longed for and expected, is never in the present where we are. By definition, happiness always eludes us. Thus, it is that happiness becomes associated with anxiety, pulled between the hope for it and the fear of its loss. Happiness being *always elsewhere* means that *if* and *when* it appears, "it can recede, becoming anxious, becoming the thing that we could lose in the unfolding of time" (2010, 161). In Ahmed, time threatens the loss of happiness, and we can add support to this analysis with *historical time* as a *paradigm*, the "never together" of the three modes, from Chapter 5, that gives rise to so much human worry. Here, then, is how Ahmed sums up the strange "intimacy" between hope and anxiety: "In having hope we *become* anxious, because hope involves wanting something that might or might not happen." While hope, she goes on, may be about the wish for the "might," the "might" negatively signals or prepares that other possibility—the "might not" (183).

"Might" or "might not," so close and yet so far apart. So often this *temporality of the hope for happiness* relies on the family structure paradigm. And if happiness is never here but *always elsewhere*, as Ahmed thinks, the "here" feels no different from the "not here" anyway. Yes, the "voice of the home" may call up the place of "lost good" to which the future, full of promise, is expected to return to us.[94] But what was achieved through cinematic enhancement had to be even bigger than this, encompassing the return–no return, like the "might" or "might not" of the "achievement" of happiness. So, all the better to align the "magic something" with moving picture melodrama, the "voice" that could talk out of "both sides of its mouth" about the most difficult social problem, but when, pressed to end, performed some miracle of amelioration and assuagement.

Now back to what *a melodrama theory of historical time* offers the film historian, which turns out to be a foregrounding of the *location-in-time quandary*, my addition to Koselleck's question as to how in the present we see the *relation* between the past and the future (2004, 2). And, as I have said, both Koselleck and Bloch urge us to think about anticipation as a historical phenomenon, in Koselleck a new facing-forward that characterizes the last several centuries. Considering women in the early film industry, it would appear, however, as though this pits *their* utopianism against ours from the vantage of the once wished-for future they looked toward in their quite different times. But, thinks Fredric Jameson, the wishful are today still waiting, left "in anticipation" of Bloch's "anticipation" (1971, 158–159).[95]

Our world *may not be* the one that these female makers anticipated and although some conditions might be better, other aspects might be found to be worse, making Gene Gauntier's "new conditions" under which she found she could not work only a preview of things to come (Smith 1924, 102). If our measure is the amount of power women wielded in the then-new image industries, the contemporary analysis might be that during a short window some did have more "control" of production conditions, but this assessment would be relative to the creative power that women in the U.S. film and television industries have today. Neither Bloch nor Koselleck, however, is finally interested in this ramification of their own theories, although Bloch did place socialism at the end of the rainbow. Koselleck studies "futures past" or past conceptions of the future, but his interest in modes of time stops at the consciousness and actions of historical players. Thus, while neither Bloch nor Koselleck was interested in the disappointed or fulfilled expectations of past figures relative to a future moment on its arrival, we, at that moment, *do* wonder who these women imagined *we* might be. In one of the most comprehensive of contemporary assessments of women producing world cinema today, Patricia White thinks across modes of time when she says that "Women's access to these influential forms of social vision—cinema and feminism—has already transformed the future" (2015, 27).

So whose utopianism are we talking about today? A utopian aspiration we have without realizing it or that we might wish we had?[96] What is at stake for the present of this writing stands revealed. Our question, once again, is what their hopes for the future have to do with ours and ours with theirs. Or, as Joan Scott explains the justification for historical research on women, by documenting change and variance in times, feminists have "sought to overturn the limits placed on our aspirations" (2011, 7). This explains the imperative to tell *this* story just as the percentage of women directors in the U.S. media industries again becomes an issue.[97] Yet if so many contemporary expectations of women in the industry are riding on this particular historical narrative, there is a danger of overinvestment in it.

To ask "what happened to them" is then to ask about *our* failures and achievements, our setbacks and dreams. Since we cannot empirically know their present, we need to have a theory of it, a theory of technological expectation *in their times relative to ours*. Here is the temporal intermingling: at the end of Chapter 6, I called this our *historical relations of coincidence*, apparently accidental but no accident—their aspirations tied to ours. Of course, we know that this "connect" is also a disconnect, a mismatch between moments like cultures awkwardly at odds. The disconnect recalls an earlier feminist theory's pessimistic critique of oppression that could not accommodate the resilient "new times" optimism that drove these women's efforts to repudiate custom and that must have buoyed them up through adversities—financial losses, dismissals, unwanted pregnancies, betrayals, and family disapprovals.[98]

While, in 1925, June Mathis puts the happiest face on their contributions, we might prefer to see, retaining a more dialectical tension, the ingenuity of their accommodation to gender norms and their acquiescence to the gross inequities of the star system. Mathis's hyperbole drowns out the downside—the fraud, swindling, and huxterism at large in those years.[99] One voice did cut through Hollywood's hyperbolic rhetoric at the time. In the "game of publicity," Anzia Yezierska confessed to *Cosmopolitan* magazine, her every interview was "twisted and distorted." The screenwriter with roots in the Jewish immigrant community of Lower East Side New York dared to write about the exploitative underside when she left Hollywood, "a tortured soul with a bank account." She realizes that, as a writer making $200 dollars per week, she has herself become a capitalist—"one of the class that I hated" (1925, 154).

There would be greedy power mongers and social climbers among them, as well as shrewd schemers and backstabbers, sexual cheaters and dissemblers, and haughty sluts and jealous wives. Then there was the ignominy of their deaths—of carcinoma of the cervix (Jeanie McPherson), of suicide by poison (Florence Lawrence), of tuberculosis (Mabel Normand and Lorna Moon), or of a heart attack that took an overworked June Mathis in 1927 in the last act of "The Squall." As she called out "Mother, I'm dying, I'm dying!" she was carried outside New York's 44th Street Theater into the street.[100]

"What happened" to them is a question of how they persisted but also how they finally relinquished the hope that they once had of participation in a creative venture that became the world-dominating industry that left them behind. But here, studying the past as it conceived of its future, silent pictures from the vantage of women's aspirations, the enormity of those aspirations are so large that they actually dwarf their achievements.

CONCLUSION
Women Made Redundant

The last chapter configured a paradigm to challenge the existing state of field knowledge—the American export of the "voice of the home," a microcosm of melodrama. If producer-screenwriter June Mathis was right, the "woman's viewpoint" was exported to the world markets opened up after World War I (1925, 115). In this time that had felt like "new times," some adventuresome women, caught up in the excitement of making these dream-factory products, grabbed chances to write, produce, and direct. Others worked behind the scenes at lower levels; some finally gave up, some tried to continue. What do we now say about the stunted ambitions of those who lost jobs? Or those who wished that they had been given a job? Or the resourcefulness of those who started the companies that were later blamed for obstructing progress? Their chance was short-lived and their expectations soon expired. They had invested in an enterprise, which by 1925, was powered by finance capital. But that is not the end of that. That is not the end, because if June Mathis was right about the irresistibility of the "something" in these films, it would not have made business sense to have changed the formula. Even with fewer female creative workers, the industry continued to exploit the "magic something," whatever that was.

Mathis implies that the "magic something," the women's viewpoint, slipped in through women working in the industry. Perhaps empirical women were conduits for a sensibility, or, now straddling the empirical and the theoretical, it is because our two constructs—"women" and "genre"—are just similarly conventionalized. But if conventionalized, the "home voice" could also be available to differently gendered workers, that is, to male writers and directors who would carry over the women's viewpoint as a genre feature. To achieve this, the studios didn't need to employ women. If we take this theoretical tack, we have then a revised question: "What happened to the woman's viewpoint?" And if it had "crept in," as Mathis says, it would *still be there* after so many women had left. Now it may seem a bit deceptive to thus reframe the issue with which I began, taking a theoretical route around a question that pleads for empirical solution: "What happened to women in the silent film industry?" Throughout I have suggested that *what* "happened" is historically contingent, and I wondered whether we should even try to offer an answer since what "actually happened" is not available to us today. And yet our "What happened?" question remains, unanswered and persistent. The past, although it does not exactly exist, still "insists," says Deleuze (1994, 82).

Where is the past more insistent than in an archival document, especially one that has just come to light? In this case, there will be those documents that dispute the hollow cheer and temper June Mathis's grand claim. There are the letters these women wrote, often accompanying the scenario submission, testifying to the irregularity of the work and the specter of unemployment. In one, scenario editor Hettie Gray Baker, in correspondence with Mr. Pribyl of the Selig Polyscope Company, encloses a screenplay for Tom Mix with a letter written on Bosworth, Inc., stationery. After the 1915 merger of the Bosworth and Morosco companies, she writes again, "I doubt if I ever go back," explaining that she is out of the scenario-editing job she had with Bosworth because the Morosco company have their own writers. Yet she hopes that Mr. Garbutt at Morosco would have more work in two months.[1] Working as a scenario editor while continuing to freelance, in a second letter to Mr. Pribyl, Baker makes freelancing into something positive: "I feel very happy at the opportunity to freelance, and know that I shall enjoy the freedom of it for a while."[2] Three weeks later, she writes to thank him again, telling him that she has accepted a job from the Reliance-Majestic studio, but adds: "However, I may be a free lance again some time, so don't forget me entirely."[3] To claim to enjoy the uncertainty of freelancing and to turn it into an idea of "freedom" suggests how adept these women were at putting the pleasantest face on an anxiety in danger of devolving into despair. Title writer Dwinelle Benthall, with Rufus McCosh, was part of a scenario-writing team beginning in the 1920s and once wrote of the talent: "Some climb up and some climb down—and some climb up and down and up and down. Poverty Row—a strange place—gray with disappointment and bitter with failure, yet shot thru with the golden gleam of hope. Work, work, work!"[4]

Such empirical evidence of the futility of optimism countered by their dogged refusal to relinquish that optimism may be beyond the capacity of Frankfurt School dialectics to grasp. How then to explain "them" to "us"? While we may concur about these women that their function as affective conduits justifies our enumeration of them, the "count" we have of them is yet unverifiable. Not only are their numbers still in dispute in the U.S. case, as we have seen (Slide 2012a, 114), but we may never know what can be said

Hettie Gray Baker, scenario editor. Courtesy Connecticut
Historical Society. Hartford, Connecticut.

with absolute certainty about the motion pictures on which they worked or, if, mailing
in scenarios, they tried to work. Beyond the question of "whether" they did or did not
work is the even more empirically unwieldy question as to how women in the new
creative pool managed the unpredictability of work, particularly as freelancers living in
Los Angeles. Finally, the very unreliability of such employment served to camouflage
the massiveness of their exodus. As in the case of a writer who had frequently been "let
go," she might never have known one termination from another and therefore would
not have known which one was her last. With temporary employment, there might
never have been a pink slip.

WHAT HAPPENED TO THE WOMAN'S VIEWPOINT?

Let me propose a theoretical solution based on *unemployment,* borrowing a term from the
British labor tradition in which workers laid off are said to be "made redundant." From
the employer's point of view, workers are "redundant" if their work is no longer needed or
a worker can be "made redundant" when he or she is replaced by a technology that does
the same work. For our purposes, we need the implications of labor redundancy in which
management considers workers to be extra and therefore unnecessary even if they are

still necessary. We can thus show that as women were phased out it was not so much that they were unnecessary as that they could easily be replaced by men, especially as producers, directors, and writers. Therefore, if the "voice of the home" was already there in the American genre film—now built into melodrama as mode—women as creative workers *would be made redundant*. Ironically, their creative contributions would also be made redundant by what they had already produced in these works—that "magic something" conventionalized into the narrative core of American world exports. Women workers were replaced by the female viewpoint that they had codified, were made unnecessary by the interchangeability of "women" and "genre," our pair of conventionalizations. In the U.S. industry, women were replaced by the motion picture narrative structure that they had helped to develop, starting from the silent scenario and its stark situations. They were replaced by the efficient machinery of production and the laboratory duplication of multiple prints, as well as their distribution. Then, delivering this viewpoint, there were the theatrical projectors that moved the pictures frame by frame and enlarged the elaborately expressive signs on the face of the screen.

Labor redundancy, however, is only the first irony in a pair of ironies. While the first irony—women workers replaced by the very "voice of the home" that they had helped to develop—belongs to the realm of the "felt," the second irony belongs to the economic. That irony turns on "respectability" as redefined by the new finance economy. For if "respectability" was what women were first employed to insure, a decade later, lack of "respectability" became a rationale for closing them out, especially if they were founders of precariously existing independent companies in the 1916–1923 period.[5] As early as 1909, exhibitors were worried about the reputability of their product and concluded that female audiences were a solution.[6] Consequently, female directors and writers were recruited on the assumption that they could help to draw in middle-class female viewers and "uplift" the seedy experience of moviegoing.[7] But cosmetic product uplifting did not, however, make a business legitimate, and, as Janet Wasko reminds us, the perception of moving pictures as unsteady and financially "risky" emerged in the next decade. This new motion picture enterprise was not considered stable enough to attract investors until around 1919, Wasko thinks (1982, 10, 13).[8] In 1925, New York bank president A. H. Giannini looked back to the "trials" in the "early and precarious life" of the motion picture business: "In those pioneer days, because of these exacerbations, we could find nothing on which to base a forecast of sensible change at any particular time in the future" (1926, 46).[9] Thus by the second decade investors were looking for another kind of "respectability" than exhibitors wanted in the first decade, a characteristic Giannini defined as management placed in "capable hands" that could produce proper financial statements (ibid., 48). Not only was it thought that women could not supply financial respectability, but there is even some evidence that they may have been blamed for the industry's disreputability in the eyes of business.[10]

Accordingly, one 1916 *Photoplay* editorial associates women's companies with the "unbusinesslike" chaos of earlier years. The editors are willing to tolerate Mary Pickford and Clara Kimball Young as producers, "But how many Youngs or Pickfords are there in America?" they ask, as though any more would be too many (63). "These alleged artists would drag film-making back to its days of solitary, suspicious feudal inefficiency" (64). But "inefficient"? Perhaps these companies were undercapitalized and impractical, ill-advised, and not exactly "business" even if they hoped to make a profit. These actress-producers may have been duped by a distributor as was Nell Shipman, exploited by a husband as was Ethel Grandin, or ignored as was Gloria Swanson by Will Hayes.[11] Some short-term independent ventures may not have produced more than a single film and thus did not last long enough to be judged in terms of "efficiency."[12] We can almost glimpse here the industry underside through the political economy question as to how so many women's companies "came and went," or a second company was attempted after the failure of the first.[13] Perhaps some *were* fantasy companies, especially since a few, although advertised, may never have shot a film. We continue to search for *Bartered Flesh*, the film the *Exhibitors' Trade Review* announced as the first picture of Lule Warrenton's "all-woman company," brainchild of the character actress who did some directing at Universal Pictures.[14] To the complete fantasy project we could add the vanity company exemplified by actress Mae Murray's Tiffany Pictures.[15]

But our goal is neither a definitive version of events nor a theory to supplant other theories. Rather, it is an intervention to encourage more engagement. New research on so many aspiring women stimulates a rethinking of assumptions in two key areas: U.S. independent and regional cinemas and the transition from global to national cinema. In U.S. studio studies, women become more integral to the story of industry independents who sought control of all aspects of production by starting up *outside* the companies that became the U.S. studios.[16] Lois Weber Productions and Alice Guy

Lule Warrenton, actress/producer/director. Courtesy Margaret Herrick Library, Academy of Motion Picture Arts & Sciences. Beverly Hills, California.

Blaché's Solax Company, among others, become the basis for considering alternative working arrangements before the studio system, organized, for instance, around the family mode of production.[17] Feminists may be forever stumped by the difference and sameness conundrum, epitomized by regional versus urban as well as class and race privilege in contrast with immigrant disadvantage. Even if these women all took risks in this new machine venture, opportunities were not equally distributed. In Oklahoma, African American Drusilla Dungee-Huston, between 1905 and into the 1930s, wrote and rewrote a screenplay that was never finally produced (Brooks-Bertram, 2013). While we know that in North Carolina, Florida, Kansas, North Dakota, and Idaho, women shot footage and distributed moving pictures; there may have been more in other regions.[18]

To accommodate what we may never know or in advance of later knowing, we throw the widest net, crediting these women for their *"expectation" despite expectations of them*, measured in the difference between what society thought possible and what some attempted, acknowledging how very low the bar was set for women at the time. Emphasis on anticipation over achievement also frames a repositioning of women at the advent, thinking, in 1895, of Antonia Dickson's vision of the technological future. Merely by asking what Gaumont secretary Alice Guy was doing in 1895 changes everything.[19] In the following decade, since the global prefaces the national stage of cinema's expansion, the "woman's viewpoint," or the "voice" of melodrama, was made a world phenomenon.[20] However, lest we be tempted to re-jig a historical chronology of "firsts," think how these examples critique the "birth of cinema," establishing, as I argue in Chapter 3, multiple "births" as well as multiple versions. To put it differently, "gender," itself a question, is integral to the *question of the technological advent* as well as the later spread of global moving image culture.[21]

Emphasis on expectation and anticipation over achievement underwrites the idea that as founders and cofounders of companies, U.S. women were situated to gain even more as independents than men. It may also be that some imagined themselves as the source of a world culture if, following our "voice of the home" export thesis, we posit that women supplied the irresistible ingredient in cinema at the post–World War I stage of global expansion. However, while June Mathis aspired to write for "one world" of viewers, today this implies an imperialist arrogance. While scholars now acknowledge women's part in national cinema-building in Europe, South America, Australia, Asia, and the Middle East, the connection between and among them is theoretical work-in-progress. Then, looking ahead to the challenge of tracing the "voice of the home" paradigm, we invariably face the doubleness of the Western strategy: to expand markets was to export images that delivered a troublesome "modern woman" ideal.[22] In addition, we will continue to ask what it was that the "export" met on arrival in so many cultures. What was unimaginable about those cultures? Still, the American "export" of the "voice of the home" may the link women across continents who were instrumental at the start of over thirty other national film industries.[23] The "voice of the home"

Mimi Derba, actress/producer.
Courtesy Museo Soumaya.
Mexico City, Mexico.

export must have found its audience in those national markets—from Europe and the Middle East to China and Japan. After all, before these women were makers they were urban center viewers.[24] As significantly, they even emerge as antagonistic to American exports, as is the case with Mimí Derba, who started Azteca Films in 1917 Mexico City as a nationalist bulwark against Hollywood expansion.[25] Given world export, the task ahead is to locate more global encounters in urban centers from Cairo to Tokyo. In the following, then, I situate non-Western women as quite beyond the Western imagination. On the eerie analogy with the historical realm itself, these women have been for too long too far out of conceptual reach, although, across uncomprehending worlds, they tried to imagine each other.

WHERE IN THE WORLD: HISTORICAL SURPRISE

Those who have followed developments in the field for forty years will not miss the dramatic reversal in which what was first unthinkable by 1970s Anglo-American feminist film theorists has now emerged as established; when what was inconceivable becomes, all of a sudden, so conceivable that few can recall ever having thought otherwise.[26]

How curious that a historical scenario, once unimaginable, can become an accepted historical narrative. Is this not sufficient reason to be somewhat suspicious of them all?

This is to theorize *historical relations of coincidence*, proposed at the end of Chapter 6, as we come to see that our two times pose inextricable questions. *Historical coincidence* makes the question as to how it was that they weren't imagined just as intriguing a question as how it was that they managed or didn't manage to complete the moving image productions that they envisioned. It is not only that we want to know how they expected that they could do this, against the odds, but why, after they imagined so much, the boldness of their gamble did not occur to us, decades later. Since we still know so little, we must imagine how they might have engineered this; we must imagine what we can't imagine. And why other than because the historical past is by definition full of unimaginabilities or surprises.[27] Yet, we run the risk of boiling the issue of the "unimaginable" historical subject down to a set of common sense ideas. Luckily, the everyday idea that there are "limits to the imagination" and the criticism of "too limited" an imagination cancel each other out. There is also something else that could stop a common sense line of reasoning in its tracks: the difference between unthinkable and unimaginable. First, however, note the proximity of "unimaginability" to the more prohibitive and dangerous "unthinkability," or that which *mustn't be* thought and can't be admitted into our conceptual repertoire. Then, let's remember how recently "gender" was "unthinkable" as a category of historical analysis (Scott 2006, 393).[28] Further afield, we detect the old Orientalist effects in addition to the dismissals closer to home in everyday unthinkableness expressed as "no such thing." This interdiction applies to historical figures, some of whom definitively *were* while others are *not supposed to have been* as "unthinkability" cordons off whole worlds. Unthinkable has its close association with the culturally disgusting and appalling as in "unspeakable horrors." This prohibition against expression stands, as power, even before an event occurs, so that, if it "shouldn't," it therefore *didn't happen at all*—our explanation for the French position on secretary Alice Guy's early fiction filmmaking. Is this not the crux of the difficulty we want to feature here? That insofar as we *can* we always want to know under what political conditions historiographic dangers can and cannot be admitted to thought.[29]

THINKING ABOUT UNTHINKABILITIES

What do we gain by thinking about earlier "unthinkabilities"? How curious that prior unthinkabilites may later become thinkable, while there is no answering the question as to who is *currently* unthinkable; by definition, whoever she/he is cannot now be thought. Recall the moment when Dorothy Arzner, as a lesbian historical figure and theoretical paradigm, was quite unthinkable, as Shelley Stamp asks us to do when she remembers how very difficult it was to "insert her" (2013a). Dorothy Arzner, formerly "unthinkable," was once a categorical blind spot and a conceptual taboo. When Claire

Johnston wrote that Dorothy Arzner and Lois Weber were effectively the "only women" to have produced a body of work in the first decades of the U.S. studio system she introduced an idea that only gradually came to the fore, albeit in a relatively progressive field (1973, 29–30). What did Johnston detect as "subversion" in Arzner's Hollywood films other than June Mathis's secretly suffused "something"? So if we argue that the "voice of the home," the women's viewpoint, was smuggled in by so many working women (and carried on by men), we can't overlook this earlier interest in theorizing a "something." Yet "subversion" in feminist film theory, further developed through the 1980s with the "invention" of the woman's film, faces new challenges and is ripe for reconsideration.[30] In the 1970s, the family melodrama became subversive as consequence of a subtle shift from subversive auteur director Douglas Sirk, a "slippage" that happened almost unnoticed entirely in the theoretical realm (Gledhill 1987, 7). Now performing a parallel critical move through June Mathis on behalf of women in the silent industry, the "voice of the home" is shifted onto melodrama, the genre umbrella. Today, with the legacy of melodrama more fully fleshed out and its purview expanded to all popular genres and extrapolated to world cinema, we are poised to enlarge feminist film theory and historiography.

So, knowing what we now know about what was once unthinkable, how do we study that which is beyond current comprehension? If nothing else, we can predict reversals and exceptions. While, for example, we may find technological aspirations in non-Western women, those who flaunted tradition paid a high social price.[31] Perhaps the most extreme case is that of Cairo actress Bahija Hafez, who made a silent version of *El Dahaya/The Victims* (1932) and then composed a score and directed the sound segments when equipment became available in Egypt. We know something of the forces aligned against her because of the lawsuit she brought against her male coworkers for discrimination (Rahman 2002, 370). As though the lawsuit was not disgraceful enough, her public visibility so offended her conservative family that they disowned her and even "accepted condolences for her death," Tunisian scholar Ouissal Mejri tells us. In response to her family's condemnation, Hafez wrote: "I am for freedom of women, freedom to do menial jobs instead of remaining locked in the house. If I followed the advice of my family I would not be anyone, but today I have learned the languages and the arts that I like. I was born a man in a woman's body" (Mejri 2010). For Hafez's Muslim family, it was prohibitive that she should have a public body, let alone that she should secretly think of herself as born a "man in a woman's body." If for her family, Bahija Hafez as a filmmaker was unthinkable, for Western feminist scholars, until recently, Bahija Hafez the filmmaker was almost as inconceivable as Dorothy Arzner was before her.

As a hypothesis to test we can at least say: "If there was one, there were others." Yes, one visible maker may eclipse others, but if there was one, there were others, even others elsewhere in the world, because, after all, motion pictures were distributed worldwide. Here, however, are contradictions due for more examination, the first being that the

West, having eclipsed the rest of the world, also transformed what it had eclipsed.[32] In current transnational feminist research, the eclipsed returns to disturb our assumptions about who was "ahead" and who was "behind," to upend those hierarchies of "modernity" organized around "the West and the rest." The project ahead calls for world cinema in reverse, *from* global cities and regions where the entertainment export arrived and where new nationalisms clashed with colonial projects. Consider, along these lines, Tazuko Sakane who, according to her biographer, Ikegawa Reiko, began in Japan in 1929 at the Nikkatsu Studio as assistant director on the Mizoguchi unit.[33] In 1937, after Japan invaded China, Sakane directed documentaries in the educational film unit at the Manchuria Film Association studio in the Japanese-controlled Manchukuo state where she found opportunities she was not allowed in Tokyo. To quote Sakane who linked herself to what she saw as a world tradition via Germany and the United States: "People thought it was really uppity for a woman to become a film director. But overseas there are already women directors such as Dorothy Arzner, and Leotine [Leontine] Sagan of *Girls in Uniform*. If many more female staff members like screenplay writers and cinematographers, appear in the Japanese film industry, I though not Sagan's equal, would like to create a cinema together with them that is filled with feminine sensitivity, a kind of cinema men are not able to create."[34] Arzner herself may not have imagined Sakane but, against an asymmetry of imaginative capacities, we

Tazuko Sakane, director. Courtesy
Museum of Kyoto. Kyoto, Japan.

Pu Shunqing, screenwriter, on set of *Mulan Joins the Army* (Minxin Film Company, China, 1928). Courtesy Mr. LAI Shek 黎錫.

now posit historically coincidental relations across times and cultures. While Arzner is translated by her Japanese counterpart, our Western lesbian paradigm, "Dorothy," is reciprocally transformed in such a way that "Tazuko Sakane," the new paradigm, now creates a transnational configuration: Japanese Tazuko Sakane "together with" American Dorothy Arzner and German Leontine Sagan.

While we posit "if there was one, there were others," we also see variation beyond the Hollywood industrial model, that is, other models that characterized other national cinemas. If, in the United States case the "star-name" company was underwritten by celebrity (Mahar 2006, ch. 2, 6), in other parts of the world we can assume neither for-profit finance nor a star system. There are instead the revolutionary Soviets like Aleksandra Khokhlova and Esfir Shub, as well as revolutionary Chinese women like Pu Shunqing, who, as writers or director-producers, built a new kind of society by means of state-run collective work.[35] The industrial model conjoined to the family system of production, however, emerges elsewhere, although in another cultural register. The foundation of Indian cinema as a national initiative is the husband-wife team Devika Rani and Himansu Rai who, in 1934, established the Bombay Talkies Studio on the pre–World War II industrial model that later became Bollywood (Mukherjee 2015, 32). With notable exceptions—the Communist state as well as educational pictures—making motion pictures was business. Thus, the many cases in which making even one motion picture required starting a company, as exemplified by Bahija Hafez, who founded the Fanar Film Company in Cairo (Mejri 2010), and Daisy Sylvan, who founded Daisy Film in Florence, Italy (Jandelli 2013). Or, also as in the U.S. model, an industry insider might branch out as an independent, as did Czech actress Thea Červenková. Only after she learned the Czech film business, beginning in 1918 at Slaviafilm, did Červenková start Filmový ústav, or Film Office, founded with her cameraman, who later recalled that the company functioned "more like a family business" (Bláhová 2013). Yet, as in U.S. regional cases, women with no connection to the new industry followed through on a story idea. In Mexico, Cándida Beltrán Rendón emerged as producer, director, set designer, and actress in the self-financed *El secreto de la abuela/The Grandmother's Secret* (1928) (Vázquez and Márquez 2013). Perhaps the most unanticipated approach to film production entailed the foundation of schools. In Lima, Peru, Polish immigrant Stefania Socha opened an "Acting for Film" academy and then directed and produced *Los abismos de la vida/The Abysses of Life* (1929) (Lucioni and Nuñez 2013). Across the continent in Buenos Aires, Argentina, Italian immigrant Emilia Saleny directed four films, the fifth of which was a production by her Academia Saleny students (Fradinger 2013).

For Italian film scholars, Elvira Giallanella is an elusive object of historical intrigue and, relative to the categories mentioned earlier, a figure exterior to the dominant sphere of motion pictures as business. I propose to see her one film as outside entertainment as industrially capitalized because it appears to have been conceived as a pacifist statement post–World War I, discovered only because it survived in the Cineteca Nazionale in Rome where it had been since its deposit in May, 1957. Describing how the film was almost missed on Vittorio Martinelli's Italian silent cinema filmography, Micaela Veronisi concludes that this film, *Umanità/Humankind* (1919), produced by Giallanella's company Liana Film, was never screened at all in the historical moment of its production after World War I (2017). Today, however, *Umanità* is celebrated as a striking, aesthetically modernist antiwar film. A single-frame enlargement indicates the poignancy of the film's abstract images, empty boots lined up in marching order encountered by two children and a gnome exploring a desert of discarded armaments. We think of the enormity of the hope, in Virginia Woolf's words, of "peace and freedom for the whole world" (as quoted in Veronisi 2010, 79). Inspired by Monica Dall'Asta's answer to the charge that these historical women are feminist fabrications, we can now answer the question as to what it is that they do for us as well as what we do for them. Thinking of Elvira Giallanella, Dall'Asta argues that historical reality "provokes" imagination. Our imagination gives them existence, she says, "for an image, a now conceivable image, is the only possible condition of existence for Giallanella here and now." Thus, she continues, "we come to the truly paradoxical conclusion that they need us as much as we need them. They need us in order to exist historically, that is, not just as lost figures of the past, but as provocative images in and for the present" (Dall'Asta and Gaines 2015, 21).

Frame enlargement, *Humanity/ Umanità* (Liana Films, Italy, 1919), Elvira Giallanella, director/producer. Courtesy Cineteca Nazionale. Rome, Italy.

WHAT FEMINISM CAN'T IMAGINE

What strikes us now that so many surviving films and photographs have surfaced is the breadth of the discrepancy between what these women imagined for themselves and what 1970s feminism hadn't imagined about them. These earlier women imagined a transcendent moment of a story "come to life" on a screen, creative participation in a project, and a passion incarnated. We, in contrast, imagined abstractly that there were few of them, if any, or none at all, even though out of the "not there" a powerful negative paradigm was forged.

Now think back to 1919. Is there any idea more utopian than the wish for world peace at the end of World War I's devastation? What is more unimaginable a century later than a world at peace? So it is in relation to Elvira that I would qualify her vision as "almost" unimaginable because in her lifetime her vision of peace instead of war while beyond the European imagination *did* occur to some pacifists.[36] "Almost," I say because she *did* complete the film and Italian scholars later realized her imagination of its exhibition. We, coming after, have been necessary to the realization of her antiwar vision and helped to achieve this by giving her motion picture film the exhibition it never had, with public screenings nearly one hundred years later (Dall'Asta and Gaines, 2015, 21).

Today, after viewing the evidence, it may be difficult to think that such moving picture recoveries were once "almost unimaginable." But as soon as they come to light, we claim them. Feminist scholars and artists, meeting moving image evidence halfway, supplement their makers' aspirations with ours, because, even given the uneven status of women today, continent to continent, there is really nothing that a more global feminism can't imagine *with* them, notwithstanding the difficulties of delivering on the promise. We are, hopefully, as "in anticipation" as they were, remembering that we are the "former future" they once anticipated. The *melodrama theory of historical time* tells us why it is that we want to see the "what once was" of their heyday as that which "might have been" for them if only they could have continued—"if only" and therefore what *could be again*. This looking toward what "could be again" is paradoxically a hope for an "almost unimaginable" future time. What, after all, was the project of the 1970s women's film festival retrospectives other than an attempt to look, as melodrama often does, to the past as the source of the "hoped for" future?[37]

There is, of course, another sense of "what feminism can't imagine," not the statement of fact but the question "What can't feminism imagine?" in which there is no limit to what can be envisioned for women given feminism's utopian legacies, with theory and history allied and no longer so estranged. Having said this, however, we must ask how to facilitate *research* that expects the absolutely unexpected—even that which cannot be accommodated by our favorite theories. Here, too, we ask what becomes of the unexpected given the "essentially domesticating effect" of most historical writing (White 1987, 256). Let us then say that historical research is a constant encounter with the strange and inscrutable. For as the image of the empty boots in *Umanità* flash an unanticipated consciousness across a century, they signal to us in a strange code we can never finally crack.[38] We are not, after all, the mothers or fathers and brothers, wives, husbands, and sisters of the millions of European soldiers who died so futilely in the Great War that did not end war. Try as we might to dispassionately explain *their* times, we will still speak of them through *our* moment. From this standpoint, we might then realize how unanswerable historical "what happened" questions really are.

APPENDIX

I. ARCHIVES ABBREVIATIONS

AMPAS-MC—Academy of Motion Picture Arts and Sciences, Margaret Herrick Library, Special Collections, Beverly Hills, Calif.

AMPAS-OH—Academy of Motion Picture Arts and Sciences, Oral History Program, Margaret Herrick Library, Beverly Hills, Calif.

Calif. BYU—Brigham Young University, Arts & Communication Archives, Harold B. Lee Library, Provo, Utah.

CUOHRO—Columbia University, Oral History Research Office, New York, N.Y.

MOMA—Museum of Modern Art, Celeste Bartos International Film Study Center, New York, N.Y.

USC-CAL—University of Southern California, Cinematic Arts Library, Los Angeles, Calif.

USC-RHC—University of Southern California, Doheny Memorial Library, Regional History Collections, Los Angeles, Calif.

II. DVD SOURCES OR ONLINE LINKS FOR TITLES REFERENCED

For further information about archival holdings and commercial availability, readers are referred to the Women Film Pioneers website: wfpp.cdrs.columbia.edu (accessed January 1, 2017).

Anna-Liisa (Suomi-Filmi, 1922). Director: Teuvo Puro, Jussi Snellman. Story: Minna Canth. DVD (Kansallinen Audiovisuaalinen Instituutti, 2014).

Ben Hur (Kalem Co., 1907). Director: Sidney Olcott, Frank Oates Rose, Screenplay/Actress: Gene Gauntier. DVD. *Spartacus* (Grapevine Video, US, 2012).

Bread (Universal Pictures, 1918). Director/Screenplay: Ida May Park. DVD. *Pioneers: First Women Filmmakers* (Kino Lorber, US, forthcoming).

Camille (Alla Nazimova Productions, 1921). Director: Ray Smallwood. Screenplay: June Mathis. Cast: Alla Nazimova. Designer: Natasha Rambova. DVD (Grapevine Video, US, 2004).

The Colleen Bawn (Kalem Co., 1911). Director: Sidney Olcott. Screenplay/Actress: Gene Gauntier. http://www.tcd.ie/irishfilm/silent/the-colleen-bawn.php (accessed June 1, 2017).

Eleanor's Catch (Rex Film Corp, US, 1916). Producer/Director: Cleo Madison. Screenplay: William Mong. DVD. *Hypocrites* (Kino Video, US, 2008).

The Four Horsemen of the Apocalypse (Metro Pictures Co., 1921). Director: Rex Ingram. Producer/Screenplay: June Mathis. DVD (Delta Entertainment Corp., US, 2006).

Golden Gate Girls (Hong Kong Art Development Council & Blue Queen Cultural Communication Ltd., 2013). Director/Screenplay/Producer: S. Louisa Wei. DVD (Women Make Movies, US, 2013).

The Hazards of Helen, Chapt. 13 (Kalem Co., 1915). Director: Leo Maloney, Helen Holmes. Screenplay: Edward Matlack. DVD. *Treasures III: Social Issues in American Film, 1900–1934* (Image Entertainment, US, 2007).

La Fée aux choux, ou La naissance des enfants (Gaumont, 1900). Director: Alice Guy. DVD. *Gaumont Treasures 1897–1913* (Kino International, 2009).

La Matelas Alcoolique/The Drunken Mattress (Gaumont, 1906). Director: Alice Guy. DVD. *Gaumont Treasures 1897–1913* (Kino International, 2009).

The Love Light (Mary Pickford Co., 1921). Director/Screenplay: Frances Marion. Producer: Mary Pickford. DVD (Milestone Films, US, 2000).

Madame a des envies/Madame Has Her Cravings (Gaumont, 1906). Director: Alice Guy. DVD. *Gaumont Treasures 1897–1913* (Kino International, 2009).

The Red Lantern (Metro Pictures, 1919). Director: Albert Cappellani. Screenplay: June Mathis, Albert Cappelani. Cast: Alla Nazimova. DVD (Cinematek Belgium, 2012; Gartenberg Media, 2017).

The Rosary (Rex Motion Picture C,o. 1913). Director/Screenplay: Lois Weber. DVD. *Pioneers: First Women Filmmakers* (Kino Lorber, US, forthcoming).

Sage-femme de première classe/First-Class Midwife (Gaumont, 1902). Director: Alice Guy. DVD. *Gaumont Treasures 1897–1913* (Kino International, 2009).

Salomy Jane (California Motion Picture Corp., 1914). Director: Lucius Henderson, William Nigh. DVD. *Treasures 5: The West, 1898–1938* (Image Entertainment, US, 2011).

Shoes (Bluebird Photoplays, Inc., 1916). Director/Producer/Screenplay: Lois Weber. DVD/Blu-Ray (Milestone Films, US, 2017).

The Single Standard (Metro/Goldwyn/Mayer, 1929). Director: John S. Robertson. Screenplay: Josephine Lovett. Story: Adela Rogers St. Johns. DVD/VHS (MGM, US, 1998).

White Water (Nell Shipman Production, 1922). Director: Bert Van Tulye, Nell Shipman. Producer/Screenplay/Actress: Nell Shipman. DVD. *The Nell Shipman Collection: The Short Films* (The Idaho Film Collection, US, 2007).

Within Our Gates (Micheaux Book and Film Co., 1920). Director: Oscar Micheaux. DVD. *Pioneers of African American Cinema* (Kino Lorber, US, 2016).

NOTES

INTRODUCTION: WHAT GERTRUDE STEIN
WONDERS ABOUT HISTORIANS

1. Slide (2012a, 114) challenges this figure mentioned by Cari Beauchamp in her introduction to a contemporary screening of *Humoresque* (dir. Frank Borzage, Cosmopolitan Pictures, 1920), with screenplay by Francis Marion adapted from the Fannie Hurst novel. The 50 percent figure has been used by a number of feminist historians. Holliday (1995, 144) estimates a 1:1 ratio between men and women in scenario writing departments in the 1910s. Mahar (2001, 101) says that both men and women were invited into the *Photoplay* Author League, established in 1914, "no doubt because just as many women as men (if not more) wrote scenarios during the silent era." Lant (2006, 549) says that half of all silent-era scenarios were written by women.

2. Appiah (2003, 122) suggests an intriguing way into the problem of knowledge when he elaborates on the philosophical "paradox of analysis," which, following G. E. Moore, can be seen as leading to a conundrum. The problem is that if we advance a statement like "To know is to believe on the basis of a reliable method," we end up with the apparently exchangeable "*knowledge* and *reliably produced true belief.*" Thus not only do we *not* have a tool of analysis but we end up with the "same statement." It would seem that we can also end up with a kind of tautology in which "to know means to know."

3. The most recent survival statistics on silent feature films are Pierce (2013, 2) who says that only 25 percent survive as complete but another 17 percent, or 5 percent of the total produced survive but are incomplete. Martin and Clark (1987) say that the survival rate of short films, numerous until around 1915, are as relevant or more so to women's contributions. At the time of their writing that number had not been estimated.

4. The reference "transfer of presence" is to Runia (2014, 82–83). Thanks to Vivian Sobchack for this reference. See ch. 4 on his theory of how one can be "moved by the presence of the

past," relative to the powers of the photographic likened to novelist W. G. Sebald's usage of historical detail and an alternative to established theories of meaning and representation.

5. Gaudreault (2011, 12) thinks the critique of traditional film history began with Jean-Louis Comolli. What today he terms a "'post-Comolli' criticism" is concerned with the way historians "approach their object of study." See Comolli (1990 [1971], 226–227) on how the multiple and fragmentary "'birth of cinema' emerges from all its 'Histories': scattered and sporadic, beginning anew with each new 'apparatus.'" The viability of Comolli is confirmed in the recent English republication of key essays edited by Fairfax (Comolli 2015) with preface by Philip Rosen. Still, see the continued intellectual viability of relatively traditional historical research in journals such as *Film History*.

6. See Strauven (2013, 68–73) for a comparison of major approaches claiming the term *media archaeology*. Elsaesser (2004) has been seminal where, on 104, he argues following Foucault that the field needs to take an "archaeological turn." The earliest use of the term in the field may be Elsaesser (1986, 246–251). See also Elsaesser (1990, 1–8). Most recently Elsaesser (2016, 22) adds to his 1990 justification for media archaeology based on the discovery of the early period of cinema and the transformations produced by "digitization." Sobchack (2011, 326–327) sees a trend that, given an emphasis on materiality and "presence," requires a new kind of historiography. See also Beltrame, Fidotta, Mariani (2014), papers from the Udine XXI International Film Studies Conference. See Somaini (2016) for an explication of Eisenstein's "Notes On a History of Cinema" as media archaeology.

7. The years 1895–1925 do not correspond perfectly with either the pre-sound years in the United States where sound came in around 1926–1927, or in other parts of the world where films were silent into the 1930s.

8. Pordenone Silent Film Festival (Giornate del Cinema Muto), Pordenone, Italy, 1982–present: http://www.cinetecadelfriuli.org/gcm/default.html (accessed August 1, 2016). Il Cinema Ritrovato, Bologna, Italy. 1986–present: http://festival.ilcinemaritrovato.it/en/ (accessed August 1, 2016). "To Save and Project: The 11th MoMA International Festival of Film Preservation," Museum of Modern Art, New York. October–November 2013: https://www.moma.org/visit/calendar/films/1429 (accessed August 1, 2016). Non Solo Dive: Pioniere del cinema italiano, conference and festival, Bologna, Italy (2007): http://thebioscope.net/2007/11/26/non-solo-dive/ (accessed August 1, 2016). Women and the Silent Screen Conferences: Utrecht (1999); Santa Cruz (2001): http://artstream.ucsc.edu/womensilentscreen/ (accessed August 1, 2016). Montreal (2004); Guadalajara (2006); Stockholm (2008); Bologna (2010): http://box.dar.unibo.it/wss2010/ocs/index.php/wss/WSS6.html (accessed August 2016). Melbourne (2013): http://wss2013.arts.unimelb.edu.au/ (accessed August 1, 2016). Pittsburgh (2015): https://wssviii.wordpress.com/ (accessed August 1, 2016).

9. See for papers from the Women and the Silent Screen conferences: Hastie and Stamp (2006), Maule (2005), Maule and Russell (2005), Bull and Söderbergh Widding (2010), and Dall'Asta and Duckett (2013). Relevant collections and overviews include Förster and Warth (1999), Bean and Negra (2002a, b), Rabinowitz (2006), Callahan (2010), and Bean, Kapse, and Horak (2014). Research websites: Women and Silent British Cinema (WSBC): http://women andsilentbritishcinema.wordpress.com (accessed August 1, 2016), History of Women in the British Film and TV Industries: http://research.ncl.ac.uk/womensworkftvi/ (accessed August 1, 2016), Asta Nielsen Kinothek: http://www.kinothek-asta-nielsen.de/ (accessed August 1, 2016).

10. For an overview of the transformation of the French academy where this began, see Dosse (1997a, b).

11. Significantly, Scott (2007, 20) reminds us that even if we live in a postmodern age, it is post-structuralism, not postmodernism, that is the critical term as well as the approach we need, and the one is "not to be confused" with the other. See also Butler (1991) on this point. More recently, Jameson (2016, 143–144) has reiterated this distinction.

12. The key texts here are Riley (2003), Scott (1996a, 2006, 2007), and Butler and Scott (1992). For an overview see Morgan (2006).

13. For an analysis of the academic success of feminist film theory relative to the "male gaze" and the centerpiece, Mulvey (1975), see Merck (2007). On the "historical turn" in the field, see Higashi (2004, 94–100). See Elsaesser (1986, 146–151) for a review of the relevant books at the time, which included Allen and Gomery (1985). More recently Baer (2015, 153) reminds us that any connection between the German historical turn or the European "New History" and film studies developments in the 1980s produced by the term *the new film history* is a loose one. However, the interest in the economic, as developed, for instance, by Lucien Febvre and Marc Bloch (1953) in France was an important aspect of Allen and Gomery's stress on the technological and industrial.

14. See Spivak (1993, 149), where she calls for undoing the "binary opposition between the 'philosophical' and the 'empirical,'" without, however, exactly demonstrating how to do this.

15. Schlüpmann (2013, 13–14) is responding to Gaudreault as representative, but she mentions Elsaesser as well. She is as concerned that the study of women in the silent era has been "subsumed in the new film history," suggesting the need for continuing to hold conferences on women and the silent screen. On these conferences, see note 8. Gledhill and Knight (2015, 3–4), in their reference to Steedman (2002), align the recent "Doing Women's Film History" conferences and initiatives with theoretical challenges to traditional approaches to evidence. For sponsorship of the conference, see Women's Film and Television History Network (NFTHN): http: //womensfilmand televisionhistory.wordpress.com (accessed August 1, 2016).

16. Petro (2004, 1277) refers to feminist film studies "'before' and 'after' the gaze," urging us to "our own histories, which we must constantly endeavor to rethink, refine, and recall." This is also in the spirit of the work of the Permanent Seminar on the Histories of Film Theories: http://filmtheories.org/ (accessed August 1, 2016).

17. Elsaesser (2012, 604–605), for example, maintains that the "new film history," especially as it became *cinema* history (in a shift to a wider context than the history of films), did not resolve theoretical issues. He says of the new research that expanded exploration to other late-nineteenth-century technologies and visual culture phenomena: "In the process, it complicated the question of 'what is cinema' as well as making it even more unlikely that there would be agreement on what its 'history' might be" (605).

18. See Scott (2007, 21–23) on U.S. historians' resistance to post-structuralism, which she thinks begins with history as it has been positioned opposite philosophy and confirms that the antagonism came to a head over "objectivity."

19. See Munslow (2003, ch. 1, especially 29–31). Jenkins and Munslow (2004, 10) refer to the predominant approach as "empiricism plus concepts."

20. See Gaines (2016, 2) where I discuss how it might be said that theory was challenged on behalf of empirical viewers.

21. In the U.S. case, the first histories are Ramsaye (1986), Hampton (1970), and Jacobs (1975); in the French case, Bardèche and Brasillach (1938), Mitry (1967–1980), and Deslandes and Richard (1968).

22. For the impact of continental theory that could translate into "postmodern history," see Jenkins (1991), although White (2009, 3) now calls Jenkins "adamantly post-postmodern," and Munslow (2009, 320) sees Jenkins as moving past "postmodern histories." See Jameson (2016, 143–144) on his reconsideration of the terms *postmodernism* and *postmodernity* in which he stresses the latter, which he sees as a periodization marking a break around 1980 and which he thinks denotes the "end of the modern" in ways ranging from "communications technologies" to "forms of art." Baumbach, Young, and Yu (2016, 16, note 7) note how postmodernism has been subject to "conflation" with post-structuralism but also with "cultural Marxism." The term *metahistory* is still associated with Hayden White (1973). Runia (2014, 50) thinks that White's *Metahistory* began a "heyday of metahistoriography." The term *metaphilosophy* or the "philosophy of the philosophy of history" is from Carr (2009, 17). For "history-writing as critique," see Scott (2007, 19–38). For an overview of the "roots" of the "new philosophy of history," see Ankersmit (1995, 278–283).

23. See Jenkins and Munslow (2004, Part Three, "Deconstructionism") under which they have reprinted, among others, Walter Benjamin, Hayden White, and Jacques Derrida. For further on the "deconstructivist historian," see Gaines (2016, 324).

24. Its coordinates have been mapped relative to the discipline-specific "linguistic turn" in the 1960s. For a more agnostic approach, see Scott (2007), who thinks that critique should not be to seen as a "turn," which has the effect of making it seem "a matter of fashion or style."

25. See Hayden White's Foreword to Koselleck (2002, x) as well as Koselleck (2004, 1), who asserts the importance of theory to history "if it still wants to conceive of itself as an academic discipline." Indicative of the coexistence of the two key terms, see Doran (2013, 1–3) on naming his edited volume, *Philosophy of History after Hayden White*, and White (2013a, 209), who in his concluding "Comment" says that although a "*philosophy* of history" could be imagined, it would entail thinking of events as concepts. He doesn't claim to have been doing "philosophy of history" because of the distinction he makes between history as having to do with events-in-time and philosophy with concepts that have a relation to one another unlike the kinds of relations events have to one another. Where events are related by "cause and effect," "similarity and contiguity," and "contingency," for example, he sees concepts as having relations of "contrariety, contradiction, and implication."

26. This move has been elaborated by Gumbrecht (2004) and Runia (2014). See Sobchack (2011, 331, note 6) where she quotes Hayden White as saying that although he thinks any experience of the "presence of the past" could only be illusory, one could have an "illusion of presence," which is what he thinks Frank Ankersmit means in making a distinction between an experience "*of*" history and his now preferred "*about*" history or an experience "of *historicality*."

27. The chronological narrative of inclusion could be said to have its "point of origin" in an article in the short-lived publication *Women and Film* (Smith 1973). Smith (1974, 1) says: "The work of woman filmmakers in the eighty-year history of motion pictures has never been chronicled."

28. See Cooper (2010, xxi) for another way of explaining the apparent lack of discrimination in the case of women working at Universal Pictures.

29. "How Twelve Famous" (1923, 31–33) mentions Anita Loos, Frances Marion, Ouida Bergere, June Mathis, Olga Printzlau, Margaret Turnbull, Clara Beranger, Jane Murfin, Belulah Marie Dix, Marion Fairfax, Eve Unsell, Sada Cowan.

30. Norden (1995, 187) also uses this quote from Grau in the first academic overview of U.S. women, picking up where Slide and Smith left off. Norden was originally published in *Wide Angle* 6:3 (1985): 58–67.

31. See articles in Kay and Peary (1977): Van Wert on Germaine Dulac, Peary on Alice Guy Blaché, Kozarski on Lois Weber.

32. On Guy Blaché and the Solax company, see McMahan (2002) and Kozarski (2004, ch. 3).

33. In the United States and Europe, there is the related phenomenon of female scientists and executives as an emerging group of seriously ambitious and powerful women. In 2015, Germany passed a law requiring a percentage of women on corporate boards. See Buckley (2015, C1) on the American Civil Liberties Union request for U.S. federal hearings on gender discrimination in the major Hollywood studios, talent agencies, and networks. See also ch. 8, note 97, on organizations compiling statistics on women in the U.S. film and television industries.

34. See White (2015, 1–27). For instance, the second of two world conferences after the first organized by Veronica Pravadelli in Rome was "Global Women's Cinema: Transnational Contexts, Cultural Difference, and Gendered Scenarios" (September 18–20, 2014), Humanities Institute at Stony Brook, Stony Brook, New York. The third was "Women, Film Culture, and Globalization" (September 2–4, 2016), Concordia University, Montreal, Canada.

35. As importantly, White (2015, 18) emphasizes how McHugh's "transnational generation" challenges "spatial as well as temporal" approaches to feminism and film, such as the traditional "second" and "third" waves, or even feminism as opposed to postfeminist configurations. McHugh's contemporary paradigm foregrounds the "transnational" aspect of some silent-era women whose careers were established on more than one continent. See Gledhill (2010, 275–282) for an overview and Dall'Asta (2010a, 311–312) on the Hungarian-Italian distributor Frieda Klug. See also National Film and Television archivists on the special issues of gender as well as transnational collection development: Dixon (2010, 304–309), Burrows (2010, 343–349).

36. Kaplan and Grewal (2002, 73) emphasize that "transnational" is useful "only when it signals attention to uneven and dissimilar circuits of culture and capital."

37. Gunning (2008, 11–13) argues that cinema was global before it was national. See also ch. 9.

38. Smith (1973, 77) mentions Gauntier as codirector of *From the Manger to the Cross* and an assistant director at Kalem, and although she says that Gauntier wrote scripts for and starred in over five hundred films, she does not mention Gauntier's memoir "Blazing the Trail." Slide (1977, 102) puts Gauntier forth not only as Kalem's "leading lady" but as having founded her own company, The Gene Gauntier Feature Players, in 1912. In addition, he says, she is credited with directing one film that she wrote, *The Grandmother* (1910).

39. See Mahar (2006, ch. 2 and 6) on women producers. See also Gaines (2016, 7–11). For updates on occupations data based on ongoing research, see: wfpp.cdrs.columbia.edu (accessed January 1, 2017).

40. Over sixty is a conservative estimate and doesn't tell us about differences between enterprises: units within larger film companies, independent companies that produced motion

pictures, companies that functioned more like agencies. The director and producer roles may have been blurred in the beginning, and there is no comprehensive account of how the term was used or the function emerged. See ch. 1, note, 28, and ch. 8, note 38. Swanson (1958, 15) describes how in her acting work with Mack Sennett "there was no such thing as a producer. The actor and the director sat around and talked about a scene, and everyone put in his two cents" CUOHRO.

41. See Kozarski (2004) and Spehr (1977) as studies of the U.S. industry in New Jersey before there was a Hollywood. See Olsson (2008) on early Los Angeles.

42. Jacob (2015, 160) makes this observation in her analysis of the first issue of the journal *Women and Film* 1.1 (1972). See especially page 74, a chart showing the percentage of women versus men who were then members of the Hollywood unions: the International Alliance of Theatrical Stage Employees (IATSE) and the local Motion Picture Operators (MPMO), and the Screen Writers, Producers, and Directors Guilds.

43. Kay and Peary (1977a, 337) frame the reprinted article: "Needless to say, most of Madame Blaché's arguments for women in film strike one today as hopelessly arcane, growing directly out of Victorian conceptions of the nature of the female—emotional, religious, sensitive, superior in 'matters of the heart.' Yet ingenious is the way Alice Blaché takes these traditionalist, often absurd, reasonings and turns them to advantage in her plea for increased participation of women in filmmaking."

44. Hine (1995, 335) defends the encyclopedic approach as a stage prefatory to opening up a field: "To make an encyclopedia is to claim a historiographical moment." McHugh (2009, 113) is quite rightly critical of feminism and film as having been stuck for too long in the phase of the encyclopedic catalog of women by name, nation, or region. I would contend that the other problem with the old encyclopedia book form was the danger of conveying that research contained between two covers was complete. We will next need to ask if online research and publication can produce the requisite open-ended indeterminability. For an extensive list of early cinema digital research projects, see "Transformations I": https://transformationsconference .net/ (accessed January 1, 2017).

45. See note 11.

46. See Gaines (2014c, 180–181) for a discussion of the legacy of anti-historicism in 1970s film theory.

47. The world recalls *Pearl White* because her films were distributed internationally so broadly. Dahlquist (2013b, 14–17) argues about her distributor that French Pathé Frère's internationalization market strategy was double: to promote itself as a global organization and to emphasize local production as "glocalized Americana" (18).

48. On Gene Gauntier's girl spy as the beginning of the serial queen in 1908–1909, see Gaines (2010, 294–298), Mahar (2001, 105), and Everett (1973, 22–25). Dall'Asta (2013, 77) says that the Protéa serials both "pre-dated and then paralleled" *Pearl White* and were first screened in 1913 in the United States. See also ch. 1, note 17.

49. This is not to say either that other serial queens were not popular or that *Pearl White* was not wildly popular. See Askari (2014, 109–114) on the reception of Ruth Roland's serial *The Tiger's Trail* in Tehran. On the reception of *Pearl White*, known in China as *Baolain* or "precious lotus," see Xiqing (2013, 250–256).

50. Musser and Sklar (1990, 3–4) comment on what they saw as an "adamant anti-historical" position and skepticism of "empiricism" dominant in the field. Although this was then changing,

Notes to Introduction

as they saw it, "historical investigation" was still undeveloped and in their analysis some scholars formerly aligned with "ahistorical structuralisms" now used *historiography* as a term too loosely. Although the issue of the American journal *Radical History Review* (Spring 1988) they coedited was aligned with current interest in working-class lives, they don't mention the British tradition in the introduction to this collection that reprinted some of the articles.

51. On first consideration, one might say that Althusser was thrown out in the 1980s along with the objectionable aspects of 1970s film theory. Foucault, whom Hayden White calls the "anti-historical historian," in contrast, continues to be invoked, and as I noted earlier, his term *archaeology* is today associated with innovations in film and media research. Yet Grieveson (2009, 183–186) has called our attention to the selective uses of Foucault in the field of cinema and media studies concentrating on his history of sexuality but only more recently building on his analysis of institutional power.

52. Elsaesser (1986) reviews Allen and Gomery (1985) and Salt (1983, 246), linking the interest in film history to the transformations in cinema itself. Further, he intimates that the "legitimation" of film history as academic pursuit may be in part responsible for the alignment, new at that time, with scientificity or empiricism (Elsaesser 1986, 247). Butler (1992, 413) notes that the "new historicism" in film studies corresponded with the falling off of the 1970s *Screen* tradition.

53. See Gaines (2014c, 184) on the anti-historicism in 1970s film theory relative to the German Frankfurt School "crisis of historicism" and French post-structuralist critiques of historicism. See Bambach (2013, 133–147) for a discussion of the relevant aspects of the German case. Thanks to Nick Baer for this reference.

54. Some examples of a more critical approach to historiography from within film and media studies include Cowie (2011) on historical writing, Gaudreault (2011), Gaudreault and Gunning (2006), Sobchack (2000), and Rosen (2001). For emerging scholarship that comes out on the other side of the "historical turn," see Baron (2014), Baer (2015), and essays in Beltrame, Fidotta, and Mariani (2014).

55. Tasker and Negra (2007, 14) explore as well what they call "popular feminism as postfeminism." McRobbie (2008, 1) identifies a "*faux*-feminism" that keeps the women's movement in check. Scott (2011, 143) calls Elizabeth Weed's "Feminist Theory Archive" a "post post institution." See also Braidotti (2005).

56. On the use of Bloch for queer theory, see Muñoz (2009), Ahmed (2004, 183–189), and Ahmed (2010, 181–183). Hansen, (2012, xii–xiii) explains the importance of the German feminist journal *Frauen ünd Film*, which introduced Critical Theory into feminism through Benjamin. Most significant, Hansen identifies *Frauen ünd Film* as the place where Mulvey (1975) was taken up and where, in addition to the critique of patriarchy, "female subjectivity" was considered in terms "other than absence and negativity."

57. On the question of Marxist feminism today, see Fraser (2013, 16), who proposes return to the "insurrectionary, anti-capitalist spirit of the second wave."

58. Scott (1996a, 4) also says that whether "women" is a "singular or radically diverse category," it is an "unresolved question." She also points out that feminism has not answered the question as to whether the category is produced by or preexists history.

59. This reassessment appears in a special issue of *The American Historical Review* (2008a, 1422–1430) devoted to her essay "Gender: A Useful Category of Historical Analysis" (1986, 1053–1075). Scott (2009, 48) updates her formulation again: "Gender is a useful category only

if differences are the question, not the answer, only if we ask what 'men' and 'women' are taken to mean wherever and whenever we are looking at them, rather than assuming we already know who and what they are."

60. Cooper (2010, xv) notes that their "collective disappearance" was not the subject of comment until "well after the fact" when women directors were largely gone (Osborne 1925, 5).

CHAPTER 1. WHAT HAPPENED TO WOMEN IN THE SILENT U.S. FILM INDUSTRY?

1. Of nine possible Gene Gauntier Feature Players films, released by Warners Features, 1912–1915, two are extant: *For Ireland's Sake* (dir. Sidney Olcott, 1914) and *Come Back to Erin* (dir. Sidney Olcott, 1914). For a complete Gautier filmography, see Bisplinghoff (2013).

2. Cleo Madison directing credits at Universal include the extant titles: *Eleanor's Catch*. Producer/director: Cleo Madison, screenplay: William Mong (Rex Film Corp. U.S. 1916), cast: Cleo Madison, Lule Warrenton; *The Power of Fascination*. Producer/director: Cleo Madison, author: Charles Saxby (Rex Film Corp. U.S. 1915), cast: Cleo Madison, Jack Holt, Thomas Chatterton, Carrie Fowler, Jack Francis, Jack Wells; *Her Defiance*. Producer/director: Cleo Madison, Joe King, screenplay: Harvey Gates (Rex Film Corp. U.S. 1916), cast: Cleo Madison.

3. For new feminist research, see Lant (2006, 547–585). Some of the first revisions of the standard narrative have been studies of the careers of the most prolific and important directors: Dorothy Arzner (Mayne 1994), Alice Guy Blaché (McMahan 2002), Nell Shipman (Armatage 2003), and Lois Weber (Stamp 2015).

4. See Kuhn and Stacey (1998) for an account of the prohibition against empirical work in the 1970s that had a direct impact on feminist film scholarship.

5. Smith (1973, 77) mentions Cleo Madison as an actress who "produced and directed" one- and two-reel films at Universal: *Liquid Dynamite* (1915), *The King of Destiny* (1915), and *Her Bitter Cup* (1916).

6. Slide (1996b, v) describes his discovery: "Back in 1972, I was hired to set up and undertake the initial research for the *American Film Institute Catalog: Feature Films, 1911–1920*. As I turned the pages of such early American trade papers as *The Moving Picture World* and *Motion Picture News*, I slowly became aware of the number of films directed by women." See Gaines (2004) for more on feminism and historical research in the 1970s.

7. More recent volumes have begun to rectify this. See Abel (2005), Bowser (1990), and Koszarski (1990).

8. See *Motion Picture World* (1912, 1169) on the formation of Gene Gauntier Feature Players. Bisplinghoff (2013) is the best source on Gauntier's career. Mahar (2006, 62) argues that we still do not have adequate evidence of the kind of work these women did within these companies.

9. Cooper (2010, xv) in reference to the kind of evidence we have and the difficulty of finding a culpable causal agent, says of the case of Universal women that their disappearance from the workplace almost suggests one of those "insoluble mysteries" with which historians grapple.

10. It is possible to think of her "revulsion" as beginning in December 1912, when she and director Sidney Olcott returned to New York from Palestine to face the Kalem executives with a print of the six-reel film they had shot—*From the Manger to the Cross*. In "Blazing the Trail" (March 1929, 142), she recalls this moment: "What lay behind the changed attitude of the Kalem officials I have never learned." On the making of *From the Manger to the Cross*, see

Henderson-Bland (1922). The importance of this film and Gauntier's contribution to it were first mentioned in Slide (1996b, 117–118; 1998, 107).

11. On the "new film history," see Introduction.

12. Gene Gauntier Letter to Colonel William Selig, June 28, 1915, William Selig Collection, AMPAS-SC.

13. Mahar (2006, 72) reads the interview in her New York apartment as disingenuous and suspects the pretense in Gauntier's raving to *Photoplay* about her love for housekeeping. But the article also says that Gauntier had only been "housekeeping" a week and that in that week she was at the studio three or four days (Condon 1915, 69). Although the titles *The Governor and His Daughter* and *The Maid of '76* are mentioned in the article, reliable sources such as Spehr (1996, 225) indicate nine titles produced by Gene Gauntier Feature Players and neither of these are among them.

14. *Moving Picture World* (March 27, 1915, 1942) reports that Gauntier and Jack Clark and their company will make three- and four-reel pictures for Universal. Branff (1999) lists five titles released under either Universal's Powers or Bison brand with Jack J. Clark as director and Gene Gauntier in the cast, writing only one of the five. Spehr (1996, 225) also lists five titles.

15. The last three films in which Gauntier appeared were produced by relatively minor companies. Slide says that Capital Film Co., headquartered in Indiana, was in business 1918–1924 (1998, 32) and that Pioneer Film Corporation was, in 1919, in its third restructuring since 1915 (1998, 159).

16. See Gaines (2012a) on the problem of attribution when we study the first decade in which all creative personnel were effectively anonymous.

17. The first historians treated her as a daredevil actress (Bardèche and Brasillach 1938, 73) and as responsible for the "working synopsis" for *Ben Hur* (1907) (Ramsaye 1986, 462). After "Blazing the Trail" became available to researchers at the Museum of Modern Art, Gauntier is referenced as one of the "first screen scenarists" (Jacobs 1975, 61), a "gifted leading woman" who adapted the classics *Tom Sawyer*, *As You Like It*, *Evangeline*, *Hiawatha*, and *The Scarlet Letter* (Wagenknecht 1962, 54); founded Gene Gauntier Feature Players; and wrote and directed one film, *Grandmother* (1910) (Slide 1977, 102). Also at Gene Gauntier Feature Players, Gauntier oversaw "everything from the dark-room to the business offices" where she is "star author, director, and technician" and, with Jack J. Clark, "equal owner of the enterprise" (Grau 1914, 363).

18. At the Kalem Company she made three girl spy titles, all extant: *The Girl Spy* (1909), *The Girl Spy before Vicksburg* (1910), and *Further Adventures of the Girl Spy* (1910). Copies of all were held in archives outside the United States until a copy of *Further Adventures of the Girl Spy* was "repatriated" from the British Film Institute around 2004. She continued this early "series" at Gene Gauntier Feature Players with at least two more, considered lost: *A Daughter of the Confederacy* (1913) and *Little Rebel* (1915). See also Judson (1913, 892).

19. Lant (2006, 562) suggests that because directing was the most highly coveted job in this period, it is a "sensitive indicator" of the opportunities and possibilities for women. She reiterates as well (559) that Dorothy Arzner was the only "prominent" director still working. On Arzner, see also Casella (2009, 243).

20. Mahar (2006, ch. 4), Singer (2001), Bean (2002b), Stamp (2000, ch. 3), and articles in Dahlquist (2013a).

21. Mahar adds that this irreverent femaleness is also there in the work of silent comedy stars, exemplified for her by Mabel Normand (2006, 110–112). Consider how many comediennes converted their popularity into enterprises: the Mabel Normand Feature Film Company, the Marie Dressler Motion Picture Corporation, Gale Henry's Model Film Company, Faye Tincher Productions, and, again, Flora Finch's two ventures. See Joyce and Putzi (2013) on Normand; Moore (2013) on Dressler; Massa (2013) on Henry; Rapf (2013) on Tincher.

22. These female action pictures reached an apex in the Grace Cunard–Francis Ford serials at Universal around 1917 but continued in a thin stream into the 1920s (Everett 1973, 22; Mahar 2006, 105–106). On the Cunard-Ford collaborations, see Cooper (2010, 121–125).

23. The reference here is to early cinema as itself transgressive, beginning with Burch (1990), further developed in the "cinema of attractions" literature, the comprehensive overview of which is Strauven (2006), in which, see Gunning (2006, 31–39).

24. Mahar (2006, 8) foregrounds the "what happened to the female filmmaker?" question. Neely (2010, 28) asks, "Why did they stop?" Cooper (2010, 24) addresses the question implicitly with the hypothesis that researchers have not produced a "how and why" explanation because the issue is less one of evidence than of methodological approach.

25. Cooper (2010, xxi) challenges us to think our way around the inevitabilities encouraged by both gender analysis and the methodology of historical causality, to admit analytically that "events might have gone otherwise."

26. Mahar (2006, 201) mentions editors, the most important of whom is Anne Bauchens. Many more writers continued at the major studios, including Gertrude Atherton, Leah Baird, Clara Beranger, Adele S. Buffington, Lenore Coffee, Kate Corbaley, Sada Cowen, Beulah Marie Dix, Winnifred Dunn, Dorothy Farnum, Agnes Christine Johnston, Bradley King, Sonya Levien, Anita Loos, Josephine Lovett, Jeanie Macpherson, Frances Marion, Sarah Y. Mason, Bess Meredyth, Jane Murfin, Olga Printzlau, Dorothy Davenport Reid, Adela Rogers St. Johns, Lillian Case Russell, Wanda Tuchock, Eve Unsell, and Dorothy Yost.

27. See Förster (2005, 12) on what she calls the "careerographies" or "reconstructions of careers" as seen in film and theater roles, films produced, and writings. Her idea is to put together a kind of "professional itinerary" of the figures she studies.

28. Anderson (2016, 15) says of the work of early producers that they might: "write scenarios, scout locations, procure costumes and properties, direct and edit films, process prints, write promotion, secure sales, ship prints, or even project motion pictures in large exhibition venues, all of this in addition to attending to budgets and the legal and financial concerns of the companies they operated." This would have described the work of J. Stuart Blackton or William Selig, his early examples, but not necessarily that of the women who put their names on units within larger companies or independent companies that broke away from larger ones.

29. Mahar (2006, 62) argues that for the first phase at least, the kinds of films they made for their own companies featured strong women. This assertion calls for analysis of many more examples.

30. See Bowser (1990, 112) who argues that Florence Turner and Florence Lawrence were effectively "tied" for the honor of first motion picture star, contrary to the popular view that the first star was Lawrence.

31. See Neely (2010) on the women who started companies financed by First National Pictures, beginning in 1917—Olga Petrova and Anita Stewart as well as Mary Pickford, Constance

and Norma Talmadge, Anita Loos, Katherine MacDonald, Mildred Harris-Chaplin, Hope Hampton, and Marguerite Clark.

32. On Mathis, see Slater (2002, 2008, 2010) and Wexman (2013); on Unsell, see Achuff and Matz (2013), Fairfax (Slater 2013), Russell (Wagner 2013), and Baird (Blaetz 2013).

33. Mahar (2006, 73) says that most had a "male partner." For a comprehensive list of male-female partnerships, see Gaines and Vatsal (2013). See Creekmur (2013) on Guinan; Ionita (2013) on Mrs. Sidney Drew; Anderson (2013) on Reid; and Lund on Barriscale (2013).

34. See Introduction note 1. Holliday (1995, notes 37, 75–76) says that although *photoplaywright, scenarist*, and *scenario writer* were first used synonymously, after the advent of sound *scenario writer* was gradually phased out in favor of *screenwriter*. See Gaines and Vatsal (2013) on women scenario editors who also supervised writing departments, and ch. 7, note 5, for a list of 18.

35. *The Curse of the Quon Gwon* was discovered in Wong's family and placed on the National Film Registry list in 2007. See Lau (2013) on Wong, Lyons (2013) on Michelina and, on Souders and Williams, see Morgan and Dixon (2013) as well as Welbon (2001, 40).

36. Mahar (2001, 73) uses this phrase, but her later book version significantly complicates the dramatic summation that I am using here for effect.

37. Mahar (2006, 170). See Koszarski (1990, 69–77) on the formation of Associated First National Exhibitors Circuit. First National was bought by Warner Brothers in 1928.

38. Yet this formulation, which appears to privilege Staiger's account over Musser's reconceptualization, is itself an example of competing narratives, although it should be noted that Musser's "collaborative system" (1991,161, 312) poses more of a challenge to the idea of an early "director system" than to the evolution of the "central producer system" that Staiger, in Bordwell, Staiger, Thompson, thinks came to dominance about 1914 (1985, 93). The standard references for the two explanatory models are Musser (1996, 85–108) and Staiger in Bordwell, Staiger, Thompson (1985, 113–141). See Mahar (2006, 170–171) on the impact of the central-producer system on independent companies. Cooper (2010, xvii) says that he, too, has been persuaded by Mahar's case for the explanatory value of finance capital, especially in the way she shows a correlation between vertical integration and the disappearance of independent women's companies. He sees that industrialization defined jobs more tightly and therefore closed off options for moving into directing.

39. An example might be the one Neely (2010, 9) gives of the novels Anita Stewart told a reporter that she wanted to adapt with her production company in 1919—Theodore Dreiser's *Sister Carrie* and *Susan Lennox: Her Rise and Fall*, the story of the prostitute who turned her life around. Greta Garbo played the role in the 1931 MGM adaptation of *Susan Lennox*.

40. Cooper (2010, xxi) reminds us that the "profit motive" does not line up perfectly with sexism. Capitalism and patriarchy may work hand in hand or at odds with one another, and, in the case of Universal, he seems to suggest, profit may have overridden sexism.

41. Cooper (2010, xvii) says of Universal in this regard that "to attribute a shift in the gendered division of labor simply to the triumph of big business risks oversimplifying that transformation to the point of mystifying it."

42. Murray here typifies the motivation of the star actress to start a company. Mahar (2006, 154) confirms that actresses were frustrated with the choices made for them and that what they wanted was to control not only the story but the distribution of the film. See also Murray (1959, 7–8) where she explains that she had a Tiffany ring, "a wonderful marquis, and I loved that

name, so when my company was put together with these great—well, the automobile people of Detroit, you know, were my backers I had my way about the name of the company and it was called Tiffany. To me that was the highest."

43. Although Mae Murray's Tiffany Productions made eight films distributed through Metro-Goldwyn-Mayer between 1922 and 1924, by this time it is likely that no actress was receiving the terms she might have negotiated a few years earlier. Murray describes how studio president Nicholas Schenck renewed her contract as an MGM player but left her husband out of it, putting an end to the marriage already suffering from what she describes as his feelings of jealousy and inadequacy (Murray n.d., 47). Although Mae Murray's appearance in the classic MGM film *The Merry Widow* (1925) is considered the pinnacle of her career, it was not a Tiffany Productions project and MGM had taken over her company name. See also Willis (2013) on Murray.

44. An example might be if we "corrected" Ramsaye and Hampton, who see the female stardom of Mary Pickford and Clara Kimball Young as integral to the development of the mature business. See Ramsaye on Adolph Zukor's negotiations with Mary Pickford in 1915, the resulting contract with whom he parlays into Paramount Pictures (1986, 745–751). In Hampton, Lewis J. Selznick's idea for a company named for actress Clara Kimball Young (Clara Kimball Young Pictures), an offshoot of his World Film Corporation, is a "daring" means of financing production through franchises sold as advances against film rentals. Buyers were wealthy investors, including mail order entrepreneur Arthur Spiegel and theatrical agent William O. Brady (1970, 135). New research suggests that both Pickford and Young found these arrangements intolerable and, although Pickford's role in starting United Artists in 1919 is well known, Young's attempt to sue Selznick and found her own company is not part of the original narrative. See Mahar (2006, 165).

45. Osborne (1925, 4) mentions two Universal women directors—Ida May Park and Lois Weber—and gets the name of a third one—Elsie Jane Wilson—incorrect.

46. Smith (1924, 102) gives us more details, referring to Gauntier's work as critic on the *Kansas City Post*, to the public record of the divorce January 30, 1918, between Mrs. Genevieve Clark and John J. Clark registered in Kansas City. In her letter to *Photoplay*, Gauntier refers to the Island of Arust on the west coast of Sweden where she was planning to write the book that must have found form in the 1928 memoir "Blazing the Trail." In conversation (October 9, 2010), Tony Tracy, codirector with Peter Flynn of *Blazing the Trail* (2010), the Irish Broadcasting System documentary on the O'Kalems, as they came to be known, confirms that the remainder of Gauntier's life was spent with her actress sister and her husband, the Swedish Electrolux heir, either in Sweden or traveling, sometimes on the family yacht, which is what might have taken her to the Caribbean where she died.

CHAPTER 2. WHERE WAS ANTONIA DICKSON?

1. The *History of Kinetograph* was originally published as a series of articles in *Cassier's Magazine*, November, 1892, through December, 1894. Antonia and W. K. L. rearranged the articles in 1894–1895 as a pamphlet and arranged printing by Albert Bunn to be used by the Raff and Gammon Kinetoscope Company in promoting the Kinetoscope. See Spehr (2008, 148–149; 394–395).

2. Hendricks (1961, 7–8) quotes a review of *Cassier's Magazine* series from the British journal *Electrical Review* (August 18, 1893), which commented satirically on the "florid language." Spehr

(2008, 286) notes that the style of *History of the Kinetograph* is consistent although "flowery, verbose and laced with classical and mythological references" in the Victorian style of the day. He thinks that W. K. L.'s writing style was unlike his sister's although he most likely wrote the Edison invention descriptions.

3. Spehr (2008, 289) notes that *Cassier's Magazine* did not print her full name in her article on the telephone (1892). Today's reader, however, will sense that *History of the Kinetograph* also reads like the promotional pamphlet that it was, more popular science than science proper.

4. Lacasse and Duigou (1987), Lacasse (2013), and Gaudreault (1993, 95).

5. See also Deleuze: "We cannot say that it was. It no longer exists, it does not exist, but it insists, it consists, it *is*. It insists with the former present, it consists with the new or present present" (1994, 82). Cohen (2006, 246), elaborating on this passage, says that the existence or nonexistence of the past is a "false problem" and to say that the past "insists" is preferable to saying that the 'past was' or that it no longer exists. As relevant is Husserl (1991, 19): "The attempt to treat the past as something nonreal and nonexistent is also highly questionable."

6. Spehr (2008, 378–379) makes the case that the Lumières *could have* based their machine on diagrams of the kinetograph since some technical descriptions and articles had been published. However, he quotes the research of Marta Braun and Laurent Mannoni who say that around the time of the first Kinetoscope showing in Paris that Georges Demenÿ had approached the Lumières about his Phonoscope and that his camera, like Dickson's prototype, also featured an intermittent movement.

7. Dickson's obituary in *Cassier's Magazine* is one of a few sources of information about her writings and lectures. Thanks to Paul Spehr for the Dickson references.

8. Dickson and Dickson (1894, 361–362), in the two-page *L' ENVOI* write: "From this union of minds, individual and racial, achieved by the junction of woman's perceptive wisdom with the rational wisdom of man, and wielded in the fire of love, sweeter and more passionate than the Epithalamium of the morning stars," these "new forms" will be born. But this is all to be brought about, as they say in the concluding sentence, by the "genius" of Thomas Alva Edison.

9. See Dickson on the telephone (1892), as well as the 1895 "Wonders of the Kinetoscope," in which she quotes Edison on the phonograph, which he calls "A young lady .. who from her birth has spoken all languages, played all instruments and imitated all sounds, cooing with the babies, whistling with the birds, singing with the operatic stars and discoursing with the philogists." As quoted in Lant (2006, 408).

10. Rich (1979, 284) says "The passive or active instrumentality of white women in the practice of inhumanity against black people is a fact of history" and even refers to "female racism" (281), a concept that has not been picked up.

11. Butler (2011, 12–13) on Scott's use of the paradox of "sexual difference" says that rather than denying the dilemma that it presents us with, Scott sees "a conundrum without which we cannot function, and it is even a constitutive conundrum of feminist theory."

12. Scott (2008b, 8) acknowledges the downside of feminist institutional success and configures the essays in the collection she introduces as an attempt to "turn feminism's critical edge upon itself." See Martin (2008, 172–173) on the predictability of gender analyses and the possibility that gender "may have outlived its usefulness."

13. Wang (2011, 2) sees contemporary transnational feminism not as offering a vision of a "future cosmopolitan utopia" as the consequence of breaking down borders but as a critique of a globalization seen as "erecting new borders even while erasing old ones." Her proposal

for considering contemporary cinema directed by women that involves "female authorship" involves acknowledging "unevenness."

14. Steedman (2002, 77) says: "The very search for what is lost and gone . . alters it, as it goes along, so that every search becomes an impossible one." But note that the" impossibility" of things is not only an insight but a deconstructive move.

15. I mean here both the literal impossibility and the term from deconstruction. See Jenkins and Munslow (2004, 12–15) and then consider the theorists they consider include in the category of "deconstructionist historian."

16. Koselleck (2004, 93), White (1999, 1), and Rancière (1994, 1–3). Bruno (1984, 54) mentions the "philological" phenomenon of the double meaning in her discussion of the critique of narrative historiography. Rosen (2001, 6) thinks of "historicity" as two "moments" in league: "*historiography*, the writing of history ('historio-graphy')" and "*history*, the actual past that the writing claims to convey." Heidegger (1996, 346) says of the "most obvious ambiguity of the term *history*: "It makes itself known in the fact that it means 'historical reality' as well as the possibility of a science of it."

17. Although *Da-sein* might mean *existence* in the German vernacular it is well known that Heidigger didn't think of the terms as synonymous in *Being in Time*. His English translator Joan Stambaugh explains that one of the reasons for leaving *Da-sein* untranslated (although capitalized and hyphenated) was that the philosopher meant to re-inflect the German word while retaining its ordinary meaning (1996, xiii–xiv). Heidegger scholar Magda King (2001, 48) thinks the term is most closely translated into English as "being-there" or "there-being," but is also open to the possibility of its meaning both "human being and way of life" (49).

18. See Dosse (1997a, 375–379) on Heidegger's explicit and implicit "influence" on Foucault, Lacan, and Derrida. See Derrida (2016, 169–170) for his seminar notes, recently published and translated, in which he demonstrates how Heidegger unravels four "tangled significations" in the concept of history.

19. See Trouillot (1995, 146–147): "That U.S. slavery as both officially ended, yet continues in many complex forms—most notably institutionalized racism and the cultural denigration of blackness—makes its representation particularly burdensome in the United States."

20. On the "linguistic turn," see Munslow (2003, 47) who says that while the historian might easily take a reflexive position toward methodology, "to expect that historical understanding begins with the historian's language rather than the past takes a heart in the mouth epistemological leap. Most historians can't do it and won't do it." On how Hayden White has continued to be influential, see Doran (2013).

21. In those fields, the conviction that the "mode of discourse" and the "product produced" by it could be made one and the same by using a similar "manner of speaking," as White would explain, is no longer questioned (1987, 57).

22. The reference to feminism is to Mulvey (1975) but the impact of Barthes (1977b) has continued in ever more sophisticated analyses like Gaudreault (2009) and Altman (2008). The tradition has become standardized in textbooks like Bordwell and Thompson (2017, ch. 3), although perhaps as less critical than astute.

23. Perhaps this is because of the critique of that critique, for which see Christopher Williams (2000), the most comprehensive discussion of narrative as it relates to notions of "realism." Still, in what other field does one find scholars foregrounding their approach as "narrative history"? See Bordwell and Thompson (2003, 9) where they explain that "More often, historians'

explanations take the form of stories. *Narrative history*, as it is called, seeks to answer *how* and *why* questions by tracing the relevant circumstances over time. It produces a chain or causes and effects, or shows how a process works, by telling a story."

24. Exceptions are Cowie (2011) and Gaudreault (2011, 11–13). Rosen (2001) has critiqued narrative history, but not turned that analysis on narrative film history specifically, which is not to say that his insights aren't highly relevant.

25. Munslow (2003, 48, 56–60) refers to the "mirror of nature or correspondence theory of truth." The question of "correspondence" or "noncorrespondence" has some advantages in considering the historian's representational practice over "realism" or "mimesis" which have more to do with the success of the effect on reader or viewer than the historian's goal of making a narrative that adequately refers. Although, see White (1987, 27): "The story told" can be understood as "a mimesis of the story lived in some region of historical reality, and insofar as it is an accurate imitation, it is to be considered a truthful account thereof."

26. See Gallagher and Greenblatt (1997, ch. 2) on what might have happened but finally did not.

27. See Runia (2014, 53) for a case for meaning as challenged by what he calls "presence," that intrigue of considering that there is something on the "denotative" side that trumps the "connotative" meaning. Although film theory might have dealt with this phenomenon as the indexical "wham" (Nichols 1991, 157), Runia (53–54) expands upon Badiou's *passion du réel*.

28. Ankersmit (2001, 237) says that "Historical time is a relatively recent and highly artificial invention of Western civilization. It is a cultural, not a philosophical notion . . . for founding narrativism on the concept of time is building on quicksand."

29. See Tribe on (2004, x–xi) on Koselleck's debt to Heidegger. See Heidegger's formulation of "having-been" (past) relative to the "futural" (1996, 349–353).

30. For Kosseleck (2004, 4), the basic question pertains to what he sees as a new "relocation" of the past relative to the future.

31. Carr (1987, 198) in his review of Koselleck uses the term *hermeneutical circle* and it is here that he sees the influence of Heidegger.

32. Tribe (2004, xi, note 13) says that in the translation of Koselleck's book to English "futures past" was selected over "former futures," which should have been the title.

33. Although to read the conclusion of the Dicksons' Edison biography (1894, 361–362), one can only conclude that the Victorians were still deferential to the past. They write that "for the promise and potency of the Future lie in the Past and Present." But finally: "The time will surely come when man and woman, standing side by side and hand in hand upon the broad sunlit heights of human progress, shall look back upon the narrow and crooked paths."

34. The question appears on the concluding page of this short pamphlet (2000, 52). Elsaesser (2012, 590) reads this question less as a prediction than as a "flight of fantasy."

35. On the relation between the kinetoscope and the cinematograph, see Spehr (2008, 378–379, note 14). On the Edison Vitascope projection system, see Spehr (2008, 376, 382).

36. On the superior Biograph image developed by W. K. L. Dickson and his partners, see Spehr (2008, 419–421) and Brown and Anthony (1999).

37. See also note 16. Among the other machines based to some degree on the Kinetoscope/ Kinetograph were the Cinématographe (Lumière), the Phonoscope (Demenÿ), the Bioskop (Skladnowsky), the Mutoscope (Casler), the Eidoloscope (Latham), and the Phantoscope (Armat), as well as Edison's Vitascope (Spehr 2008, 378–382).

38. Morin (2005, ch. 3) was early to note how the cinematograph was not immediately but had to become cinema, the institution. Gaudreault (2011, ch. 2) gives this more precision. See Streible (2013) on "digital film" as an oxymoron.

39. Altman (2004, 19, 21) complicates this reconfiguration as an ongoing "*crisis of identity*" which a technology experiences at every stage, its social construction "*ongoing*" and "*multiple*" thus never final.

40. The references are to Bazin (2009), Andrew (2010), and Rodowick (2007). See also Tsivian (2008). The 2009 Barnard translation does somewhat more than the Gray translation to situate Bazin's "The Myth of Total Cinema" essay as weighing in on the digital moment. Compare the recent translation: "In this way, every new improvement to cinema merely brings it paradoxically closer to its origins. Cinema has yet to be invented!" (2009, 17) with the Gray translation: "Every new development added to the cinema must, paradoxically, take it nearer and nearer to its origins. In short, cinema has not yet been invented!" (2005 [1967], 21).

41. Gaudreault and Marion (2015, 105) problematize these issues by positing that cinema is "born twice," emerging as a device between 1890 and 1895 and then as an institution around 1910–1915. As a challenge to the "birth" metaphor, however, they prefer "emergence" and want to foreground the complexity involved. However, I would contend that we also need to ask what this paradigm contributes to contemporary technological emergence from the vantage of those thinking this set of questions.

42. Danto (2007, 170) refers to "asymmetry in our concept of Past and Future." Ankersmit (2007, 364) says that the idea that the past and present are in a relation of "asymmetry" was completely new in 1965 when Danto's *Analytical Philosophy of History* was first published, and remains so to this day. Note, however that Deleuze, in *Difference and Repetition,* three years later, theorizes the "living present" that puts the past and the future into "asymmetrical elements" of the present (1994, 81). Deleuze scholars will note the philosopher's debt here to Bergson, *Matter and Memory* from which he takes the concept of the "pure past," a concept that has no easy equivalent in the philosophy of history (2002). Patton, Deleuze's translator and editor, finds the "pure past" as synonymous with "pure memory," the antithesis of the represented "image-memory" (1994, 314). See Bergson (2002, ch. 3). And yet, if Bergson's paradoxes are redolent of Heidegger's *Being and Time*, Deleuze's expansion of them is more so. Boundas (2009, 326) even thinks that Deleuze's title *Difference and Repetition* (1994) was intended as a response to *Being and Time.*

43. Williams (2003, 85) urges the importance of Deleuze's philosophy of time and finds it a reaction against a linearity that posits an "irreversible" past relative to future directionality but sees it as unusually complex and resistant to summary. Deleuze's indebtedness to Bergson (Grosz 2005, 3) explains the conception of time in *Matter and Memory* as divided into two rather than three, and the split produces the one of two "trajectories" that makes the present pass and the other as "preserving" the present as past. Bergson (2002, 137–138) might be perceived in Deleuze's two "paradoxes," the one positing the past as "contemporaneous" with the present that it once was and the other, following from the first, the "coexistence" of all of the past with the new present that makes it past (1994, 81–82).

44. See Cohen (2006, 229) on how he thinks Deleuze's philosophical system might use the "time out of joint" paradigm as an alternative to get around "common and good sense," made

"workable for dynamic logics." Williams (2003, 112), clarifying that Deleuze is at odds with both good sense and common sense, explains that philosophy "runs the risk" of falling back onto either of these senses and might better not take up this "task" at all.

45. As to the metaphor of "coexistence" of past and present, this would seem to be more in line with Koselleck's idea of historical time as not singular but rather "many forms of time superimposed on one another" (2004, 2). In the following I have not attempted to resolve the difference between the metaphors of "superimposition" and "asymmetry," but have rather favored the latter, borrowing Danto for its proximity to Deleuze's time as "out of joint."

46. For an example of how fraught consider the "where" question relative to the place of Marxism today in Derrida (1994, xix): "Without this *noncontemporaneity with itself of the living present*, without that which secretly unhinges it, without this responsibility and this respect for justice concerning those who *are not there*, of those who are no longer or who are not yet *present and living*, what sense would there be to ask the questions: 'where?' 'where tomorrow?' 'whither?'" The answer to which is that when and if it arrives the consideration becomes one of how it "proceeds *from* [*provident* de] the future."

47. For a new generation taking up the project of writing on feminism and film in the 1970s, see Jacob (2015) and Warren (2008, 2012).

48. Mink (1987, 93) was not convinced that "space" was usefully analogized with "time," and I am inclined to agree, especially since the phrase "space and time" often covers up the difficulties of inequivalence.

49. The charge of "making things up" has been leveled famously against Hayden White. See Ginsburg (1991). More recently, White (2010, 337), speaking of the professional historian's "constructed" past (and not the "practical past" from Oakeshott), says that "The historical past is and will be whatever historians decide to make of it," and further that "history does not teach anything at all, consisting as it does of a body of statements about what might have happened in the past, could never happen again, and even if it did, could not happen in precisely the same way as before."

50. Bean (2002b, 4) confirms this when she comments that the "appeal to history went largely unnoticed in academic circles." Filling out the early 1970s she reminds us that Marjorie Rosen's *Popcorn Venus* (1973) referenced Francis Marion, Lois Weber, and Anita Loos. See Mulvey (2004b) and Butler (2008) on the feminist 1970s.

51. The subheading of his ch. 4 is "Outline of a Concept of Historical Time" (1979, 89–118).

52. "Not only our own resources but those of the entire world will be at our command, nay, we may even anticipate the time when sociable relations will be established between ourselves and the planetary system, when the latest doings in Mars, Saturn and Venus will be recorded by enterprising kinetographic reporters" (2000, 51).

53. Jameson finds "the modern" to be a "pseudo-concept" that contains no sense of either past or future, and although he suggests that "modernity" could be read as "capitalism," he declines to insist on this (2002, 214–215).

54. Jameson (2002, 214) after a lengthy discussion of "modernism as ideology" concludes that "modernity" might still be used productively as a "trope" insofar as it can produce new historical narratives.

55. Here, I further follow Koselleck who traces the way the term *modernus* came into being (2004, 228).

56. This might also mean, following Koselleck, that we see figures of the early twentieth century as newly "in anticipation" of a "future" present and in which we hear something of the philosophical legacy of Heidegger. To recall, Heidegger thought of history in terms of human orientation toward "possibilities," postulating the future as projected out of the past. Or, in his terms, a future full of "possibilities" is interpreted in the past understood as a "having-been" (Bambach 2013, 144).

57. This capacity to live according to more than one configuration of historical time would be Koselleck's answer to Gumbrecht who thinks that historical time is part of an old construct and who, borrowing both Danto and Koselleck, argues that the "asymmetry" between the "horizon of expectations" (the future) and the "space of experience" (the past) sets the present up to learn from the past (2004, 120). While I concur with Gumbrecht's wariness of "lessons" from history, I would argue that he has read Koselleck selectively.

58. The critique is Comolli's (1990, 226–227): "In effect, the birth of the cinema, in all the 'histories' dedicated to it, can be read as a multiple and fragmentary phenomenon: disseminated, shattered, started over with each new 'instrument' perfected, with each new supplementary detail, with each new patent, and, at the same time, deferred, delayed due to the lack, in one after another of these instruments, of some technical detail, with a new solution for each new problem—to the extent that what changes from one instrument to another is often infinitesimal, as is what is found to be lacking." Comolli further sees the "long gestation period of the cinema" and the "period of its birth" as the "site where the majority of phantasms and myths are anchored and reinforced."

59. Gunning (1997, 9) thus begins his article on early documentary under the subheading "A deferred discovery": "The recent re-evaluation of early cinema springs from a determination to approach the films of cinema's first decades on their own terms. While recognizing that a historiographic project which attempts to fully reproduce the past 'as it really was' is doomed to a naive historicism, nonetheless, a responsible historian must try to recreate the original horizon of expectation in which films were reproduced and received."

60. See Gunning (2006, 34) for an account of how viewing archival film prints figured in formulating the "cinema of attractions" paradigm. For challenges to the "attractions" paradigm also supported by reconsidering archival evidence, see Garncarz (2012) and Musser (1994).

CHAPTER 3. MORE FICTIONS

1. See Gaumont Co. website: http://www.gaumont.fr/fr/qui.html (accessed August 1, 2016). Breton (1984, 12), an early source in French, cites the reference in Alice Guy Blaché's memoirs to *La Fée aux choux*, saying that although she is now considered the first "*metteur en scène de fiction*," it should not be forgotten that Méliès was associated with "féeries." To my knowledge, no other source, however, has associated Guy Blaché's cabbage fairies with the Méliès "féerie" films. Thanks to Laura Wexler and Lynn A. Higging for comments on this chapter.

2. McMahan (2002, 12) says that feminists have "interpreted" Guy Blaché's memoirs as though she thought of herself as the first fiction filmmaker. Tomadjoglou (2015, 96–97) provocatively suggests that we consider the fantasy function Alice Guy performs for feminists and even that "a feminist Alice Guy" is imagined.

3. See Lenk and McMahan (1999) for a detailed account of that discovery, as well as Lenk (2002) and McMahan (2002, 22), who refer to having "positively identified" the film Guy re-

ferred to as *La Fée aux choux* in August, 1996, but several pages earlier says that she was "able to document the tentative identification" by other scholars of "a version of this film" (19). The archival language of "positive identification," however, leaves no room for uncertainty and even the possibility McMahan herself opens up (253, note 50) where she suggests that there may have been three versions of the film and that the Swedish Archive Sieurin collection print would be the second, made between 1897 and 1900.

4. *The Lost Garden: The Life and Cinema of Alice Guy Blaché* (dir. Marquise Lepage, National Film Board of Canada, 1995), distributed by Women Make Movies.

5. See Tomadjoglou (2015, 107) for the analysis of this selection, which includes the rejection of one baby (doll) with Indian feathers and another who is remarkably black.

6. Here, compare the original and one translation of the 1964 Alice Guy Blaché interview:

Original Bachy question: "En regardant ailleurs dans son livre, il cite par exemple, parmi vos films *La Fée aux Choux* et *Les aventures d'une sage-femme* quelque chose comme ça. Il les réunit en 1902 d'un côté, ailleurs, il cite les 2 films séparément. *L'histoire d'une sage femme* et *La Fee aux choux* sont deux films?" (1985, 32).

Original A. G. B. answer to Bachy: "*L'histoire d'une sage femme? À ce moment là je n'aurais jamais osé parler de cela!* La Fée aux Choux, *ça fait partie de mon histoire*" (1985, 32).

Translation V. B. question: "Sadoul refers to both *La Fée aux choux* and *Les Aventures d'une sage femme* or some such. At one point he lumps them together giving 1902 as the date. In another passage he alludes to them separately. Are they really two distinct films?" (Simon 2009b, 10).

Translation A. G. B. answer: "The story of a midwife? At that moment in time, I would never have dared speak of such a thing. *La Fée aux choux*—that is a part of history" (Simon 2009b, 9).

7. Alternative translation Bachy (1985, 32) A. G. B. answer to V. B. question: "The story of a midwife? At the time, I would never have dared speak of that. *La Fée aux choux*—that is a part of my history." Thanks to Aurore Spiers for the second translation and French language expertise. Note: Because the Simon translation that leaves out the French modifier "*mon*" better supports my theoretical point, I have relied upon it here, although I would further comment on the curious difference that one word can make in such a case.

8. McMahan (2002, 12–13) speculates that Alice Guy's first filming was connected to Gaumont's development, the 60mm *chronophotographe* based on Georges Demenÿ's patents, which would have been "perfected" in early 1896. While the likelihood that she used the 60mm camera is not in dispute, McMahan's reference to May 1896, is perplexing as the memoir makes no mention of a month.

9. See Gaines (2006, 235) on the versions of the Lumière *L'Arroseur arrosé* of which the company made at least three. Guy Blaché herself thought that this Lumière title was the first story film (McMahan 2002, 12). See Ezra (2000, 13) on Méliès's first film, shot in either May or June of 1896, *Une Partie de cartes/Playing Cards*, an imitation of the Lumière's *Partie de Cartes*.

10. I concur with McMahan (2002, 10), who argues that Guy Blaché would have been among those who helped the move from "motion studies" and in the direction of fiction.

11. Gaudreault and Gunning (2009, 4) nominate this event as arguably more of a "first" for the Lumière device than the December 28, 1895, date, that is, if one wants to invest in

inaugural moments. They give more unqualified support to the idea that, since the "first" is in dispute, the range of possibilities remains open when they also argue, "These questions about origins, it must be said, also carry with them a certain degree of subjectivity (and emotions and national sentiment sometimes enter into the matter as well)," and go on to say that one's position is invariably tied to an idea of an "inaugural moment" (2).

12. McMahan (2004, 23–40) challenges the order of "sound after silent" by arguing that Alice Guy's chronophones made for the Gaumont studio change this chronology.

13. Tomodjoglou (2015, 100) describes the production at this time as based less on rigid division of labor than of "loosely functioning collaborative teams in which the players and technicians could perform different roles." The directorial credit for *Le Matelas alcoolique* (1906), she says, is divided between Alice Guy and Romeo Bozzetti, but see her memoir on the origin of her idea for the comedy and her assertion that "I had personally directed it" (Slide 1996b, 39–40). Williams (1992, 56), however, was early to credit Alice Guy as not only the earliest producer/director to scout for locations but attributes to her the "visual style" that distinguished a Gaumont film from, for example, one produced by Pathé Frères from the same period.

14. Slide adds to this in his editor's footnote that daughter-in-law Simone Blaché disagreed with Lacassin and affirmed that *La Fée aux choux* was made in 1896, and further, he says that, like her mother-in-law, she distrusted the Gaumont catalogs (1996b, 147–148).

15. The 1897 date is the one McMahan gives for when Guy was made head of Gaumont film production. Her resignation came in 1907 when she married Herbert Blaché and left for the United States (2009b, 125–126).

16. McMahan (2002, 22) refers to the new "glass-roofed studio" built in 1905. Jacobson (2015, 7) says that the "glass-enclosed studio" Gaumont built in 1904 was the largest in the world before World War I. Williams (1992, 56–57) argues that Guy was also the first director/producer to systematically scout locations and even credits her with beginning a French tradition of "photographic verisimilitude," linking this location shooting to other kinds of economies she instituted.

17. See Gaudreault (2001) as exemplifying an empirical approach to answering the question of the Lumière edit and Salt (1983) as foundational in the statistical contribution to questions of cinema style.

18. See Gaudreault and Gunning (2009, 2). Cosandey (1996) challenges the advancement of the Lumière first exhibition as a French nationalist project.

19. See the series of articles, Jean-Louis Comolli, "Technique et Idéology," appearing in *Cahiers du Cinéma*, nos. 229–241 (May 1971–September-October 1972) translated together in 2015.

20. The phrase from the preface of von Ranke's 1824 book has been variously translated from the German. Tribe has translated von Ranke in Koselleck as "The task of judging the past for the benefit of future generations has been given to History: the present essay does not aspire to such an elevated task; it merely seeks to show the past as it once was" (2004, 36).

21. Rosen (2001, 11–12) argues that MacCabe (1976), in aligning Bazin with empiricism, may have contributed to the Anglo-American rejection of the theorist in this moment of antipathy to historicism.

22. In defense of von Ranke, Kellner (1995, 10) wonders if we are not all naive realists when we try to speak about the historical past. We want to think that something did happen and

we want to find a way to say what we think it was that "actually" transpired. Then again, says Kellner, qualifying his assertion that we all slip into naive realism, there is a contradiction between naivete and a more political understanding of what it is to be a realist. Yet he puts his own analysis in check, arguing that in the balance we might also acknowledge such a thing as naive *antirealism* by which he must mean an extreme constructivism.

23. See Hayden White (1992), the article considered his answer to the charge of holocaust denial.

24. Foner (2014, 27) gives as an example, R. R. Palmer's two-volume *The Age of Democratic Revolution* (1959–1964) in which the words "Haiti," "slavery," and "Saint-Dominique," for instance, are not found in the index.

25. One might wonder why I focus on "unthinkability" rather than "repression." See Foucault on the "inadequacy of repression," especially for grasping the productivity of power (2012, 61).

26. Construed by contemporaries who participated in these events as well as those who configured them to "fit" narratives for Western readers, the revolt was "trivialized," "banalized," and even canceled (Trouillot 1995, 96).

27. See Hastie (2002) for an astute analysis of Guy Blaché's "own recollective processes" (34), leading to the observation that in the memoirs as well as texts by others, it is not that "history" is a corrective but that "memory is instead suspicious of history."

28. Considering "constructivism" and so-called "realism" as having extreme forms, as he does, Trouillot wants to see instead "how history works," although I would argue that he has to subscribe more to constructivism than to its antithesis in order to pose the questions he does about how power precedes the narrative of the event (1995, 29). It is unclear to me how an outcome that was decided in advance of its "having happened," that is, constructed even before an event took place, relates to the "autonomy" that he also wants to grant events in the past (6).

29. "Un des frères s'en va en bas, va tourner une manivelle, et nous voyons arriver sur la toile les ateliers Lumière à Lyon. Des gens qui sortaient, qui couraient. Nous étions absolument éberlués" (Bachy 1985, 37). Thanks to Aurore Spiers for the translation.

30. The fact that a Gaumont film shot in 1896 would have been shot in 60mm leads archivist Kim Tomadjoglou to argue that the most critical evidence we could have in hand would be a 60mm version of a film depicting a fairy among cabbages (Simon 2009, 23). McMahan (2002, 38) refers to Guy Blaché's assertion that they sold eighty copies of the fairy film but also says that the film was remade two times because the original disintegrated. Yet this doesn't tell us the years in which the film was remade or what versions with which titles.

31. In her memoir, Guy Blaché both corrects Sadoul's dates for a film titled *Le Matelas* to 1897–1898 (Slide 1996a, 36) and describes witnessing a comic scene involving a drunk and a mattress maker that gave her the idea for the film *Matelas alcoolique* that she dates as 1906 (ibid., 39–40). Yet there was the earlier Lumière film *Querelle de matelassirères / The Quarrel of the Mattress Makers*, now dated 1897; although it features the mattress maker and a heckler, it is not a comic chase as is the extant Gaumont film, *Le Matelas alcoolique / The Drunken Mattress* (1906), now attributed to Guy Blaché. However, the Gaumont is strikingly similar to the Méliès title *The Tramp and the Mattress Maker / La Cardeuse de Matelas* (1906), from the same year. McMahan says that *Le Matelas alcoolique* was also most likely after the Lumière *Querelle de matelassirères / The Quarrel of the Mattress makers* (2002, 28).

32. That she herself was aware of the importance of film material evidence is there in her remark in the memoir in reference to that first film she calls *La Fée Aux choux*: "Today it is a classic of which the Cinémathèque française preserves the negative" (Slide 1996b, 28).

33. In the definitive study of female cross-dressing and lesbianism in silent cinema Horak (2016, 2–3), admits that while the open-endedness of these figures explains their "appeal," there is a danger that our contemporary enthusiasm might "obscure" or even "misrepresent" their function in their time.

34. Williams (1992, 55–56), while crediting Alice Guy with developing the Gaumont "house style," contrasts these productions with that of their competitor Pathé Frères where the "true authors" were the set designers.

35. See *La Fée Aux choux* streamed on YouTube:. https://www.youtube.com/watch?v=MTd 7roVkgnQ (accessed August 1, 2016).

CHAPTER 4. OBJECT LESSONS

1. Doane (2007b, 132) refers to the indexicality of the photochemical basis of film as having been used to "guarantee" such a "privileged relation to the real."

2. Fossati (2009, 115) discusses this phenomenon as the "indexical argument" often utilized when a film is recruited as historical evidence as in a documentary. Here she asks if this argument can be made for fiction film where the indexical relation may be to a real world scene utilized in a fiction. The point is to take into account how photosensitive film is thought to index whatever was put before the camera—whether the artificial set of the fiction film or the unrehearsed event of documentary.

3. Cherchi Usai (2000, 66) makes this distinction between restoration and preservation: Restoration involves practices "compensating for the loss or degradation of the moving image artifact" in an attempt to return it to "a state as close as possible to its original condition." Preservation, while involving the restoration of content, is additionally aimed at "maintaining" the moving image on a "permanent basis."

4. See Cherchi Usai (2000, 1–4) beginning with a chapter he titles "The Romance of Celluloid."

5. "Because a camera happened to record them, the moments film was exposed to thus became historical moments of a new order. In a sense, therefore, film turned the present into a kind of immediate history; it made history out of the present" (Chanan 1980, 15–16).

6. Consider Bordwell (1997) for whom film history is a narrative of stylistic evolution.

7. See ch. 2, note 16 for the definition of *historicity* I am using, which differs from that used by some archivists.

8. As Eco (1976, 604) has it: "Confronted with a conventionalization so much richer, and hence a formalization so much subtler than anything else, we are shocked into believing we stand before a language which restores reality to us."

9. I simplify here and must grant the variance within the archival community relative to theoretical issues raised by restoration. See Busche (2006, 15) who contrasts Cherchi Usai's approach which privileges "original" artifact integrity with that of João Socrates de Oliveira whose restoration goal is the "original" viewing experience.

10. See Gartenberg (1984) for specifics. Elsaesser (1990, 3–6) explains the connection between the 1978 and Brighton Conference, the rediscovery of silent cinema, and what he calls "the new film history."

11. Cherchi Usai (2000, 147) gives as a rule of restoration: "Every print of a film is a unique object, with its own physical and aesthetic characteristics, and should not be treated as identical to other prints with the same title."

12. Here, where the index proves existence, is Rosen's justification for exploring the proximity between film theory and the historian's method. Most elementary in this comparison is the historian's reliance on documentary sources, which Rosen groups together as "species of indexical sign" (2001, 112). It is not at all, however, that historians use the notion of index derived from the semiotics of Charles Sanders Peirce. It is rather that Rosen uses the theoretical concept of the *indexical trace* to give precision to the historian's investment in the artifact based on the idea that its referent had a past presence. He then parallels these investments—the historian's in the artifact and Bazinian film theory's in objects whose imprint is registered on a strip of film of objects that existed in the past "presence" of the camera (20). The relevance of Peirce to the question of actual existence is there in statements like: "An Index is a sign which refers to the Object that it denotes by virtue of being really affected by that Object" (1955, 102).

13. Marks (2002, 93), in response to Cherchi Usai's often-quoted "Cinema history is born of an absence," goes on to interpret him as commenting on how "images take on history as a function of loss: if not of their physical materiality, then of their initial conditions of viewing. Cinema history, then, is a melancholic act from the start, for even in the presence of the fullness of the image we are aware that it is disappearing before our eyes."

14. For other readings of this film, see Balides (2002), Stamp (2015, 101–118), Cooper (2010, 133–134, 150–152, 163–164). Herron (1916, 8), author of the *Colliers* short story on which the film was based, quotes Chicago social worker Jane Addams from her book on prostitution: "When the shoes became too worn to endore [*sic*] a third soling and she possessed but 90 cents toward a new pair, she gave up the struggle; to use her own contemptuous phrase, she 'sold out for a new pair of shoes.'"

15. But later Steedman (2002, 11) quotes Derrida from *Mal d'archive* to the effect that we mistake "nothing" found in a place with nothing at all, and might rather see "that an absence is not *nothing*, but is rather the space left by what has gone." What appears to be the "emptiness" left "indicates how it was filled and animated."

16. Actually, Rodowick describes the conflict in popular culture between analog and digital over which is more "real," which has the effect of "dissembling" the imaginariness of both (2007, 5).

17. See Marks (2002, 91) where she argues that it is not just the deteriorating film but old videotapes that "flaunt their tenuous connection to the reality they index."

18. We say the digital is constituted by 0's and 1's often, but may remain mystified by the process and may even think that we're talking about something immaterial although magnetic inscription is not immaterial. See Sterne (2012, 7) who notes that it is strange that we might think our files are immaterial when we know that they take up space.

19. See Schmidt (2003, 60) for detailed background on the fate of the Mary Pickford collection at the U.S. Library of Congress after negotiations for the deposit of which began in 1943. A complete Pickford filmography listing archival sources is in Schmidt (2012, 241–249).

20. See Rodowick (2007 14–16) on Nelson Goodman's allographic two-stage arts in which the composition and the performance are separate stages. Another analogy would be that of the orchestral score, which only becomes music in performance mode. The player piano and the player piano roll come to mind because of the U.S. Supreme Court case in which the court

was asked to decide whether the roll was a "copy" of the musical composition and therefore a "work" protectable by copyright. See *White-Smith Music Co. v. Apollo Co.*, 209 U.S. 1, 28 S. Ct. 319, 52 L. Ed. 655 (1908). However, any study of U.S. intellectual property only indicates the historical variability of the legal concept of "the work."

21. According to the *Shoes* press kit for the 2017 DVD release, *Shoes*, one of the most popular Bluebird Photoplays releases, was booked in over 2,000 theaters (2017, 3). Pierce (1997, 17) gives statistics on the number of prints struck for domestic and foreign distribution in the 1920s, citing the highest number reported in *Forbes* in 1927, as sixty for foreign and one hundred for domestic. Ten years earlier the number of prints struck might have been lower.

22. See Thompson (1985, 72) on how in these years Universal Pictures was the only U.S. company to target the Asian market, beginning with Japan. See Sato (1982, 33) on the popularity of Universal's Bluebird, the brand under which Lois Weber's films were released in 1916.

23. On the cinephillic obsession with print quality, see Cherchi Usai (2000, 147). Elsaesser (2012, 604–605) insists on the distinction between history of films and cinema history, which "lives of prints" would observe. For an example of a comprehensive "lives of prints" study based on surviving "race films," see Horak (2016, 199–214).

24. A search of the international silent film holdings database, Treasures from the FIAF Archives, yields the following archives as holding at least one print of *The Birth of a Nation* (D. W. Griffith, U.S., 1915): Bulgarska Nacionalna Filmoteka (Sofia), Cineteca Italiana (Milano), Cinémathèque Royale (Bruxelles), Cinemateca Brasileira (São Paulo), Cinemateca Do Museu de Arte Moderne (Rio de Janeiro), Danish Film Institute (København), National Film and Sound Archive, Australia (Canberra), Cineteca del Friuli (Gemona), Deutsches Filminstitut-DIF (Wiesbaden), Filmmuseum des Münchner Stadtmuseum (München), Filmoteka Narodowa (Warszawa), George Eastman Museum (Rochester), Gosfilmofond Russia (Moscow), Library of Congress (Washington), Museum of Modern Art (New York), BFI/National Film and Television Archive (London), Eye Film Institute (Amsterdam), Öesterreichisches Filmmuseum (Wien), Arhiva Nationala de Filme (Bucuresti), Cinémathèque Québécoise (Montréal), Cinemateca Nacional de Angola (Luanda), Norsk Filminstitutt (Oslo), UCLA Film and Television Archive (Los Angeles), Academy Film Archive (Beverly Hills), Filmoteca Española (Madrid), Svenska Filminstitutet (Stockholm), Harvard Film Archive (Cambridge), Jugoslovenska Kinoteka (Beograd), Cinémathèque Française (Paris).

25. The classic case is *Citizen Kane* (Orson Welles, U.S., 1941).

26. See Veronesi (2010, 72–74) on Giallanella's production company Liana Films. Dall'Asta (2010b, 39) stresses the possibility that *Umanità* was never screened in public, which raises the question of its status as a historical film print if we are defining that object as "to-be-exhibited." If the motion picture film print never had a performative "life" as a properly screened motion picture film and was never therefore "seen as a film," we want to know how this changes its exhibition history position.

27. Cherchi Usai (2000, 66) also explains that motion picture film "restoration" entails the "reproduction of a source copy." The goal is a duplication that produces a "satisfactory imitation of the source copy."

28. Email correspondence, EYE Institute head curator Giovanna Fossati, Annike Kross (restorer), and Elif Rongen-Kaynakci (silent film specialist) (July 11, 2011).

29. One is reminded of the realm of intellectual property in which an entity can have rights in the "work" without physically having "the work" as object. See Gaines (1991, ch. 2).

30. The reference is to Benjamin (2008, 24–25): "From a photographic plate, for example, one can make any number of prints; to ask for the 'authentic' print makes no sense." Except that one cannot make any number because either the plate will wear out or today the edition will be limited so as to produce rarity, so, "No," contrary to Benjamin, it now *does* make sense to ask for an "authentic print" except that the "authentic print" is still complete nonsense. Rosen (2001, 167–168) insightfully notes the tension in the apparently opposite function of the index: mass distribution of "imaged objects" and yet the "transmission" of that "object" that may be taken to have an origin.

31. Email correspondence, EYE Institute head curator Giovanna Fossati, Annike Kross (restorer), and Elif Rongen-Kaynakci (silent film specialist) (July 11, 2011).

32. Manovich (2013, 156) argues that when "media becomes software" the logic becomes one of "permanent extendability." If the logic of the copy is no longer operative, then reproducibility is subsumed into ever-increasing compression, or ever-increasing speed of transferability, or ever-increasing ease of migration, or it dissolves into the techniques of data manipulation: capture, copy, paste. If it is the other way around and compression is subsumed under reproducibility, we have something that could be called *reproductive compression*.

33. See ch. 2, note 16, for the definition of "historicity" I am using, which differs from that used by some archivists.

34. Cherchi Usai (2000, 44) describes the pattern left on the 435 buried prints caused by the temperature change when they were taken from the frozen ground. Both light and humidity produced a "melting" of the emulsion on the reel edges. See also Gaines (2007, 172), where I refer to the print *Little Lindy Learns to Sing* (Lule Warrenton, Universal, 1916), which, along with *Bread* (Ida May Park, Universal, 1916), was part of the Dawson City cache of prints.

35. But in *Within Our Gates* (Oscar Micheaux, 1919), the archival decision was to make an alteration. In Micheaux's controversial film one close-up within the scene in which a black man and his wife are lynched by a white mob appeared upside down as seen in the surviving 35mm print titled *La Negra*, found with Spanish intertitles in the Filmoteca in Madrid in the 1990s. The first U.S. Library of Congress restoration reversed this shot so that the rope hung down from the pole, as seen in the first VHS tape release from Smithsonian video.

36. Thompson (1985, 194–195) explains that historically continuity "stood for the smoothly flowing narrative, with its technique constantly in the service of the causal chain, yet always effacing itself."

37. We can explain the continuity error as the result of the economy of motion picture production in the 1910s. Such a discontinuity produced by "cutting in" a shot that didn't "match" the background would be found in lower-budget films made at this time. The fact that this frame is there in the extant 35mm print, however, does not necessarily mean that it would be found in the original print or later prints since there is always the possibility that a film could have been reedited.

38. Email correspondence, EYE Institute head curator Giovanna Fossati, Annike Kross (restorer), and Elif Rongen-Kaynakci (silent film specialist) (July 11, 2011).

39. *Shoes* press kit. Milestone Films, 2016.

40. Nichols (1991, 151) wryly argues that "The indexical quality of the image proclaims its authenticity. but this is also a self-substantiating claim akin to the remonstration by the Cretan that he is telling the truth as he tells us that Cretans always lie."

41. Fossati (2009, 139) explains the thinking that "human mediation can be the carrier of authenticity from an original film artifact to its restoration."

42. "Le scandale c'était un peu d'être renoiro-rossellinien et beaucoup d' être 'hitch-cocko-hawksien," as quoted in Costa (1994, 185).

43. The Hugh Gray translation is less radical: "All the arts are based on the presence of man, only photography derives an advantage from his absence" (Bazin 2005, 13).

44. See Fossati (2009, 123–126) on how the "film as art" framework has bonded with the concept of originality and authenticity via the medium specificity argument as with the "film as original." But the shift is toward the conceptual artifact (film style) not material film artifact except where closely associated with the auteur.

45. See Bordwell (1997, 49) on Alexandre Astruc's analogy between the camera and the writer's pen as seen in the latter's term *caméra-stylo* that prepared the way for an idea of "authorship" that developed in the 1950s in the journal *Cahiers du cinéma*.

46. See Horwath (Cherchi Usai et al. 2008, 114) on how, if the film is no longer a physical object, it could still be licensed by rights holders who transferred data streams after payment.

47. See Horwath and Cherchi Usai (Cherchi Usai et al. 2008, 210). Although the term "art of reproduction" is Cherchi Usai's, the two archivists appear to disagree in this exchange.

48. Although some, like Mitchell (1992, 52) would argue against the comparison with the mass circulation side of the photographic image—that position aligned with Walter Benjamin. Instead he sees both the high speed of circulation and the infinite recombinant potential of the digital.

49. The reference is to the impact of Foucault's " What Is an Author?" (1979). See papers from the English Institute reevaluation of authorship in their 2010 conference (McGill 2013). Also see my critique of authorship and female directors, Gaines (2002) and MacCabe (2003) for one of the most devastating challenges. For a comprehensive auteur theory today update, see Elsaesser (2012, especially ch. 21).

50. Cooper (2010, 135–137) discusses a contemporary review of Weber's *Even as You and I* (1917) that makes a case for the director's "genius" but which he finds is less an auteur than a genre analysis in its attempt to make sense of the recurring motifs and themes in the films she had directed and often written. The review, he concludes, is a defense of the profitable success of Weber's "message" films.

51. Fosatti (2009, 231) says that the "film as art" paradigm that informs some restoration practices raises the question of the auteur's intentions. In Gaines (2012b), I challenge the idea of the "hand" of the female director.

52. Ernst (2013, 59) thinks digital systems can be credited, since media archaeology can be performed as calculation and measurement "by means of such machines."

53. See Doane (2007b, 133–134) on Peirce's association of indexicality with the use of demonstrative pronouns such as "this" or "that."

54. Kessler-Harris (2012, 14), discussing Lillian Hellman, refers to Rachel Brownstein on literary biography in these terms.

55. See Fossati (2012) for how archivists deal with the conditions and the concept of multiple originals.

CHAPTER 5. THE MELODRAMA THEORY OF HISTORICAL TIME

1. Ermarth here explains how the conventions used by historians are so "naturalized" that we use the them as basic "tools of thought," and "history" comes to seem no different from time itself. See ch. 2.

2. Granted, we're looking at what Louis Althusser considered "complex and peculiar" (1979, 103). For discussion of Althusser's challenge to the "continuum" of linear time (103) and his proposal of a more paradoxical structure, see ch. 2, as well as Ankersmit (2007, 364) for the relevance of the term "asymmetry" from Danto (2007). See ch. 2, note 42.

3. Brooks (1985, 28–29) lays out his theory that melodrama begins with the "space of innocence" and that narrative structure follows the "struggle" for the "recognition of the sign of virtue and innocence."

4. Wright (1986, 10–11) reprints the advertising poster for *The Woman Suffers* (1918, Southern Cross Feature Film Co.) a collaboration between actress Lottie Lyell and director Raymond Longford who, in 1922, started Longford-Lyell, Australian Picture Productions Ltd.

5. See Gaines, "Moving Picture Melodrama," in Williams (forthcoming); Gaines, "Even More Tears: The *Historical Time* Theory of Melodrama," in Gledhill and Williams, eds. (2018).

6. Gumbrecht (2004, 120) says of historical time that it "now seems to lie behind us." See ch. 2 for my justification for using the concept in this study.

7. For more on the fallen woman genre, see Staiger (1995) and Jacobs (2008).

8. More thinking needs to be done about how this elongation in which the past "does not go away" might be a hold over from an earlier moment, today "out of step." Thanks to Matthew Buckley for this insight as well as for his in-depth responses to this chapter.

9. Tribe (2004, xi) in the introduction to his translation of Koselleck, *Futures Past*, says that the German *vergangene Zukunft* should have been translated as "former future(s)" and been the book title. This might have helped to foreground the once "anticipated future" idea.

10. Deleuze's second paradox of coexistence is the one relevant here: "If each past is contemporaneous with the present that it was, then *all* of the past coexists with the new present in relation to which it is now past" (1994, 81–82).

11. The term *defect* is from Macherey (1978, 197).

12. Gledhill (1987, 31) refers to the "material of the world melodrama seeks to melodramatize." In Gaines (2014a), I consider melodrama as historically working on the contradiction between the biological and the familial in *Way Down East* (D. W. Griffith, U.S., 1920) and *4 Months, 3 Weeks and 2 Days* (Christian Mungiau, Romania, 2006), updating the Marxist feminist analysis of the contradictions of patriarchy and capitalism developed in 1970s film melodrama theory. See Mulvey (1987, 75) on melodrama as a "safety valve for social contradictions centered on sex and the family."

13. Gledhill (1987, 7) explains that the interest in the contradictions of bourgeois ideology was originally developed as a reading of the Hollywood films of Douglas Sirk and was only later applied to melodrama. Elsaesser (1987, 67) says of Hollywood melodrama's "playing out" of contradictions characteristic of American society that a "gap opens between the emotions and the reality they seek to reach." More recently, Berlant (2008, 179) explains the "therapeutic" function of popular genres directed to women and illustrates this with the ideological function of love: "Love is supposed to transcend or at least neutralize the contradictions of history."

14. For example: *East Lynne*. Director: Bertram Bracken, screenplay: Mary Murillo (Fox Film Corp. U.S. 1916), cast: Theda Bara; *East Lynne*. Director: Emmett Flynn, screenplay: Lenore Coffee, Emmett Flynn (Fox Film Corp. U.S. 1925).

15. In Brooks, the innocent's virtue is unacknowledged but finally recognized, making visible what he terms the "drama of recognition" (1985, 27). See also Gledhill (1987, 30).

16. See Gledhill (2000, 240) on the "polarizing" aspect of melodrama that "drives" signifiers in the direction of oppositions. This is not negative here but rather the work of convention as signs are forced to take sides in a struggle.

17. The *locus classicus* of this idea is Watt (1957).

18. The evolution of crosscutting in U.S. cinema has focused on early D. W. Griffith melodramas like *The Lonedale Operator* (1911) or *The Lonely Villa* (1909). But if crosscutting is, by definition, a patterned alternation, then other filmmakers were using a variant of the device in these years. See titles directed by Frances Marion (*The Love Light*, 1921) and by Nell Shipman (*White Water*, 1922). Lest we make the mistake of taking fast cutting pace to be a Griffith signature, we need to reconsider the serial queens. See ch. 1.

19. Eisenstein (1977, 200) uses the term *cut-back* to describe the device Griffith used in *After Many Years* (1908), the earlier version of *Enoch Arden*.

20. Brooks sees literary and theatrical melodrama as fostering a "moment of astonishment," often when the evidence of the innocent's virtue is revealed and is unequivocally recognized (1985, 26).

21. Relevant here, Singer (2001, 46) thinks that this is one of the places that melodrama shows itself to be nonclassical in its narrative structure. That is, in contrast with tight cause and effect, melodrama has "far greater tolerance" for "outrageous coincidence, implausibility, convoluted plotting, deus ex machina resolutions, and episodic strings of action."

22. See Gaines (2018) in Gledhill and Williams, eds. *A'santanotte* (Elvira Notari, Italy, 1922) is discussed in these terms.

23. Trouillot (1995, 13), says that what he calls "the historical process" has "some autonomy" relative to the narrative of it yet (15) he goes on to say that "the past does not exist independently from the present."

CHAPTER 6. ARE THEY "JUST LIKE US"?

1. White (2010, 315) says of Foucault that in contrast to histories of the past he thought it was "much more interesting and ultimately more productive to imagine the history of the present."

2. The reference is to Nancy K. Miller's theorization of authorial gender-or-race-specified criticism (1986, 113), for instance, where she describes Charlotte Brontë's character Lucy Snowe as writing "as a woman."

3. For another example, see Spivak's discussion of the Rani of Simur (1999, 209–247), an important discursion on historical interpretation followed by an important theoretical digression that includes a sharp political critique of empirical historiography: "It has helped positivist empiricism—the justifying foundation of advanced capitalist neocolonialism—to define its own arena as 'concrete experience,' 'what actually happens'" (255).

4. See Jenkins (2003, 39–40) on the difficulty with present assumptions.

5. I concur with Rosen (2001, 390) that Barthes "The Discourse of History" (1986a) is "seminal" in the analysis of the discourse of the historian, but wonder why it has been cited less often than "The Reality Effect" (1986b) in film and media studies scholarship.

6. See White (2010, 316) for the political critique of the genealogical: "By providing for the nation an equivalent of what the genealogist provided for the family, professional historians of the nineteenth century not only established the purity of the group's bloodlines but also confirmed the claim of the dominant ethnic group within the nation to the land it ruled." See Gaines (2015, 324–328) for the relevance to film and media history.

7. Consider Doane, Mellencamp, and Williams (1983, 7) as discussed in Dall'Asta and Gaines (2015, 15–16).

8. We should recall the importance of rereading the nineteenth-century British women writers at the time, as Gayatri Spivak's (1985) juxtaposition of *Jane Eyre* and the *Wide Sargasso Sea* that critiqued the British tradition through the figure of West Indian mixed-race Bertha Mason, hidden in the attic.

9. See Gaines (2012b, 22–23) for a reading of Kaplan's position as the lament that "If only there had been more women," that also reconsiders the feminist "subversive" reading of female authorship.

10. See Beauchamp (2006, 73–77) on Marion's attempts to work with and against male directors on this film.

11. See Rich (1998, ch. 4) on the first U.S. Women's Film Festivals.

12. This is not to say that actresses were not recruited as subversive. See Kaplan (1983a) on Marlene Dietrich.

13. But see Holliday (1995, 115) who says that there were more actresses who were also writers.

14. See Gaines (2004, 117) on what looking for feminist precursors in the U.S. film industry first yielded.

15. Jenkins (1991, 7; 2003, 39–40) uses the term "before now" and I have borrowed this throughout.

16. This is a variation on Gaudreault (2011, 2) who finds in the naming of other times an indication of the assumptions held by the "historian's 'historicizing' present."

17. There are difficulties with finding the "abject" everywhere. Similarly, as concerns the word "subaltern," Spivak (1999, 336) complains that the word has become generalized.

18. See Scott (1999, ch. 4) for the feminist critique of E. P. Thompson.

19. For an anthropologist's analysis of how the category *transgender* has rapidly grown and is controverted when gender and sexuality don't line up, see Valentine (2007). Identity politics has had its continual critics, among them Stuart Hall who has argued that "It is an immensely important gain when one recognizes that all identity is constructed across difference and begins to live with the politics of difference" (1987, 45).

20. See note 6 on the relation between the new nineteenth-century "science" of history and the new nation state's need for genealogy.

21. The "modernized" lives of Catherine the Great (Massie 2011) and Cleopatra (Schiff 2010) are best sellers in the contemporary book market.

22. We might also consider those career aspects brought to the fore after the academic phase and into the public phase of recognition thinking of Alice Guy Blaché, now in that second phase at the moment of U.S. and European public discovery exemplified by the documentary *Be Natural* (forthcoming) as well as retrospectives at the Whitney Museum in New York (January 2011) and the Cinema Ritrovato in Bologna, Italy (July 2011).

23. On Michelina, see Lyons (2013); on Wong, see Lau (2013); on Aoki, see Ross (2013); on Dungee-Huston, see Brooks-Bertram (2013); on Williams, see Welbon (2001). Morgan and

Dixon (2013), in their essay "African American Women in the Silent Film Industry," give more examples of Black women who saw opportunities for cultural outreach in motion pictures.

24. On the impasse in feminist film theory, see Kaplan (1985, 243). Casetti (2007, 35) suggests that the "impasse" that film theory encountered in the 1990s can be explained as well by the demise of its object. It was not only that no new model to replace the old was developed but that the object of study was gone.

25. See Munslow (2003, 77) on the question of the historian's use of "empathy" to explain historical actors relative to Collingwood's idea of "empathetic re-enactment," which is not without its detractors. Collingwood (1993, 288) thus formulates the function of the historian's imagination: "To know someone else's activity of thinking is possible only on the assumption that this same activity can be re-enacted in one's own mind."

26. What is worse, Jenkins argues, in a move that turns the criticism of presentism against itself, every defense against present-centeredness is epistemologically impossible. In the end, he even thinks that if the historian is dedicated to guarding against presentism, *that* position is itself presentist. This is because, as he puts it, "the claim in the present that you should not be present-centered is no less a present-centered claim than the claim that you should" (2003, 12).

27. To be more precise, Jenkins (2009a, 15–16), swears off histories "of either the modernist or postmodernist kind," although he would prefer histories to be "postmodern." I am not convinced that the fields referenced here are in agreement about what they want "postmodern" to represent. Interesting in this regard is Hayden White's introduction to Jenkins in which he concludes that the author is more "post-postmodern," given that he thinks postmodernism retains "the past" by ironic means (2009, 3).

28. The source of the metaphor we have borrowed is Benjamin (1999, 462–463): "It is not that what is past cast its light on the present, or what is present its light on what is past; rather, image is that wherein what has been comes together in a flash with the now to form a constellation."

29. Mink would consider this as a problem in what was "conceptually available" to those at the time just as we may attempt to reconstruct that time using terms that are only "conceptually available" to us via our historical research. Hence the inevitable "conceptual asymmetries," as he says, consequence of changes in entire systems of thought, theirs as well as ours (1987, 140).

30. Buckley (2015, C1) reports that in 2015 only 4 percent of the largest-grossing U.S. films were directed by women. Setting a precedent, the A.C.L.U. of Southern California requested state and federal agencies to open up an investigation of major Hollywood studios, talent agencies, and networks, charging gender discrimination in their hiring practices.

31. See Runia (2014, 104), who takes inspiration from W. G. Sebald (2011), for whom photographs as well as physical remains "can remember us."

32. The documentary *Golden Gate Girls* (Wei 2013) finds Eng functioning in enclaves, especially the Hong Kong community entertainment underground inhabited by Peking Opera performers, gamblers, and high livers. On Eng, also see Wei (2011, 15–17; 2013).

CHAPTER 7. WORKING IN THE DREAM FACTORY

1. See Stamp (2015, 2–3) on the "staging" of work as she analyzes four photographs of Lois Weber working with and without her secretary at the typewriter, as labor "performed" for the camera in a publicity shoot. She further observes that these photo shoot images are a reminder of the difficulty for the historian of studying this work, now so untraceable.

2. Screenwriter Josephine Lovett was making $500 a week and her secretary Nesta Charles $25 a week; Alice Duher Miller, screenwriter, made $250 a week and her secretary Jean Harrison, $25 a week. Payroll ending August 25, 1926, Metro/Goldwyn/Mayer Pictures Weekly Payroll, AMPAS-SC. See Morey (2013) on Barnard College graduate Alice Duher Miller and Salerno on Josephine Lovett (2013).

3. Mahar (2006, 6) begins with the "relatively egalitarian culture of work" in the American theater, which she finds carried over into the earliest motion picture "companies."

4. See Hill (2016, 28–38) on the "efficiency" measures that companies were beginning to take as early as 1913, involving not only the "continuity script" that organized production but the blueprints for studio buildings. After 1917, however, she locates some resistance to these measures in what she calls the "efficiency backlash" (note 78, 235).

5. See Gaines and Vatsal (2013) for a list of 18 female scenario editors by company; Hettie Gray Baker: Bosworth, Fox; F. Marion Brandon: Éclair; Ashley Miller (and Edwin S. Porter): Edison; Louella Parsons: Essanay: Josephine Rector: Essanay; Florence Strauss: First National; Lillian Spellman Stone: Lubin; Kate Corbaley: Metro; June Mathis: Metro; Catherine Carr: North American; Ouida Bergère: Pathé; Eve Unsell: R. C. Pictures; Bradley King: Thomas A. Ince; Miriam Meredith: Thomas A. Ince; Beta Breuil: Vitagraph; Margeurite Bertsch: Vitagraph; Gertrude Thanhouser: Thanhouser; Eugenie Magnus Ingleton (wih Eugene B. Lewis): Universal.

6. In "Reminiscences of Frances Marion" (1958, 3) the writer recalls Lois Weber, Anita Loos, Adela Rogers St. Johns, Bess Meredith, and June Mathis as the early scenario writers: "There were a few men; they were newspapermen, and they were a little bit ashamed of it. They were writing on the side," CUOHRO.

7. A good example of this would be Mahar (2001), the first publication of her argument that women were more highly placed in the silent-era U.S. film industry than in any other business. Since this study appeared in the journal *Enterprise & History*, her research helps to make a place for the historical study of women and wealth.

8. Ramsaye (1986 [1926], 442–443) says that "It was accepted practice then to impress actors into service as carpenters, scene painters and the like."

9. Mahar (2006, 38), finds the term referenced by J. Stuart Blackton, the origin of which was the minstrel team. Often cited is Beulah Marie Dix's recollection of the informality in Brownlow (1968, 22): "Anybody on the set did anything he or she was called upon to do. I've walked on as an extra, I've tended lights—and anybody not doing anything else wrote down the director's notes on the script. I also spent a good deal of time in the cutting room." Brownlow goes on: "A solid core of first-class writers, nearly all of them women, grew up as the importance of the work began to be recognized: Frances Marion, Eve Unsell, Clara Beranger, Edith Kennedy, Bess Meredyth, Ouida Bergere, Beulah Marie Dix, Marion Fairfax, Jeanie Macpherson, Lenore Coffee, Hector and Margaret Turnbull, and June Mathis were to remain top scenarists throughout the silent era" (23). Alma Young, who started at Robertson-Cole in 1921, recalls working as script girl, translator, switchboard operator, and taking on jobs in the property department as well as answering fan mail. Interview (January 30 and February 20, 1977), AMPAS-OH.

10. Blackton (n.d.), AMPAS-MC.

11. Gauntier, "Blazing the Trail" *Women's Home Companion* (October 1928, 183).

12. Mary Pickford letter to Francis Boggs (April 12, 1910). William Selig Papers. AMPAS—MC. According to Slide (1998, 183) Boggs was a stage director who went West in 1908 for the

Selig Co. where his company is thought to have shot the first moving picture narrative in the vicinity of Los Angeles.

13. Holliday (1995, 115), says that more actresses than actors were also writers in the silent era. The Women Film Pioneers Project count to date of U.S. actresses who also had screenwriting credits stands at 44 of 103 total screenwriters (also tagged as coscreenwriters, scenario writers, and scenarists). The majority of the 476 female names the project classifies as still "unhistoricized," that is, as yet "unresearched," appear to be women who worked as screenwriters.

14. Thanks to Martin Norden for this source. See also Norden (2014).

15. See ch. 1, note 9. Others who directed at Universal Pictures Manufacturing Company were Cleo Madison, Ida May Park, Lule Warrenton, Elsie Jane Wilson, and Ruth Stonehouse.

16. Stamp (2015, 67) tells us that when the *Universal Weekly* in 1916 declared Weber the "Greatest Woman Director in the World," some argued that the title needed to drop the word "woman."

17. See Jacobson (2015, 105–107) on the new Vitagraph Co. studio, built in 1911 in Brooklyn, divided into workshops and laboratories, studio stages and designated publicity and business offices. *Moving Picture World* (1912, 907) published a promotional image including "Wardrobe Department" and "The Joining Room" filled by female workers.

18. See note 5 earlier for a list of 18 women scenario editors by studio.

19. Agnes Christine Johnson to [Albert] Smith (July 26, 1914). Box 12647. Warner Bros. Collection, USC-RHC.

20. Holliday (1995, 45) says that Bradley King began as a stenographer for the Lubin Co. before she became chief scenario writer for Thomas H. Ince in the 1920s. On Bradley King, see Taves (2013). Virginia Van Upp later wrote *Cover Girl* (1944) and produced the film noir classic *Gilda* (1946). Van Upp is listed on the Metro/Goldwyn/Mayer Pictures Weekly Payroll for December 30, 1925, as making $50 a week as payroll clerk.

21. The estimated total numbers are based on the most recent count on the Women Film Pioneers Project website: wfpp.cdrs.columbia.edu (accessed September 1, 2016).

22. See the introduction, note 1, on the question of the percentage of female to male screenwriters. Slide (2012a, 114) is referring to the two published volumes of the American Film Institute Catalog covering the silent era.

23. It was the fruitlessness of research on the thousands of anonymous writers, who can only be indicated by reports as to the bulk of submissions that many studios used as evidence of fan interest, that led me to ask about these workers. See Gaines (2012a, 445–446).

24. Slide challenges the 50 percent figure (2012a, 114). See also the introduction, notes 1 and 22 in this chapter.

25. But Valeria also appeared ambivalent about the marriage. Of the friend making her a white satin nightgown with matching negligee, she writes on August 7, 1928, to Irma: "I really think she is more excited than I am about it. Somehow or other I just can't seem to get terribly excited over the prospect of being married" (Beauchamp 2006, 194).

26. Cecil B. DeMille Weekly Payroll records. (April 17, 1928). Box 277, folder 8. Cecil B. DeMille Collection, BYU.

27. See: www.wfpp.cdrs.columbia.edu (accessed July 7, 2017). Taken over in 2010 by the Columbia University Libraries Center for Digital Research and Scholarship when the contracted publisher concluded that the material was too massive to be accommodated by the

projected print volumes, the Women Film Pioneers Project data, although published officially in 2013, continues to grow and is thus constantly in the process of being "published" as it is expanded and updated.

28. At publication, the Women Film Pioneers Project listed a total of 164 different terms for occupations.

29. Metro Pictures Weekly Payroll (July 2, 1921), AMPAS-MC.

30. Metro/Goldwyn/Mayer Weekly Payroll (December 30, 1925), AMPAS-MC. See ch. 8, note 2, on the Goldwyn/Metro Pictures merger. Slide (1998, 125) says that the Loew's Inc. theater circuit had already acquired Metro Pictures Corp. in 1919 and brought in Louis B. Mayer. After Loew's took over the failing Goldwyn Pictures Corporation and brought in Mayer's company, Metro/Goldwyn/Mayer was created on May 17, 1924 and moved into the Goldwyn Studios in Culver City.

31. At publication, the Women Film Pioneers Project lists a U.S. total of 55 directors, including codirectors and assistant directors and 60 producers, including coproducers and executive producers. The count is 32 in the category of producer-director, including those tagged as producer, executive producer, director, codirector, coproducer, assistant director. Mark Lynn Anderson (2016, 17), in his focus on the evolution of the executive producer, opens up the "producer" category for reconsideration, noting that the difference between director and producer was not always there in practice, especially in the first decade as the structure of what became the studio was in formation. Since so many women were credited with (or claimed) some variant of the term "producer" we need to rethink the work (or the symbolics if no real work) associated with that category in the silent era. See also ch. 1, note 28.

32. Valeria writes to Irma on July 19, 1928, that she is taking dictation from Mr. MacMahon who is writing the novelization of *The Godless Girl* (1928) from the screenplay by Jeanie Macpherson (Beauchamp 2006, 191).

33. Morgenson (2015) writes that, in 1965, the CEO pay as multiple of average worker pay was 20 times, while in 2013 it was nearly 300. https://www.nytimes.com/2015/08/09/business/why-putting-a-number-to-ceo-pay-might-bring-change.html (accessed August 1, 2016). Yezierska (1925, 647) is the only period source that draws attention to such discrepancies when she recalls that "eminent authors," stars, and directors "got fortunes for their work; the others drudged from morning till night for less than their bread."

34. DeMille Weekly Payroll (April 17, 1928) lists Cecil B. DeMille (Administrative) as making $2,500, Jeanie Macpherson as making $1,000 per week as the highest paid Scenario Writer, and Valeria Belletti on the same page as one of the 3 Secretaries making $5, the lowest weekly pay, also earned by a few men—7 classified as Labor, 1 as Driver, and 1 as Mechanic. Cecil B. DeMille Collection. Box 277, folder 8, BYU.

35. Valeria's letter letter dated January 16, 1928, describes: "Things quiet at the studios. Warner Brothers has closed its studio and I don't think it will reopen until spring. United Artists has laid off a lot of people. MGM has laid off about 200. DeMille has laid off about 100—other girls who have been here longer . have been dismissed" (174). On March 13, 1928, she writes that she is "still at the studio, although my days are numbered. Pathé has bought DeMille and whole crowd is being let out. Pathé will bring in their own" (181). Beauchamp (2006, 181) confirms this in reference to a *Variety* article that reports that Joseph P. Kennedy, the Pathé special advisor, would let go employees after current productions had been completed.

36. See note 32.

37. See *Variety*, 1916, on the new "jobbing" system that meant actors were hired as temporary workers.

38. On the Leah Baird Co., see Blaetz (2013); on the Flora Finch Company, 1916–1917, followed by Flora Finch Film Frolics Pictures Corporation in 1920, see Miller (2013a); on the Drew Pictures, see Ionita (2013).

39. On the history of extras, see Slide (2012b) and McKenna (2008, ch. 3).

40. See ch. 1, note 38 on the case Mahar makes for finance capital as an explanation and Cooper's concurrence. Wasko (1982, 10–14) is an important reevaluation of the evidence. For the standard industry history account, see Hampton (1970, 311–316). Jacobs (1975, 170) assumes that motion pictures is "big business" by 1918. Further, he discusses the rise in costs in the 1920s, referring to Wall Street bankers as bringing in the producer-supervisor to control costs, but puts less emphasis than Hampton on the "waste and inefficiency" issues that made investors dubious (293–295).

41. On March 13, 1928, Valeria writes that buying the house has put her in "considerable debt," but that the rents she will take in will pay the mortgage interest. We can calculate the amount of her mortgage as $9,500, or the difference between the $13,500 cost and her $4,000 cash down payment (Beauchamp 2006, 183). For an analysis of contemporary women who still struggled to balance home life and careers based on the Stanford class of 1994, see Kantor (2014).

42. Foucault (1972, 130–131) sees the archive as to be analyzed in terms of the "discontinuity" or "gap" between us and "what we can no longer say." While he would challenge the ease of our "continuities" he would also caution that there is no undoing of the "discontinuities of history."

43. Ricoeur (2004, 201–202), commenting on what he sees in Foucault as the "theme of discontinuity" wonders: "Should we reproach Foucault for having substituted the ideology of the continuous for one of the discontinuous?"

44. For the shape of computationally enabled historiographic research in the so-called "digital age" see Anderson (2011), Lundemo (2014), and articles in *CinéMas* special issue, ed. Blümlinger (2014).

45. See note 25.

46. See Derrida (1996) and Foucault (1972, ch. 5).

CHAPTER 8. THE WORLD EXPORT OF "THE VOICE OF THE HOME"

1. *Film Daily* (June 7, 1925): 115, as quoted in Lant (2006, 664–665, and 798, note 149) where she lists the nine women who like Mathis wrote back in answer to the *Film Daily* question about "The Feminine Mind in Picture Making": Eve Unsell, Mary Pickford, Clara Beranger, Marion Fairfax, Leah Baird, Jane Murfin, Anita Loos, and Josephine Lovett Robertson. See Wexman (2013) who counts Mathis as either screenwriter or cowriter on 114 feature films that went into production between 1918 and 1927.

2. For instance, see Jacobs (1975, 159): "When war broke out in Europe in 1914, American motion picture production constituted more than half of the total movie production of the world; by 1917 America was making nearly all the world's motion pictures." Especially triumphant is *Motography* in 1914: "When peace reigns once more in Europe, one of the first har-

bingers of the return to normal living will be the reopening of the picture theaters. And their programs will be made up of American-made films. Then will come the greatest prosperity the American manufacturers have ever known . and with the domestic market bigger than ever, American-made films will not only lead the world—they will constitute it," as quoted in Thompson (1985, 54). Wasko (1982, 32) says that Hollywood "clearly dominated" and, by 1927, was effectively the "world center" for motion picture production and the source of "80% of the world's output of exposed film."

3. Lant (2006, 32) later picks up on Mathis's claim: "It was even mooted, in 1925, that women's presence in American film production, and their louder voices in American culture more generally, might explain the international dominance of American cinema; in Europe women had less to say." Hampton (1970, 135) credits Selznick with the strategic use of Clara Kimball Young in the formation of a company but is critical of executive decisions made by Mathis (310–312). Hampton's version of Mathis's career contradicts the case she appears to be making for the kind of film she thought had been successful. In his analysis, as a Goldwyn producer Mathis assembled a committee of intellectuals to advise her who dismissed "melodrama" and "hokum" as well as proven popular subject matter (312).

4. In the introduction to the most comprehensive study of women workers in silent-era Hollywood, Mahar (2006, 4–5) reiterates that publicity departments emerged in the 1910s, and scholars of U.S. motion picture history must always consider star personas and behind-the-scenes stories as specially constructed for public consumption. See Anderson (2016, 26–29) for the argument that the image of the studio chief executive as talented producer and business-man needs consideration relative to the development of studio public relations, beginning as early as the U.S. entry into World War I.

5. Cooper (2013c, 120) has argued that the justification for archival research might best be not to "preserve or recover" the past but to "transform present day institutions and their relationships." But Anderson (2016, 33), glossing Cooper, emphasizes something else here—the goal of archival projects to "pervert the present." This, in contrast to the use of archival research to "render irrelevant" what has been said or written, is a use of records deployed to "correct and discipline" misconstrual by sources but presuming that archival documents are somehow pristine relative to any earlier "historicizing function."

6. See Hochschild (2005) on the Belgian outrage after the publication of his 1999 *King Leopold's Ghost*, history of African genocide, 1885–1908, in the Belgian king's plundered Congo.

7. Recent examples in silent-era U.S. cinema research of how categories have produced significant knowledge shifts might be Anderson (2011, Ch. 3) who uses the category "queer" to transform thought about Rudolph Valentino. The idea new to twentieth-century American studies of a female migration to California is opened up by the use of *gender*, the category, in Hallett (2013).

8. Gender is even thought by some Western governments to need balancing in areas like sports, although not as yet in the area of moving image culture. Although in October 2013, five of the most powerful women in the French government signed "A Charte de L'Egalite for the French Film Industry," demanding a 50 percent gender balance film production funding rule, a response to the report "The Place of Women in Art and Culture: The Time Has Come to Move to Action."

9. Keynote, "Feminist Media Historiography and the Work Ahead," Women and the Silent Screen Conference, October 1, 2013, University of Melbourne, Australia.

10. See Anderson (2011, 77) who cites Studlar on Valentino as "the woman-made man." He then goes on to address Valentino's "queerness" relative to American mass culture as less about his sexual identity than the "types of sexualities his stardom made possible, gratified, or otherwise indulged" (101).

11. Slater (2002, 203) explains that Metro was her second job, so she entered Metro in 1919 as head of the scenario department. But later (2010, 103), he says that by 1918 she was the "main writer" at Metro Pictures. Schmidt (1982, 50), in his history of Metro Pictures, 1915–1920, says that Mathis started at Metro in May, 1918, as part of an effort to build up the scenario department as a way of de-emphasizing the star system.

12. Lipke (1923, III,13), quotes another source on Mathis, then Goldwyn Studios editorial director, who is said to be "the woman with the most important job in the world." Slater (2002, 213) says that she began work at First National in late 1924 and there began a second successful career phase in which she developed screenplays that promoted Colleen Moore and wrote the acclaimed *Classified* for Corinne Griffith. However, by 1926 she was again doing freelance work for MGM (Slater 2002, 215). See also Wexman on Mathis (2013), Slater on Griffith (2013), notes 1 and 12.

13. Kozarski (1990, 241). Slater (2002, 204) says that in 1923 Goldwyn producer Mathis undertook negotiations for the adaptation of *McTeague*, which would become *Greed*, as well as for *Ben Hur*. She had already left for Italy to begin *Ben-Hur* when Louis B. Mayer, Harry Rapf, and Irving Thalberg secured control of Metro-Goldwyn-Mayer in its newly merged form. See Brownlow (1968, 451–453) on how MGM took over all aspects of the *Ben-Hur* production, pushing out Mathis's team. Only after they had replaced the lead actors and director, as well as the crew, did they release the explanation that the Goldwyn and Metro merger had required the overhaul. Kell (1924, 32–33) describes how Mathis, who had written the script, arrived in Rome expecting to supervise the production, but her authority was reduced to approval of some scenes.

14. Slater (2002, 202) refers to the American Film Institute figure of 113 titles on which she worked as screenwriter, coscreenwriter, or editorial director over an eleven-year career. June Mathis credits include: *The Red Lantern*. Director: Albert Capellani, screenplay: June Mathis, Albert Capellani (Nazimova Productions U.S. 1919), cast: Alla Nazimova; *Camille*. Director: Ray C. Smallwood, screenplay: June Mathis (Nazimova Productions U.S. 1921), cast: Alla Nazimova; *Blood and Sand*. Director: Fred Niblo, screenplay: June Mathis (Famous Players—Lasky Corp. U.S. 1922), cast: Rudolph Valentino; *The Four Horsemen of the Apocalypse*. Director: Rex Ingram, screenplay: June Mathis (Metro Pictures Corp. U.S. 1921), cast: Alice Terry, Rudolph Valentino; *The Conquering Power*. Director: Rex Ingram, screenplay: June Mathis (Metro Pictures Corp. Metro Special U.S. 1921), cast: Alice Terry, Rudolph Valentino; *Classified*. Director: Alfred Santell, screenplay/editor: June Mathis (Corinne Griffith Productions U.S. 1925), cast: Corinne Griffith; *Sally*. Director: Alfred E. Green, screenplay/editorial director: June Mathis (First National Pictures Inc. U.S. 1925), cast: Colleen Moore; *Irene*. Director: Alfred E. Green, editorial director/continuity: June Mathis (First National Pictures Inc U.S. 1926), cast: Colleen Moore.

15. At the time, Thompson offered as support for this the number of world cinema auteurs who acknowledged their debt to the Hollywood style, whether negative or positive influence, as well as the point that popular genres appeared to have their origin in the U.S. (1985, ix).

16. Bordwell, in Bordwell, Thompson, Staiger (1985, 3), first says that "classical" as a term may seem a strange term to use to describe American mass culture, but that it is French in origin, and in use even before Bazin (2005, 29). More recently, Williams (2018) argues that Bazin's first translator Hugh Gray left the quotation marks off of the term "classical." See, alternatively, Bazin as translated by Timothy Barnard, who includes the quotation marks (2009, 94): "In short, we are in every sense in the presence of a 'classical' art at its peak." Bordwell, in Bordwell, Thompson, and Staiger (1985, 4) lists as the aspects critics have traditionally used to evaluate the classically canonical: "decorum, proportion, formal harmony, respect for tradition, mimesis, self-effacing craftsmanship, and cool control of the receivers' response."

17. Kaplan (2012, 72), for example, thinks feminist critics used the industry notion of "genre" to develop another genre, the "women's picture" or "woman's film." They were effectively "drawing attention to aspects of Hollywood melodrama" that male critics had overlooked. Gledhill (2000, 239) puts it somewhat differently, referring to the "woman's film" as like film noir, which she sees as relatively "unarticulated" in earlier decades. See Elsaesser (2012, 9–10) on postclassical cinema as "classical-plus" as well as Section IV (223–304).

18. But see Schlüpmann (1994, 83) on the 1970s German position in the journal *Frauen ünd Film*, which she characterizes as "contradictory" given that "feminist film theories scrupulously analyzed the systematic oppression of the female subject in film, contributions to film history celebrated the strengths of women as directors and cutters, the subversiveness of actresses, and the wealth of experience of an older generation of female spectators."

19. To be precise, it was classical narrative that was said to have been exported, but although feminist film theory understood this narrative as "patriarchial," the position was never exactly that "patriarchial cinema" was exported.

20. See Gaines (2001, 71) for the case that, although Mulvey (1975) introduced the term "male gaze," she used the term one time in her seminal essay. It was, however, developed by Kaplan (1983, ch. 1).

21. It has become accepted in the field that female writers and directors were first sought in an effort to improve the class of filmgoers by attracting female audiences on the theory that women would "uplift" the new entertainment. See also "Play to the Ladies" (1909, 34), which quotes "one of the most successful exhibitors" as having said "I play to the ladies," as though showing the kind of story women enjoy explains that success. After the number of women in creative positions increased, however, the idea that they were writing for women becomes implied, although it is sometimes stated explicitly in interviews. See Beranger (1919).

22. But Slater (2002, 202), argues that Mathis "used her power to establish a voice for women within the industry," an analysis that could push an interpretation of Mathis's claim as self-serving. This interpretation, however, would have to discount the possibility that with her support other women's positions were given "voice."

23. Slide (2012a, 114) describes the "gasps from the audience" at the Academy of Motion Picture Arts and Sciences in response to Cari Beauchamp's statement that women wrote 50 percent of silent-era films. But see Introduction, note 1 on Slide's challenge to this statistic.

24. On the "cinema of attractions," see Gunning (1986, 2006); for silent cinema female audiences, see Mayne (1990), Staiger (1995), Hansen (1991), Rabinovitz (1998); on the rediscovery of the serial queens, see Stamp (2000, ch. 3), Singer (1996, 2001, 1996), Bean (2002a), Dahlquist (2013a,b). On the "first global vernacular" see Hansen (2000a, 12; 2000b, 340), also

theorized by Hansen as "vernacular modernism." Elsewhere I have taken issue with the term "modernism" in this formulation given the history of "high" modernism and its antipathy to the popular, which does not go away if we introduce other "modernisms." A term like *popular modernism,* however, would still seem strange (Gaines, "What Did Hollywood Export to the Rest of the World?" forthcoming).

25. Mercer and Shingler (2004, 83) cite Gledhill on the genres informed by "melodramatic rhetoric" (1987, 13) and then they make a case for "male melodrama" (Mercer and Shingler 2004, 98–104).

26. See Gledhill (1987, 33–35) for an explanation of how the addition of speech completed the cinema's orientation toward an idea of realism (aligned with the masculine), contributing to the disconnection from its melodrama "origins." Yet, she goes on, the gangster and the western genres never really, as she says, "veered from their melodramatic predispositions." And the motion picture film industry even acknowledged the legacy in a term like *crime melodrama,* for instance. On the historical use of the term *melodrama* in U.S. press and industry promotion, see Neale (1993).

27. Here is the place to ask whether classical continuity narrative and melodrama as a mode are mutually exclusive or not. Indeed, melodrama conventions work off from classical formality, and melodrama's aesthetic excess as ironic commentary requires there to be a classical text on which to comment. See Mercer and Shingler (2004). Buckley (2012, 430), in his introduction to the special issue of *Modern Drama* on melodrama, thinks that the best theoretical work on melodrama has been done within film and television studies and references theater historians as now repositioning melodrama as central to the Victorian stage. Gledhill (2000, 232), posits that it has been the dedication to arguing for cinema as "modernist break with past traditions" that has contributed to the "neglect" of theatrical legacies. See also Gledhill, "Domestic Melodrama," forthcoming.

28. Williams (2012, 529) allows that "vernacular modernism" is currently used to describe what she sees as melodrama, and thus there would be no mutual exclusivity. However, the too easy merger of these two paradigms could forestall deeper consideration of what each attempts to achieve. Also, both melodrama and "attractions" here become "body genres" in the argument that they are the rule rather than the exception to it, suggesting a way of approaching a commonality in these paradigms beyond the mutual challenge to the dominance of classicism.

29. Williams (2001, 16) also puts it that melodrama has historically been the "norm not the exception." Jacobs (2012, 397) rereads critics in the 1920s and 1930s for their disparaging attitude toward "old-fashioned melodrama" in reference to the memory of stage play versions of *Madame X* and *East Lynne.* Film reception of what she calls the "maternal melodrama" genre broke down along rural as opposed to urban lines. Furthermore, examples of the contemporary melodrama canon, she says, would not have been understood in the 1920s as "women's pictures" (398). But see Gledhill (1987, 35) on how the "woman's film" later came to be associated with melodrama after sound, which meant that the negative connotations could be directed away from masculine genres. She further suggests that women as both "cultural producers and consumers" need to be considered relative to the gendering of our critical categories. Here is caution about taking the "woman's film" as synonymous with melodrama.

30. Kaplan (1992, 62) says that if one follows the definition of melodrama in Brooks (1985) then "all main Hollywood genres are melodrama," especially as they attempt an "ethical recentering" as a response to the "decentering of modern consciousness."

31. The connection between *melos* or *music* and melodrama was made as early as Elsaesser (1987, 50), who in the section "Putting Melos into Drama" offers the definition that "melodrama is a dramatic narrative in which musical accompaniment marks the emotional effects."

32. See Dall'Asta (2010b). Scott (1996a, 4) says that "To the extent that feminist history serves the political ends of feminism, it participates in producing this essentialized common identity of women." In other words, she thinks that "essentialism" is an unavoidable pitfall.

33. The literature on the "feminine aesthetic" in literary studies is vast, and for a time was carried over into film aesthetics, but was quickly challenged for its essentialist potential. See De Lauretis (1986, 2).

34. See also Gaines (2012b, 24–27) where I critique the approach in which the "hand" of Alice Guy Blaché can be read in aesthetic choices made in *The New Love and the Old* (Solax, 1912), a short film she most likely directed and produced.

35. See Dyer (1991, 187–188). While I can agree with Dyer that it "does matter" who makes a film, I still take what I call an "anti-auteurist" position (Gaines 2002, 91–101).

36. Beranger (1919, 662) says that "In the writing of picture stories women seem to have the call and just why this should be is easily understood. The largest proportion of motion picture 'fans' are women. Women writers know better what pleases their sisters than men." Holliday (1995, 145) thinks that the silent-era studios had no way of knowing whether the audience was female or male but assumed that women comprised the majority.

37. An unusual case is a *Photoplay* article relaying Cleo Madison's version of how when she asked if she could direct her own moving pictures in response to the Universal company's refusal, she complained that every male director she was assigned was "unsatisfactory." As a consequence, the company allowed her to choose her own company and to work as director. Asked if this frightened her she replied: "Why should I be? I had seen men with less brains than I have getting away with it, and so I know that I could direct if they'd give me the opportunity" (Henry 1916, 111). For Madison's directing credits, see ch.1, note 2.

38. See Neely (2010; 2013) for Louis B. Mayer—Anita Stewart, and Mahar (2013b, 2006, 164–165), and Anderson (2017) for Selznick—Clara Kimball Young. Anderson's most recent answer to the question as to how much "creative control" as well as "economic control" Young had as an actress-producer was finally no more than "limited autonomy within the larger industrial context." On Gloria Swanson, see Buck (2013) and Staiger (2013, 205–206) who analyzes Swanson's challenges with Will Hays who, refusing to recognize that she was the producer on *Sadie Thompson* (1928), persisted in corresponding with executive producer Joseph Schenck.

39. See Musser (2009, 82–84) on Alice Guy Blaché and Herbert Blaché as well as Ida May Park and Joseph DeGrasse. On Lovett, see Salerno (2013). See Gaines and Vatsal (2013) for a list of male-female creative teams.

40. Grimstead maintains that the move to align women rather than men with certain moral value was a nineteenth-century development, as quoted in Gledhill (1987, 34).

41. See Kaplan (1992, ch. 2) for a lineage that traces the separate male (public) and female (private) spheres to Rousseau's *Emile* (1762), citing Nancy Cott (1977) on how women came to be identified with the "heart" and the consequent construction of women as dependent on men, the basis of sexual inequality. Kaplan (1992, 82) further recapitulates Rousseau on this point to underscore how the "very survival of the human race depends on the woman's function in cementing the family through her skills in emotions and relationships."

42. See Dickson and Dickson (2000, 14) on the technological ideal, the "establishment of harmonious relations between kinetograph and phonograph"; Dickson and Dickson (as quoted in Lant 2006, 6), on the motion picture film as promising "new forms of social and political life" based on collaboration between the sexes; See Dickson and Dickson (1894, 361–362).

43. Lant (2006, 252–253) has also noted Bertsch's "Christian millennialism."

44. Hansen (2000b), 337 includes "theatrical melodrama" with its deployment of "spectacle and coincidence" in her list of what is left out of the classical cinema paradigm—along with genres—horror, comedy, and pornography. In her analysis of Chinese silent film (2000a, 20), she allows that "melodramatic and sentimental" readings would be possible, but perhaps more importantly, her approach to these films follows the methodology of melodrama analysis, here, significantly in the way that the contradictions that arise in the modern moment are figured in the lives of women (15).

45. A key text here is Benjamin (1970, 257): "To articulate the past historically does not mean to recognize it 'the way it really was' (Ranke)." Again in the *Arcades Project* (1999, 463), he writes: "The history that showed things 'as they really were' was the strongest narcotic of the century."

46. Huyssen (1986) points out the early association of the feminine with mass culture as a way of denigrating it as well as excluding women from a masculinized high modernism, although, he concludes (205), that women could finally not be excluded from high culture.

47. See Gaines (2000, 107–109) for an overview of the influential paradigm for analyzing mass culture that connects cultural studies with Ernst Bloch via Stuart Hall's "double movement of the popular" (1981, 228).

48. Readers may detect a replay of some of the issues around the contemporary "modernity thesis" debates in the field, and they would be correct since I am also returning to a Frankfurt School–informed theorization of the relation between moving pictures and the moment of their emergence. However, where Kracauer and Benjamin were associated with a hypothesis that saw changes in perception or cinema analogized with urban modernity, I am more interested in refining a theory that takes "the modern" in a direction that avoids the pitfalls of studying a historical sensorium. For a comprehensive overview of the "modernity thesis," see Singer (2001, ch. 4).

49. Zizek (2013, xx) in his preface to a recent collection of essays on Bloch says that "fundamentally, with regard to what really matters, he was right, he remains our contemporary, and maybe he belongs even more to our time than to his own."

50. Jameson here restates Bloch's "without the utopian function, class ideologies would only have managed to create transitory deception" (Bloch 1995, 156). See also Gaines (2000, 107–109).

51. Koselleck (2004, 3) measures "modernity" as the way in which time is experienced as a "new time," and relative to his theory of "relocation," the more times are felt to be "new times" the higher the expectation placed on a future time. Sounding somewhat like Bloch he sees the "new" as not just new but as "even better than what has gone before" (228).

52. Bloch starts in 1915–1916 with the *Spirit of Utopia* as World War I begins, but the *Principle of Hope* project was completed in 1938–1947. Koselleck looks back from the decades after World War II.

53. Koselleck (2002, 84) in "The Temporalization of Utopia," makes a rare reference to Bloch, whom he credits with having assigned a positive valence to "utopia."

54. Schlüpmann (2013, 18), goes further, in developing her theory of "play" to find an "intermediate zone" or space in which film and audience are inseparable. See Altenloh (2001), the 1914 German sociological study of female filmgoers that gives credence to this theory.

55. Schlüpmann (2012, 47–48), says that, in 1916, Nielsen did return to Berlin and made eight more productions with her own money, and even started her own company, Art-Film GmbH, with which she produced *Hamlet* (1921), casting herself in trousers. Loiperdinger and Jung (2013) collect essays on Nielsen as the first internationally marketed star during the 1910–1914 period when she had the most control. As Schlüpmann (2012, 47) says of that time, "all the freedom was hers."

56. On Fern Andra, see http://f-films.deutsches-filminstitut.de/biographien/f_andra_b.htm (accessed August 1, 2016). Schlüpmann (2010, 72) also mentions Luise del Zopp who wrote an estimated forty films between 1911 and 1914. For Schlüpmann, however, Nielsen is the complete paradigm, one aligned with a "countermovement" in the history of film that extends through creative personnel to the audience and culminates in a theory of "embodied perception," counter to the 1970s feminist theory of the cinematic male gaze (2010, 220).

57. See ch. 2 for the Heideggerian notion of "possibilities" that gives a boost to historical aspiration and future orientation in Koselleck (Carr 1987, 198).

58. The term *emancipatory* implies a connection to suffrage. Lant (2006, 560) quotes Beranger who thought that in 1920, the year the U.S. federal government approved the vote for women, the film industry led others in the number of opportunities for women.

59. Singer (1996, 192) traces the "New Woman" in U.S. culture to Winchester, 1902. Roberts (2008, 78) finds the term earlier in 1894, the creation of British journalist Sarah Grand. One of the most astute analyses of the New Woman is Staiger (1995, 181) who thus articulates the middle class "fascination" with her sexuality: "Who was the New Woman and what did she want?"

60. "A New Woman was necessary for a new order," argues Staiger (1995, 179), which includes a labor market with both men and women and women as potential consumers for an enlarged vision of newly marketable things.

61. Staiger (1995, xi, xvi), looking at the 1907–1915 period sees the question of the Bad Woman as opposed to the "Good" New Woman who might or might not replace the Victorian Domestic Woman as a "debate." Otto and Rocco (2011, 7) ask "Was the New Woman flesh and blood, a metaphor or both concurrently"? White (1987, 47) refers to the "logic of figuration itself" or "tropology." For his original theorization, see 1973, 31–38, where he explains that the characterizing metaphor is dangerous insofar as its use is an investment in the belief that language can grasp things figuratively.

62. Lant (2006, 563) says that women could be "found entwined with, or alongside, equipment in promotional images, as a way or expressing, allegorically, the wonder of the machines."

63. See Gaines and Koerner (2013) for a list that includes Grace Davison, Francelina Billington, and Margery Ordway.

64. Synon (1914, 59) quotes actress-camera operator Francelia Billington: "I suppose that it is still a novelty to see a girl more interested in a mechanical problem than in make-up."

65. Dixon (1916, 61) in an article featuring Grace Davison asks: "And does Miss Davison understand all about trick photography?" and goes on to reassure the reader that she can do triple as well as double exposure.

66. Stamp (2015, 240) reads Lois Weber's advice to "aspiring" filmmakers as "Don't try it," not as discouragement but as a more realistic assessment of the difficulties in store for women who tried.

67. Lant (2006, 559) uses the "closed door" metaphor but also refers to the "see-sawing" of careers, especially of women directors.

68. De Lauretis (1986, 14–15), theorizes what I have been calling feminism's sameness-difference conundrum as "its inherent and at least for now irreconcilable contradiction," which means that there is no feminism as a "coherent and available image." The *female subject of feminism*" thus defined by these differences among and between women is thus structurally contradictory.

69. Of the U.S. serial queens, Kathleen Williams, Helen Holmes, and Helen Gibson had production companies. See Dall'Asta (2010a, 319–321) on how Pearl White produced one film, not in the United States but in Paris.

70. See Berlant (2008, ch. 1) on *Uncle Tom's Cabin*, first published in 1852. Williams (2001, ch. 1) begins her discussion of American race melodrama with the multiple theatrical productions of Stowe's novel, making the point of the close correspondence between these productions and motion pictures, from *Uncle Tom's Cabin* (Edwin S. Porter, Edison Co., U.S., 1903) to *The Birth of a Nation* (D. W. Griffith, U.S., 1915).

71. Undoubtedly, this sentiment would have been anathema to Bloch, the Marxist, and neither is it part of Frigga Haug's Marxist feminist revision of him. Haug thinks Bloch's vision is largely male (1992, 65). A disdain might be found in his description of old wishes as "spinsterish," for example (1995, 370).

72. Haug (1992, 68) interjects the Marxist warning about "false" as opposed to genuine needs.

73. Singer (1996, 184) convincingly argues that the serial queen cast as the resourceful, risk-taking action heroine could also be read as an experiment in gender reversal designed to draw crowds to the "novelty and curiosity" of a woman doing what men usually do.

74. See Gaines, forthcoming, on the composite score for films like *The Red Lantern* (1919) as exemplifying American cultural amalgamation.

75. See Kuleshov (1974, 128–129) and Tsivian (1996, 39–41). In Gaines (2010, 296–298), I develop Eisenstein's fascination with the serial queens from Tsivian and also from Peterson (2013, 117–118).

76. Tsivian (1996, 39–41) also mentions Pearl White's *The House of Hate* (1918) as an Eisenstein favorite.

77. Hansen (2000b) develops the influential thesis as "mass production of the senses," an exported "sensorium" that summarized modernity. For theorization of the double meaning of "moving" as in pictures that both "move" their audiences and are themselves "moving," see Williams (2001, 13).

78. See Altman (2004) on how silent cinema was never exactly silent and Gaines (2013b) on silent cinema as largely "wordless."

79. See introduction, note 13 on the "male gaze" in feminist film theory.

80. Studlar analyzes Valentino as caught between Old World male sexuality and the New as "utopian feminine ideal" (1996, 12, 13).

81. In "Reminiscences of Frances Marion: oral history" (June 1958), 2, Marion refers to writers as "middlemen" who "translated the plays onto the screen" and later, as she says, became known as "scenario writers." This cryptic reference could mean that they took ideas from the

theater or just that they used whatever stories they found—even those already on the screen in nickelodeons.

82. Mayer (2009, 29) has characterized the connection between late Victorian and Edwardian theater as a "fluid" one marked by "mutual rip-offs." Explaining the deep American familiarity with plots, he refers to the multiple stage versions of *Uncle Tom's Cabin* and says of the Boucicault stage version of the Washington *Irving Rip Van Winkle* that it was "pirated and emulated" into the twentieth century (50). Finally, one need only think of all of the drowning attempts and ice floe "sensation scenes" that predated *Way Down East* (D. W. Griffith, 1920), including *Uncle Tom's Cabin* (1860) as well as "The Colleen Bawn" (1860) (Mayer 2009, 195–195). See note 70.

83. For the connection between "the Victorian" and melodrama as carried over into the film adaptations of *East Lynne*, see Barefoot (1994, 94–98). Kaplan (1992, ch. 5) discusses the *East Lynne* theatrical adaptations from which the film versions drew. On Mrs. Henry Wood's novel as "sensation fiction" as well as the world translation of *East Lynne*, see Jay (2005, vii–ix, xiv).

84. *The Colleen Bawn* (Kalem, 1911). Adaptation: Gene Gauntier. Director: Sydney Olcott, cast: Gene Gauntier, Sydney Olcott; *Camille*. screenplay: Frances Marion (Schubert/World U.S., 1915), cast: Clara Kimball Young; *Camille* (Alla Nazimova Productions, 1921). Director: Ray C. Smallwood, screenplay: June Mathis, cast: Alla Nazimova, Rudolph Valentino, costumes: Natasha Rambova; *Camille*. screenplay: Olga Printzlau (Norma Talmadge Productions/First National U.S. 1927). Director: Fred Niblo. cast: Norma Talmadge; *East Lynne* (Fox, 1916), screenplay: Mary Murillo; *East Lynne* (Fox, 1925), screenplay: Lenore Coffee.

85. *Stella Dallas* (Goldwyn, 1925). Director: Henry King, screenwriter: Frances Marion, adapted from Prouty (2005 [1923]). Beauchamp (1997, 60), thus describes Marion's work at the World Company in New Jersey where she was head of the scenario department: "as a rule, the stories were boilerplate—five-reel melodramas of love lost and found that World spewed out at a rate of at least two a month." On *Stella Dallas* as a classic melodrama and the "politics" of "sentimentality," see Berlant (2008, 24–25).

86. Interviewed by Lipke (1923, 16), Mathis says of Europeans: "They can appreciate the grimness of an unhappy ending. It is the spirit of the American people—perhaps the blessing, perhaps the curse—that we are optimistic. Even our motion pictures have to have happy endings. We are trying to get away from the final clinch, but it is a struggle." Although, she says, the people love it, she goes on, "In their hearts they know there can't always be a happy ending. They know that there are divorce courts, the insane asylums and jails, typical institutions of unhappy endings."

87. See Franck (2012), Moon (2012), and articles in the Royal Belgian Film Archive publication on *The Red Lantern* (Franck, 2012).

88. In film melodrama theory since the 1970s, this feature has been tied to the representation of contradictions. As Geoffrey Nowell-Smith put it, the more the drama attempts to "realistically" portray social problems, the more it will generate something which "cannot be accommodated" (1987, 73). This essay is the source of the related idea that the attempt to proceed "realistically" produces an "excess," a concept important in the development of melodrama theory. However, in deference to challenges to the psychoanalytic framework Nowell-Smith uses, as well as to the notion of "excess" that is borrowed to write off the entire mode as a "mode of excess," I don't carry over these aspects of this important essay.

89. Laying theoretical groundwork for the counter-ideological that goes against the expected story Nowell-Smith says: "The tendency of melodramas to culminate in a happy end is not unopposed" (1987, 73). However, this 1970s theory was developed in the context of the 1950s melodramas directed by Douglas Sirk, and scholars at the time were invested in finding a Brechtian undermining moment in the ideologically complicit family melodrama (Mulvey 1987; Elsaesser 1987; Kaplan 1992). Gledhill (1987, 7) observed that via a "slippage," the idea of Sirk as subversive auteur schooled in the German theatrical tradition of Bertolt Brecht was transposed onto family melodrama. An auteur theory approach was taken over by a genre theory, a point I will return to in the final chapter.

90. This failure would seem to be explained by the introduction of an unmotivated or "uncaused" event in the last scene, Bordwell's example of narrative failure. But the "uncaused" would be one of the hallmarks of melodrama in this period according to Singer (2001, 46), to which he adds "outrageous coincidence, implausibility, convoluted plotting, dues ex machina resolutions, and episodic strings of action that stuff too many events together to be able to be kept in line by a cause-and-effect chain of narrative progression."

91. More needs to be written on the many screenwriting manuals published by women who began work in the silent era, among them Bertsch (1917), Carr (1914), Corbaley (1920), Marion (1937), Parsons (1917), Beranger (1950), and Patterson (1920, 1928). For a more complete list, see Gaines and Vatsal (2013).

92. See Grieveson (2004), 90–91, on the social significance of "moral domestic dramas" exemplified by *A Drunkard's Reformation*, involving a contrast between the home and the saloon.

93. U.S. temperance films should here be contrasted with the European: *A Drunkard's Reformation* (D. W. Griffith, U.S. 1909), *What Drink Did* (D. W. Griffith, U.S., 1909), as opposed to *Les Victimes de l'alcoolisme/Victims of Drink* (Pathé, France, 1902) and *Ein vergeudetes Leben/A Life Wasted* (Germany, 1910).

94. In her analysis of melodrama's use of "familial values" across so many genres and subgenres, Gledhill (1987, 21) sees the way in which "home and family" is consistently "nostalgic." See Gaines in Gledhill and Williams, eds. (2018) on the question as to whether or not melodrama is reactionary in its apparent wish for the future to be just as the past had been.

95. Updating his analysis of Bloch, Jameson (2005, 10), is mildly critical of Bloch for seeing the Utopian in too many places because he assumed that it was part of human nature. On the connection between socialism and the Utopian, however, he says that these are still "unresolved topics," noting that today Utopia appears to have "recovered its vitality," seen in its stimulation of the political (xii).

96. Mulvey (2004b, 1288–1289) thinks that the "utopian aspiration" ceased to be important in Britain in the 1980s. As to the question of the commodification of affect, Brian Massumi says flat out that affect is now completely industrial, its own elusive sloppiness no natural protection: "The ability of affect to produce an economic effect more swiftly and surely than economics itself means that affect is a real condition, an intrinsic variable of the late capitalist system, as infrastructural as a factory" (2002, 45).

97. For analysis of the status of contemporary women in the industry, see Rich (2013) and Tasker (2010). In 2012, the Sundance Institute and Women in Film Los Angeles created a mentorship program, in 2013 announcing what it called a "first-of-its-kind" study looking at Sundance gender participation 2002–2012, in which it found a continued "gender disparity,"

in American independent film. See Smith, Choueiti, and Pieper (2015) and Lauzen, (2016). Buckley (2015, C1) reports that in 2015 only 4 percent of the largest grossing U.S. films were directed by women. Lauzen's "Celluloid Ceiling" reported: "In 2016, women comprised 17% of all directors, writers, producers, executive producers, editors, and cinematographers working on the top 250 domestic grossing films. This represents a decline of 2 percentage points from last year and is even within the percentage achieved in 1998." http://womenintvfilm.sdsu.edu (accessed January 1, 2017).

98. On her son Richard de Mille's account of Lorna Moon's unwanted pregnancy, see de Mille (1998).

99. Fuld (1915, 107) in a warning to would-be investors and uninitiated moving picture producers, details the ways in which the greenhorn can be scammed: "But to him who would be connected with the manufacturing of films there opens up a big and alluring prospect and an almost infinite number or ways of having his money taken from him."

100. "June Mathis Dies While at Theatre" headlined an article on the first page of the *New York Times* on July 27, 1927. Slater (2002, 215–216) refers to the surgery she had undergone earlier the same year and the will she wrote in the hospital. Her sudden death of heart failure he attributes to overwork.

CONCLUSION: WOMEN MADE REDUNDANT

1. Letter from Hettie Gray Baker to Mr. [John F.] Pribyl. n.d. AMPAS-MC.

2. Letter from Hettie Gray Baker to Mr. [John F.] Pribyl. February 3, 1915. AMPAS-MC.

3. Letter from Hettie Gray Baker to Mr. [John F.] Pribyl. February 3, 1915. AMPAS-MC. On Baker, see Gordon (2013).

4. Benthall, "Poverty Row," (typescript, 26, n.d.) AMPAS-MC. Slide (1998, 161) says that although "Poverty Row" first referred to the Sunset Blvd. and Gower Street area of Hollywood where minor companies produced films, from about 1924, it later came to mean the cheaper productions among which he lists Tiffany Productions, named by Mae Murray after the jewelers. Slide (207) says that around 1930 the jewelry company filed an injunction against the use of the name.

5. Mahar (2006, 154) uses 1916–1923 to delineate the second period of independent companies. On independent companies, see Kozarski (1990, 69–77).

6. See "Play to the Ladies" (1909, 33–34).

7. On how women got a "foot in the door" when exhibitors wanted to make motion pictures more respectable, see Mahar (2006, 6). Stamp (2015, 30), however, also notes that even as Lois Weber's "feminine hand" was associated with "refinement," the topics that she took up could be seen as challenging "genteel uplift."

8. It was not until the Supreme Court in *Mutual Pictures v. Ohio* (1915) that motion pictures were ruled "a business pure and simple" (Wasco 1982, 14).

9. Giannini's negative assessment of that period continues: "The machinery equipment employed in the business, the kind of theatres in use, the poor stories, the inexperienced director, the caliber of the cast, the incompetent title-writer." (1926, 46).

10. Mahar (2006, 168–169) adds to this the analysis that the studios had come to fear the independence of stars and that their aim was to reclaim their power for the studio, a move that has had little to no attention in studio industry history. Also see "Abolish the Star System."

11. On Shipman, see Shipman (1987, 103–107); on Grandin, see Askari (2013) and Mahar (2006, 73–74); and on Swanson, see Staiger (2013).

12. Mahar (2006, 185) calls our attention to the one-film phenomenon. Examples of U.S. production companies that may have made only one film include Margery Wilson Productions on which, see Walker (2013) and Vera McCord Productions (WFPP). Slide (1977, 114) mentions that McCord "produced and directed" *The Good-Bad Wife* (1921) but refers to Ruth Bryan Owen only as having written, directed, and starred in *Once Upon a Time* (1923), missing the fact that she had to have formed a company in order to mount the production. See Lane (2013a). Since emphasis at the time of Slide's writing was on women as directors, the phenomenon of their having both named themselves producers and undertaken producing responsibilities gets overlooked. However, Edyth Totten "produced, 'picturized' and starred" in *A Factory Magdalen* (1914), Slide says (1996b, 114). Other cases of companies "announced" but for which there is no evidence of films completed include: Lule Warrenton's Frieder Film Corporation, see Gaines (2013c); the Valda Valkyrien Production Company, on which, see Liu (2013).

13. Examples of women whose names were associated with more than one U.S. company (often in partnership with men) include: Bessie Barriscale (Howard Hickman): Bessie Barriscale Feature Company, 1917, B. B. Features, 1918–1920; Alice Guy-Blaché (Herbert Blaché): Solax Company, 1910–1922; Blaché American Features, 1913; Marion Davies: Marion Davies Film Corporation, 1918–1920; Marion Davies (William Randolph Hearst) Cosmopolitan Productions, 1918–1923; Mrs. Sidney Drew (Sidney Drew) Mr. and Mrs. Sidney Drew Comedies, 1917–1919; Mrs. Sidney Drew Comedies, 1920; Flora Finch: Flora Finch Company, 1916–1917; Flora Finch Film Frolics Pictures Corporation, 1920; Helen Gardner (Charles L. Gaskill): Helen Gardner Picture Players, 1912–1914; Helen Gardner Picture Players, 1918; Helen Holmes (J. P. McGowan): Signal Film Corporation, 1915; Helen Holmes Production Corporation, 1919; Helen Holmes (J. P. McGowan): S. L. K. Serial Corporation, 1919; Gene Gauntier (Sydney Olcott): Olcott-Gauntier Unit Kalem Co., 1910–1912; Gene Gauntier (Sydney Olcott): Gene Gauntier Feature Players, 1912–1915; Gene Gauntier (Jack C. Clark): Gene Gauntier Feature Players, 1915; Ethel Grandin (Ray C. Smallwood, Arthur Smallwood): Smallwood Film Corporation, 1913; Ethel Grandin (Ray C. Smallwood): Grandin Films, 1913–1915; Marion Leonard (Stanner E. V. Taylor): Gem Motion Picture Company, 1911; Monopol Film Company, 1912; Mar-Leon Company, 1913; Mary Pickford: Pickford Film Corporation, 1916–1919; Mary Pickford: (Charles Chaplin, D. W. Griffith, Douglas Fairbanks): United Artists, 1919; Gloria Swanson: Gloria Swanson Productions, 1926–1926; Gloria Swanson (Joseph P. Kennedy): Gloria Films, 1928; Lois Weber (Philip Smalley): Rex, 1912–1914; Lois Weber Productions, 1917–1921; Clara Kimball Young (Lewis J. Selznick): Clara Kimball Young Film Corporation, 1916–1917; Clara Kimball Young (Adolph Zukor): C. K. Y. Film Corporation, 1917–1919; Clara Kimball Young (Harry Garson): Equity Pictures Corporation, 1919–1924.

14. Slide (1996, 48), uses this phrase. It likely came from the headline "An All-Woman Company" from *The Story World and Photodramatist* (1923, 79).

15. See ch. 1, notes 42, 43, on Murray's role in "Tiffany Productions." Here, by "vanity company," I want to point to the self-aggrandizement and name-exploitation without suggesting that the star was uninvolved. Slide (2012a, 114–115) gives Mae Murray's screenwriting credit on *Modern Love* (1918) as one example of what he thinks is the kind of "vanity credit"

given to star actresses like Theda Bara and Mary Pickford. Although he grants that it is "impossible to know," his implication is that the actress most likely did not do the writing for which she was credited.

16. Jacobs (1975, 295) lists women as well as men who, as stars, attempted to form "their own" production companies, although in his analysis, because they lacked distribution and exhibition or the company was subject to "poor management," they lost their fortunes in these producing ventures. He lists Anita Stewart, Norma Talmadge, Clara Kimball Young, and Agnes Ayres, along with the better known William S. Hart, Charles Chaplin, Douglas Fairbanks, Sessue Hayakawa, and Roscoe Arbuckle. See Kozarski (1990, 69–77) on the independents. See Mahar (2006, 160), for another list of stars who either formed or announced the formation of companies after 1917. Independence for actresses, she says, meant that they could select directors as well as the scenarios that they put into production, or delegate this work. This second "star-producer movement" she finds was defined more by women than men. For more on the conditions of production of these independent companies, see "Reminiscences of Sessue Hayakawa: Oral History," April 1959, 1–33. See also Introduction, note 40; ch. 1, note 28; ch. 8, note 38.

17. On Weber, see Stamp (2015, 142–148); on Guy Blaché, see Mahar (2006, 74–76) and McMahan (2009a, 52–59). As a family history model, see Thanhauser (2016).

18. On Elizabeth P. Grimball in North Carolina, see Hendershott (2013); on Ruth Bryan Owen in Florida, see Lane (2013a). For Kansas City, Missouri, and African Americans Tressie Sauders and Maria P. Williams, see Morgan and Dixon (2013) and Welbon (2001, 40). On Angela Murray Gibson and North Dakota, see Grimm (2017). For Idaho and Shipman, see Armatage (2003), Mahar (2006, 162–164), and Shipman (1987).

19. See ch. 2 on how Gaumont secretary Alice Guy attended early Lumière screenings and sought to improve the product by shooting "stories" for the French company. She also directed *phonocénes* before the conversion to sound in the late 1920s. See McMahan (2004, 23, 30–33) for an alternative approach to the events of film history based on the drive to mechanize in which, because animation and motion studies are the centerpiece and sound-image synchronization an offshoot, Guy's production of postsynchronized sound films between 1902 and 1906 for Gaumont Chronophone become pivotal. For more on Guy and the Chronophone, see McMahan (2009a, 50–52).

20. Gunning (2008, 11–13) argues that early cinema was global before it was national. However, the phenomenon of women's work directing and producing in the United States as well as Europe and Asia corresponds with later phases in which national film industries helped form national identity. See Abel, Bertellini, and King (2008, 2–3) who raise some relevant issues around cinema as "new venue for 'imagining the nation' as an 'imagined community.'"

21. On gender as a "question," see Scott (2008a, 1422). In the first of her three-part periodization of the silent era, Mahar (2006, 6) sees 1896–1908 as the "technological" decade, which, because of the emphasis on invention, did not involve women who would not figure until the second period, 1908–1916, which she terms "uplift." My emphasis on women at the advent suggests that we can find ways to figure them in the earlier technological period.

22. Weinbaum et al. (2008, 7), in the introduction to the collection *The Modern Girl Around the World* take as their project a challenge to what they call a "conflation of 'modern' and 'Western'" that has organized the hierarchy in which some societies are more "modern" than

others that are seen as "catching up." While the project is an important starting point for further research into the export question, in these essays motion pictures are taken too uncritically as purveyors of "modern" styles replicated by viewers.

23. On early women who had two-continent careers, see Gaines (2010) and Dall'Asta, (2010a). The Women Film Pioneers Project phase two has taken up silent-era and early national film industry examples from the following countries: Australia, Austria, Belgium, Canada, China, Czech Republic and Slovakia, Denmark, Egypt, Finland, France, Germany, Hungary, India, Ireland, Italy, Japan, Korea, the Netherlands, Norway, the Philippines, Poland, Portugal, Spain, Sweden, Switzerland, Tunisia, Turkey, the United Kingdom (Ireland, Scotland, and Britain), the former Union of Soviet Socialist Republics, and the former Yugoslavia.

24. In 1916, U.S. companies were exporting motion pictures to Cuba, Jamaica, Venezuela, Columbia, and Panama. Fox opened offices in Buenos Aires, São Paulo, and Rio de Janiero. In 1916, Universal Pictures opened offices in Japan, India, and Singapore and, the next year, in Java. Famous Players–Lasky signed an agent for Argentina, Paraguay, and Uruguay that same year. For more examples, see Thompson (1985, 196–197; 204–209). Metro Pictures was slower than others to establish world exchanges. *The Red Lantern* (1919), a candidate for Metro Pictures' new global export strategy, was, however, handled by Export and Import Film Co, Inc., for Latin America and Europe, although a Paris company won the bidding for this and all future Nazimova productions. See "Handsome Offers" (1919, 1207).

25. On Mimí Derba, see Miguel (2000) and Torres San Martín and Hershfield (2013). On how global cinema predated the Hollywood studio system, see López (2000, 420).

26. But it should be noted that the Germans were an exception. See Schlüpmann (1994, 83) who might be describing the German feminist journal *Frauen ünd Film in the 1970s* when she identifies the contradiction in feminism and film as "analyzing the oppression of the female subject in film while at the same time celebrating the achievements of directors and editors, the 'subversiveness' of actresses and the experiential knowledge of female spectators."

27. Koselleck (2002, 135) says that "history is always new and replete with surprise."

28. See Rubin (2011, 34–35) for the introduction of the "sex/gender system" into feminist theory in the 1970s, facilitating the replacement of the term "sex" with "gender."

29. Readers may hear an echo of Deleuze, "How can the unthinkable not lie at the heart of thought?" (1994, 227). However, Dorothy Arzner as director may still be "unthinkable" in Paris. See Mayne (2017), who reviews the Cinémathèque Française retrospective of the work of Dorothy Arzner in March and April, 2017, and the introductory essay to the retrospective, which she thinks exhibits an old misogyny and "lesbophobia." Philippe Garnier, she goes on, effectively "downplays her achievements," downgrading her to a "B" director. According to Mayne, Garnier attributes Arzner's success to her wealth and suggests that to view her work through lesbianism and feminism is to "misinterpret" that work.

30. Altman (1999, 72–77) credits feminism with "inventing" the woman's film as a genre and Kaplan picks this up (2012, 71–73). Also see Gledhill (1987, 35) on the complicated historical relation between melodrama and the woman's film. On an earlier tendency to find subversion in so many places, see Williams (2012, 527), who writes: "Today, because we are less likely to think any interruption is subversive we are left with an awkward heritage." In Gaines (2012b, 22–23), I critique the feminist tendency to see "subversion" everywhere in the text.

31. Much more work needs to be done contrasting the "New Woman" phenomenon world-

wide in its apparent "contradictoriness" and double message to young women as well as re-thinking the export-import relation: See Williams (2014, 31) on the French *nouvelle femme* and Germaine Dulac's editorials on "figures" of women in mid-1907. Hansen (2000a, 16) introduces the "New Woman" as contested in Shanghai but see Harris (1997, 279), who says that both the film *The New Woman* (1935) and the suicide of the actress Ruan Lingyu raise the issue of Chinese popular culture at a "moment of crisis over the degree to which women would be agents, symbols, or victims of modernity." Otto and Rocco (2011, 8) associate the New Woman with both profound "changes in gender relations" and the shallowness of "passing fashion." Thanks to Briand Gentry for this last citation.

32. Gerow (2010, 23), writing on Japan, 1895–1925, suggests the need to challenge the idea of Hollywood as the "center" that is then "translated" into a non-Western culture.

33. See Zhao (2017b) and Wei (2011, 17–18). Sakane directed *Brides of the Frontier* (1943) a "dramatic documentary" propaganda film for training the brides-to-be of the Japanese soldiers stationed in Manchuko. For historical background on the studio, see Zhao (2017a). Thanks to Xinyi Zhao for her Japanese translation.

34. As quoted in Ikegawa (2012) [*Maedchen in Uniform*, Germany, 1931]. See also Ikegawa (2012).

35. On Aleksandra Khokhlova, see Olenina (2013); on Esfir Shub, see Dogo (2013); on Pu Shunqing, see Wei (2013).

36. See Williams (2014, 29) on Germaine Dulac's dedication to internationalist and pacifist causes.

37. This point echoes the observation that melodrama is conservative in that its future always resembles the past. For the progressive as opposed to reactionary worldview of melodrama, see Gaines (2018).

38. Elsaesser (1996, 13) on early German cinema puts it better when he laments that "At times, one has the feeling of no longer possessing the cultural or emotional key to unlock their brittle charm."

BIBLIOGRAPHY

I. GENERAL BIBLIOGRAPHY

Abel, Richard. 1984. *French Cinema: The First Wave, 1919–1929*. Princeton, N.J.: Princeton University Press.

———. 1994. *The Ciné Goes to Town: French Cinema, 1896–1914*. Berkeley: University of California Press.

———, ed. 2005. *Encyclopedia of Early Cinema*. New York: Routledge.

———. 2016. "Newspaperwomen and the Movies in the USA, 1914–1925." In *Women Film Pioneers Project*. eds. Jane M. Gaines, Radha Vatsal, and Monica Dall'Asta. New York: Center for Digital Research and Scholarship, Columbia University Libraries. https://wfpp.cdrs.columbia.edu/essay/newspaperwomen-and-the-movies-in-the-usa-1914-1925/.

Abel, Richard, Giorgio Bertellini, and Rob King. 2008. Introduction. In *Early Cinema and the 'National'*. eds. Richard Abel, Giorgio Bertellini, and Rob King. 1–7. New Barnet (North London): John Libbey.

Achuff, Charlie, and Madeline Matz. 2013. "Eve Unsell." In *Women Film Pioneers Project*. eds. Jane M. Gaines, Radha Vatsal, and Monica Dall'Asta. New York: Center for Digital Research and Scholarship, Columbia University Libraries. https://wfpp.cdrs.columbia.edu/pioneer/ccp-eve-unsell/.

Acker, Ally. 2011a [1991]. *Reel Women: Pioneers of the Cinema, The First Hundred Years*. Vol. 1. 1890s–1950s. 3rd ed. New York: Reel Women Media Publishing.

———. 2011b [1991]. *Reel Women: Pioneers of the Cinema, The First Hundred Years*. Vol. 2. 1960–2010. 3rd ed. New York: Reel Women Media Publishing.

Ahmed, Sara. 2004. *The Cultural Politics of Emotion*. Edinburgh: Edinburgh University Press.

———. 2010. *The Promise of Happiness*. Durham: Duke University Press.

Allen, Robert C., and Douglas Gomery. 1985. *Film History: Theory and Practice*. New York: Alfred Knopf.

Althusser, Louis. 1970. *For Marx*. trans. Ben Brewster. London: Verso.

———. 1979 [1966] *Reading Capital*. trans. Ben Brewster. London: Verso.

Altman, Rick. 1992. "Dickens, Griffith, and Film Theory Today." In *Classical Hollywood Narrative: The Paradigm Wars*. ed. Jane M. Gaines. 9–48. Durham: Duke University Press.

———. 2004. *Silent Film Sound*. New York: Columbia University Press.

Anderson, Mark Lynn. 2011. *Twilight of the Idols: Hollywood and the Human Sciences in 1920s America*. Berkeley: University of California Press.

———. 2013. "Dorothy Davenport Reid." In *Women Film Pioneers Project*. eds. Jane M. Gaines, Radha Vatsal, and Monica Dall'Asta. New York: Center for Digital Research and Scholarship, Columbia University Libraries. https://wfpp.cdrs.columbia.edu/pioneer/ccp -dorothy-davenport-reid/.

———. 2016. "The Silent Screen, 1895–1927." In *Producing*. ed. Jon Lewis. 15–35. New Brunswick, N.J.: Rutgers University Press.

———. 2017. "The Clara Kimball Young Film Corporation v. Clara Kimball Young: A Picture of Restraint." Unpublished paper, "Women and Silent Screen International Conference IX." Shanghai, China (June).

Anderson, Steve F. 2011. *Technologies of History: Visual Media and the Eccentricity of the Past*. Hanover, N.H.: Dartmouth College Press.

Andrew, Dudley. 2010. *What Cinema Is!* London: Wiley-Blackwell.

Ankersmit, F. R. 1995. "Bibliographical Essay." In *A New Philosophy of History*. eds. Frank Ankersmit and Hans Kellner. 278–283. Chicago: University of Chicago Press.

———. 2001. "Six Theses on Narrativist Philosophy of History." in *The History and Narrative Reader*. ed. Geoffrey Roberts. 237–245. London: Routledge.

———. 2007. "Danto's Philosophy of History in Retrospective." In Arthur C. Danto, *Narration and Knowledge*. 364–393. New York: Columbia University Press.

Ankersmit, Frank, and Hans Kellner, eds. 1995. *A New Philosophy of History*. Chicago: University of Chicago Press.

Ankersmit, Frank, Ewa Domańska, and Hans Kellner, eds. 2009. *Re-figuring Hayden White*. Stanford: Stanford University Press.

Appiah, Kwame Anthony. 2003. *Thinking It Through*. New York: Oxford University Press.

Armatage, Kay. 2003. *The Girl from God's Country: Nell Shipman and the Silent Cinema*. Toronto: University of Toronto Press.

Armstrong, Nancy. 2002. *Fiction in the Age of Photography: The Legacy of British Realism*. Cambridge: Harvard University Press.

Aronowitz, Stanley. 2003. *How Class Works: Power and Social Movement*. New Haven: Yale University Press.

Askari, Kaveh. 2013. "Ethel Grandin." In *Women Film Pioneers Project*. eds. Jane M. Gaines, Radha Vatsal and Monica Dall'Asta. New York: Center for Digital Research and Scholarship, Columbia University Libraries. https://wfpp.cdrs.columbia.edu/pioneer/ccp -gene-gauntier/.

———. 2014. "An Afterlife for Junk Prints: Serials and Other 'Classics' in Late-1920s Tehran." eds. Jennifer M. Bean, Anupama Kapse, and Laura Horak. *Silent Cinema and the Politics of Space*. 99–120. Bloomington: University of Indiana Press.

Astruc, Anthony. 1969 [1948]. "The Birth of a New Avant-Garde: Le Caméra-Stylo," In *The New Wave*. ed. Peter Graham. 17–23. London: British Film Institute/New York: Doubleday.

Bachy, Victor. 1985. "Entretiens avec Alice Guy." In *Les Premiers ans du cinéma français: Actes du Ve colloque international de l'institut Jean Vigo*. 31–42. Perpignan, France: Institut Jean Vigo. Conversations with Alice Guy." trans. Lois Grjebine. Reprint *Les Premiers ans du cinema Francais: Proceedings of the Fifth International Colloquium of the Institute Jean Vigo*. 31–42. Perpignan: Institut Jean Vigo.

Baer, Nicholas. 2015. "Historical Turns: On Caligari, Kracauer, and New Film History." In *Film and History: Producing and Experiencing History in Moving Images and Sounds*. eds. Delia González de Reufels, Rasmus Greiner, and Winifried Pauleit. 153–164. Bremen: City 46/Kommunalkino.

Bakhtin, M. M. 1981. *The Dialogic Imagination*. Austin: University of Texas.

Balides, Constance. 2002. "Making Ends Meet: 'Welfare Films' and the Politics of Consumption during the Progressive Era." In *A Feminist Reader in Early Cinema*. eds. Jennifer M. Bean and Diane Negra. 166–194. Durham: Duke University Press.

Bambach, Charles R. 1995. *Heidegger, Dilthey, and the Crisis of Historicism*. Ithaca: Cornell University Press.

———. 2013. "Weimar Philosophy and the Crisis in Historical Thinking." In *Weimar Thought: A Contested Legacy*. eds. Peter E. Gordon and John P. McCormick. 133–149. Princeton, N.J.: Princeton University Press.

Bao, Weihong. 2013. "From Pearl White to White Rose Woo: Tracing the Vernacular Body of *Nüixia* in Chinese Silent Cinema, 1927–1931." In *Exporting Perilous Pauline: Pearl White and the Serial Film Craze*. ed. Marina Dalquist. 187–221. Urbana: University of Illinois.

———. 2015. *Fiery Cinema: The Emergence of an Affective Medium in China, 1915–1945*. Minneapolis: University of Minnesota Press.

Bardèche, Maurice, and Robert Brasillach. 1938 [1935]. *The History of Motion Pictures*. trans. and ed. Iris Barry. New York: W. W. Norton and the Museum of Modern Art.

Barefoot, Guy. 1994. "*East Lynne* to *Gaslight*: Hollywood, Melodrama and Twentieth-Century Notions of the Victorian." In *Melodrama: Stage/Picture/Screen*. eds. Jacky Bratton, Jim Cook, and Christine Gledhill. 94–105. London: British Film Institute.

Barlow, Tani, 2004a. Introduction. In *The Question of Women in Chinese Feminism*. ed. Tani Barlow. 1–14. Durham: Duke University Press.

———, ed. 2004b. *The Question of Women in Chinese Feminism*. Durham: Duke University Press.

Baron, Jaimie. 2014. *The Archive Effect. Found Footage and the Audiovisual Experience of History*. New York: Routledge.

Barthes, Roland. 1977a. "The Death of the Author." In *Image/Music/Text*. trans. Stephen Heath. 142–148. New York: Hill and Wang.

———. 1977b. "Introduction to the Structural Analysis of Narratives," In *Image/Music/Text*. trans. Stephen Heath. 79–124. New York: Hill and Wang.

———. 1977c. "The Rhetoric of the Image." In *Image/Music/Text*. trans. Stephen Heath. 32–51. New York: Hill and Wang.

———. 1986a [1967]. "The Discourse of History." In *The Rustle of Language*. trans. Richard Howard. 141–148. New York: Hill and Wang.

———. 1986b [1968]. "The Reality Effect." In *The Rustle of Language*. trans. Richard Howard. 127–140. New York: Hill and Wang.

Baumbach, Nico, Damon R. Young, and Genvieve Yu. 2016. "Introduction: For a Political Critique of Culture." *Social Text* 127–34.2 (June): 1–20.

Bazin, André. 2005 [1967]. *What Is Cinema? Vol. I.* trans. Hugh Gray. Berkeley: University of California Press.

———. 2009 [1967]. *What Is Cinema? Vol. I.* trans. Timothy Barnard. Montreal: Caboose.

Bean, Jennifer M. 2002a. "Technologies of Stardom and the Extraordinary Body." In *A Feminist Reader in Early Cinema*. eds. Jennifer M. Bean and Diane Negra. 404–443. Durham: Duke University Press.

———. 2002b. "Introduction: toward a Feminist Historiography of Early Cinema." In *A Feminist Reader in Early Cinema*. eds. Jennifer M. Bean and Diane Negra. 1–26. Durham: Duke University Press.

———. 2014. *Silent Cinema and the Politics of Space*. eds. Jennifer M. Bean, Anupama Kapse, and Laura Horak, Bloomington: University of Indiana Press.

Beauchamp, Cari. 1997. *Without Lying Down: Frances Marion and the Powerful Women of Early Hollywood*. Berkeley: University of California Press.

———, ed. and annotated. 2006. *Adventures of a Hollywood Secretary*. Berkeley: University of California Press.

Beltrame, Alberto, Giuseppe Fidotta, and Andrea Mariani, eds. 2014. *At the Borders of (Film) History: Temporality, Archaeology, Theories*. XXI International Film Studies Conference. University of Udine, Italy.

Benjamin, Walter. 1970 [1950]. "Theses on the Philosophy of History." In *Illuminations*. ed. Hannah Arendt. trans. Harry Zohn. 255–266. New York: Fontana/Collins.

———. 1999 [1982]. *The Arcades Project*. trans. Howard Eiland and Kefin McLaughlin. Cambridge: Harvard University Press.

———. 2008. *The Work of Art in the Age of Its Technological Reproducibility, and Other Writings on Media*. eds. Michael Jennings et al. trans. Edmund Jephcott, Rodney Livingstone, Howard Eiland et al. Cambridge: Harvard University Press.

Bentley, Eric. 1964. *The Life of the Drama*. New York: Athenaeum.

Bergson, Henri. 2002 [1908]. *Matter and Memory*. trans. N. M. Paul and W. S. Palmer. Cambridge: MIT Press.

Berlant, Laura. 2008. *The Female Complaint: The Unfinished Business of Sentimentality in American Culture*. Durham: Duke University Press.

Bethel, Amy. 2013. "Henderina Victoria Scott." In *Women Film Pioneers Project*. eds. Jane M. Gaines, Radha Vatsal, and Monica Dall'Asta. New York: Center for Digital Research and Scholarship, Columbia University Libraries. https://wfpp.cdrs.columbia.edu/pioneer/ccp-henderina-victoria-scott/.

Bisplinghoff, Gretchen. 2013. "Gene Gauntier." In *Women Film Pioneers Project*. eds. Jane M. Gaines, Radha Vatsal, and Monica Dall'Asta. New York: Center for Digital Research and Scholarship, Columbia University Libraries. https://wfpp.cdrs.columbia.edu/pioneer/ccp-gene-gauntier/.

Blaché, Alice Guy. 1996 [1914]. "Woman's Place in Photoplay Production." *The Memoirs of Alice Guy Blaché.* ed. Anthony Slide. 139–142. Lanham, Md.: The Scarecrow Press.

Blaetz, Robin. 2013. "Leah Baird." In *Women Film Pioneers Project.* eds. Jane M. Gaines, Radha Vatsal, and Monica Dall'Asta. New York: Center for Digital Research and Scholarship, Columbia University Libraries. https://wfpp.cdrs.columbia.edu/pioneer/ccp-leah-baird/.

Bláhová, Jindřiška. 2013. "Thea (Terezie) Červenková." In *Women Film Pioneers Project.* eds. Jane M. Gaines, Radha Vatsal, and Monica Dall'Asta. New York: Center for Digital Research and Scholarship, Columbia University Libraries. https://wfpp.cdrs.columbia.edu/pioneer/ccp-thea-cervenkova/.

Bloch, Ernst. 1995 [1938–1947]. *The Principle of Hope, Vol. I.* trans. Neville and Stephen Plaice and Paul Knight. Cambridge: MIT Press.

———. 2006 [1969]. *Traces.* trans. Anthony A. Nassar. Stanford: Stanford University Press.

Bloch, Marc. 1953. *The Historian's Craft.* trans. Peter Putnam. New York: Random House.

Blümlinger, Christa. 2014. "The Starry Archive." *CinéMas* 24.2/3 (Spring): 7–16, 263.

Bolter, Jay David, and Richard Grusin. 2000. *Remediation: Understanding New Media.* Cambridge: MIT Press.

Bordwell, David. 1982. "Happily Ever After Part I. " *The Velvet Light Trap* 19: 2–7.

———. 1997. *On the History of Film Style.* Cambridge: Harvard University Press.

Bordwell, David, and Kristin Thompson. 1983. "Linearity, Materialism and the Study of Early American Cinema." *Wide Angle* 5.3: 4–15.

———. 2003. *Film History, An Introduction.* 2nd ed. Boston: McGraw Hill.

———. 2017. *Film Art: An Introduction.* 11th ed. New York: McGraw Hill.

Bordwell, David, Janet Staiger, and Kristin Thompson. 1985. *The Classical Hollywood System: Film Style and Mode of Production to 1960.* New York: Columbia University Press.

Boschi, Alberto, and Giacomo Manzoli. 1995. "Beyond the Author." *Fotogenia* 2: 148–151.

Boundas, Constantin V. 2009. "Martin Heidegger." In *Deleuze's Philosophical Lineage.* eds. Graham Jones and Jon Roffe. 321–338. Edinburgh: Edinburgh University Press.

Bowser, Eileen. 1990. *The Transformation of Cinema, 1907–1915.* Berkeley: University of California Press.

Boyda, James. 2013."Preserving the Immaterial: Digital Decay and the Archive." *The Spectator* 33.2 (Fall): 6–10.

Braidotti, Rosi. "A Critical Cartography of Feminist Post-Postmodernism." *Australian Feminist Studies* 20.47 (2005): 1–15.

Branff, Richard E. 1999. *The Universal Silents: A Filmography of the Universal Motion Picture Manufacturing Company, 1912–1929.* Jefferson, N.C.: McFarland.

Braudel, Ferdinand. 1980. "History and the Social Sciences: The Longue Durée." In *On History.* trans. Sarah Matthews. 25–54. Chicago: University of Chicago Press.

Breton, Emile. 1984. *Femmes d'images.* Paris: Editions Merridor.

Brooks, Peter. 1985 [1976]. *The Melodramatic Imagination: Balzac, Henry James, Melodrama, and the Mode of Excess.* New York: Columbia University Press.

Brooks-Bertram, Peggy. 2013. "Drusilla Dungee-Huston." In *Women Film Pioneers Project.* eds. Jane M. Gaines, Radha Vatsal, and Monica Dall'Asta. New York: Center for Digital Research and Scholarship, Columbia University Libraries. https://wfpp.cdrs.columbia.edu/pioneer/drusilla-dunjee-houston-2/.

Brough, John Barnett. 1991. "Translator's Introduction." In Edmund Husserl, *On the Phenomenology of the Consciousness of Internal Time* (1893–1917). trans. John Barnett Brough. xii–lvii. Dordrecht: Kluwer Academic Publishers.

Brown, Kelly R. 1999. *Florence Lawrence, the Biograph Girl: America's First Movie Star.* Jefferson, N.C.: McFarland and Company, Inc.

Brown, R., and B. Anthony. 1999. *A Victorian Enterprise: The History of the British Mutoscope and Biograph Company, 1897–1915.* Trowbridge: Flick Books.

Browne, Nick. 1990. "Introduction: The Politics of Representation: Cahiers du Cinéma, 1969–72." In *Cahiers du Cinéma, 1969–72: The Politics of Representation.* ed. Nick Browne. 1–20. Cambridge: Harvard University Press.

Brownlow, Kevin. 1968. *The Parade's Gone By.* New York: Knopf.

Bruneta, Gian Piero. 1996. "Reveal the Author!" *Fotogenia* 3: 154–160.

Bruno, Giuliana. 1984. "Towards a Theorization of Film History." *Iris* 2.2: 41–55.

———. 1993. *Streetwalking on a Ruined Map: Cultural Theory and the City Films of Elvira Notari.* Princeton, N.J.: Princeton University Press.

Buck, Julie. 2013. "Gloria Swanson." In *Women Film Pioneers Project.* eds. Jane M. Gaines, Radha Vatsal, and Monica Dall'Asta. New York: Center for Digital Research and Scholarship, Columbia University Libraries. https://wfpp.cdrs.columbia.edu/pioneer/ccp-gloria-swanson/.

Buckley, Matthew. 2012. Introduction. *Modern Drama* 55.4: 429–436.

Bull, Sofia, and Astrid Söderberg Widding, eds. 2010. *Not So Silent: Women in Cinema before Sound.* Stockholm: Acta Universitatis Stockholmiensis.

Burch, Noël. 1978/9. "Porter, or Ambivalence." *Screen* 19.4 (Winter): 91–105.

———. 1990. *Life to Those Shadows.* trans. and ed. Ben Brewster. Berkeley: University of California Press.

Burrows, Elaine. 2010. "A Historical Overview of NFTVA/BFI Collection Development Policies with Regard to Gender and Nation Questions." *Framework* 51.2 (Fall): 343–357.

Busche, Andreas. 2006. "Just Another Form of Ideology? Ethical and Methodological Principles in Film Restoration." *The Moving Image* 6: 1–29.

Butler, Alison. 1992. "New Film Histories and the Politics of Location." *Screen* 33.4 (Winter): 413–426.

———. 2002. *Women's Cinema: The Contested Screen.* London: Wallflower.

———. 2008. "Feminist Perspectives in Film Studies." In *The Sage Handbook of Film Studies.* eds. James Donald and Michael Renov. 391–407. Los Angeles: Sage.

Butler, Judith. 1991. "Imitation and Gender Insubordination." In *Inside/Out: Lesbian Theories, Gay Theories.* ed. Diana Fuss. 13–31. New York: Routledge.

———. 2004. *Undoing Gender.* New York: Routledge.

———. 2006. "Contingent Foundations: Feminism and the Question of 'Postmodernism.'" In *The Feminist History Reader.* ed. Sue Morgan. 195–202. New York: Routledge.

———. 2011. "Speaking Up, Talking Back: Joan Scott's Critical Feminism." In *The Question of Gender: Joan W. Scott's Critical Feminism.* eds. Judith Butler and Elizabeth Weed. 11–18. Bloomington: Indiana University Press.

Butler, Judith, and Joan Scott, eds. 1992. *Feminists Theorize the Political.* New York: Routledge.

Callahan, Vicki, ed. 2010. *Reclaiming the Archive: Feminism and Film History*. Detroit: Wayne State University Press.

Carr, David. 1987. Review of *Futures Past: On the Semantics of Historical Time*. *History and Theory* 26.2 (May): 197–204.

———. 2009. "Metaphilosophy of History." In *Re-figuring Hayden White*. eds. Frank Ankersmit, Ewa Domanska, Hans Kellner. 15–33. Stanford: Stanford University Press.

Carr, E. H. 1964. *What Is History?* New York: Alfred A. Knopf.

Casella, Donna. 2009. "What Women Want: The Complex World of Dorothy Arzner and Her Cinematic Women." *Framework* 50.1–2 (Fall): 235–270.

———. 2017. "Shaping the Craft of Screenwriting: Women Screen Writers in Silent Era Hollywood." In *Women Film Pioneers Project*. eds. Jane M. Gaines, Radha Vatsal, and Monica Dall'Asta. New York: Center for Digital Research and Scholarship, Columbia University Libraries. https://wfpp.cdrs.columbia.edu/essay/shaping-the-craft-of-screenwriting -women-screen-writers-in-silent-era-hollywood/.

Casetti, Francesco. 2007. "Theory, Post-theory, Neo-theories: Changes in Discourses, Changes in Objects." *Cinémas* 17.2–3 (Spring): 33–45.

Casetti, Francesco, and Jane M. Gaines. 2009. "Introduction: In the Beginning and at the Very End." In *Proceedings from Dall'inizio, alla fineo/In the Beginning and at the Very End*. eds. Francesco Casetti and Jane M. Gaines. 17–18. Udine International Film Studies Conference, XVI. Udine, Italy.

Chanan, Michael. 1980. *The Dream That Kicks: The Prehistory and Early Years of Cinema in Britain*. London: Routledge and Kegan Paul.

Cherchi Usai, Paolo. 1994. "The Philosophy of Film History." *Film History* 6:3–5.

———. 2000. *Silent Cinema: An Introduction*. London: British Film Institute.

———. 2001. *The Death of Cinema: History, Cultural Memory and the Digital Dark Age*. London: British Film Institute.

———. 2006. "The Demise of the Digital (Print # 1)." *Film Quarterly* 59.3 (Spring): 3.

Cherchi Usai, Paolo, et al., eds. 2008. *Film Curatorship: Archives, Museums, and the Digital Marketplace*. Wein: Austrian Film Museum and SYNEMA.

Chion, Michel. 2009. *Film, a Sound Art*. trans. Claudia Gorbman. New York: Columbia University Press.

Cohen, Sande. 2006. *History out of Joint*. Baltimore: Johns Hopkins University Press.

Coissac, Guillaume Michel. 1925. Histoire du cinématographe de ses origins a nos jours. Paris: Editions du "Cineopse."

Collingwood, R. G. 1993 [1946]. *The Idea of History*. Rev. ed. London: Oxford University Press.

Comolli, Jean-Louis. 1999. "Documentary Journey to the Land of the Head Shrinkers." *October* 90: 36–49.

———. 1990 [1971]. "Technique and Ideology: Camera, Perspective, Depth of Field, " in *Cahiers du Cinéma, 1969–1972: The Politics of Representation*. ed. Nick Browne. 213–247. Cambridge: Harvard University Press. Reprinted 2015. *Cinema against Spectacle: Technique and Ideology Revisited*. trans. and ed. Daniel Fairfax. 147–193. Amsterdam: Amsterdam University Press.

Cooper, Mark Garrett. 2010. *Universal Women: A Case of Institutional Change*. Urbana: University of Illinois Press.

———. 2013a. "Cleo Madison." In *Women Film Pioneers Project*. eds. Jane M. Gaines, Radha Vatsal, and Monica Dall'Asta. New York: Center for Digital Research and Scholarship, Columbia University Libraries. https://wfpp.cdrs.columbia.edu/pioneer/ccp-cleo -madison/.

———. 2013b. "Kathlyn Williams." In *Women Film Pioneers Project*. eds. Jane M. Gaines, Radha Vatsal, and Monica Dall'Asta. New York: Center for Digital Research and Scholarship, Columbia University Libraries. https://wfpp.cdrs.columbia.edu/pioneer/ccp-kathlyn -williams/.

———. 2013c. "Archive, Theater, Ship: The Phelps Sisters Film the World." In *Researching Women in Silent Cinema: New Findings and Perspectives*. eds. Monica Dall'Asta, Victoria Duckett, and Lucia Tralli. 120–129. Bologna: University of Bologna. http://wss2013 .arts.unimelb.edu.au/wp-content/uploads/2013/10/0_RESEARCHING-WOMEN _SILENT-CINEMA.pdf.

Cosandey, Roland. 1996. "9 Back to Lumiére, or the Dream of an Essence: Some Untimely Considerations about a French Myth." In *Cinema: the Beginnings and the Future*. ed. Christopher Williams. 82–96. London: University of Westminster Press.

Costa, Antonio. 1994. "Francois, Eric, Claude, Jean-Luc, Jacques and the Authors." *Fotogenia* 2: 183–190.

Cott, Nancy. 1977. *The Bonds of Womanhood: Woman's Sphere in New England 1780–1835*. New Haven: Yale University Press.

Cowie, Elizabeth. 2011. *Recording Reality, Desiring the Real*. Minneapolis: University of Minnesota Press.

Crafton, Donald. 2005. "Gaumont." In *Encyclopedia of Early Cinema*. ed. Richard Abel. 265–266. London: Routledge.

Creekmur, Corey K. 2013. "Texas Guinan." In *Women Film Pioneers Project*. eds. Jane M. Gaines, Radha Vatsal, and Monica Dall'Asta. New York: Center for Digital Research and Scholarship, Columbia University Libraries. https://wfpp.cdrs.columbia.edu/pioneer/ccp-texas -guinan/.

Dahlquist, Marina, ed. 2013a. *Exporting Pauline: Pearl White and the Serial Film Craze*. Champaign-Urbana: University of Illinois Press.

———. 2013b. "Introduction: Why Pearl?" In Marina Dahlquist ed. *Exporting Pauline: Pearl White and the Serial Film Craze*. 1–23. Champaign-Urbana: University of Illinois Press.

———. 2013c. "Pearl White." In *Women Film Pioneers Project*. eds. Jane M. Gaines, Radha Vatsal, and Monica Dall'Asta. New York: Center for Digital Research and Scholarship, Columbia University Libraries. https://wfpp.cdrs.columbia.edu/pioneer/ccp-pearl -white/.

Dall'Asta, Monica, ed. 2008. *Non Solo Dive: Pioniere Del Cinema Italiano*. Bologna: Cineteca Bologna.

———. 2010a. "On Frieda Klug, Pearl White, and Other Traveling Women Film Pioneers," *Framework* 51.2 (Fall): 310–323.

———. 2010b. "What It Means to Be a Woman: Theorizing Feminist Film History beyond the Essentialism/Constructionism Divide." In *Not So Silent: Women in Cinema before Sound*. eds. Astrid Söderberg Widding and Sofia Bull. 39–47. Stockholm: Acta Universitatis Stockholmiensis.

———. 2013. "Pearl, the Swift One, of the Extraordinary Adventures of Pearl White in France." In *Exporting Pauline: Pearl White and the Serial Film Craze*. ed. Marina Dahlquist. 71–98. Champaign-Urbana: University of Illinois Press.

Dall'Asta, Monica, and Jane M. Gaines. 2015. "Constellations: When Past and Present Collide in Feminist Film History." In *Doing Women's Film History: Reframing Cinema's Past and Future*. eds. Christine Gledhill and Julia Knight. 13–25. Champaign-Urbana: University of Illinois Press.

Dall'Asta, Monica, and Victoria Duckett. 2013. "Kaleidoscope: Women and Cinematic Change from the Silent Era to Now." In *Researching Women in Silent Cinema: New Findings and Perspectives*. eds. Monica Dall'Asta, Victoria Duckett, and Lucia Tralli. 2–11. Bologna: University of Bologna. http://amsacta.unibo.it/3827/.

Danto, Arthur C. 1965. *Analytical Philosophy of History*. Cambridge: Cambridge University Press.

———. 2007 [1985]. *Narration and Knowledge*. New York: Columbia University Press.

De Groat, Greta. 2013. "The Talmadge Sisters." In *Women Film Pioneers Project*. eds. Jane M. Gaines, Radha Vatsal, and Monica Dall'Asta. New York: Center for Digital Research and Scholarship, Columbia University Libraries. https://wfpp.cdrs.columbia.edu/pioneer/ccp-constance-talmadge-and-norma-talmadge/.

De Kuyper, Eric. 1994. "Anyone for an Aesthetic of Film History?" *Film History* 6: 100–109.

De Lauretis, Teresa. 1986. "Feminist Studies/Critical Studies: Issues, Terms, and Contexts." In *Feminist Studies/Critical Studies*. ed. Teresa de Lauretis. 1–19. Bloomington: Indiana University Press.

Deleuze, Gilles. 1994 [1968]. *Difference and Repetition*. trans. Paul Patton. New York: Columbia University Press.

De Mille, Richard. 1998. *My Secret Mother, Lorna Moon*. New York: Farrar, Strauss and Giroux.

Derrida, Jacques. 1994. *Specters of Marx: The State of the Debt, the Work of Mourning, and the New International*. New York: Routledge.

———. 1996. *Archive Fever: A Freudian Impression*. Chicago: University of Chicago Press.

———. 2016. *Heidegger: The Question of Being and History*. trans. Geoffrey Bennington. Chicago: University of Chicago Press.

Deslandes, Jacques, and Jacques Richard. 1968. *Histoire comparée du cinéma Vol. 2, du cinématographe au cinéma (1986–1906)*. Tournai, Belgium: Casterman.

Dickson, Antonia. 1892. "Nine Hundred and Fifty Miles by Telephone." *Cassier's Magazine* 71–74.

———. 1895. "Wonders of the Kinetoscope." *Frank Leslie's Monthly* (February): 245–251. Excerpted 2006. *The Red Velvet Seat: Women's Writing on the First Fifty Years of Cinema*. eds. Antonia Lant with Ingrid Periz. 405–410. New York: Verso.

Dickson, Antonia, and W. K. L Dickson. 1894. *Life and Inventions of Thomas Alva Edison*. New York: Thomas Y. Crowell.

———. 2000 [1895]. *History of the Kinetograph, Kinetoscope, and Kineto-Phonograph*. New York: Museum of Modern Art.

Dickson, W. K. L. 1933. "A Brief History of the Kinetograph, the Kinetoscope and the Kineto-phonograph." *Journal of the Society of Motion Picture Engineers* (December): 9–16.

Dixon, Bryony. 2010. "Women's Film History Project: Issues of Transnationalism." *Framework* 51.2 (Fall): 304–309.

Doane, Mary Ann. 2002. *The Emergence of Cinematic Time: Modernity, Contingency, the Archive*. Cambridge: Harvard University Press.

———. 2007a. "Indexicality: Trace and Sign: Introduction." *differences* 18.1: 1–6.

———. 2007b. "The Indexical and the Concept of Medium Specificity." *differences* 18.1: 129–152.

Doane, Mary Ann, Patricia Mellencamp, and Linda Williams, eds. 1983. "Feminist Film Criticism: An Introduction." In *Re-Vision: Essays in Feminist Film Criticism*. eds. Mary Ann Doane, Patricia Mellencamp, and Linda Williams. 1–17. Los Angeles: The American Film Institute.

Dogo, Dunja. 2013. "Esfir Shub." *Women Film Pioneers Project*. eds. Jane M. Gaines, Radha Vatsal, and Monica Dall'Asta. New York: Center for Digital Research and Scholarship, Columbia University Libraries. https://wfpp.cdrs.columbia.edu/pioneer/ccp-esfir-shub/.

Doran, Robert. 2013. "Choosing the Past: Hayden White and the Philosophy of History." In *Philosophy of History after Hayden White*. ed. Robert Doran. 1–33. London: Bloomsbury.

Dosse, François. 1997a. *History of Structuralism, Vol. 1*. trans. Deborah Glassman. Minneapolis: University of Minnesota Press.

———.1997b. *History of Structuralism, Vol. 2: The Sign Sets, 1967-Present*. trans. Deborah Glassman. Minneapolis: University of Minnesota Press.

Dreiser, Theodore. 2000 [1900]. *Sister Carrie*. Reprinted New York: First Signet Classic.

Dyer, Richard. 1991. "Believing in Fairies: The Author and the Homosexual." In *Inside/Out: Lesbian Theories, Gay Theories*. ed. Diana Fuss. 185–201. New York: Routledge.

———. 2007. *Pastiche*. New York: Routledge.

Eco, Umberto. 1976. "Articulations of the Cinematic Code." In *Movies and Methods*. ed. Bill Nichols. 590–607. Berkeley: University of California Press.

Eisenstein, Sergei. 1977. *Film Form*. ed. and trans. Jay Leyda. New York: Harcourt Brace Jovanovich.

Elsaesser, Thomas. 1986. "The New Film History." *Sight and Sound* 55.4: 246–251.

———. 1987 [1972]. "Tales of Sound and Fury: Observations on the Family Melodrama." In *Home Is Where the Heart Is*. ed. Christine Gledhill. 43–69. London: British Film Institute.

———. 1990. "General Introduction: Early Cinema: From Linear History to Mass Media Archaeology." In *Early Cinema: Space/Frame/Narrative*. eds. Thomas Elsaesser with Adam Barker. 1–8. London: British Film Institute.

———. 1996. "Early German Cinema: A Second Life?" In *A Second Life: German Cinema's First Decades*. eds. Thomas Elsaesser with Michael Wedel. 9–37. Amsterdam: Amsterdam University Press/Brussels, November.

———. 2004. "The New Film History as Media Archaeology." *Cinémas* 14.2–3 (Spring): 75–117.

———. 2012. *The Persistence of Hollywood*. New York: Routledge.

———. 2014. "Le Mélodrame: entre globalization de l'empathie et standardization de l'intime." In *Le mélodrama filmique revisité/Revisiting Film Melodrama*. eds. Dominique Nasta, Muriel Andrin, and Anne Gailly. 31–45. Brussels: Peter Lang.

———. 2016. *Film History as Media Archaeology: Tracking Digital Cinema*. Amsterdam: Amsterdam University Press.

Erens, Patricia. 2013. "Anzia Yezierska." In *Women Film Pioneers Project*. eds. Jane M. Gaines, Radha Vatsal, and Monica Dall'Asta. New York: Center for Digital Research and Scholarship, Columbia University Libraries. https://wfpp.cdrs.columbia.edu/pioneer/ccp/ -anzia-yezierska/.

Ermarth, Elizabeth Deeds. 2007. "The Closed Space of Choice: A Manifesto on the Future of History." *Manifestos for History*. eds. Keith Jenkins, Sue Morgan, and Alun Munslow. 50–66. London: Routledge.

Ernst, Wolfgang. 2011. "Media Archaeology: Method and Machine versus History and Narrative of Media." In *Media Archaeology: Approaches, Applications, and Implications*. eds. Erkki Huhtamo and Jussi Parikka. 239–255. Berkeley: University of California Press.

———. 2013. *Digital Memory and the Archive*. ed. Jussi Parikka. Minneapolis: University of Minnesota Press.

Everett, Eldon K. 1973. "The Great Grace Cunard—Francis Ford Mystery." *Classic Film Collector* (Summer): 22–25.

Ezra, Elizabeth. 2000. *Georges Méliès*. Manchester: Manchester University Press.

Felski, Rita. 2003. *Literature after Feminism*. Chicago: University of Chicago Press.

Foner, Eric. 2014. Review of R. R. Palmer, *The Age of Democratic Revolution. The Nation*: 27.

Förster, Annette. 2005. *Histories of Fame and Failure. Adriënne Solser, Musidora, Nell Shipman: Women Acting and Directing in The Netherlands, France and North America*. Utrecht: Utrecht University.

———. "A Pendulum of Performances: Asta Nielsen on Stage and Screen." In *Researching Women in Silent Cinema: New Findings and Perspectives,* eds. Monica Dall'Asta and Victoria Duckett. 303–317. Bologna: University of Bologna.

Förster, Annette, and Eva Warth. 1999. "Feminist Approaches to Early Film History: An Overview." *Tijdschrift voor Mediageschiedenis* 2.1: 114–128.

Fossati, Giovanna. 2009. *From Grain to Pixel: The Archival Life of Film in Transition*. Amsterdam: Amsterdam University Press.

———. 2012. "Multiple Originals: The (Digital) Restoration and Exhibition of Early Films." In *A Companion to Early Cinema*. eds. Andre Gaudreault, Nicholas Dulac, and Santiago Hidalgo. 550–567. New York: John Wiley and Sons.

Foster, Gwendolyn Audrey. 1995. *Women Film Directors: An International Bio-Critical Dictionary*. Westport, Conn.: Greenwood Press.

Foucault, Michel. 1972. *The Archaeology of Knowledge*. New York: Pantheon Books.

———. 1973. *The Order of Things*. New York: Random House.

———. 1979. "What Is an Author?" *Screen* 20.1 (Spring): 13–23.

———. 1980. *Power/Knowledge: Selected Interviews and Other Writings, 1972–1977*. ed. Colin Gordon. New York: Pantheon Books.

———. 2012 [1984]. *The Foucault Reader*. ed. Paul Rabinow. New York: Vintage Books.

Fradinger, Moira. 2013. "Emilia Saleny." In *Women Film Pioneers Project*. eds. Jane M. Gaines, Radha Vatsal, and Monica Dall'Asta. New York: Center for Digital Research and Scholarship, Columbia University Libraries. https://wfpp.cdrs.columbia.edu/pioneer/emilia -saleny/.

Franck, Stef. 2012. "Contextualizing *The Red Lantern*." *To Dazzle Eye and to Stir the Heart: The Red Lantern, Nazimova, and the Boxer Rebellion.* ed. Stef Franck. Brussels: Royal Belgian Film Archive, 4–11.

Fraser, Nancy. 2013. *Fortunes of Feminism: From State-Managed Capitalism to Neoliberal Crisis.* New York: Verso.

Frow, John. 2006. *Genre.* New York: Routledge.

Gaines, Jane M. 1991. *Contested Culture: The Image, the Voice, and the Law.* Chapel Hill: University of North Carolina Press.

———. 1996. "The Melos in Marxist Theory." In *The Hidden Foundation: Cinema and the Question of Class.* eds. David E. James and Rick Berg. 56–71. Minneapolis: University of Minnesota Press.

———. 1999. "Introduction: The Real Returns." In *Collecting Visible Evidence.* eds. Jane M. Gaines and Michael Renov. 1–18. Minneapolis: University of Minnesota Press.

———. 2000. "Dream/Factory." In *Reinventing Film Studies.* eds. Christine Gledhill and Linda Williams. 100–113. London: Arnold.

———. 2001. *Fire and Desire: Mixed Race Movies in the Silent Era.* Chicago: University of Chicago Press.

———. 2002. "Of Cabbages and Authorship." In *A Feminist Reader in Early Cinema.* eds. Jennifer M. Bean and Diane Negri. 88–118. Durham: Duke University Press.

———. 2004. "Film History and the Two Presents of Feminist Film Theory." *Cinema Journal* 44.1: 113–117.

———. 2005. "First Fictions." *Signs* 30.1 (Winter): 1293–1317.

———. 2006. "Early Cinema's Heyday of Copying: The Too Many Copies of L'Arroseur arrosé." *Cultural Studies* 20.2–3 (May): 227–244.

———. 2007. "Sad Songs of Nitrate." *Camera Obscura* 66.22.3 (Fall 2007): 171–178.

———. 2010. "World Women: What Silent-Era Circulating Film Prints Tell Us about Two-Continent Careers." *Framework* 51.2 (Fall): 283–303.

———. 2011. "The Inevitability of Teleology: From *le dispositif* to Apparatus Theory to *dispositifs* Plural." *Recherches sémiotiques/Semiotic Inquiry* 31.1–2–3: 101–114.

———. 2012a. "Anonymities: Uncredited and Unknown in Early Cinema." In *A Companion to Early Cinema.* eds. André Gaudreault, Nicolas Dulac, and Santiago Hidalgo. 443–459. West Sussex: Wiley-Blackwell.

———. 2012b. "The Ingenuity of Genre and the Genius of Women." In *Gender Meets Genre in Postwar Cinema.* ed. Christine Gledhill. 15–28. Champaign-Urbana: University of Illinois Press.

———. 2013a. "What Happened to the Philosophy of Film History?" *Film History* 25.1–2: 70–80.

———. 2013b. "Wordlessness, to Be Continued . . ." *Researching Women in Silent Cinema: New Findings and Perspectives.* eds. Monica Dall'Asta and Victoria Duckett. 288–301. Bologna: University of Bologna. http://amsacta.unibo.it/3827/.

———. 2013c. "Lule Warrenton." In *Women Film Pioneers Project.* eds. Jane M. Gaines, Radha Vatsal, and Monica Dall'Asta. New York: Center for Digital Research and Scholarship, Columbia University Libraries. https://wfpp.cdrs.columbia.edu/pioneer/ccp-lule-warrenton/.

————. 2014a. "*Four Months, Three Weeks, and Two Days*: Where Is the Marxism in Melo-drama Theory?" *Le mélodrama filmique revisité/Revisiting Film Melodrama.* eds. Domi-nique Nasta and Muriel Andrin. 277–291. Brussels: Peter Lang.

————. 2014b. "Twins, Triplets and Quadruplets: Copying Early Film Pillow Fights 1897–1905." In *Whose Right? Authorship, Media and Intellectual Property in the Digital Era.* eds. Alberto Beltrame, Ludovica Fales, and Guiseppe Fidotta. 141–152. Proceedings of International Film Studies Conference XX. University of Udine, Italy.

————. 2014c. "Why We Took the 'Historical Turn': The Poisons and Antidotes Version." In *At the Borders of (Film) History: Temporality, Archaeology, Theories.* eds. Alberto Beltrame, Ludovica Fales, Giuseppe Fidotta. 179–190. Proceedings of International Film Studies Conference XXI, University of Udine, Italy.

————. 2015. "Eisenstein's Absolutely Wonderful, Totally Impossible Project." In *Sergei M. Eisenstein: Notes for a General History of Cinema.* eds. Naum Klejman and Antonio Somaini. 323–332. Amsterdam: University of Amsterdam Press.

————. 2016. "On Not Narrating the History of Feminism and Film." In *Feminist Me-dia Histories* 2.2. eds. Yvonne Tasker et al. http://fmh.ucpress.edu/content/2/2/6.full .pdf+html.

————. 2017. "What Was 'Women's Work' in the Silent Film Era?" *Routledge Companion to Cinema and Gender.* eds. Kristin Hale, Dijana Jelaca, E. Ann Kaplan, and Patrice Petro. 266–278. New York: Routledge.

————. 2018. "Even More Tears: The *Historical Time* Theory of Melodrama." In *Melodrama Un-bound.* eds. Christine Gledhill and Linda Williams. New York: Columbia University Press.

————. forthcoming. "Moving Picture Melodrama." In *Cambridge Companion to English Melodrama.* ed. Carolyn Williams. Cambridge: Cambridge University Press.

————. forthcoming. "What Did Hollywood Export to the Rest of the World?" In *Theorizing Colonial Cinemas.* eds. Aimee Kwon et al.

Gaines, Jane M., and Michelle Koerner. 2013. "Woman as Camera Operators or 'Cranks.'" In *Women Film Pioneers Project.* eds. Jane M. Gaines, Radha Vatsal, and Monica Dall'Asta. New York: Center for Digital Research and Scholarship, Columbia University Librar-ies. https://wfpp.cdrs.columbia.edu/essay/how-women-worked-in-the-us-silent-film -industry/.

Gaines, Jane M., and Radha Vatsal. 2013. "Women Worked in the Silent Film Industry!" *Women Film Pioneers Project.* eds. Jane M. Gaines, Radha Vatsal, and Monica Dall'Asta. New York: Center for Digital Research and Scholarship, Columbia University Libraries. https://wfpp .cdrs.columbia.edu/essay/how-women-worked-in-the-us-silent-film-industry/.

Gaines, Jane M., Radha Vatsal, and Monica Dall'Asta, eds. 2013. *Women Film Pioneers Project.* New York: Center for Digital Research and Scholarship, Columbia University Libraries. http://wfpp.cdrs.columbia.edu.

Gallagher, Catherine, and Stephen Greenblatt. 1997. *Practicing New Historicism.* Chicago: University of Chicago Press.

Garncarz, Joseph. 2012. "The European Fairground Cinema: (Re)defining and (Re)contex-tualizing the 'Cinema of Attractions.'" In *A Companion to Early Cinema.* eds. André Gaudreault et al. 318–333. Chichester: Wiley-Blackwell.

Gartenberg, John. 1984. "The Brighton Project: The Archives and Research." *Iris* 2.1 (1984): 5–16.

Gaudreault, André. 1993. "The Cinematograph: A Historical Machine." In *Meanings in Texts and Actions: Questioning Paul Ricoeur*. eds. David E. Klemm and William Schweiker. 90–97. Charlottesville: University of Virginia Press.

———. 2001. "Fragmentation and Assemblage in the Lumière Animated Pictures." *Film History* 13: 76–88.

———. 2009. *From Plato to Lumière: Narration and Monstration in Literature and Cinema*. trans. Timothy Barnard. Toronto: Toronto University Press.

———. 2011. *Film and Attraction: From Kinematography to Cinema*. trans. Timothy Barnard. Champaign-Urbana: University of Illinois Press.

Gaudreault, André, and Philippe Marion. 2015. *The End of Cinema? Medium in Crisis in the Digital Age*. New York: Columbia University Press.

Gaudreault, André, and Tom Gunning. 2006 [1989]. "Early Cinema as a Challenge to Film History." In *The Cinema of Attractions Reloaded*. ed. Wanda Strauven. 365–380. Amsterdam: Amsterdam University Press.

———. 2009. "Introduction: American Cinema Emerges (1890–1909). In *American Cinema, 1890–1909: Themes and Variations*. eds. André Gaudreault and Tom Gunning. 1–21. New Brunswick, N.J.: Rutgers University Press.

Gerow, Aaron. 2010. *Visions of Japanese Modernity: Articulations of Cinema, Nation, and Spectatorship, 1895–1925*, Berkeley: University of California Press.

Giannini, A. H. 1926. "Financing the Production and Distribution of Motion Pictures." *Annals of the American Academy of Political and Social Science* 128 (November): 46–49.

Ginsburg, Carlo. 1991. "Checking the Evidence: The Judge and the Historian." *Critical Inquiry* 18.1: 79–82.

Gledhill, Christine. 1987. "The Melodramatic Field." In *Home Is Where the Heart Is*. ed. Christine Gledhill. 5–39. London: British Film Institute.

———. 2000. "Rethinking Genre." In *Reinventing Cinema*. eds. Christine Gledhill and Linda Williams. 219–243. London: Arnold.

———. 2010. "Introduction: Transnationalizing Women's Film History." *Framework* 51.2 (Fall): 275–282.

———. 2012. Introduction. In *Gender Meets Genre in Postwar Cinema*. ed. Christine Gledhill. 1–11. Champaign-Urbana: University of Illinois Press.

———. 2014. Introduction. *Le mélodrama—filmique revisité/Revisiting Film Melodrama*. eds. Dominique Nasta and Muriel Andrin. 17–30. Brussels: Peter Lang,

———. forthcoming. "Domestic Melodrama." In *Cambridge Companion to English Melodrama*. ed. Carolyn Williams. Cambridge: Cambridge University Press.

Gledhill, Christine, and Julia Knight. 2015. "Introduction." In *Doing Women's Film History: Reframing Cinemas, Past and Future*. eds. Christine Gledhill and Julia Knight. 1–12. Champaign-Urbana: University of Illinois Press.

Gledhill, Christine, and Linda Williams, eds. 2018. *Melodrama Unbound*. New York: Columbia University Press.

Gordon, Marsha. 2013. "Hettie Gray Baker." In *Women Film Pioneers Project*. eds. Jane M. Gaines, Radha Vatsal, and Monica Dall'Asta. New York: Center for Digital Research and

Scholarship, Columbia University Libraries. https://wfpp.cdrs.columbia.edu/pioneer/ccp-hettie-gray-baker/.

Gramann, Karola, Eric de Kuyper, Sabine Nessel, Heide Schlüpmann, and Michael Wedel, eds. 2009. *Sprache der Liebe: Asta Nielsen ihre Filme, ihr Kino 1910–1933/Language of Love: Asta Nielsen, Her Films, Her Cinema 1910–1933*. Vienna: Filmarchiv Austria.

Grewal, Interpal. 2005. *Transnational America: Feminisms, Diasporas, Neorealisms*. Durham: Duke University Press.

Grieveson, Lee. 2004. *Policing Cinema: Movies and Censorship in Early Twentieth-Century America*. Berkeley: University of California Press.

———. 2009. "On Governmentality and Screens." *Screen* 50.1: 180–187.

Grimm, Charles. 2017. "Angela Murray Gibson." In *Women Film Pioneers Project*. eds. Jane M. Gaines, Radha Vatsal, and Monica Dall'Asta. New York: Center for Digital Research and Scholarship, Columbia University Libraries.

Gumbrecht, Hans Ulrich. 2004. *Production of Presence: What Meaning Cannot Convey*. Stanford: University of California Press.

Gunning, Tom. 1986. "The Cinema of Attraction[s]: Early Film, Its Spectator and the Avant-Garde." *Wide Angle* 8.3–4 (Fall): 63–70.

———. 1991. *D. W. Griffith and the Origins of American Narrative Film: The Early Years at Biograph*. Urbana: University of Illinois Press.

———. 1997. "Before Documentary: Early Nonfiction Films and the 'View' Aesthetic." In *Uncharted Territory: Essays on Early Nonfiction Film*. eds. Daan Hertogs and Nico de Klerk. 9–24. Amsterdam: Netherlands Filmmuseum.

———. 2003. "Re-newing Old Technologies: Astonishment, Second Nature, and the Uncanny in Technology from the Previous Turn-of-the-Century." In *Rethinking Media Change: The Aesthetics of Transition*. eds. David Thornburn and Henry Jenkins. 39–60. Cambridge: MIT Press.

———. 2006. "Attractions: How They Came into the World." In *The Cinema of Attractions Reloaded*. ed. Wanda Strauven. 31–39. Amsterdam: Amsterdam University Press.

———. 2008. "Early Cinema as Global Cinema: The Encyclopedic Ambition." In *Early Cinema and the "National."* eds. Richard Abel, Giorgio Bertellini, and Rob King. 11–16. New Barnett: John Libbey,

Hall, Jacquelyn Dowd. 1983. "'The Mind that Burns in Each Body': Women, Rape, and Racial Violence." In *Powers of Desire: The Politics of Sexuality*. eds. Jacquelyn Dowd Hall, Anne Snitow, and Christine Stansell. 328–349. New York: Monthly Review Press.

Hall, Stuart. 1981. "Notes on Deconstructing 'The Popular.'" In *People's History and Socialist Theory*. ed. Raphael Samuel. 227–240. Boston: Routledge and Kegan Paul.

———. 1987. "Minimal Selves." In *The Real Me: Post-Modernism and the Question of Identity. ICA Documents 6*. ed. Lisa Appignanesi. 44–46. London: The Institute of Contemporary Arts.

Hallett, Hilary A. 2013. *Go West, Young Women!* Berkeley: University of California Press.

———. 2018. "Melodrama and the Making of Hollywood." In *Melodrama Unbound*. eds. Christine Gledhill and Linda Williams. New York: Columbia University Press.

Hampton, Benjamin. 1970 [1931]. *History of the American Film Industry from Its Beginnings to 1931*. New York: Dover Publications.

Hansen, Miriam. 1991. *Babel and Babylon: Spectatorship in American Silent Film*. Cambridge: Harvard University Press.

———. 1997. Introduction. *Siegfried Kracauer, A Theory of Film: The Redemption of Physical Reality*. vii–xlv. Princeton, N.J.: Princeton University Press.

———. 2000a. "Fallen Women, Rising Stars, New Horizons: Shanghai Silent Film as Vernacular Modernism." *Film Quarterly* 54.1 (2000): 10–22.

———. 2000b. "The Mass Production of the Senses: Classical Cinema as Vernacular Modernism." In *Reinventing Film Studies*. eds. Christine Gledhill and Linda Williams. 332–350. London: Arnold.

———. 2010. Foreword. In Heide Schlüpmann, *The Uncanny Gaze: The Drama of Early German Cinema*. trans. Inga Pollmann. ix–xv. Urbana: University of Illinois Press.

Harner, Gary. 1998. "The Kalem Company, Travel, and On-Location Shooting." *Film History* 10: 118–207.

Harris, Kristine. 1997. "The New Woman Incident: Cinema, Scandal, and Spectacle in 1935 Shanghai." In *Transnational Chinese Cinemas: Identity, Nationhood, Gender*. ed. Sheldon Hsiao-peng Lu. 277–302. Honolulu: University of Hawaii Press.

Haskell, Molly. 1973. *From Reverence to Rape: The Treatment of Women in the Movies*. New York: Holt, Rinehart and Winston.

Hastie, Amelie. 2002. "Circuits of Memory and History: The Memoirs of Alice Guy-Blaché." In *A Feminist Reader in Early Cinema*. eds. Jennifer M. Bean and Diane Negra. 29–59. Durham: Duke University Press.

Hastie, Amelie, and Shelly Stamp, eds. 2006. *Women and the Silent Screen*. Special issue of *Film History* 18.2.

Haug, Frigga. 1992. *Beyond Female Masochism*. trans. Rodney Livingstone. New York: Verso. Stephen Heath.

Hediger, Vinzenz. 2005. "The Original Is Always Lost: Film History, Copyright Industries and the Problem of Reconstruction." In *Cinephilia: Movies, Love and Memory*. eds. Marijke de Valck and Malte Hagener. 135–149. Amsterdam: Amsterdam University Press.

———. 2010. "Benjamin's Challenge: If Art Is No Longer the Same after Cinema, then What about History?" In *Proceedings from Dall'inizio, alla fine / In the Beginning and at the Very End*. eds. Francesco Casetti and Jane M. Gaines. 455–463. Udine International Film Studies Conference, XVI. Udine, Italy.

Heidegger, Martin. 1996 [1927]. *Being and Time*. trans. Joan Stambaugh. Albany: SUNY Press.

Hemmings, Clare. 2005. "Telling Feminist Stories." *Feminist Theory* 6.2: 115–139.

Hendershott, Carmen. 2013. "Elizabeth B. Grimball." In *Women Film Pioneers Project*. eds. Jane M. Gaines, Radha Vatsal, and Monica Dall'Asta. New York: Center for Digital Research and Scholarship, Columbia University Libraries. https://wfpp.cdrs.columbia.edu/pioneer/ccp-elizabeth-b-grimball/.

Hendricks, Gordon. 1961. *The Edison Motion Picture Myth*. Berkeley: University of California Press.

Hesford, Victoria, and Lisa Diedrich, 2014. "Experience, Eco, Event: Theorizing Feminist Histories, Historicising Feminist Theory." *Feminist Theory*. 15.2: 103–117.

Higashi, Sumiki. 2004. "In Focus: Film History, or a Baedeker Guide to the Historical Turn." *Cinema Journal* 44.1: 94–100.

Hill, Erin. 2016. *Never Done: A History of Women's Work in Media Production.* New Brunswick, N.J.: Rutgers University Press.

Hine, Darlene Clark. 1995. "The Making of Black Women in America: An Historical Encyclopedia." In *U.S. History as Women's History: New Feminist Essays.* eds. Linda K. Kerber, Alice Kessler-Harris, and Kathryn Kish Sklar. 335–347. Chapel Hill: University of North Carolina Press.

Hochschild, Adam. 2005. "A Monument to Denial." *Los Angeles Times* (March 2). http:// articles.latimes.com/2005/mar/02/opinion/oe-hochschild2.

———. 2006. *King Léopold's Ghost: A Story of Greed, Terror, and Heroism in Colonial Africa.* London: Macmillan.

Holliday, Wendy. 1995. "Hollywood's Modern Women: Screenwriting, Work Culture, and Feminism, 1910–1940." Unpublished PhD dissertation, New York University.

———. 2013a. "Beulah Marie Dix." In *Women Film Pioneers Project.* eds. Jane M. Gaines, Radha Vatsal, and Monica Dall'Asta. New York: Center for Digital Research and Scholarship, Columbia University Libraries. https://wfpp.cdrs.columbia.edu/pioneer/ccp-beulah -marie-dix/.

———. 2013b. "Olga Petrova." In *Women Film Pioneers Project.* eds. Jane M. Gaines, Radha Vatsal, and Monica Dall'Asta. New York: Center for Digital Research and Scholarship, Columbia University Libraries. https://wfpp.cdrs.columbia.edu/pioneer/ccp-olga-petrova/.

Horak, Jan-Christopher. 2007. "The Gap between 1 and 0: Digital Video and the Omissions of Film History." *Spectator* 27.1 (Spring): 29–41.

———. 2016. "Preserving Race Films." In *Early Race Filmmaking in America.* ed. Barbara Tepa Lupack. 199–230. New York: Routledge.

Horak, Laura. 2016. *Girls Will Be Boys: Cross-Dressed Women, Lesbians, and American Cinema.* New Brunswick, N.J.: Rutgers University Press.

Horne, Jennifer. 2013. "Alla Nazimova." In *Women Film Pioneers Project.* eds. Jane M. Gaines, Radha Vatsal, and Monica Dall'Asta. New York: Center for Digital Research and Scholarship, Columbia University Libraries. https://wfpp.cdrs.columbia.edu/pioneer/ccp -alla-nazimova/.

Huhtamo, Erikki, and Jussi Parikka, eds. 2011. *Media Archaeology: Approaches, Applications, and Implications.* Berkeley: University of California Press.

Husserl, Edmund. 1991. *On the Phenomenology of the Consciousness of Internal Time* (1893– 1917). trans. John Barnett Brough. Dordrecht: Kluwer Academic Publishers.

Hori, Hikari. 2005. "Migration and Transgression: Female Pioneers of Documentary Filmmaking in Japan." *Asian Cinema* vol. 16.1 : 89–97.

Huyssen, Andreas. 1986. "Mass Culture as Woman: Modernism's Other." In *Studies in Entertainment.* ed. Tania Modleski. 188–207. Bloomington: Indiana University Press.

Ikegawa, Reiko. 2011. *"Teikoku" no Eiga Kantoku Sakane Tazuko: "Kaitaku no hanayome," sen-kyūhyaku-shijūsannen, Man'ei.* Tokyo: Yoshikawa Kōbunkan.

———. 2012. "Japanese Female Director Sakane Tazuko, the Manchurian Film Association, and Archival Materials for Japanese Colonial Films." Unpublished talk,

Makino Symposium, Columbia University, 2012. https://www.youtube.com/watch?v
=G97MMeKzQuU.

Ionita, Casiana. 2013. "Mrs. Sidney Drew." In *Women Film Pioneers Project*. eds. Jane M. Gaines, Radha Vatsal, and Monica Dall'Asta. New York: Center for Digital Research and Scholarship, Columbia University Libraries. https://wfpp.cdrs.columbia.edu/pioneer/ccp-mrs -sidney-drew/.

Jackson, Victoria. 2017. "Maude Adams." In *Women Film Pioneers Project*. eds. Jane M. Gaines, Radha Vatsal, and Monica Dall'Asta. New York: Center for Digital Research and Scholarship, Columbia University Libraries. https://wfpp.cdrs.columbia.edu/pioneer/maude -adams/.

———. 2014. "Maude Adams from Stage to Screen: Her Research into Lighting and Color for Film in the 1920s." Unpublished paper delivered at "Doing Women's Film History" Conference, University of East Anglia, April.

Jacob, Clarissa K. 2015. "*Women & Film*: The First Feminist Film Magazine," *Feminist Media Histories* 1.1 (Winter 2015): 153–162.

Jacobs, Lea. 1991. *The Wages of Sin: Censorship and the Fallen Woman Film, 1928–1942*. Madison: University of Wisconsin Press.

———. 2008. *The Decline of Sentiment: American Film in the 1920s*. Berkeley: University of California Press.

———. 2012. "Unsophisticated Lady: The Vicissitudes of the Maternal Melodrama." In *The Wiley-Blackwell History of American Film*. eds. Roy Grundeman, Cynthia Lucia, and Art Simon. 397–416. London: Blackwell.

Jacobs, Lewis. 1975 [1939]. *The Rise of American Film*. New York: Columbia University Press.

Jacobson, Brian R. 2015. *Studios before the System: Architecture, Technology, and the Emergence of Cinematic Space*. New York: Columbia University Press.

Jameson, Fredric. 1971. *Marxism and Form*. Princeton, N.J.: Princeton University Press.

———. 2002. *A Singular Modernity: Essay on the Ontology of the Present*. New York: Verso.

———. 2005. *Archaeologies of the Future: The Desire Called Utopia and Other Science Fictions*. London: Verso.

———. 2016. Interview: "Revisiting Postmodernism." *Social Text* 127–34.2 (June): 143–160.

Jandelli, Cristina. 2013. "Daisy Sylvan." In *Women Film Pioneers Project*. eds. Jane M. Gaines, Radha Vatsal, and Monica Dall'Asta. New York: Center for Digital Research and Scholarship, Columbia University Libraries. https://wfpp.cdrs.columbia.edu/pioneer/daisy -sylvan/.

Jay, Elisabeth, ed. 2005. Introduction. In Ellen Wood, *East Lynne*. [1861]. vii–xxxix. Oxford: Oxford University Press.

Jenkins, Keith. 1991. *Re-Thinking History*. New York: Routledge.

———. 2003. *Refiguring History*. New York: Routledge.

———. 2009a. *At the Limits of History: Essays on Theory and Practice*. New York: Routledge.

———. 2009b. "'Nobody Does It Better': Radical History and Hayden White." In *Re-figuring Hayden White*. eds. Frank Ankersmit, Ewa Domańska, and Hans Kellner. 105–123. Stanford: Stanford University Press.

Jenkins, Keith, and Alun Munslow, eds. 2004. *The Nature of History Reader*. New York: Routledge.

Johnston, Claire. 1973. "Women's Cinema as Counter-Cinema." In *Notes on Women's Cinema*. ed. Claire Johnston. 24–31. London: Society for Education in Film and Television.

——. 1975a. "Feminist Politics and Film History," *Screen* 16.3: 115–124.

——. 1975b. *The Work of Dorothy Arzner: Towards a Feminist Criticism*. London: BFI.

Jones, Graham, and Jon Roffe, eds. 2009. *Deleuze's Philosophical Lineage*. Edinburgh: Edinburgh University Press.

Joyce, Simon, and Jennifer Putzi. 2013. "Mabel Normand." In *Women Film Pioneers Project*. eds. Jane M. Gaines, Radha Vatsal, and Monica Dall'Asta. New York: Center for Digital Research and Scholarship, Columbia University Libraries. https://wfpp.cdrs.columbia.edu/pioneer/ccp-mabel-normand/.

Kantor, Jodi. 2014. "A Brand New World in Which Men Ruled." *New York Times* (December 23). http://www.nytimes.com/interactive/2014/12/23/us/gender-gaps-stanford-94.html.

Kaplan, Caren, and Inderpal Grewal. 2002. "Transnational Practices and Interdisciplinary Feminist Scholarship: Refiguring Women's and Gender Studies." In *Women's Studies on Its Own: The Next Wave Reader in Institutional Change*. ed. Robyn Wiegman. 66–105. Durham: Duke University Press.

Kaplan, E. Ann. 1983a. *Women and Film: Both Sides of the Camera*. New York: Routledge.

——. 1983b. "Theories of Melodrama: A Feminist Perspective." *Women and Performance* 1.1 (1983): 40–48.

——. 1985. Review of *Re-Vision*. *Camera Obscura* 13/14: 235–249.

——. 1987. "Mothering, Feminism, and Representation: The Maternal in Melodrama and the Woman's Film from 1910 to 1940." In *Home Is Where the Heart Is*. ed. Christine Gledhill. 113–137. London: British Film Institute.

——. 1992. *Motherhood and Representation: The Mother in Popular Culture and Melodrama*. New York: Routledge.

——. 2012. "Troubling Genre/Reconstructing Gender." In *Gender Meets Genre in Postwar Cinema*. ed. Christine Gledhill. 71–83. Champaign-Urbana: University of Illinois Press.

Katz, Ephraim. 1979. *The Film Encyclopedia*. New York: Cowell, 319.

Kay, Karen, and Gerald Peary, eds. 1977a. *Women and the Cinema: A Critical Anthology*. New York: E. P. Dutton.

——. 1977b. Preface. In *Women and the Cinema: A Critical Anthology*. eds. Karen Kay and Gerald Peary. xiii–xvi. New York: E. P. Dutton.

Keil, Charlie. 2001. *Early American Cinema in Transition: Story, Style, and Filmmaking, 1907–1913*. Madison: University of Wisconsin Press.

Kellner, Hans. 1995. "Introduction: Describing Redescription." In *A New Philosophy of History*. eds. Frank Ankersmit and Hans Kellner. 1–18. Chicago: University of Chicago Press.

Kessler-Harris, Alice. 2012. *A Difficult Woman: The Challenging Life and Times of Lillian Hellman*. New York: Bloomsbury Press.

King, Magda. 2001. *A Guide to Heidegger's Being and Time*. ed. John Llewelyn. Albany: SUNY Press.

Koselleck, Reinhart. 2002. *The Practice of Conceptual History: Timing History, Spacing Concepts*. trans. Todd Presner and others. Stanford: Stanford University.

——. 2004. *Futures Past: On the Semantics of Historical Time*. trans. Keith Tribe. New York: Columbia University Press.

Koszarski, Richard. 1977. "The Years Have Not Been Kind to Lois Weber." In *Women and the Cinema: A Critical Anthology*. eds. Karyn Kay and Gerald Peary. 146–152. New York: Dutton.

———. 1990. *An Evening's Entertainment: The Age of the Silent Feature Picture, 1915–1928*. Vol. 3. *History of the American Cinema*. New York: Scribner's.

———. 2004. *Fort Lee: The Film Town*. Rome, Italy: John Libbey.

Kracauer, Siegfried. 1969. *History: The Last Things before the Last*. New York: Oxford University Press.

———. 1995 [1963]. "Photography." In *The Mass Ornament*. ed. and trans. Thomas Y. Levin. 47–63. Cambridge: Harvard University Press.

———. 1997 [1960]. *Siegfried Kracauer, A Theory of Film: The Redemption of Physical Reality*. Princeton, N.J.: Princeton University Press.

Kuhn, Annette, with Elizabeth Radstone, eds. 1990. *Women in Film: An International Guide*. New York: Fawset Colombine.

Kuhn, Annette, and Jackey Stacey. 1998. "Screen Histories: An Introduction." In *Screen Histories: A Screen Reader*. eds. Annette Kuhn and Jackey Stacey. 1–10. Oxford: Clarendon Press.

Kuleshov, Lev. 1974. "Americanitis." In *Kuleshov on Film*. ed. and trans. Ron Levaco. 127–130. Berkeley: University of California Press.

Lacasse, Germain. 2013. "Marie de Kerstrat." In *Women Film Pioneers Project*. eds. Jane M. Gaines, Radha Vatsal, and Monica Dall'Asta. New York: Center for Digital Research and Scholarship, Columbia University Libraries. https://wfpp.cdrs.columbia.edu/pioneer/marie-de-kerstrat/.

Lacasse, Germain, and Serge Duigou. 1987. *Marie de Kerstrat l'aristocrate du cinématographe*. Quimper: Éditions Ressac.

Lane, Christina. 2013a. "Ruth Bryan Owen." In *Women Film Pioneers Project*. eds. Jane M. Gaines, Radha Vatsal, and Monica Dall'Asta. New York: Center for Digital Research and Scholarship, Columbia University Libraries. https://wfpp.cdrs.columbia.edu/pioneer/ccp-ruth-bryan-owen/.

———. 2013b. "Vera McCord." In *Women Film Pioneers Project*. eds. Jane M. Gaines, Radha Vatsal, and Monica Dall'Asta. New York: Center for Digital Research and Scholarship, Columbia University Libraries. https://wfpp.cdrs.columbia.edu/pioneer/ccp-vera-mccord/.

Lant, Antonia, ed. 2006. *The Red Velvet Seat: Women's Writing on the First Fifty Years of Cinema*. London: Verso.

Lau, Jenny. 2013. "Marion E. Wong." In *Women Film Pioneers Project*. eds. Jane M. Gaines, Radha Vatsal, and Monica Dall'Asta. New York: Center for Digital Research and Scholarship, Columbia University Libraries. https://wfpp.cdrs.columbia.edu/pioneer/ccp-marion-e-wong/.

Lauzen, Margaret. 2016. "MPAA Must Lead—or Be Led—in Battle to Improve Diversity." http://womenintvfilm.sdsu.edu.

Law, Kar. 2011. "In Search of Esther Eng: Border-Crossing Pioneer in Chinese-Language Filmmaking." In *Chinese Women's Cinema: Transnational Contexts*. trans. Chris Tong. ed. Lingzhen Wang. 313–329. New York: Columbia University Press.

Lenk, Sabine. 2002. "A Standard Identification Process of How the Work of Alice Guy Has Benefited from Increased Communication between Researchers." trans. Alison McMahan. In Alison McMahan, *Alice Guy Blaché: Lost Visionary of the Cinema.* 277–280. New York: Continuum Books.

Lenk, Sabine, and Alison McMahan. 1999. "À la recherché d'objets filmiques non identifiés: Autoour de l' oeuvre d' Alice Guy-Blaché." Archives 81 (août).

Liu, Jia. 2013. "Valda Valkyrien." In *Women Film Pioneers Project.* eds. Jane M. Gaines, Radha Vatsal, and Monica Dall'Asta. New York: Center for Digital Research and Scholarship, Columbia University Libraries. https://wfpp.cdrs.columbia.edu/pioneer/ccp-valda -valkyrien/.

Loiperdinger, Martin, and Uli Jung, eds. 2013. *Importing Asta Nielsen: The International Film Star in the Making 1910–1914.* New Barnet (London): John Libbey.

López, Ana M. 2000. "Facing Up to Hollywood." In *Reinventing Film Studies.* eds. Christine Gledhill and Linda Williams. 419–437. London: Arnold.

Lovink, Geert. 2013. "Archive Rumblings: An Interview with Wolfgang Ernst." In Wolfgang Ernst, *Digital Memory and the Archive.* ed. with introduction by Jussi Parrika. 193–203. Minneapolis: University of Minnesota Press,

Lucioni, Mario, and Irela Nuñez. 2013. "Stefanía Socha." In *Women Film Pioneers Project.* eds. Jane M. Gaines, Radha Vatsal and Monica Dall'Asta. New York: Center for Digital Research and Scholarship, Columbia University Libraries. https://wfpp.cdrs.columbia.edu/ pioneer/ccp-stefania-socha/.

Lund, Maria Fosheim. 2013. "Bessie Barriscale." In *Women Film Pioneers Project.* eds. Jane M. Gaines, Radha Vatsal, and Monica Dall'Asta. New York: Center for Digital Research and Scholarship, Columbia University Libraries. https://wfpp.cdrs.columbia.edu/pioneer/ ccp-bessie-barriscale/.

Lundemo, Trond. 2014. "Archives and Technological Selection," *CiNéMAS* 24.2–3: 17–39.

Lyons, Mary Ann. 2013. "Beatriz Michelina." In *Women Film Pioneers Project.* eds. Jane M. Gaines, Radha Vatsal, and Monica Dall'Asta. New York: Center for Digital Research and Scholarship, Columbia University Libraries. https://wfpp.cdrs.columbia.edu/pioneer/ ccp-beatriz-michelena/.

MacCabe, Colin. 1974. "Realism and the Cinema: Notes on Brechtian Theses." *Screen* 15.2: 7–27.

———. 1976. "Theory and Film: Principles of Realism and Pleasure." *Screen* 17.3 (Autumn): 7–27.

———. 2003. "The Revenge of the Author." In *Film and Authorship.* ed. Virginia Wexman. 30–41. New Brunswick, N.J.: Rutgers University Press.

Macherey, Pierre. 1978. *Theory of Literary Production.* trans. Geoffrey Wall. London: Routledge and Kegan Paul.

Mahar, Karen Ward. 2001. "True Womanhood in Hollywood: Gendered Business Strategies and the Rise and Fall of the Woman Filmmaker, 1896–1928." *Enterprise & History* 2: 72–110.

———. 2006. *Women Filmmakers in Early Hollywood.* Baltimore: Johns Hopkins University Press.

———. 2013a. "Helen Holmes." In *Women Film Pioneers Project.* eds. Jane M. Gaines, Radha Vatsal, and Monica Dall'Asta. New York: Center for Digital Research and Scholarship,

Columbia University Libraries. https://wfpp.cdrs.columbia.edu/pioneer/ccp-helen
-holmes/.

———. 2013b. "Clara Kimball Young." In *Women Film Pioneers Project.* eds. Jane M. Gaines,
Radha Vatsal, and Monica Dall'Asta. New York: Center for Digital Research and Scholarship, Columbia University Libraries. https://wfpp.cdrs.columbia.edu/pioneer/ccp
-clara-kimball-young/.

Mahar, Karen Ward, and Kathryn Fuller-Seeley. 2013. "Exhibiting Women: Gender, Show-
manship, and Professionalization of Film Exhibition in the United States, 1900–1930." In
Women Film Pioneers Project. eds. Jane M. Gaines, Radha Vatsal, and Monica Dall'Asta.
New York: Center for Digital Research and Scholarship, Columbia University Libraries. https://wfpp.cdrs.columbia.edu/essay/exhibiting-women-gender-showmanship
-and-the-professionalization-of-film-exhibition-in-the-united-states-1900-ndash-1930/.

Manovich, Lev. 2001. *The Language of New Media.* Cambridge: MIT Press.

———. 2013. *Software Takes Command.* New York: Bloomsbury.

Marks, Laura. 2002. *Touch: Sensuous Theory and Multisensory Media.* Minneapolis: University of Minnesota Press.

Márquez, Kenya, and Luis Bernardo Jaime Vázquez. 2013. "Cándida Beltrán Rendón." In
Women Film Pioneers Project. eds. Jane M. Gaines, Radha Vatsal, and Monica Dall'Asta.
New York: Center for Digital Research and Scholarship, Columbia University Libraries.
https://wfpp.cdrs.columbia.edu/pioneer/ccp-candida-beltran-rendon/.

Martin, Ann, and Virginia Clark. 1987. "Introduction." In *What Women Wrote: Scenarios,
1912–1929.* Fredrick, Md.: University Publications of America, Cinema Microfilm Series.

Martin, Biddy. 2008. "Success and Its Failures." In *Women's Studies on the Edge.* ed. Joan W.
Scott. 169 -197. Durham: Duke University Press.

Martin, Biddy, and Chandra Talpede Mohanty. 1986. "Feminist Politics: What's Home
Got to Do with It?" *Feminist Studies/Critical Studies.* ed. Teresa de Lauretis. 191–212.
Bloomington: Indiana University Press.

Massa, Steve. 2013. "Gale Henry." In *Women Film Pioneers Project.* eds. Jane M. Gaines, Radha
Vatsal, and Monica Dall'Asta. New York: Center for Digital Research and Scholarship,
Columbia University Libraries. https://wfpp.cdrs.columbia.edu/pioneer/ccp-gale-henry/.

Massie, Robert K. 1967. *Nicholas and Alexandra.* New York: Random House.

———. 2011. *Catherine the Great: Portrait of a Woman.* New York: Random House.

Massumi, Brian. 2002. *Parables for the Virtual: Movement, Affect, Sensation.* Durham: Duke
University Press.

Maule, Rosanna, ed. 2005. *Femmes et Cinéma muet: nouvelles problématiques, nouvelles
methodologies/Women and the Silent Cinema: Methods, Approaches, Issues.* Special
issue of *Cinémas* 16.1.

Maule, Rosanna, and Catherine Russell, eds. 2005. *Cinephilia and Women's Cinema in the
1920s.* Special issue of *Framework* 46.1.

Mayer, David. 2009. *Stagestruck Filmmaker: D. W. Griffith and the American Theatre.* Iowa
City: University of Iowa Press.

Mayne, Judith. 1990. *The Woman at the Keyhole.* Bloomington: Indiana University Press.

———. 1993. *Cinema and Spectatorship.* London: Routledge.

———. 1994. *Directed by Dorothy Arzner.* Bloomington: Indiana University Press.

———. 2017 "Scandale! Dorothy Arzner in Paris." *Film Quarterly* (July 12). https://film quarterly.org/2017/07/12/scandale-dorothy-arzner-in-oaris/.

McGill, Meredith L., ed. 2013. *Taking Liberties with the Author: Selected Essays from the English Institute*. Cambridge: English Institute and American Council of Learned Societies.

McHugh, Kathleen. 2009. "The World and the Soup: Historicizing Media Feminisms in Transnational Contexts." *Camera Obscura* 72 (2009): 110–151.

McKenna, Denise. 2008. "The City That Made the Pictures Move: Gender, Labor, and the Film Industry in Los Angeles, 1908–1917." Unpublished PhD dissertation, New York University.

McMahan, Alison. 2002. *Alice Guy Blaché: Lost Visionary of Cinema*. New York: Continuum.

———. 2004. "Beginnings." In *European Cinema*. ed. Elizabeth Ezra. 23–40. Oxford: Oxford University Press.

———. 2009a. "Madame Blaché in America: Director, Producer, Studio Owner." In *Alice Guy Blaché: Cinema Pioneer*. ed. Joan Simon. 47–76. New Haven: Yale University Press.

———. 2009b. "Key Events and Dates: Alice Guy Blaché." In *Alice Guy Blaché: Cinema Pioneer*. ed. Joan Simon. 124–131. New Haven: Yale University Press.

McRobbie, Angela. 2008. *The Aftermath of Feminism: Gender, Culture and Social Change*. London: Sage.

Mejri, Ouissal. 2010. "Women in Egyptian Silent Cinema: the 1920s Pioneers." Unpublished paper delivered at Women and the Silent Screen VI. Bologna: Manifattura delle Arti.

Mellen, Joan. 1977. *Women and Their Sexuality in the New Film*. Liberty, N.J.: Horizon Press.

Mercer, John, and Martin Shingler. 2004. *Melodrama: Genre, Style, Sensibility*. London: Wallflower.

Merck, Mandy. 2007. "Mulvey's Manifesto." *Camera Obscura* 22 (2007): 1–23.

Miguel, Ángel. 2000. *Mimí Derba*. Mexico: Archivo Fílmico Agrasánchez/Filmoteca de la UNAM.

Miller, April. 2013a. "Flora Finch." In *Women Film Pioneers Project*. eds. Jane M. Gaines, Radha Vatsal, and Monica Dall'Asta. New York: Center for Digital Research and Scholarship, Columbia University Libraries. https://wfpp.cdrs.columbia.edu/pioneer/ccp-flora-finch/.

———. 2013b. "Agnes Christine Johnson." In *Women Film Pioneers Project*. eds. Jane M. Gaines, Radha Vatsal, and Monica Dall'Asta. New York: Center for Digital Research and Scholarship, Columbia University Libraries. https://wfpp.cdrs.columbia.edu/pioneer/ccp-agnes-christine-johnston/.

Miller, Nancy K. 1986. "Changing the Subject: Authorship, Writing, and the Reader." in *Feminist Studies/Critical Studies*. ed. Teresa de Lauretis. 102–120. Bloomington: Indiana University Press.

Mink, Louis O. 1987. *Historical Understanding*. Ithaca: Cornell University Press.

Mitchell, William J. 1992. *The Reconfigured Eye: Visual Truth in the Post-Photographic Era*. Cambridge: MIT Press.

Mitry, Jean. 1967–1980. *Historie du cinéma*. 5 vols. Paris: Èditions Universitaires.

Moon, Krystyn R. 2012. "The Creation of *The Red Lantern*: American Orientalism and the Beginning of the 20th Century." In *To Dazzle Eye and to Stir the Heart: The Red*

Lantern, Nazimova, and the Boxer Rebellion. ed. Stef Franck. 45–58. Brussels: Royal
Belgian Film Archive.

Moore, Paul. 2013. "Marie Dressler." In *Women Film Pioneers Project.* eds. Jane M. Gaines,
Radha Vatsal, and Monica Dall'Asta. New York: Center for Digital Research and Scholarship, Columbia University Libraries. https://wfpp.cdrs.columbia.edu/pioneer/ccp
-marie-dressler/.

Morey, Anne. 1997. "'Have You the Power?'": The Palmer Photoplay Corporation and the
Film Viewer/Author in the 1920s," *Film History* 9: 300–319.

———. 2003. *Hollywood Outsiders: The Adaptation of the Film Industry, 1913–1934.* Minneapolis: University of Minnesota Press.

———. 2010. "A New Eroticism or Merely a New Woman? Cecil B. DeMille's Adaptation of
Alice Duer Miller's *Manslaughter.*" *Framework* 51.2 (Fall): 388–403.

———. 2013. "School of Scandal: Alice Duer Miller, Scandal, and the New Woman." In *Researching Women in Silent Cinema: New Findings and Perspectives.* eds. Monica Dall'Asta
and Victoria Duckett. 163–175. Bologna: University of Bologna. http://wss2013.arts
.unimelb.edu.au/wp-content/uploads/2013/10/0_RESEARCHING-WOMEN_SILENT
-CINEMA.pdf.

Morgan, Kyna. 2013a. "Tressie Souders." In *Women Film Pioneers Project.* eds. Jane M. Gaines,
Radha Vatsal, and Monica Dall'Asta. New York: Center for Digital Research and Scholarship, Columbia University Libraries. https://wfpp.cdrs.columbia.edu/pioneer/tressie
-souders-2/.

———. 2013b. "Maria P. Williams." In *Women Film Pioneers Project.* eds. Jane M. Gaines,
Radha Vatsal, and Monica Dall'Asta. New York: Center for Digital Research and Scholarship, Columbia University Libraries. https://wfpp.cdrs.columbia.edu/pioneer/maria
-p-williams-2/.

Morgan, Kyna, and Aimee Dixon. 2013. "African American Women in the Silent Film Industry." In *Women Film Pioneers Project.* eds. Jane M. Gaines, Radha Vatsal, and Monica
Dall'Asta. New York: Center for Digital Research and Scholarship, Columbia University
Libraries. https://wfpp.cdrs.columbia.edu/essay/african-american-women-in-the-silent
-film-industry/.

Morgan, Sue. 2006. "Introduction: Writing Feminist History: Theoretical Debates and
Critical Practices." In *The Feminist History Reader.* ed. Sue Morgan. 1–48. New York:
Routledge.

Morgenson, Gretchen. 2015. "Why Putting a Number to C.E.O. Pay Might Bring Change."
New York Times (August 6): BU1. https://www.nytimes.com/2015/08/09/business/why
-putting-a-number-to-ceo-pay-might-bring-change.html.

Morin, Edgar. 2005 [1956]. *Cinema, or The Imaginary Man.* trans. Lorraine Mortimer. Minneapolis: University of Minnesota Press.

Mukherjee, Debashree. 2015. "Scandalous Evidence: Looking for the Bombay Film Actress in
an Absent Archive (1930s-1940s)." In *Doing Women's Film History: Reframing Cinemas,
Past and Future.* eds. Christine Gledhill and Julia Knight. 29–41. Urbana: University
of Illinois Press.

Mulvey, Laura. 1975. "Visual Pleasure and Narrative Cinema," *Screen* 16.3 (Autumn): 6–18.

———. 1987. "Notes on Sirk and Melodrama." In *Home Is Where the Heart Is.* ed. Christine
Gledhill. 75–79. London: British Film Institute.

———. 1989. "British Feminist Film Theory's Female Spectators: Presence and Absence." *Camera Obscura* 20–21: 69–81.

———. 2004a. "Passing Time: Reflections on Cinema from a New Technological Age." *Screen* 45.2: 142–155.

———. 2004b. "Looking at the Past from the Present: Rethinking Feminist Film Theory of the 1970s." *Signs* 30.1: 1286–1292.

———. 2006. *Death 24 x a Second: Stillness and the Moving Image*. London: Reaktion Books.

Muñoz, José Esteban. 2009. *Cruising Utopia: The Then and There of Queer Futurity*. New York: New York University Press.

Munslow, Alun. 2003. *The New History*. Harlow, England: Pearson.

———. 2006. *Deconstructing History*. New York: Routledge.

———. 2009. "Afterword." Keith Jenkins. *At the Limits of History: Essays on Theory and Practice*. 315–321. New York: Routledge.

Musser, Charles. 1990. *The Emergence of Cinema: The American Screen to 1907*. Berkeley: University of California Press.

———. 1991. *Before the Nickelodeon: Edwin S. Porter and the Edison Manufacturing Company*. Berkeley: University of California Press.

———. 1994. "Rethinking Early Cinema: The Cinema of Attractions and Narrativity." *Yale Journal of Criticism* 7.2 (Fall): 203–232.

———. 1996. "Pre-Classical American Cinema: It's Changing Modes of Production." In *Silent Film*. ed. Richard Abel. 85–108. New Brunswick, N.J.: Rutgers University Press.

———. 2004. "Historiographic Method and the Study of Early Cinema." Cinema Journal 44.1: 101–107.

———. 2009a. "1896–1897: Movies and the Beginnings of Cinema." In *American Cinema. 1890–1909: Themes and Variations*. eds. André Gaudreault and Tom Gunning. 45–65. New Brunswick, N.J.: Rutgers University Press.

———. 2009b. "The Wages of Feminism: Alice Guy Blaché and Her Late Feature Films." In *Alice Guy Blaché: Cinema Pioneer*. ed. Joan Simon. 81–100. New Haven: Yale University Press.

Musser, Charles, and Robert Sklar. 1990. Introduction. In *Resisting Images Essays on Cinema and History*. eds. Charles Musser and Robert Sklar. 3–11. Philadelphia: Temple University Press.

Neale, Steve. 1986. "Melodrama and Tears." *Screen*. 27.6 (November/December): 6–22.

———. 1993. "Melo Talk: On the Meaning and Use of the Term 'Melodrama' in the American Trade Press." *The Velvet Light Trap* 32 (Fall): 66–89.

Neely, Hugh. 2010. "A Studio of Her Own: Women Producers at First National, 1917–1927." Unpublished paper delivered at Women and the Silent Screen V., July, Bologna, Italy.

———. 2013. "Anita Stewart." In *Women Film Pioneers Project*. eds. Jane M. Gaines, Radha Vatsal, and Monica Dall'Asta. New York: Center for Digital Research and Scholarship, Columbia University Libraries. https://wfpp.cdrs.columbia.edu/pioneer/ccp-anita-stewart/.

Negra, Diane, and Yvonne Tasker. 2007. *Interrogating Post-Feminism: Gender and the Politics of Popular Culture*. Durham: Duke University Press.

Nichols, Bill. 1991. *Representing Reality*. Bloomington: Indiana University Press.

Nochlin, Linda. 1973. "Why Have There Been No Great Women Artists?" In *Art and Sexual Politics: Why Have There Been No Great Women Artists?* eds. Thomas B. Hess and Elizabeth C. Baker. 1–43. New York: Collier.

Norden, Martin F. 1995. "Women in the Early Film Industry." In *The Studio System*. ed. Janet Staiger. 187–199. New Brunswick, N.J.: Rutgers University Press. Reprinted *Wide Angle*.

———. 2014. "Listening for Lois: Reconstructing the Public Utterances of Lois Weber." Unpublished paper. "Doing Women's Film History II." University of East Anglia, Norwich, United Kingdom (April 2014).

Nowell-Smith, Geoffrey. 1987. "Minnelli and Melodrama." In *Home Is Where the Heart Is*. ed. Christine Gledhill. 70–74. London: British Film Institute.

Olenina, Ana. 2013. "Aleksandra Khokhlova." In *Women Film Pioneers Project*. eds. Jane M. Gaines, Radha Vatsal, and Monica Dall'Asta. New York: Center for Digital Research and Scholarship, Columbia University Libraries. https://wfpp.cdrs.columbia.edu/pioneer/aleksandra-khokhlova-2/.

Olsen, Niklas. 2012. *History in the Plural: An Introduction to the Work of Reinhart Koselleck*. New York: Berghahn Books.

Olsson, Jan. 2008. *Los Angeles before Hollywood: Journalism and American Film Culture, 1905–1915*. Stockholm: National Library of Sweden.

Orr, Linda. 1990. *Headless History: Nineteenth-Century French Historiography of the Revolution*. Ithaca: Cornell University Press.

Otto, Elizabeth, and Vanessa Rocco, eds. 2011. *The New Woman International*. Ann Arbor: University of Michigan Press.

Parikka, Jussi. 2012. *What Is Media Archaeology?* Malden, Mass.: Polity Press.

Paul, Herman. 2009. "Hayden White and the Crisis of Historicism." In *Re-figuring Hayden White*. eds. Frank Ankersmit, Ewa Domańska, and Hans Kellner. 54–73. Stanford: Stanford University Press.

Pearson, Keith Ansell. 1999. *Germinal Life: The Difference and Repetition of Deleuze*. New York: Routledge.

Peary, Gerald. 1977. "Alice Guy Blaché: Czarina of the Silent Screen." In *Women and the Cinema: A Critical Anthology*. eds. Karyn Kay and Gerald Peary. 139–145. New York: Dutton.

Peirce, Charles Sanders. 1955. *Philosophical Writings of Peirce*. ed. Justus Buchler. New York: Dover.

Peterson, Christina. 2013. "'The Most Assassinated Woman in the World': Pearl White and the First Avant-Garde." In *Exporting Perilous Pauline: Pearl White and the Serial Film Craze*. ed. Marina Dahlquist. 99–159. Urbana: University of Illinois Press.

———. 2016. "Mary Murillo." In *Women Film Pioneers Project*. eds. Jane M. Gaines, Radha Vatsal, and Monica Dall'Asta. New York: Center for Digital Research and Scholarship, Columbia University Libraries. https://wfpp.cdrs.columbia.edu/pioneer/mary-murillo/.

Petro, Patrice. 2004. "Reflections on Feminist Film Studies, Early and Late." *Signs* 30.1: 1272–1278.

Pierce, David. 1997. "The Legion of the Condemned—Why American Silent Films Perished." *Film History* 9: 5–22.

———. 2007. "Forgotten Faces: Why Some of Our Cinema Heritage Is Part of the Public Domain." *Film History* 19: 125–143.

———. 2013. *The Survival of American Silent Feature Films: 1912–1929*. Washington, D.C.: Council on Library and Information Resources and the Library of Congress.

Pollock, Griselda. 1999. *Differencing the Canon. Feminist Desire and the Writing of Art's Histories*. New York: Routledge.

Prouty, Olive Higgins. 2015 [1923]. *Stella Dallas*. New York: The Feminist Press at the City University of New York.

Quart, Barbara. 1988. *Women Directors: The Emergence of a New Cinema*. New York: Praeger.

Rabinowitz, Lauren. 1998. *For the Love of Pleasure: Women, Movies, and Culture in Turn-of-the-Century Chicago*. New Brunswick, N.J.: Rutgers University Press.

———. 2006. "The Future of Feminism and Film History." *Camera Obscura* 61: 39–44.

Rahman, Magdi Abdel. 2002. "Al-Dahaia—An Egyptian Case History in the Restoration of Nitrate Film." In *This Film Is Dangerous: A Celebration of Nitrate Film*. ed. Roger Smither. 369–374. London: Fédération Internationale des Archives du Film.

Ramsaye, Terry. 1986 [1926]. *A Million and One Nights*. New York: Simon and Schuster.

Rancière, Jacques. 1994. *The Names of History: On the Poetics of Knowledge*. trans. Hassan Melehy. Minneapolis: University of Minnesota Press.

———. 2006. *Film Fables*. trans. Emiliano Battista. Oxford: Berg.

Rapf, Joanna E. 2013. "Fay Tincher." In *Women Film Pioneers Project*. eds. Jane M. Gaines, Radha Vatsal, and Monica Dall'Asta. New York: Center for Digital Research and Scholarship, Columbia University Libraries. https://wfpp.cdrs.columbia.edu/pioneer/ccp-fay-tincher/.

Rich, Adrienne. 1979. "Disloyal to Civilization: Feminism, Racism, Gynephobia." In *On Lies, Secrets, and Silence*. 275–310. New York: W. W. Norton.

Rich, B. Ruby. 1998. *Chick Flicks: Theories and Memories of the Feminist Film Movement*. Durham: Duke University Press.

———. 2013. "The Confidence Game." *Camera Obscura* 82: 157–165.

———. 2014. *New Queer Cinema*. Durham: Duke University Press.

Ricoeur, Paul. 1985. *Time and Narrative Vol. 3*. trans. Kathleen Blamey and David Pellauer. Chicago: University of Chicago Press.

———. 2004. *Memory, History, Forgetting*. trans. Kathleen Blamey and David Pellauer. Chicago: University of Chicago Press.

Riley, Denise. 2003 [1988]. *"Am I That Name?" Feminism and the Category of "Women" in History*. Minneapolis: University of Minnesota Press.

———. 2006 [1988]. "Does Sex Have a History?" In *The Feminist History Reader*. ed. Sue Morgan. 149–159. New York: Routledge.

Roberts, Geoffrey. 2001a. "Introduction: The History and Narrative Debate, 1960–2000." In *The History and Narrative Reader*. ed. Geoffrey Roberts. 1–21. New York: Routledge.

———, ed. 2001b. *The History and Narrative Reader*. New York: Routledge.

Roberts, Mary Louise. 2008. "Making the Modern French Girl." In *The Modern Girl Around the World*. eds. Alys Eve Weinbaum et al. The Modern Girl around the World Research Group. 77–95. Durham: Duke University Press.

Rodgers, Daniel T. 1990. "Before Postmodernism." *Reviews in American History* 18: 77–81.

Rodowick, D. N. 1984. "Historical Knowing in Film." *Iris* 2.2: 2–4.

———. 2007. *The Virtual Life of Film*. Cambridge: Harvard University Press.

Rosen, Marjorie. 1973. *Popcorn Venus*. New York: Coward, McCann and Geoghegan.

Rosen, Phillip. 2001. *Change Mummified: Cinema, Historicity, Theory*. Minneapolis: University of Minnesota Press.

Rosenstone, Robert A. 1996. "The Future of the Past: Film and the Beginnings of Postmodern History." In *The Persistence of History*. ed. Vivian Sobchack. 201–218. New York: Routledge.

Ross, Sara. 2013. "Tsuru Aoki." In *Women Film Pioneers Project*. eds. Jane M. Gaines, Radha Vatsal, and Monica Dall'Asta. New York: Center for Digital Research and Scholarship, Columbia University Libraries. https://wfpp.cdrs.columbia.edu/pioneer/ccp-tsuru -aoki/.

Rowbotham, Sheila. 1973. *Hidden from History: 300 Years of Women's Oppression and the Fight against It*. London: Pluto Press.

Rubin, Gayle S. 2011 [1975]. "The Traffic in Women: Notes on the 'Political Economy' of Sex." In *Deviations*. 3365. Durham: Duke University Press.

Runia, Eelco. 2006. "Presence." *History and Theory* 45 (February): 1–26.

———. 2014. *Moved by the Past: Discontinuity and Historical Mutation*. New York: Columbia University Press.

Sadoul, Georges. 1948. *Histoire générale du cinéma, vol. 2: Les Pioneers du cinéma. 1897–1909*. 3rd ed. Paris: Denoël.

———. 1946. *Histoire générale du cinema*. Paris: Denoël.

Salerno, Abigail. 2013. "Josephine Lovett." In *Women Film Pioneers Project*. eds. Jane M. Gaines, Radha Vatsal, and Monica Dall'Asta. New York: Center for Digital Research and Scholarship, Columbia University Libraries. https://wfpp.cdrs.columbia.edu/pioneer/ccp-josephine -lovett/.

Salt, Barry. 1983. *Film Style and Technology: History and Analysis*. London: Starwood.

Sato, Tado. 1982. *Currents in Japanese Cinema*. trans. Gregory Barrett. Tokyo: Kodansha International.

Schiff, Stacy. 2010. *Cleopatra: A Life*. New York: Little, Brown and Company.

Schlüpmann, Heide. 1994. "Re-reading Nietzsche through Kracauer: Towards a Feminist Perspective on Film History." *Film History* 6: 80–92.

———. 2010. *The Uncanniness of the Gaze: The Drama of Early German Cinema*. trans. Ingrid Pollman. Champaign-Urbana: University of Illinois Press.

———. 2012. "27 May 1911: Asta Nielsen Secures Unprecedented Artistic Control." In *A New History of German Cinema*. eds. Jennifer M. Kapczynski and Michael D. Richardson. 44–50. Rochester: Camden House.

———. 2013. "An Alliance between History and Theory." In *Researching Women in Silent Cinema: New Findings and Perspectives*. eds. Monica Dall'Asta and Victoria Duckett. 13–26. Bologna: University of Bologna.

Schmidt, Christel. 2003. "Preserving Pickford: The Mary Pickford Collection and the Library of Congress." *The Moving Image* 3.1: 59–81.

———, ed. 2012. *Mary Pickford: Queen of the Movies*. Washington, D.C.: Library of Congress and University of Kentucky Press.

Schmidt, Jackson. 1982. "On the Road to MGM: A History of Metro Pictures Corporation, 1915–1920." *The Velvet Light Trap* 19: 46–52.

Scott, Joan Wallach. 1986. "Gender: A Useful Category of Historical Analysis." *American Historical Review* 91.5 (December): 1053–1075.

———. 1996a. "Introduction." In *Feminism and History*. ed. Joan Scott. 1–13. New York: Oxford University Press.

———, ed. 1996b. *Feminism and History*. New York: Oxford University Press.

———. 1999 [1988]. *Gender and the Politics of History*. New York: Columbia University Press.

———. 2004. "After History." In *The Nature of History Reader*. eds. Keith Jenkins and Alun Munslow. 260–270. London: Routledge.

———. 2006. "Feminism's History." In *The Feminist History Reader*. ed. Sue Morgan. 388–398. London: Routledge.

———. 2007. "History-writing as Critique." In *Manifestoes for History*. eds. Keith Jenkins, Sue Morgan, and Alun Munslow. 19–38. New York: Routledge.

———. 2008a. "Unanswered Questions." In *American Historical Review Forum*: "Revisiting Gender: A Useful Category of Historical Analysis." *American Historical Review* 113.5 (December): 1422–1430.

———, ed. 2008b. *Women's Studies on the Edge*. Durham: Duke University Press.

———. 2009. "Finding Critical History." In *Becoming Historians*. eds. James Banner and John Gillis. 26–53. Chicago: University of Chicago Press.

———. 2011. *The Fantasy of Feminist History*. Durham: Duke University Press.

Sebald, W. G. 2011 [2001]. *Austerlitz*. New York: Modern Library.

Sennett, Richard, and Jonathan Cobb. 1973. *The Hidden Injuries of Class*. New York: Vintage Books.

Shipman, Nell. 1987. *The Silent Screen and My Talking Heart*. Boise: Boise State University.

Shoes press kit. 2017. Milestone Films.

Simanowski, Roberto. 2016. *Data Love: The Seduction and Betrayal of Digital Technologies*. New York: Columbia University Press.

Simon, Joan, ed. 2009a. *Alice Guy Blaché: Cinema Pioneer*. New Haven: Yale University Press.

———. 2009b. "The Great Adventure: Alice Guy Blaché, Cinema Pioneer." In *Alice Guy Blaché: Cinema Pioneer*. ed. Joan Simon. 1–32. New Haven: Yale University Press.

Singer, Ben. 1996. "Female Power in Serial-Queen Melodrama: The Etiology of an Anomaly." In *Silent Film*. ed. Richard Abel. 163–193. New Brunswick, N.J.: Rutgers University Press.

———. 2001. *Melodrama and Modernity: Early Sensational Cinema and Its Context*. New York: Columbia University Press.

Sklar, Robert. 1990 [1988]. "Oh! Althusser! Historiography and the Rise of Cinema." In *Resisting Images Essays on Cinema and History*. eds. Charles Musser and Robert Sklar. 12–35. Philadelphia: Temple University Press.

Slater, Thomas J. 2002. "June Mathis: A Woman Who Spoke through Silents." *American Silent Film: Discovering Marginalized Voices*. eds. Greg Bachman and Thomas J. Slater. 201–216. Carbondale: Southern Illinois University Press. Reprint of "June Mathis: A Woman Who Spoke through Silents." *Griffithiana* 18.53 (May 1995): 133–155.

———. 2008. "June Mathis's *The Legion of Death* (1918): Melodrama and the Realities of Women in World War I." *Women's Studies: An Interdisciplinary Journal* (October): 833–844.

———. 2010. "June Mathis's Valentino Scripts: Images of Male 'Becoming' after the Great War." *Cinema Journal* 50.1 (Fall): 99–120.

———. 2013. "Marion Fairfax." In *Women Film Pioneers Project*. eds. Jane M. Gaines, Radha Vatsal, and Monica Dall'Asta. New York: Center for Digital Research and Scholarship, Columbia University Libraries. https://wfpp.cdrs.columbia.edu/pioneer/ccp-marion-fairfax/.

Slide, Anthony. 1977. *Early Women Directors*. South Brunswick: A. S. Barnes and Co.

———. 1978. *Aspects of American Film History Prior to 1920*. Metuchen, N.J.: Scarecrow Press.

———. 1987. *The Big V: A History of the Vitagraph Company*. Metuchen, N.J.: Scarecrow Press.

———. 1992. *Nitrate Won't Wait*. Jefferson, N.C.: McFarland.

———. 1996a. *The Silent Feminists: America's First Women Directors*. Lanham, Md.: Scarecrow Press.

———, ed. 1996b. *The Memoirs of Alice Guy Blaché*. trans. Roberta and Simone Blaché. Lanham, Md.: Scarecrow Press.

———. 1998. *The Historical Dictionary of the American Film Industry*. Lanham, Md.: Scarecrow Press.

———. 2012a. "Early Women Filmmakers: The Real Numbers." *Film History* 24.1: 114–121.

———. 2012b. *Hollywood Unknowns: A History of Extras, Bit Players, and Stand-Ins*. Jackson: University of Mississippi Press.

Smith, Sharon. 1973. "Women Who Make Movies." *Women and Film* 1.3/4: 77–90. Reprinted in the following: http://ejumpcut.org/archive/WomenAndFilm/WF3-4/77.

———. 1974. *Women Who Make Movies*. New York: Hopkinson and Blake.

Smith, Stacy L., Marc Choueiti, Katherine Pieper. 2015. "Inequality in 800 Popular Films: Examining Portrayals of Gender, Race/Ethnicity, LGBT, and Disability from 2007 to 2015." Media, Diversity & Social Change Initiative, USC Annenberg School for Communication and Journalism. http://annenberg.usc.edu/pages/~/media/MDSCI/Dr%20Stacy%20L%20Smith%20Inequality%20in%20800%20Films%20FINAL.ashx.

Smither, Roger, ed. 2002. *This Film Is Dangerous: A Celebration of Nitrate Film*. London: Federation Internationale des Archives du Film.

Smoodin, Eric. 2007. "Introduction: The History of Film History." In *Looking Past the Screen: Case Studies in American Film History and Method*. eds. Jon Lewis and Eric Smoodin. 1–33. Durham: Duke University Press.

Snitow, Ann. 1996. "A Gender Diary." In *Feminism and History*. ed. Joan Wallach Scott. 505–544. New York: Oxford University Press.

———. 2016. *The Feminism of Uncertainty*. Durham: Duke University.

Sobchack, Vivian. 1996. "Introduction: History Happens." In *The Persistence of History: Cinema, Television, and the Modern Event*. ed. Vivian Sobchack. 4–20. New York: Routledge/American Film Institute.

———. 1997. "The Insistent Fringe: Moving Images and the Palimpsest of Historical Consciousness." *History and Theory: Studies in the Philosophy of History* 36.4: 4–20.

———. 2000. "What Is Film History? Or, the Riddle of the Sphinxes." In *Reinventing Film Studies*. eds. Christine Gledhill and Linda Williams. 300–315. London: Arnold.

———. 2011. "Afterword: Media Archaeology and Re-presencing the Past." eds. Erkki Huhtamo and Jussi Parikka. *Media Archaeology: Approaches, Applications, and Implications*. 323–333. Berkeley: University of California Press.

Somaini, Antonio. 2016. "Eisenstein's Notes as Media Archaeology," In *Sergei Eisenstein, The Eisenstein Cabinet*. eds. Naum Klejman and Antonio Somaini. 19–105. Amsterdam: University of Amsterdam Press.

Spehr, Paul. 1977. *The Movies Begin: Making Movies in New Jersey, 1887–1920*. Newark, N.J.: The Newark Museum.

———. 1996. *American Film Personnel and Company Credits, 1908–1920: Filmographies Reordered by Authoritative Organizational and Personal Names from Lauritzen and Lundquist's American Film-Index*. Jefferson, N.C.: McFarland.

———. 2008. *The Man Who Made Movies: W. K. L. Dickson*. New Barnet, Herts: John Libbey.

Spiers, Aurore. 2014. "Looking for Berthe Dagmar: A Case Study of the Mythology of the *Femme Nouvelle* in France." Unpublished MA thesis, Columbia University.

Spivak, Gayatri. 1985. "Three Women's Texts and a Critique of Imperialism." *Critical Inquiry* 21.1 (Autumn): 243–261.

———. 1993. *Outside in the Teaching Machine*. New York: Routledge.

———. 1999. *A Critique of Postcolonial Reason*. Cambridge: Harvard University Press.

Staiger, Janet. 1985. "The Hollywood Mode of Production to 1930." In *The Classical Hollywood Cinema: Film Style and Mode of Production to 1960*. eds. David Bordwell, Janet Staiger, and Kristin Thompson. 243–261. New York: Columbia University Press.

———. 1995. *Bad Women: Regulating Sexuality in Early American Cinema*. Minneapolis: University of Minnesota Press.

———. 2013. "'Because I Am a Woman': Thinking Identity and Agency for Historiography." *Film History* 25.1–2: 205–214.

Stamp, Shelley. 2000. *Movie-Struck Girls: Women and Motion Picture Culture after the Nickelodeon*. Princeton, N.J.: Princeton University Press.

———. 2004. "Lois Weber, Progressive Cinema and the Fate of 'The Work-A-Day Girl' in *Shoes*." *Camera Obscura* 56: 140–169.

———. 2006. "Presenting the Smalleys, 'Collaborators in Authorship and Direction.'" *Film History* 18.2: 119–128.

———. 2010b. "'Exit Flapper, Enter Woman': Or Lois Weber in Jazz Age Hollywood." *Framework* 51.2 (Fall): 358–387.

———. 2013a. Keynote lecture, "Feminist Media Historiography and the Work Ahead" (October). University of Melbourne, Australia.

———. 2013b. "Lois Weber." In *Women Film Pioneers Project*. eds. Jane M. Gaines, Radha Vatsal, and Monica Dall'Asta. New York: Center for Digital Research and Scholarship, Columbia University Libraries. https://wfpp.cdrs.columbia.edu/pioneer/ccp-lois-weber/.

———. 2015. *Lois Weber in Early Hollywood*. Berkeley: University of California Press.

Steedman, Carolyn. 1992. *Past Tenses: Essays on Writing, Autobiography and History*. London: Rivers Oram Press.

———. 2002. *Dust: The Archive and Cultural History*. New Brunswick, N.J.: Rutgers University Press.

Stein, Gertrude. 1993 [1935]. *Narration: Four Lectures by Gertrude Stein*. Chicago: University of Chicago Press.

Sterne, Jonathan. 2012. *MP3: The Meaning of a Format*. Durham: Duke University Press.

Strauven, Wanda, ed. 2006. *The Cinema of Attractions Reloaded*. Amsterdam: Amsterdam University Press.

———. 2013. "Media Archaeology: Where Film History, Media Art, and New Media (Can) Meet." *Preserving and Exhibiting Media Art: Challenges and Perspectives*. eds. Julia Noodegraaf et al. 68–73. Amsterdam: University of Amsterdam Press.

Streible, Dan. 2013. "Moving Image History and the F-Word: Or, 'Digital Film' Is an Oxymoron." *Film History* 25.1–2: 227–235.

Studlar, Gaylyn. 1996. *This Mad Masquerade: Stardom and Masculinity in the Jazz Age*. New York: Columbia University Press.

Sturtevant, Victoria. 2013. "Sarah Y. Mason." In *Women Film Pioneers Project*. eds. Jane M. Gaines, Radha Vatsal, and Monica Dall'Asta. New York: Center for Digital Research and Scholarship, Columbia University Libraries. https://wfpp.cdrs.columbia.edu/pioneer/ccp-sarah-y-mason/.

Talbot, Frederick A. 1912. *Moving Pictures: How They Are Made and Worked*. Rev. ed. Philadelphia: J. B. Lippincott.

Tasker, Yvonne, and Diane Negra. 2007. *Interrogating Post-Feminism: Gender and the Politics of Popular Culture*. Durham: Duke University Press.

Taves, Brian. 2013. "Bradley King." In *Women Film Pioneers Project*. eds. Jane M. Gaines, Radha Vatsal, and Monica Dall'Asta. New York: Center for Digital Research and Scholarship, Columbia University Libraries. https://wfpp.cdrs.columbia.edu/pioneer/ccp-bradley-king/.

Thanhouser, Ned. 2016. "All in the Family: The Thanhouser Studio." In *Women Film Pioneers Project*. eds. Jane M. Gaines, Radha Vatsal, and Monica Dall'Asta. New York: Center for Digital Research and Scholarship, Columbia University Libraries. https://wfpp.cdrs.columbia.edu/essay/all-in-the-family-the-thanhouser-studio/.

Thomas, Rosie. 2013. "Not Quite (Pearl) White: Fearless Nadia, Queen of the Stunts." In *Exporting Pauline: Pearl White and the Serial Film Craze*. 160–186. Urbana: University of Illinois Press.

Thompson, E. P. 1966. *The Making of the English Working Class*. New York: Vintage.

Thompson, Kristin. 1985. *Exporting Entertainment: America in the World Film Market, 1907–1934*. London: British Film Institute Publishing.

———. 1998. "Narrative Structure in Early Classical Cinema." In *Celebrating 1895: The Centenary of Cinema*. ed. John Fullerton. 225–237. London: John Libbey.

Thompson, Peter, and Slavoj Zizek, eds. 2013. *The Privatization of Hope: Ernst Bloch and the Future of Utopia*. Durham: Duke University Press.

Tomadjoglou, Kimberly. 2009. "Wonderment-Seeing the World through the Eyes of Alice Guy Blaché." In *Alice Guy Blaché: Cinema Pioneer*. ed. Joan Simon. 101–112. New Haven: Yale University Press.

———. 2013. "Elvira Notari." In *Women Film Pioneers Project*. eds. Jane M. Gaines, Radha Vatsal, and Monica Dall'Asta. New York: Center for Digital Research and Scholarship, Columbia University Libraries. https://wfpp.cdrs.columbia.edu/pioneer/ccp-elvira-notari/.

———. 2015. "Alice Guy's Great Cinematic Adventure." In *Doing Women's Film History: Reframing Cinemas, Past and Future*. eds. Christine Gledhill and Julia Knight. 95–109. Urbana: University of Illinois Press.

Torres Saint Martín, Patricia, and Joanne Hershfeld. 2013. "Writing the History of Latin American Women in the Silent Film Industry." In *Women Film Pioneers Project*. eds. Jane M. Gaines, Radha Vatsal, and Monica Dall'Asta. New York: Center for Digital Research and Scholarship, Columbia University Libraries. https://wfpp.cdrs.columbia.edu/essay/writing-the-history-of-latin-american-women-working-in-the-silent-film-industry/.

Tribe, Keith. 1977/1978. "History and the Production of Memories." *Screen* 18.4 (Winter): 9–22.

———. 2004. "Translator's Introduction." In *Futures Past: On the Semantics of Historical Time*. trans. Keith Tribe. vi–xx. New York: Columbia University Press.

Trouillot, Michel-Rolph. 1995. *Silencing the Past: Power and the Production of History*. Boston: Beacon Press.

Tsivian, Yuri. 1989. "Some Preparatory Remarks on Russian Cinema." In *Silent Witnesses: Russian Films 1908–1919*. eds. Paolo Cherchi Usai et al. 24–40. London: British Film Institute.

———. 1996. "Between the Old and the New: Soviet Film Culture in 1918–1924," *Griffithiana* 55/56: 39–41.

———. 2008. "'What Is Cinema?' An Agnostic Answer." *Critical Inquiry* 34.4 (Summer): 754–776.

Valentine, David. 2007. *Imagining Transgender: An Ethnography of a Category*. Durham: Duke University Press.

Vasey, Ruth. 1997. *The World According to Hollywood, 1919–1939*. Exeter: University of Exeter Press.

Vattimo, Gianni. 2013. "From the Problem of Evil to Hermeneutic Philosophy of History: For Hayden White." In *Philosophy of History after Hayden White*. ed. Robert Doran. 201–207. London: Bloomsbury.

Verhoeven, Deb. 2013. "Mrs. Señora Spencer." In *Women Film Pioneers Project*. eds. Jane M. Gaines, Radha Vatsal, and Monica Dall'Asta. New York: Center for Digital Research and Scholarship, Columbia University Libraries. https://wfpp.cdrs.columbia.edu/pioneer/ccp-senora-spencer/.

Veronesi, Micaela. 2010. "A Woman Wishes to 'Make A New World.' Umanità and Elvira Giallanella." In *Not So Silent: Women in Cinema before Sound*. eds. Astrid Söderberg Widdig and Sofia Bull. 67–79. Stockholm: Acta Universitatis Stockholmiensis.

———. 2013. "Elvira Giallanella." In *Women Film Pioneers Project*. eds. Jane M. Gaines, Radha Vatsal, and Monica Dall'Asta. New York: Center for Digital Research and Scholarship, Columbia University Libraries. https://wfpp.cdrs.columbia.edu/pioneer/elvira-giallanella/.

Von Ranke, Leopold. 1973. *The Theory and Practice of History*. eds. and trans. Georg G. Iggers and Konrad von Moltke. Indianapolis: Bobbs-Merrill.

Wagenknecht, Edward. 1962. *Movies in the Age of Innocence*. Norman: University of Oklahoma Press.

Wagner, Kristen Anderson. 2013. "Lillian Case Russell." In *Women Film Pioneers Project*. eds. Jane M. Gaines, Radha Vatsal, and Monica Dall'Asta. New York: Center for Digital Research and Scholarship, Columbia University Libraries. https://wfpp.cdrs.columbia.edu/pioneer/ccp-lillian-case-russell/.

Walker, Janet. 2013. "Margery Wilson." In *Women Film Pioneers Project*. eds. Jane M. Gaines, Radha Vatsal, and Monica Dall'Asta. New York: Center for Digital Research and Scholarship, Columbia University Libraries. https://wfpp.cdrs.columbia.edu/pioneer/ccp-margery-wilson/.

Walker, Janet, and Diane Waldman. 1999. Introduction. In *Feminism and Documentary*. eds. Janet Walker and Diane Waldman. 1–35. Minneapolis: University of Minnesota Press.

Walker, Michael. 1982. "Melodrama and the American Cinema." *Movie* 29/30: 2–38.

Wallace, Michelle. 1990. *Invisibility Blues*. London: Verso.

Wang, Lingzhen. 2011. "Introduction: Transnational Feminist Reconfiguration of Film Discourse and Women's Cinema." In *Chinese Women's Cinema: Transnational Contexts*. ed. Lingzhen Wang. 1–43. New York: Columbia University Press.

Warhol, Andy. 1975. *The Philosophy of Andy Warhol*. New York: Harcourt, Brace, Jovanovich.

Warren, Shilyh. 2008. "By, For, and About: The 'Real" Problem in the Feminist Film Movement," *Mediascape* (Fall). http: www.tft.ucla.edu/mediacape/Fall08.

——. 2012. "Consciousness-raising and Difference in *The Woman's Film* (1971) and *Self-Health* (1974)." *Jump Cut* 54 (Fall). http://www.jumpcut.

Wasko, Janet. 1982. *Movies and Money: Financing the American Film Industry*. New Jersey: Ablex Publishing Co.

——. 2008. "The Hollywood Industry Paradigm." In *The Sage Handbook of Film Studies*. eds. James Donald and Michael Renov. 287–311. Los Angeles: Sage.

Watt, Ian P. 1957. *The Rise of the Novel: Studies in Defoe, Richardson, and Fielding*. Berkeley: University of California Press.

Wei, Louisa. 2011. "Women's Trajectories in Chinese and Japanese Cinemas: A Chronological Overview." In *dekalog: On East Asian Filmmakers*. ed. Kate E. Taylor. 13–44. Brighton: Wallflower Press.

——. 2013a. "Esther Eng." In *Women Film Pioneers Project*. eds. Jane M. Gaines, Radha Vatsal, and Monica Dall'Asta. New York: Center for Digital Research and Scholarship, Columbia University Libraries. https://wfpp.cdrs.columbia.edu/pioneer/pu-shunqing. https://wfpp.cdrs.columbia.edu/pioneer/esther-eng.

——. 2013b. "Pu Shunqing." In *Women Film Pioneers Project*. eds. Jane M. Gaines, Radha Vatsal, and Monica Dall'Asta. New York: Center for Digital Research and Scholarship, Columbia University Libraries. https://wfpp.cdrs.columbia.edu/pioneer/.

Weinbaum, Alys Eve, et al. 2008. "The Modern Girl as Heuristic Device: Collaboration, Connective Comparison, Multidirectional Citation." In *The Modern Girl around the World*. eds. The Modern Girl Around the World Research Group. 1–24. Durham: Duke University Press.

Welbon, Yvonne. 2001. "Sisters in Cinema: Case Studies of Three First-Time Achievements Made by African American Women Feature Film Directors in the 1990s." Unpublished PhD dissertation, Northwestern University.

Welsch, Tricia. 2013. *Gloria Swanson: Ready for Her Close-Up*. Jackson: University Press of Mississippi.

Wexman, Virginia. 1995. "Film as Art and Filmmakers as Artists: 100 Years." *Arachné* 2.2: 265–278.

———. 2013. "June Mathis." In *Women Film Pioneers Project*. eds. Jane M. Gaines, Radha Vat-sal, and Monica Dall'Asta. New York: Center for Digital Research and Scholarship, Columbia University Libraries. https://wfpp.cdrs.columbia.edu/pioneer/ccp-june-mathis/.

Wheery, Edith. 1911. *The Red Lantern: Being the Story of the Goddess of the Red Lantern Light*. New York: John Lane Company.

White, Hayden. 1973. *Metahistory: The Historical Imagination in Nineteenth Century Europe*. Baltimore: Johns Hopkins University Press.

———. 1987. *The Content of the Form: Narrative Discourse and Historical Representation*. Baltimore: Johns Hopkins Press.

———. 1992. "Historical Emplotment and the Problem of Truth." In *Probing the Limits of Representation*. ed. S. Friendlander. 37–53. Berkeley: University of California Press.

———. 1999. *Figural Realism: Studies in the Mimesis Effect*. Baltimore: Johns Hopkins Press.

———. 2001. "The Historical Text as Literary Artifact." In *The History and Narrative Reader*. ed. Geoffrey Roberts. 221–236. New York: Routledge.

———. 2002. Foreword. In Reinhart Koselleck, *The Practice of Conceptual History: Timing History, Spacing Concepts*. trans. Todd Presner and Others. ix–xiv. Stanford: University of California Press.

———. 2007. "Manifesto Time." *Manifestos for History*, eds. Keith Jenkins, Sue Morgan, and Alun Munslow. 220–231. London: Routledge.

———. 2008. "The Historical Event," *differences: A Journal of Feminist Cultural Studies* 19.2: 9–34.

———. 2009. "Foreword: The Postmodern Messenger." In Keith Jenkins, *At the Limits of History: Essays in Theory and Practice*. 1–3. New York: Routledge.

———. 2010. *The Fiction of Narrative*. ed. Robert Doran. Baltimore: Johns Hopkins University Press.

———. 2013a. " Comment." In *Philosophy of History after Hayden White*. ed. Robert Doran. 209–213. London: Bloomsbury.

———. 2013b. "History as Fulfillment." In *Philosophy of History after Hayden White*. ed. Robert Doran. 35–46. London: Bloomsbury.

———. 2014. *The Practical Past*. Evanston: Northwestern University Press.

White, Patricia. 2015. *Women's Cinema, World Cinema: Projecting Contemporary Feminisms*. Durham: Duke University Press.

Williams, Alan. 1992. *Republic of Images: A History of French Filmmaking*. Cambridge: Harvard University Press.

———. 2009. "The *Sage Femme* of Early Cinema." In *Alice Guy Blaché: Cinema Pioneer*. ed. Joan Simon. 33–46. New Haven: Yale University Press.

Williams, Carolyn, ed. forthcoming. *Cambridge Companion to English Melodrama*. Cambridge: Cambridge University Press.

Williams, Christopher. 2000. "After the Classic, the Classical and Ideology: The Differences of Realism." In *Re-inventing Film Studies*. eds. Christine Gledhill and Linda Williams. 206–220. London: Arnold.

Williams, James. 2003. *Gilles Deleuze's Difference and Repetition: A Critical Introduction and Guide*. Edinburgh: University Press.

Williams, Linda. 2001. *Playing the Race Card: Melodramas of Black and White from Uncle Tom to O. J. Simpson.* Berkeley: University of California Press.

———. 2004. "Why I Did Not Want to Write This Essay." *Signs*: 1264–1271.

———. 2012. "Mega-Melodrama! Vertical and Horizontal Suspensions of the 'Classical'" *Modern Drama* 55.4 (Winter): 523–543.

———. 2018. "'Tales of Sound and Fury . . ' or, the Elephant of Melodrama." In *Melodrama Unbound.* eds. Christine Gledhill and Linda Williams. New York: Columbia University Press.

Williams, Raymond. 1977. *Marxism and Literature.* Oxford: Oxford University Press.

Williams, Tami. 2014. *Germaine Dulac: A Cinema of Sensations.* Urbana: University of Illinois Press.

Williamson, Alice M. 1927. *Alice in Movieland.* London: A. M. Philpot.

Willis, Artemis. 2013. "Mae Murray." In *Women Film Pioneers Project.* eds. Jane M. Gaines, Radha Vatsal, and Monica Dall'Asta. New York: Center for Digital Research and Scholarship, Columbia University Libraries. https://wfpp.cdrs.columbia.edu/pioneer/mae-murray/.

Winchester, Boyd. 1902. "The New Woman." *Arena* (April): 367.

Wood, Mrs. Henry. 2005 [1861]. *East Lynne.* ed. Elisabeth Jay. Oxford: Oxford University Press.

Wright, Andree. 1986. *Brilliant Careers.* Sidney, Australia: Pan Books.

Xiqing, Qin. 2013. "Pearl White and the New Female Image in Chinese Early Silent Cinema." In *Researching Women in Silent Cinema: New Findings and Perspectives.* eds. Monica Dall'Asta and Victoria Duckett. 246–262. Bologna: University of Bologna.

Zhao, Xinyi. 2017a. "A National Cinema in Search of a Nation: The Manchuria Film Association." Unpublished MA Thesis, Columbia University.

———. 2017b. "Tazuko Sakane." In *Women Film Pioneers Project.* eds. Jane M. Gaines, Radha Vatsal, and Monica Dall'Asta. New York: Center for Digital Research and Scholarship, Columbia University Libraries.

Zizek, Slavoj. 2013. "Preface: Bloch's Ontology of Not-Yet-Being." In *The Privatization of Hope: Ernst Bloch and the Future of Utopia.* eds. Peter Thompson and Slavoj Zizek. xv–xx. Durham: Duke University Press.

II. SILENT-ERA: PERIODICALS, UNPUBLISHED MANUSCRIPTS, ORAL HISTORIES, AND BOOKS

"Abolish the Star System." 1920. *New York Times* (October 31): 22.

Addams, Jane. 2002 [1912]. *A New Conscience and an Ancient Evil.* ed. and intro. Katherine Joslin. Champaign-Urbana: University of Illinois Press.

Altenloh, Emilie. 2001 [1914]. "A Sociology of the Cinema: The Audience." trans. Kathleen Cross. *Screen* 42.3 (Autumn): 249–293. From *Zur Soziologie des Kino.* Jena: Diedrihs.

"An All-Woman Film Company." 1914. *The Story World and Photodramatist* 5:5 (July 1923): 79.

Benthall, Dwinelle. n.d. "Poverty Row" typescript. Dwinelle Benthall and Rufus McCosh Collection. AMPAS-MC.

Beranger, Clara. 1918. "Are Women the Better Script Writers?" *Moving Picture World* (August 24): 1128.

———. 1919. "Feminine Sphere in the Field of Movies Is Large Indeed, Says Clara Beranger." Interview. *Moving Picture World* (August 2): 662.

———. 1950. *Writing for the Screen*. Dubuque, Iowa: Wm C. Brown Co.

Bertsch, Marguerite. 1917. *How to Write for Moving Pictures: A Manual of Instruction and Information*. New York: George H. Doran Co. https://hdl.handle.net/2027/mdp.39015000 37653622006.

Blaché, Alice Guy. 1914. "Women's Place in Photoplay Production." *Moving Picture World* (July 11): 195.

Blackton, J. Stuart. 1926. "The Happy Ending." *The Motion Picture Director* 2.8 (March): 3.

———. n.d. "Hollywood with Its Hair Down." Unpublished manuscript, Box 3, folder 31. J. Stuart Blackton Collection. AMPAS-MC.

"Business." 1914. *Motography* (September 19): 407–408.

Carr, Catherine. 1914. *The Art of Photoplay Writing*. New York: Hannis Jordan.

"Close-ups." 1916. *Photoplay* (December): 63–64.

Condon, Mabel. 1915. "Hot Chocolate and Reminiscences at Nine in the Morning." *Photoplay* (January): 69–72.

Corbaley, Kate. 1920. *Selling Manuscripts in the Photoplay Market*. Los Angeles: Palmer Photoplay Corporation.

Dennison, Mabel Rhea. 1909. "Actresses in Moving Picture Work." *The Nickelodeon* 1.1 (January): 19–20.

Denton, Frances. 1918. "Lights! Camera! Quiet! Ready! Shoot! *Photoplay* (February): 48–50.

Dixon, A. J. 1916. "The Only Camera Woman." *Picture Play Magazine* (January 1): 59–65.

Emerson, John, and Anita Loos. 1920. *How to Write Photoplays*. New York: McCann.

Farnum, Dorothy. 1926. "Heart Interest Success Secret of Film Writer." *Los Angeles Times* (May 5): C29.

Fuld, Horace A. 1915. "The Fakes andç Frauds in Motion Pictures." *Motion Picture Magazine* (October): 107–110.

Gauntier, Gene. 1915. "Blazing the Trail." Typescript of memoir. MOMA-CB.

———. 1928–1929. "Blazing the Trail." *Women's Home Companion* (October): 7–8, 181–184, 186; (November): 25–26, 166, 168–170; (December): 15–16, 132, 134; (January): 13–14, 94; (February): 20–21, 92, 94, 97; (March): 18–19, 142, 146. Excerpted in Antonia Lant, ed. 2006. 624–627. The *Red Velvet Seat: Women's Writing on the First Fifty Years of Cinema*. New York: Verso. Complete issues online. https://wfpp.cdrs.columbia.edu/pioneer/ccp -gene-gauntier/.

Gebhart, Myrtle. 1923. "Business Women in Film Studios." *Business Woman* (December): 26–28, 66–68.

———. 1924. "The Girls Who Do Not Act." *Picture-Play Magazine* (December): 102, 119.

"Gene Gauntier Feature Players." 1912. *Moving Picture World* (December 12): 1169.

"Gene Gauntier with Universal." 1915. *Moving Picture World* (March 27): 1942.

Gilliams, E. Leslie. 1923. "Will Woman's Leadership Change Movies?" *Illustrated World* (February): 860, 956.

Grau, Robert. 1914. *The Theatre of Science*. New York: Broadway Publishing.

"Handsome Offers Had to Be Turned Down." 1919. *Moving Picture World* (International Section) (May 24): 1207.

Hayakawa, Sessue. 1959. Reminiscences of Sessue Hayakawa, oral history, April. CUOHRO.

Henderson-Bland, R. 1922. *From Manger to Cross: The Story of the World-Famous Film of the Life of Jesus*. London: Hodder and Stoughton.

Henry, William M. 1916. "Cleo, the Craftswoman." *Photoplay* (January): 110–111.

Herron, Stella Wynne. 1916. "Shoes." *Collier's National Weekly* (January 1): 8–9; 25.

"How Twelve Famous Women Scenario Writers Succeeded." 1923. *Photoplay* (August): 31–33.

Judson, H. C. 1913. "A Daughter of the Confederacy." *Moving Picture World* 15.4: 892.

"June Mathis Dies while at Theatre." 1927. *New York Times* (July 27): 1.

Kell, A. Chester. 1924. "The Fiasco of Ben Hur." *Photoplay* (November): 32–33, 101.

Lipke, Katherine. 1923. "The Most Important Job Ever Held by a Woman" *Los Angeles Times* (June 3): III, 13–16. (June Mathis).

Marion, Frances. 1937. *How to Write and Sell Film Stories*. New York: Covici-Friede.

———. 1958. Reminiscences of Frances Marion, oral history, June. 1–30. CUOHRO.

Mathis, June. 1925. "The Feminine Mind in Picture Making." *Film Daily* (June 7): 115. Reprinted in Lant (2006, 665–667).

Murray, Mae. n.d. "Life Stories." Unpublished manuscript. AMPAS-MC.

———. 1916. "New 'Jobbing' System Hires Actors as Temps." *Variety*. (August 11).

———. 1959. Reminiscences of Mae Murray, oral history, December. CUOHRO.

Osborne, Florence M. 1925. "Why Are There No Women Directors?" *Motion Picture Magazine* (November): 5.

Parsons, Louella O. 1917. *How to Write for the "Movies."* Rev. ed. Chicago: A. C. McClurg.

Patterson, Frances Taylor. 1920. *Cinema Craftsmanship*. New York: Harcourt, Brace and Howe.

———. 1928. *Scenario and Screen*. New York: Harcourt, Brace.

Petrova, Olga. 1996 [1914]. "A Remembrance." In *The Memoirs of Alice Guy Blaché*. ed. Anthony Slide. 107–110. Lanham, Md.: Scarecrow Press.

"Play to the Ladies." 1909. *The Nickelodeon* I.2: 33–34.

Sargent, Epes Winthrop. 1914. "The Literary Side of the Motion Picture World." *Moving Picture World* 21.2 (July 11): 199–202.

———. 1928. "Gene Gauntier Again." Introduction to "Blazing the Trail." *Women's Home Companion* (October): 4.

Smith, Fredrick James. 1924. "Unwept, Unhonored, and Unfilmed." *Photoplay* (July): 64–76, 101–104.

Swanson, Gloria. 1958. Reminiscences of Gloria Swanson, oral history, September. CUOHRO.

Synon, Katherine. 1914. "Francelia Billington Who Can Play Both Ends of a Camera against the Middle." *Photoplay* (December): 58–60.

"The Vitagraph Company of America." 1912. *Moving Picture World* (June 8): 907.

Weber, Lois. 1928a. "Many Women Well Fitted by Film Training to Direct Movies, Lois Weber Claims." *San Diego Evening Tribune* (April 24): 3.

———. 1928b. "Hostility of Men Drawback to Women Making Success in Picture Directing, Claim." *San Diego Evening Tribune* (April 25): 13.

Yezierska, Anzia. 1925. "This Is What $10,000 Did to Me." *Cosmopolitan* (October): 40–41, 154; excerpted in Antonia Lant. ed. 2006. 643–648. *The Red Velvet Seat: Women's Writing on the First Fifty Years of Cinema*. New York: Verso.

Young, Alma, 1977. Interview with Anthony Slide and Robert Gitt (January 30 and February 20). AMPAS-OH.

INDEX

history, 1–2; adequation in, 39–40; ambiguities of, 37–40, 64; artifact as historical index, 73–76; asymmetry in, 100–101, 102, 222n42; from below, 11; critical approach to, 6; digital turn in, 90; of the kinetograph, 34–37; paradox of analysis in, 207n2; point of researching, 159–162; post-structuralism in, 4, 12; separating historical past from the usable past in, 15; textual existence as only existence in, 126–128; theories of, 3–6, 45–46; and theory as no longer estranged, 3–6; what happened versus what is said to have happened in, 64–68

history-as-critique, 6, 159, 180

historylessness, 83–84, 85

History of the Kinetograph, Kinetoscope and Kineto-Phonograph, 33

Holliday, Wendy, 27, 141, 142, 166

Holmes, Helen, 16–17, 180, *181*; "no woman in 1925" and, 23

How to Write for Moving Pictures, 169

Humanity/Umanità, 81, 128, 201, *202, 203*

Hungry Hearts, 133

Husserl, Edmund, 102, 104–105, 109, 126

ideology of historical loss, 77–79, 94; historylessness and, 83–84, *85*

ideology of masculinity, 182–183

indexical certainty, 74, 84, 228n2; real-before-the-camera to real materiality and, 88–89

Indian cinema, 200

Ingleton, Eugenie Magnus, 29

irreversibility of time, 102, 106–107

Jacobs, Lewis, 8

Jameson, Fredric, 74, 170, 176

Jane Eyre, 115

Japanese cinema, 199–200

Jenkins, Keith, 6, 78, 124, 125; on textual existence, 126–127

Johnson, Agnes Christine, 142, *142*

Johnston, Claire, 197–198

Kalem Company, 20, 21, 23, 137

Kaplan, E. Ann, 116, 164

Kay, Karyn, 8

Kellner, Hans, 64

Khokhlova, Aleksandra, 200

Kimball Young, Clara, 20, 26, 166, 193, 218n44

kinetograph: Antonia Dickson and the anticipation of the future of the, 48–50; history of the, 34–37, 41

King, Bradley, 142

King, Henry, 150

Kluge, Frieda, 178

knowledge effects, 5

Koselleck, Reinhart, 38, 108, 125, 170, 171, 188; on chance, 111; on fiction of actuality, 126; former future, 41, 44, 49, 99; on historical time, 40–42, 48–50, 223n45, 224n57

Kozarski, Richard, 151

Kuhn, Annette, 12

La Fée aux choux, 51–53, 70; Alice Guy's authorship of, 60–61; critiques of birth of cinema narrative of, 62–64; 1896 date of, 56–59; identifying the print of, 53–55; reprints of, 68–69; what happened versus what is said to have happened and, 64–68

Lant, Antonia, 34, 135, 177

L'arroseur arrosé, 68–69

Lawrence, Florence, 16–17, 19, 25–26

Leblanc, Georgette, 29

Le Jardinier, 56

Leonard, Marion, 16, *25*

Leonard, Robert Z., 30

Liana Film, 201

Life and Inventions of Thomas Edison, 34

"Life Stories," 30

Little Rebel, The, 20

lived aspect of historical time, 97

location-in-time quandary, 44, 96, 111, 113–114, 117, 124, 130

Loebenstein, Michael, 81, 83–84

Loos, Anita, 141, 142, 144

Lord of the Rings, 39

Loring, Hope, 140, *140*

modernity thesis, 246n48

moments of the historical operation, 40

moral schemes, 96, 97

Morey, Anne, 142

Motion Picture News, 7

Motion Picture Patents Company, 48

Moving Picture World, The, 7, 21, 139

Mulan Joins the Army, 200

Mulvey, Laura, 43, 102

Murray, Mae, 30, 217–218n42

Museum of Modern Art, Los Angeles, 79

Muslow, Alan, 6

Musser, Charles, 80, 217n38

My Madonna, 110

Mystery of the Yellow Room, The, 21

naive realism, 226–227n22

narrating of the feminist 1970s, 45–47

narrative, addiction, 186

narrative mode of knowing, 32

Nazimova, Alla, 26, *27*, 185, *185*

Neely, Hugh, 30

New Jersey Star, 68

"New Woman," 48, 175, 254–255n31

Nickelodeon, The, 135

Nielsen, Asta, 112, 121, 172–173, *173–174*

Nietzsche, Friedrich, 74

Nikkatsu, Studio, 199

Nochlin, Linda, 117

Norton, Stephen S., 91

Notari, Elvira, 112, 128

"no woman in 1925," 23–24

now-time, 102–105

Oakeshoot, Michael, 15

objectlessness and mixed ontologies, 81–83

Olcott, Sidney, 16, 20, 22–23, 214–215n10

Ordway, Marjorie, *176*

Orr, Linda, 155

others, historical, 121–125

"over by 1925," 28–30

paradox of analysis, 207n2

Paramount Pictures DeMille, 134, 145, 147, 150–151

Park, Ida May, 29, *79, 177*

Parsons, Louella, 142, 143

Pearl White, 11

Peterson, Mrs. H., 148, 157

Petrova, Olga, 26, *26*, 128

Philosophy of History after Hayden White, 210n25

Photoplay, 16–18, 28, 193, 245n37; on Gene Gauntier, 19–21

Pickford, Mary, 8, 20, 137, 193, 218n44

Picture-Play Magazine, 135

Pillow Fight, A, 69

political economic explanation of "over by 1925," 28–30

postmodern history, 6

post-postfeminist feminism, 12–13, 36

post-structuralism, 4, 12

power relations and daydream-as-resistance, 180

present, histories of the, 125–126

presentism, 113, 236n26

Prina, Irma, 133, 144, 149

Prouty, Olive Higgins, 116

Pu Shunqing, *200*

Rai, Himansu, 200

Ramsaye, Terry, 8, 28, 63, 136–137; on emotional commodity, 166–167

Rancière, Jacques, 37, 129

Rani, Devika, 200

realism, 3, 73–74, 227n28; naive, 226–227n22; thesis of, 94

reciprocity, historical, 121–122

Red Lantern, The, 185–186

redundancy, 193–197

re-familiarization of the historical past, 121

Reid, Dorothy Davenport, 26

Reiko, Ikegawa, 199

restitution, 78–79

restoration: as restitution, 78; to what it had never been, 93–94

retroactive causality, 43

Rich, Adrienne, 36

Ricoeur, Paul, 40, 93

rigged occurrence, 109

Riley, Denise, 9–10

Roads That Lead Home, The, 186–187

Roberts, Geoff, 32

Tolkien, J. R. R., 39
transfer of presence, 207–208n4
Tribe, Keith, 11, 41, 97
Trouillot, Michel-Rolf, 64–67, 126
Turner, Florence, 16, *17,* 136–137
Turner Films, Inc., 16

uncertainties of historical time, 97–98;
    everyday, 95, 99–100, 104
Uncle Tom's Cabin, 179
unequal distribution of narrative wealth,
    22
Universal Film Manufacturing Company,
    17, 19, 21, 24, 29
Universal Pictures, 80, 194
Unsell, Eve, 26
unthinkabilities, 197–201
"Unwept, Unhonored, and Unfilmed," 16
Unwritten Law, 122
utopianism, 170–172, 176; feminist, 37,
    173–174; for whom, 188–189

Valentino, Rudolph, 160, 183
Van Upp, Virginia, 142
vernacular modernism, 244n28
Veronisi, Micaela, 201
Victor Company, 16–17, 26
Vitagraph Company, 16, 26, *27,* 137–138,
    139, 142, 151–152, 171
voice of the home, 158–159, 162–170,
    181–187, 193, 198
von Ranke, Leopold, 31, 64

Wang, Lingzhen, 8
Warner Brothers, 239n35
Warrenton, Lule, 26, 29, *194*
Wasko, Janet, 193
Way Down East, 98, 106–107, 108
Weber, Lois, 23, 26, 29, 72, 76, 79, 121, 132,
    137, 144, 194–195, 198; contemporary
    feminist historians on, 112; continuity
    mistake by, 86–88, 91; film authorship
    of, 89–93; on gender mattering, 138;
    "nows that never meet" used by, 103–
    104; real-before-the-camera work of,
    88–89; start as an actress, 142; under-
    standing of textual existence, 127–128

Wei, Louisa, 130
Welles, Orson, 90
Wheery, Edith, 185
White, Hayden, 15, 32, 39, 46, 63, 113,
    210n25; on historicizing the present,
    125; on the "New Woman," 175; on rec-
    ollection of past events, 104–105
White, Patricia, 188
White, Pearl, 11, 23, 182
Whitney Museum, 57, 58
Williams, Alan, 61, 68, 136
Williams, Jesse L., *124*
Williams, Kathlyn, 182
Williams, Linda, 97, 106, 164
Williams, Maria P., 28, 121, *124*
Williams, Raymond, 165
Williams, Tami, 121
women: as authority on emotions, 10,
    164–167; expectation despite expecta-
    tions of them, 195; as genre, 164–167,
    191; terminology of, 37; as voice of the
    home, 158–159, 162–170, 181–187, 193, 198
Women and Film, 18
Women Film Pioneers, 149, 157, 238n13,
    239n31
women in the silent-film industry, 16–18;
    advanced by doing "women's work,"
    138–144; answers sought in understand-
    ing what happened to, 24–28; archives
    from storage to transmission, 155–157;
    Black, 10, 28, 118, 160; competing para-
    digms of, 162–164; deaths of, 189; disap-
    pearance of women's viewpoint and,
    192–196; film festivals and, 116; futility
    of optimism of, 191–192; historical sur-
    prise on, 196–197; how to say what hap-
    pened to, 31–32; invisibility to visibility
    metaphor of, 11, 198–199; irregularity of
    work for, 191; at its heart, 160–161; loss
    as rhetorical device of, 76–77; made
    redundant, 193–197; "magic something"
    and the "world-improving dream" of,
    170–174, 190–191; Margaret Herrick
    Library and, 6–9; from "no woman in
    1925" to the heyday of, 23–24; outside
    the U.S., 199–201; overestimation and
    underestimation of evidence on, 9–12;

women in the silent-film industry (*continued*): political economy explanation for "over by 1925" status of, 28–30; telling versus counting on, 147–155; "they were there" thesis on, 135–138; unequal distribution of narrative wealth and, 22; using new technologies, 175–180, *181*; Valeria Belletti as example of, 144–146; "voice of the home" thesis on, 158–159, 162–170, 181–187; as workers in the dream factory, 132–135, 172

"Women's Place in Photoplay Production," 8

"women's work," 138–144

Wong, Marion E., 27–28, 121, *123*

Wood, Mrs. Henry, 102, 185

Woolf, Virginia, 201

"world-improving dream," 170–174

World War I, 202, 203, 240n1

Wyler, William, 90

"Yellow Wallpaper, The," 115

Yezierska, Anzia, 133, 189

Zukor, Adolph, 28

JANE M. GAINES is a professor of film at Columbia University. She is the award-winning author of *Contested Culture: The Image, the Voice and the Law* and *Fire and Desire: Mixed Race Movies in the Silent Era*.

WOMEN AND FILM HISTORY INTERNATIONAL

The University of Illinois Press
is a founding member of the
Association of American University Presses.

University of Illinois Press
1325 South Oak Street
Champaign, IL 61820-6903
www.press.uillinois.edu